TAXATION
IN
UTOPIA

TAXATION
IN
UTOPIA

REQUIRED SACRIFICE

AND THE

GENERAL WELFARE

DONALD MORRIS

SUNY PRESS

Cover: *Anemone*, designed by William Morris, 1876. Jacquard-woven silk and wool or silk damask fabric.

Published by State University of New York Press, Albany

For information, contact State University of New York Press, Albany, NY
www.sunypress.edu

Library of Congress Cataloging-in-Publication Data

Names: Morris, Donald, 1945– author. | State University of New York.
Title: Taxation in utopia : required sacrifice and the general welfare /
    Donald Morris.
Description: Albany : State University of New York, 2020. | Includes
    bibliographical references and index.
Identifiers: LCCN 2020000964 (print) | LCCN 2020000965 (ebook) | ISBN
    9781438479477 (hardcover : alk. paper) | ISBN 9781438479484 (pbk. : alk.
    paper) | ISBN 9781438479491 (ebook)
Subjects: LCSH: Taxation. | Political science—Philosophy. | Utopias—Economic
    aspects.
Classification: LCC HJ2305 .M67 2020 (print) | LCC HJ2305 (ebook) | DDC
    336.2001—dc23
LC record available at https://lccn.loc.gov/2020000964
LC ebook record available at https://lccn.loc.gov/2020000965

10 9 8 7 6 5 4 3 2 1

To Keith and Sarah

Shigaloyov continued: "Having devoted my energies to the question of social organization in any future society . . . I've come to the conclusion that all creators of social systems, from ancient times down to our own in 187_, were dreamers, story-tellers and fools who . . . understood absolutely nothing about natural science or that strange animal called man. . . . I'm proposing my own system of world organization. . . . Moreover, I must declare in advance that my system is not yet complete. . . . I became lost in my own data and my conclusion contradicts the original premise from which I started. Beginning with the idea of unlimited freedom, I end with unlimited despotism."

—Dostoevsky, *Devils*

Fyodor Dostoevsky, *Devils*, trans. Michael R. Katz (Oxford: Oxford University Press, 1992), 426.

CONTENTS

ACKNOWLEDGMENTS   xi

INTRODUCTION   1

CHAPTER ONE
Taxation as a Moral Quest   5

    Part One: Taxation: The Tail Wags the Dog   5
       An Experiment in Shared Sacrifice   5
       Ends and Means   9
       Practicality   15
       Taxation as a Moral Question of Sacrifice   17

    Part Two: The Construal of Taxation and of Utopia   21
       The Sinews of Taxation   21
       Beyond Revenue: Defining a Tax   28
       Defining Utopia   37

CHAPTER TWO
Privacy Deprivation as Taxation   41

    The Nature and Role of Privacy   41
    Thomas More (1478–1535): No Spots for Secret Meetings   45
    Big Brother's Eyes in *Nineteen Eighty-Four*   47
    H. G. Wells (1866–1946): Indexing Humanity   50
    Zamyatin (1884–1937): Who Are "They" and Who Are "We"?   54
    Expectations of Privacy   59

CHAPTER THREE
Taxing Access to Truth   63

  Part One: Plato and Bacon   63
    Opaque Government   63
    Plato (c. 428–c. 348 BCE): The Republic of Lies   65
    Francis Bacon (1561–1626): The Sacrifice to Science   68

  Part Two: Orwell and Godwin   76
    Totalitarian Methodologies: Orwell (1903–1950)   76
    William Godwin (1756–1836): Anarchist Tax Policy   81

CHAPTER FOUR
Taxation by Required Work or Occupation

  Part One: Plato and More   91
    Work and Inequality   91
    Matching Specialized Abilities to Society's Needs   93
    Plato (c. 428–c. 348 BCE): The Ideal Job in the *Republic*   94
    Thomas More (1478–1535): The Common Obligation of
      Common Daily Toil   99

  Part Two: Bellamy, Gilman, Wells, and Skinner   106
    Edward Bellamy (1850–1898): The Industrial Army   106
    Charlotte Perkins Gilman (1860–1935): Half the Human Race
      Is Denied Free Productive Expression   114
    H. G. Wells (1866–1946): Labor Laws and the Insult of
      Charity   119
    B. F. Skinner (1904–1990): We Have Created Leisure
      Without Slavery   122

  Part Three: Saint-Simon and Campanella   125
    Henri Saint-Simon (1760–1825): The Human Spirit Follows
      a Predetermined Course   125
    Tommaso Campanella (1568–1639): Assigned Labor in
      The City of the Sun   135

CHAPTER FIVE
Taxing the Family: Marriage, Childrearing, and Eugenics   139

  Part One: Plato, More, Bacon, Wells, and Le Guin   139
    Marriage Restrictions   139

Francis Bacon (1561–1626): Marriage Except for the Wise 144
H. G. Wells (1866–1946): Motherhood as a Service to
    the State 147
Le Guin (1929–2018): Anarchism and the Tax-Free Family
    in *The Dispossessed* 152

Part Two: Owen and Gilman 156
    Robert Owen (1771–1858): The Tax on Childrearing 156
    Charlotte Perkins Gilman (1860–1935): Motherhood and
        Eugenics in *Herland* 167

Part Three: Skinner, Eugenic Tax Procedures 173
    B. F. Skinner (1904–1990): Eliminating the Meaner
        Emotions in *Walden Two* 173
    Eugenic Tax Procedures: Campanella, Bellamy, Zamyatin,
        Huxley 186

CHAPTER SIX
Taxation and Land Proprietorship 197

    Part One: Harrington, Godwin, and Owen 197
        The Land Question 197
        James Harrington (1611–1677): Inheritance Tax in *Oceana* 206
        William Godwin (1756–1836): Anarchy and Private
            Property 209
        Robert Owen (1771–1858): Peaceful Revolution 210

    Part Two: George, Tolstoy, Wells, and Nozick 212
        Henry George (1839–1897): Progress, Land, and Poverty 212
        Tolstoy (1828–1910): A Landowner's Struggle with the
            Land Problem 220
        Wells (1866–1946): The Land Question in *A Modern Utopia* 227
        Robert Nozick (1938–2002): Entitlement Theory 230

CHAPTER SEVEN
Taxation Purged from Utopia 237

    Part One: Ayn Rand (1905–1982): *Atlas Shrugged* 237
        Disparate Social Systems 237
        Rand's Four Utopias 240
        Rand's "Tax" System 253

Part Two: Robert Nozick (1938–2002): Utopia of Utopias   257
   The Most Extensive State that Can Be Justified   257
   The Developing State: The First Four Stages   259
   The Fifth Stage   263
   Taxes, Forced Labor, and the Minimal State   265
   Utopia: The Minimal State Framework   276
   Taxation in Nozick's Utopia of Utopias   278
   In Closing   281

Bibliography   283

Index   305

ACKNOWLEDGMENTS

I would like to thank the librarians at the Newberry Library in Chicago, the Supreme Court Library in Springfield, Illinois, and the Brookins Library at the University of Illinois, Springfield for affording access to scarce and out-of-print materials. I am also grateful for the observations and suggestions of the three anonymous reviewers enlisted by SUNY Press as well as the encouragement and guidance of Andrew Kenyon, Senior Acquisitions Editor, philosophy, in implementing the reviewers' recommendations. Also from SUNY Press, I extend my appreciation to Ryan Morris, Senior Production Editor, for her expertise and to Holly Rogers for her editorial enhancements. The engaging meetings of The Society for Utopian Studies and the compelling investigations in its journal *Utopian Studies* have kindled my interest in the role of utopias as stimulants to the moral imagination. The editorial efforts of Sabrina Leroe improved the precision and readability of the text and reduced, to a considerable degree, potential strain on the reader's patience. James Bockmier's editorial assistance enhanced the work's organization and clarity as well as its stylistic consistency. I would also like to express my appreciation to my colleague Rosina Neginsky, my friend Dana Plank, my brother Jim, and my son Keith for reading slices of developmental versions of this work. Their critical comments and stimulating counsel provided early insights into the challenges I faced. The discussion of Orwell's *Nineteen Eighty-Four* in chapters two and three includes portions adapted from my article "Privacy and Control in Orwell's *Nineteen Eighty-Four*," in *Critical Insights: Nineteen Eighty-Four*, edited by Thomas Horan (Ipswich, MA: Salem Press, Grey House Publishing, 2016), 213–27. Cover design image by William Morris from rawpixel.com / The Metropolitan Museum of Art.

INTRODUCTION

Judge Learned Hand observed, "it is hard to imagine any tax whose imposition was not in some degree dictated by its effect on the public interest."[1] On November 6, 2017, as the US Congress prepared to complete work on a wide-ranging tax bill, the House chaplain, Reverend Patrick J. Conroy, SJ, offered a prayer.

> As legislation on taxes continues to be debated this week and next, may all Members be mindful that the institutions and structures of our great Nation guarantee the opportunities that have allowed some to achieve great success, while others continue to struggle. May their efforts these days guarantee that there are not winners and losers under new tax laws, but benefits balanced and shared by all Americans.[2]

The prayer angered some members of Congress who sought the chaplain's dismissal; they perceived the prayer as a political rather than a religious invocation. Like Mustapha Mond, the World Controller in Huxley's *Brave New World*, they preferred "God in the safe and Ford on the shelves."[3] Gandhi, a practitioner of both religion and politics, advises, however, that "those who say that religion has nothing to do with politics do not know

---

1. Learned Hand, *The Bill of Rights* (New York: Atheneum, 1979), 47.

2. *Congressional Record*, November 6, 2017, 115th Congress, 1st Session, Issue: Vol. 163, No. 180, https://www.congress.gov/congressional-record/2017/11/6.

3. Aldous Huxley, *Brave New World* (New York: Harper Collins, 2004), 207–8.

what religion means."[4] While the chaplain emphasized balancing tax benefits, the primary moral challenge of taxation is balancing sacrifices. Tax laws limiting opportunities and picking winners and losers impose sacrifices on some people for the profit of others. When lawmakers seek to camouflage their handiwork—obfuscating its self-interested dispersion of sacrifice—they evince Hayek's concern when he counseled that "the whole practice of public finance has been developed in an endeavor to outwit the taxpayer and to induce him to pay more than he is aware of, and to make him agree to expenditure in the belief that somebody else will be made to pay for it."[5]

This book addresses utopian political philosophy and its ethical underpinnings from the neglected perspective of taxation, defined in its broadest terms. As I explain more fully in the text, I chose utopias for the same reasons that investigators exploring other problems control variables, adopt simplifying assumptions, and develop conceptual models. And while moral concerns permeating taxation are illustrated in the context of utopian literature, this is not an argument for a stand-alone tax utopia or a practical treatise on tax reform.

The ethical contours of political entities—whether utopian or actual—are determined by the relation of citizens to each other and to the state. One indicator of these relations is exposed by examining the modes of taxation society employs. In this study I view taxation more broadly than "government revenue" to include "governmental impositions on the person, property, privileges, occupations, and enjoyment of the people."[6] These nonpecuniary government-required sacrifices I brand *constructive taxes* (constructive in the sense of construed, expressing the concept of substance over form). It is in this sense that the law speaks of constructive assent, constructive contract, and constructive fraud, for example. My focus in this work is on restrictions utopias place on 1) privacy, 2) access to truth, 3) the assignment of work (eliminating "useless trades" and conscripting workers, for example), 4) marriage and childrearing (including marriage proscriptions

---

4. M. K. Gandhi, *An Autobiography*, trans. Mahadev Desai (Ahmedabad: Navajivan Publishing House, 1927), 463.

5. Friedrich A. Hayek, *Law Legislation and Liberty*, vol. 3 *The Political Order of a Free People* (Chicago: University of Chicago Press, 1979), 51–52.

6. *Black's Law Dictionary*, 9th ed. (St. Paul MN: West Publishing Co., 2009), 1594.

and eugenic procedures), and 5) the proprietorship of land (common vs. private ownership).

Most utopians devote little time to describing their pecuniary tax systems. In More's *Utopia* and Bellamy's *Looking Backward*, for example, there is no pecuniary taxation because there is no money. Hertzka's *Freeland* and Wells's *A Modern Utopia* are exceptions. But ridding one's utopia of pecuniary taxes is not a utopian triumph, for—as I attempt to show—this merely transforms the nature of the required sacrifice, resulting in a new mode of taxation. The body of this text traces the moral dimensions of taxation through the utopian writings of political theorists, including Plato, More, Campanella, Bacon, Harrington, Godwin, Owen, Saint-Simon, Spencer, George, and Nozick, as well as novelists and other literary figures, including Tolstoy, Bellamy, Hertzka, Morris, Wells, London, Gilman, Zamyatin, Huxley, Orwell, Skinner, Rand, and Le Guin.

Since I define taxation more broadly than government revenue to include other potentially unrequited sacrifices government demands from its citizens, taxation is placed in its wider historical and functional contexts as a political device for promoting government's vision of the general welfare. Though this is a discussion of taxation in utopias, it is reinforced by conventional political and philosophical sources, including political economists and illustrations from morally relevant contemporary events and discussions.

Throughout, I have attempted to avoid the political labels frequently littering utopian exposition—including anarchist, communist, conservative, liberal, libertarian, progressive, socialist, and so on—though not always with success. Labels are a convenient shorthand but dangerous in the wrong hands. Using the term libertarian in a discussion of utopian writers, for example, juxtaposes works as distinct as William Morris's *News from Nowhere* and Ayn Rand's *Atlas Shrugged*. William Godwin, the anarchist, was a critic of anarchy; socialists Bellamy and Orwell were critics of socialism. Commentators pigeonhole Henry George both as a socialist and as a defender and purifier of capitalism. My attempt to avoid labels breaks down in the final chapter, where I use the term libertarian to encompass the utopias of Ayn Rand (*Atlas Shrugged*) and Robert Nozick (*Anarchy, State and Utopia*). While few utopians dwell on questions of taxation, Rand and Nozick express openly anti-tax sentiments.

For those interested in individual authors, this grid is designed to facilitate your reading.

Reading Guide

Utopian	Taxes, Utopia, the Context	Privacy	Access to Truth	Required Work or Occupation	Marriage, Childrearing, and Eugenics	Taxation and Land Ownership	Purging Utopia of Taxation
	Chap. 1	Chap. 2	Chap. 3	Chap. 4	Chap. 5	Chap. 6	Chap. 7
Bacon	1.1, 1.2		3.1		5.1		
Bellamy	1.1, 1.2		3.2‡	4.2	5.3		
Butler	1.1, 1.2				5.3‡		
Campanella	1.1, 1.2			4.3	5.3		
George	1.1, 1.2					6.2	
Gilman	1.1, 1.2			4.2	5.2		
Godwin	1.1, 1.2		3.2			6.1	
Harrington	1.1, 1.2					6.1	
Hertzka	1.1, 1.2	2‡		4.2‡, 4.3‡		6.2‡	
Huxley	1.1, 1.2	2‡			5.3‡		
Le Guin	1.1, 1.2	2‡		(7.2)*	5.1		7.2*
London	1.1, 1.2		3.2‡	4.2‡			
More	1.1, 1.2	2		4.1	5.1‡		
Morris	1.1, 1.2			4.2‡	5.1‡, 5.2‡		
Nozick	1.1, 1.2			(7.2)*		6.2	7.2*
Orwell	1.1, 1.2	2	3.2				
Owen	1.1, 1.2				5.2	6.1	
Plato	1.1, 1.2	2‡	3.1	4.1	5.1		
Proudhon	1.1, 1.2					6.1‡	
Rand	1.1, 1.2						7.1
Saint-Simon	1.1, 1.2			4.3			
Skinner	1.1, 1.2			4.2	5.3		
Spence	1.1, 1.2					6.1‡, 6.2‡	
Spencer	1.1, 1.2				5.3		
Tolstoy	1.1, 1.2					6.2	
Wells	1.1, 1.2	2		4.2	5.1	6.2	
Zamyatin	1.1, 1.2	2			5.3		

‡Generally minor or only footnote reference.

*Topic addressed in Chap. 4 is covered in Chap. 7.

CHAPTER ONE

TAXATION AS A MORAL QUEST

Part One:
Taxation: The Tail Wags the Dog

AN EXPERIMENT IN SHARED SACRIFICE

> The greatest, most important power entrusted to the Government is the power to tax the citizens. All its other powers spring from this right.

—Henri Saint-Simon (1760–1825), *Selected Writings*[1]

In *Looking Backward*, Edward Bellamy's Dr. Leete boasts: "We have no revenue service, no swarm of tax assessors and collectors."[2] It is an idle boast, however. Taxation is an integral component of public policy, and in their book on taxes and justice, Murphy and Nagel report that the ethical dimensions of public policy represent an "underpopulated area in philosophical discussion."[3] Examining the contours of these dimensions entails viewing taxation more broadly than "government revenue"—as enforced modes of

---

1. Henri Saint-Simon, *Henri Saint-Simon (1760–1825): Selected Writings on Science, Industry and Social Organization*, ed. and trans. Keith Taylor (New York: Holmes and Meier Publishers, 1975), 189.

2. Edward Bellamy, *Looking Backward: 2000–1887* (New York: Penguin Books, 1982), 167.

3. Liam Murphy and Thomas Nagel, *The Myth of Ownership: Taxes and Justice* (Oxford: Oxford University Press, 2002), 4.

sacrifice sustaining society. A government's tax system is a political experiment in shared sacrifice; its outcome is measured by the lives of the citizens whose welfare it affects. Bentham frames the problem I am addressing in its broadest context:

> Society is held together only by the sacrifices men can be induced to make of the gratifications they demand: to obtain these sacrifices is the great difficulty, the great task of government.[4]

Utopias are experiments in what sacrifices people can be induced to make; the state's measures for levying these sacrifices embody its system of taxation. Taxation, therefore, poses an ethical quandary as it requires (coerces) people to sacrifice for the benefit of others, whether or not they also benefit themselves.[5]

Assessing utopian tax systems affords a metric for inter-utopian as well as extra-utopian exploration. Though there are many such measures—for example, scientific advancement or racial equality—few are displayed across the eclectic array of utopian authors. Regarding the future of the utopian undertaking, Kateb affirms, "the point has not been reached which would allow us to conclude that the most that can be 'made' of man had already been announced in the works of the major modern utopian writers."[6] In this discussion I argue that when envisioning "the most that can be 'made' of man," some form of enduring social entity is required, and the tax structure designed to support that ideal society cannot be an incidental consideration.

A central goal of this work is to explore the connections utopias establish that link their visions or ends to the financial or other means established for their achievement. In pursuing this goal, I emphasize these "other means" that are surrogates for conventional pecuniary tax systems and common staples of utopias. Examples include 1) privacy deprivation, 2) limitations on access to truth, 3) mandatory work assignments, 4) marriage and family restrictions, and 5) conventions governing land ownership. These nonpecuniary levies

---

4. Jeremy Bentham, *Anarchical Fallacies*, in *'Nonsense upon Stilts,': Bentham, Burke, and Marx on the Rights of Man*, ed. Jeremy Waldron (London: Methuen, 1987), 48.

5. I follow Sidgwick in using *ethical* and *moral* as synonyms. Henry Sidgwick, *Outlines of the History of Ethics* (Indianapolis: Hackett Publishing Company, 1988), 11.

6. George Kateb, *Utopia and Its Enemies* (New York: The Free Press, 1963; Schocken Books, 1972), 218–19.

allocate sacrifice in addition to or in place of their pecuniary counterparts, and like other forms of taxation their charge may be narrowly targeted or broadly imposed. My discussion addresses these required sacrifices in order of their relative scalability and corresponding impact on moral autonomy. In examining taxation in utopias, one point of emphasis is the relative harmony or conflict arising between the ends the utopia espouses (values such as equality or liberty) and the means it proposes to realize these ends (its imposed forms of sacrifice). Goodwin expresses the significance of this exercise when she writes, "The different attitudes to utopian taxation are indicative of markedly different concepts of society."[7]

The arguments I propose in these chapters are illustrated in the context of utopian literature, in states that are nowhere. The same arguments can be posed in the context of actual states, whether existing or historical.[8] I chose utopias for the same reasons that investigators exploring other disciplines control variables, adopt simplifying assumptions, and develop conceptual models as abstract representations and explanatory tools. Keynes describes a model as a tool for segregating the relatively permanent factors in a problem from those that are temporary. Doing so, he says, permits the development of a framework for thinking about the transitory factors, leading ultimately to a better understanding of particular cases.[9] Segregating the permanent from the transitory also advances our understanding of a utopia and its tax regime; it does so in two ways.

On an obvious level, a utopian state offers a contrast between its permanent factors—its static laws and customs—and the transient workings of an actual state. Bacon's *New Atlantis*, for example, though subject to conflicting interpretations, is a fixed set of descriptions in an atemporal narrative. Like frozen specimens, utopias permit us to examine their tax

---

7. Barbara Goodwin, "Taxation in Utopia," *Utopian Studies* 19, no. 2 (2008): 313–31, 313.

8. In this book, I exercise my utopian license and use the term *state* in a general and intentionally noncommittal sense to mean either government or a territory governed by a particular nation (country, commonwealth) or a body of people politically organized under the governing authority in a society, in whatever form, or the specific political arrangement constituting a society's governing apparatus, including unique utopian arrangements that may evolve or devolve from such arrangements.

9. John Maynard Keynes, "Economic Model Construction and Econometrics," in *The Philosophy of Economics*, 2nd ed., ed. Daniel M. Hausman (Cambridge: Cambridge University Press, 1994), 287.

(and other economic, legal, and social) systems without reference to specific historical events, dates, or persons. Unlike actual states, there are no sudden shifts in power or policy leading to new taxes or the elimination of the old. Second, and less obvious, each utopia's hypothesis (at least implicitly) designates which factors in human nature are relatively permanent and which are transitory. The transitory (or conditional) factors are those that emerge when a state's political institutions are replaced by those proposed as ideal. Thus, Godwin says of people, "Take them out of their shackles, bid them enquire, reason and judge, and you will soon find them very different beings."[10] The "different beings" that utopias depict are the products of the underlying permanent factors of human nature modified by exposure to a new social and political environment. "The utopian ideal man," explains Gerber, "is such as we could be if only we had not been hindered in our natural development by the trammeling old-fashioned institutions of an outworn society."[11] This is Morris's assumption in *News from Nowhere*, for example, where a change in basic economic principles and the abolition of private property and government transforms the citizens into cheerful, creative, and cooperative souls. The conditions under which his citizens perform their daily work are altered from the coercive "burden of unnecessary production" to "the freedom for every man to do what he can do best."[12]

In discussing the design of experimental communities, B. F. Skinner explains that a utopian community may be thought of as a small state where some of the problems facing utopian thinkers can be reduced to a manageable size. "It is in relation to government," he says, that a speculative community "serves something of the function of a pilot experiment in science."[13] Because of the community's smaller scale, problems arising from sheer size can be overlooked; but the primary benefit, he says, is our ability

---

10. William Godwin, *Enquiry Concerning Political Justice and Its Influence on Modern Morals and Happiness*, 3rd ed. (New York: Viking Penguin, 1985), bk. 7, chap. 8, 692–93.

11. Richard Gerber, *Utopian Fantasy: A Study of English Utopian Fiction since the End of the Nineteenth Century* (London: Routledge and Kegan Paul, 1955), 17.

12. William Morris, *News from Nowhere* in *News from Nowhere and Other Writings* (New York: Penguin Books, 1993), 123–24.

13. B. F. Skinner, *Cumulative Record*, 3rd ed. (New York: Appleton-Century-Crofts, 1959), 59.

to focus on the lives of its individual members.[14] It is on this personal level that a utopia displays which aspects of human nature are permanent and which are transient.

ENDS AND MEANS

> To stir the reader, the artist must speak not of means but of ends, of the great goal toward which mankind is moving.
>
> —Yevgeny Zamyatin (1884–1937), *A Soviet Heretic*[15]

One of Popper's criticisms of utopias is that they "demand that we must determine our ultimate political aim, or the Ideal State, before taking any practical action." Once the end is in place, he says, utopians "consider the best ways and means for its realization, and to draw up a plan for practical action."[16] Levitas, in contrast, sees utopian thought as a method for exploring and debating potential frontiers of human flourishing, as utopian prospecting is not about discovering a blueprint but "entails holistic thinking about the connections between economic, social, existential and ecological processes in an integrated way."[17] I argue that a state's tax system is a critical component in this mix.

---

14. Skinner, 59. Olson reports that research does not support the idea that what is true of small groups with a "common, collective interest" can be made applicable to larger groups "merely by multiplying these results by a scale factor." Mancur Olson, *The Logic of Collective Action: Public Goods and the Theory of Groups* (Cambridge: Harvard University Press, 1965), 57–58. Skinner's *Walden Two* (discussed in chapters four and five) describes a small community that is meant to be replicated only by creating other small communities; it is not a blueprint for a larger community. A blueprint is not necessary or helpful, he says. "Progress and improvement are local changes. We better ourselves and our world as we go." Skinner, *Cumulative Record,* 49.

15. Yevgeny Zamyatin, *A Soviet Heretic: Essays by Yevgeny Zamyatin,* ed. and trans. Mirra Ginsburg (Chicago: The University of Chicago Press, 1970), 130.

16. Karl Popper, *The Open Society and Its Enemies,* one vol. ed. (Princeton, NJ: Princeton University Press, 2013), 148.

17. Ruth Levitas, *Utopia as Method: The Imaginary Reconstruction of Society* (New York: Palgrave Macmillan, 2013), xi, 18–19.

If the purpose of utopias is to encourage "the best that can be 'made' of man," this must be evinced in both the utopia's ends as well as its means. Thus, though we commonly speak of ends and means separately—and sometimes of means becoming ends or ends justifying means—Dewey advises that the two terms represent a distinction of judgment and not of reality. Specifically, he explains, " 'End' is a name for a series of acts taken collectively. . . . 'Means' is a name for the same series taken distributively. . . . Only as the end is converted into means is it definitely conceived, or intellectually defined, to say nothing of being executable."[18] In this context, we may assume that taxation—a means to diverse ends—will, in utopia, be designed to promote the ends of an ideal state, and that the system's effectiveness will be determined by examining the quality of the ends as affected by the means.

Ends viewed in isolation from the means to their attainment may have value as inspirational ideals, but what may appear as a laudable end may, when paired with unsuitable means, turn repugnant. Thus, in writing of certain political arrangements in Plato's *Republic*, Barker says: "It is easy to agree with the aims which Plato proposes to himself, but it is somewhat difficult to accept the means."[19] Though Mill praises Saint-Simon's ideal as "desirable and rational," saying its proclamation "could not but tend to . . . bring society . . . nearer to some ideal standard," he criticizes the means as "inefficacious."[20] Once the means are made explicit, what appear as expressions of the same abstract ideal—be it freedom, equality, peace, security, leisure, or harmony with nature—will each show itself as the unique consequence of the means proposed for its attainment. Consider, for example, that More,[21] Bacon,[22] Owen,[23] and other utopian philosophers and poets—expressing

---

18. John Dewey, *Human Nature and Conduct* (New York: The Modern Library, 1950), 36.

19. Ernest Barker, *The Political Thought of Plato and Aristotle* (Mineola, NY: Dover Publications, 1959), 148.

20. John Stuart Mill, *Autobiography* (New York: Penguin Books, 1989), 133.

21. More's utopians "define virtue as living according to nature." Thomas More, *Utopia*, trans. Robert M. Adams (Cambridge: Cambridge University Press, 1975), bk. 2, 67.

22. Bacon advises, "nor can nature be commanded except by being obeyed." Francis Bacon, "Plan of the Work," *The Great Instauration*, in *The Works of Francis Bacon*, ed. James Spedding, Robert Leslie Ellis, and Douglas Denon Heath, vol. 4 (Cambridge: Cambridge University Press, 2011), 32.

23. Owen speaks of "the immutable laws of nature" that "must be made known to the public." Robert Owen, *Lectures on An Entire New State of Society* (London: J. Brooks, 1830; repr., Kessinger), 86. (Page references same as original.)

the common ideal that we should pattern our lives in accord with nature's principles—were finally joined by Adolf Hitler, with his unconscionable interpretation of nature's plan for evolution, twisted into a blueprint for his ideal world and the horrific eugenic tax for effecting it.[24] Once the means are made clear, similar-sounding ends, such as "follow nature," show themselves as pathways to irreconcilable worldviews. " 'According to Nature' you want to *live?*," says Nietzsche, "what deceptive words these are!"[25]

Reflecting on ends and means in this light should make us wary of claims, such as Kateb's, that any utopian end can be achieved through an assortment of activities or practices.[26] Following Dewey's warning we should recognize in these claims the isolation of ends that have not yet been "converted into means," indicating they are, therefore, not "definitely conceived, or intellectually defined."[27] Using one of Kateb's examples, consider the dramatic difference between the meaning of *leisure* in More's *Utopia* and in Huxley's *Brave New World*. For More, leisure is created for Utopians to use in devoting themselves "to the freedom and culture of the mind,"[28] while the citizens of Huxley's London are encouraged to attend the "feelies," engage in state-sanctioned casual sex and take soma. Certainly, the end called leisure and its value to these utopian societies is transformed by the means they employ in its realization, illustrating Dewey's point. It is not leisure, referring to what a person does when she is not working or sleeping, that has changed meaning between More and Huxley, but the fact that each values this time for what can be done with it; and the alternate uses of utopian free time are one index of "the most that can be 'made' of man."

TAXES AS MEANS

Taxation is a means when viewed in isolation, but when its procedures are made explicit—who is taxed, in what medium, and for what purpose—the

---

24. Hitler declares, "one of the most patent principles of Nature's rule [is]: the inner segregation of the species of all living beings on this earth. . . . Nature's restricted form of propagation and increase is an . . . expression of her vital urge. Every animal mates only with a member of the same species." Adolf Hitler, *Mein Kampf*, trans. Ralph Manheim (Boston, Houghton Mifflin Company, 1971), 284.

25. Friedrich Nietzsche, *Beyond Good and Evil*, trans. Walter Kaufmann (New York: Vintage Books, 1966), 15.

26. Kateb, *Utopia and Its Enemies*, 83.

27. Dewey, *Human Nature and Conduct*, 36.

28. More, *Utopia*, bk. 2, 53.

importance of the integration of this means with its ends becomes evident. For taxes do not just produce revenue; they affect economic, social, existential, ecological, and ethical processes as well, influencing whether these are integrated or not. Piketty asserts that "taxation is neither good nor bad in itself. Everything depends on how taxes are collected and what they are used for."[29] For this reason, he continues, "Taxation is not a technical matter. It is preeminently a political and philosophical issue, perhaps the most important of all political issues."[30] When taxation is defined as enforced modes of sacrifice—what Murphy and Nagel assert of a capitalist economy holds also for any economy—taxes are "the most important instrument by which the political system puts into practice a conception of economic or distributive justice."[31] Whether one believes that equal or unequal wealth or income distribution is a desirable outcome, understanding the conditions that contribute to either result is a meaningful goal—for social philosophers and utopians alike. Unfortunately, as Piketty advises, "Intellectual and political debate about the distribution of wealth has long been based on an abundance of prejudice and a paucity of fact."[32]

To illustrate the importance of connecting societal goals to well-suited means, compare the different forms taxes would take between two states (utopian or otherwise). In the first, the founders announce that the primary goods for the state's laws to uphold are life, liberty, and the pursuit of happiness. The second state retains liberty but substitutes equality for life (because life is assumed, for example) and fraternity for the pursuit of happiness (perhaps, again, it is thought happiness is the natural byproduct of fraternity). In light of de Tocqueville's observation that "the taste which men have for liberty, and that which they feel for equality, are, in fact, two different things,"[33] it is apparent that a tax system designed to promote equality and fraternity, for example, should look quite distinct from one promoting liberty and the pursuit of happiness. At first glance, more utopias appear

---

29. Thomas Piketty, *Capital in the Twenty-First Century*, trans. Arthur Goldhammer (Cambridge, MA: The Belknap Press of Harvard University Press, 2014), 481.

30. Piketty, 493.

31. Murphy and Nagel, *The Myth of Ownership: Taxes and Justice*, 3. Distributive (or economic) justice is in opposition to corrective (or punitive) justice.

32. Piketty, *Capital in the Twenty-First Century*, 2.

33. Alexis de Tocqueville, *Democracy in America*, trans. Henry Reeve (New York: W. W. Norton and Co., 2007), vol. 2, bk. 2, chap. 1, 444.

to promote equality than liberty.[34] As we will see, however, designing a tax system for either goal is challenging because assigning a single meaning to either *equality* or *liberty* is a contentious matter.[35]

The substance of this approach to taxation is not new, as Montesquieu illustrates on a far grander scale in *The Spirit of Laws*. When he speaks of the "spirit" of laws he means their coordinating purpose or activating principle. Thus, he argues for a deliberate synergy between each form of government and its doctrines, institutions, and laws. When the spirit of laws promotes the general welfare, means are unified in pursuit of society's ends.[36] It is for this reason that he says, for example, "taxes may be heavier in proportion to the liberty of the subject."[37] Burke illustrates the failure to achieve a coordinated spirit of laws in his depiction of the early constitution and supporting tax system adopted in the wake of the French Revolution. "I do not see a variety of objects, reconciled in one consistent whole, but several contradictory principles reluctantly and irreconcilably brought and held together . . . like wild beasts shut up in a cage, to claw and bite each other to their mutual destruction."[38] He concludes that as the French have contrived matters, "their taxation does not so much depend on their constitution, as their constitution on their taxation."[39]

---

34. For a discussion of the prominence of utopias promoting equality over liberty, see Kateb, *Utopia and Its Enemies*, 220ff. Sargent explains, "Many utopias are, from the perspective of individual freedom, dystopias. Some have this appearance because the author wants to emphasize a value seen to be in conflict with freedom. This value is usually equality, order, or security." Lyman Tower Sargent, "Authority and Utopia: Utopianism in Political Thought," *Polity* 14, no. 4 (Summer 1982): 573.

35. Cohen notes, for example, "It is a familiar right-wing claim that freedom and equality are conflicting ideals. . . . Most leftists," however, "reply either that there is no real conflict between equality and freedom . . . or that to the extent that there indeed is one, freedom should give way to equality." G. A. Cohen, *Self-Ownership, Freedom, and Equality* (Cambridge: Cambridge University Press, 1995), 111.

36. Montesquieu declares, "I shall first examine the relations which laws bear to the nature and principle of each government . . . and if I can but once establish it, the laws will soon appear to flow thence as from their source." Charles de Montesquieu, *The Spirit of Laws*, trans. Thomas Nugent and J. V. Prichard, in *Great Books of the Western World*, ed. Robert Maynard Hutchins and Mortimer J. Adler, vol. 38 (Chicago: Encyclopaedia Britannica, 1952), bk. 1, chap. 3, 3.

37. Montesquieu, bk. 13, chap. 12, 99.

38. Edmund Burke, *Reflections on the Revolution in France* (1790) (Oxford: Oxford University Press, 1993), 182.

39. Burke, 180.

CRITICS OF UTOPIA

Among those critical of utopian thinking are Burke,[40] Hayek,[41] Hume, Malthus,[42] Marx,[43] Nietzsche,[44] Popper, and Sumner.[45] According to Hume, "All plans of government,"—citing Plato's *Republic* and More's *Utopia*—"which suppose great reformation in the manner of mankind, are plainly imaginary." In spite of this, he does not dismiss their value out of hand, adding that "in all cases, it must be advantageous to know what is most perfect in the kind, that we may be able to bring any real constitution or form of government as near as possible."[46] Popper complains of a prejudice in favor of social experiments involving the whole of a society. He favors "piecemeal social experiments" and cites the introduction of a "new kind of taxation" as a social experiment "with repercussions through the whole of society without remodelling society as a whole."[47]

---

40. Burke, 165.

41. See, for example, Chris Matthew Sciabarra, *Marx, Hayek, and Utopia* (SUNY Press, 1995).

42. Malthus was critical of Godwin in particular. He argues, "in cases where the perfection of the model is a perfection of a different and superior nature from that towards which we should naturally advance . . . we shall in all probability impede the progress which we might have expected to make had we not fixed our eyes upon so perfect a model." Thomas Malthus, *An Essay on the Principle of Population* (Oxford: Oxford University Press, 1993), 115.

43. See, for example, Roger Paden, "Marx's Critique of the Utopian Socialists," *Utopian Studies* 13, no. 2 (2002): 67–91.

44. Nietzsche declares, "The man *who has become free* . . . spurns the contemptible sort of well-being dreamed of by shopkeepers, Christians, cows, women, Englishmen and other democrats." Friedrich Nietzsche, *Twilight of the Idols*, in *The Twilight of the Idols and The Anti-Christ*, trans. R. J. Hollingdale (New York: Penguin Books, 1968), 104 (italics in original).

45. Sumner criticizes Bellamy and other social reformers. William Graham Sumner, "The Absurd Effort to Make the World Over," in *War and Other Essays* (New York: AMS Press, 1970), 206.

46. David Hume, "Idea of a Perfect Commonwealth," in *Essays, Moral, Political, and Literary*, ed. Eugene F. Miller (Indianapolis, IN: The Liberty Fund, 1985), 513–14.

47. Popper, *The Open Society and Its Enemies*," 152.

PRACTICALITY

The utterance of a single word could negative the generalizations of a lifetime of serious research and thought. Such a word was the adjective UTOPIAN. The mere utterance of it could damn any scheme, no matter how sanely conceived, of economic amelioration or regeneration.

—Jack London (1876–1916), *The Iron Heel*[48]

In *Anarchy, State, and Utopia*, Nozick exclaims, "I do not laugh at the content of our wishes that go not only beyond the actual and what we take to be feasible in the future, but even beyond the possible."[49] Among the attractions of utopian literature are its unbounded expressions of human potential and its attempts to get at the roots of societal problems standing in the way of this potential's fulfillment by offering novel solutions often unfettered by questions of practicality. But *impractical*, even when it is an apt description, does not have to mean aimless or without purpose. Paraphrasing Plato's response to the accusation that philosophers' ideas are useless, the blame for the purported impracticality of utopian ideas should rest on those who refuse to consider them—not on the ideas themselves.[50] Thus Musgrave, in *The Theory of Public Finance*, after announcing he will next discuss the distribution of income and related problems, "begs" his readers "not to discard this somewhat utopian scheme with the sterile objection of 'utterly impracticable.'" He recommends testing its practicability not by the promise of its speedy enactment but by its potential contribution "to orderly thinking about the basic issues of budget policy."[51] Utopia, according to Frye, is a social conception expressible in terms of a vision or

48. Jack London, *The Iron Heel* (New York: The Macmillan Company, 1908, repr., n.p., n.d.), 57n42. (Page references are to reprint.)

49. Robert Nozick, *Anarchy, State, and Utopia* (New York, Basic Books, 1974), 308. Though his own utopia falls prey to this charge, Nozick observes that "many criticisms [of utopia] focus upon utopians' lack of discussion of *means* for achieving their vision or their concentration upon means that will not achieve their ends" (Nozick, 326, italics in original).

50. Plato, *Republic*, bk. 6, 489.

51. Robert A. Musgrave, *The Theory of Public Finance* (New York: McGraw-Hill Book Company, 1959), vii.

myth that imagines the purpose of social life. The value of such a vision, he explains, "depends on the depth and penetration of the social analyses which inspires it."[52] Taxes—broadly conceived, and as defined later in this chapter—are a central means for achieving the ends at which society aims; accordingly, a social analysis that ignores taxation risks exposing its lack of "depth and penetration."

What advocates of utopia see as the benefits of its freedom of thought, including its unselfconscious forays into realms of unexplored human potential, others see as threats leading toward menacing outcomes. In *Utopia and Its Enemies*, Kateb describes objections against utopias that require the violent overthrow of the current governing structure. Every revolution, he declares, "consumes the dreams which set it in motion."[53] One reason for this, observes Proudhon, is that a revolution "is always split by parties and sects, which work to pervert it."[54] To this, Orwell adds his cynical insight that "every revolutionary opinion draws part of its strength from a secret conviction that nothing can be changed."[55] Though *utopian* frequently serves as a term of derision, there can be nothing wrong with utopias when their purpose is to explore alternatives to a societal condition that few believe is perfect or even adequate. In describing More's *Utopia*, Hexter says he "investigates the social evils of his own time until he discovers what he believes to be their roots, and then he systematically elaborates the regimen necessary to eradicate those evils."[56] Societies will continue to evolve and change; regarding the direction of this change, Skinner asks, "Are we to be controlled by accident, by tyrants, or by ourselves in effective cultural design?"[57]

---

52. Northrop Frye, "Varieties of Literary Utopias," in *Utopias and Utopian Thought*, ed. Frank E. Manuel (Boston, MA: Houghton Mifflin Company, 1965), 25.

53. Kateb, *Utopia and Its Enemies*, 48.

54. Pierre-Joseph Proudhon, *General Idea of the Revolution in the Nineteenth Century*, trans. John Beverley Robinson (Mineola, New York: Dover Publications, 2003), 168.

55. George Orwell, *The Road to Wigan Pier* (New York: A Harvest Book – Harcourt, 1958), 158.

56. J. H. Hexter, *More's Utopia: The Biography of an Idea* (New York: Harper Torchbooks, 1965), 58.

57. Skinner, *Cumulative Record*, 11.

TAXATION AS A MORAL QUESTION OF SACRIFICE

Taxing was originally, I assume, a way of raising money. When did it begin to be used to manipulate the behavior of the taxed?

—B. F. Skinner (1904–1990), *Notebooks*[58]

Must there be taxes *even* in utopia? If so, the tax system should mesh with, and integrate into, the spirit of the envisioned ideal society; failing to do so, I argue, will inevitably alter that spirit. Skipping until later to define either *tax* or *utopia*, there exist models of apparently tax-free utopias, with More's Utopia as one example. Unfortunately, but unsurprisingly, the resulting societies pay heavily for this outcome in other ways—in what I call nonpecuniary or *constructive* taxes.

While taxation may at first appear a dry and colorless topic for utopian inquiry, Cicero declares that "revenues are the sinews of the commonwealth,"[59] and one recent text on the economics of tax systems claims that modern tax regimes can affect "the choice of religion, timing of marriages, births, and even deaths."[60] If this is so, then envisioning an ideal—or even an improved—state without considering its tax structure is to see its coordinated operations as a black box; it is conceiving an end—the general welfare—while ignoring the means to its attainment, be it the financing or whatever sacrifices may substitute for financing. "If one wills an end," Nietzsche declares, "one must also will the means to it,"[61] and doing so requires making the means explicit. Despite this, as noted, few utopias directly address questions of taxation as a foundational issue. Perhaps this lack of interest in matters of public finance is, for many utopian theorists, a natural effect of assuming taxes to be one of those odious problems to be eliminated from utopia rather than as another societal problem in need of an innovative solution.

---

58. B. F. Skinner, *Notebooks*, ed. Robert Epstein (Englewood Cliffs, NJ: Prentice-Hall, 1980), 356.

59. Cicero, "On the Manilian Law," in *Cicero Orations*, trans. H. Grose Hodge (Cambridge, MA: Harvard University Press; Loeb Classical Library (LCL 198), 1927), §7, 29.

60. Joel Slemrod and Christian Gillitzer, *Tax Systems* (Cambridge, MA: MIT Press, 2014), 4.

61. Nietzsche, *Twilight of the Idols*, sec. 40, 106.

Concerning the framework of utopian thought, Lasky advises, "Utopias are written out of both hope and despair. They are models of stability conceived in the spirit of contradiction."[62] If a condition of stability, whether static or dynamic, is the common goal, the sinews must be designed to accommodate the state's operations within its ideal mandate.[63] As we explore diverse utopias, it will become apparent that most of their authors have not given serious thought to taxes as an underlying ethical issue. Exceptions include Saint-Simon's hierarchy of ability, George's *Progress and Poverty*, Hertzka's *Freeland*, and Wells's *A Modern Utopia*.[64] The fact that utopias seldom propose specific tax regimes is, in itself, instructive. In Plato's *Republic*, for example, Socrates does not stop the discussion of justice and say, "Before we get too far along in our discovery of the ideal state, we should decide how it will be paid for, because once we make that decision, it will shed important light on what kind of government we propose and what its relation will be to the citizens. What will be the basis for the Republic's tax policy?" The closest hint of such a discussion comes in the description of the life conditions imposed on the guardians. Regarding these protectors of a just state, Socrates explains: "they will receive a wage annually from the others consisting of the bare subsistence required for their guarding, and for this wage they must take care of themselves and the rest of the city."[65] Commenting on this fact Garnsey notes, "The only material resources to which [the guardians] have access are provided by others: they receive payments towards their livelihood from the rest of the citizenry. . . . This is in effect a tax regime."[66] But even as it is a tax regime, no explanation is

---

62. Melvin J. Lasky, *Utopia and Revolution: On the Origins of a Metaphor* (Chicago: University of Chicago Press, 1976; republished, New Brunswick, NJ: Transaction Publishers, 2004), 9.

63. Nagel asserts, "Political theory has always been concerned to design systems which generate the psychological conditions of their own stability." Thomas Nagel, *Equality and Partiality* (New York: Oxford University Press, 1991), 149.

64. In *Freeland*, for example, Hertzka's narrator explains that the "public expenditure of the community should be covered by a contribution from each individual exactly in proportion to his net income." Theodor Hertzka, *Freeland: A Social Anticipation*, trans. Arthur Ransom (London: Chatto and Windus, 1891, repr. University of California Libraries), 109. The tax system of Henri Saint-Simon is discussed in chapter four, of Henry George in chapter six, and of H. G. Wells in chapters two, four, five, and six.

65. Plato, *Republic*, trans. Allan Bloom, 2nd ed. (Basic Books, 1968), bk. 8, 543c.

66. Peter Garnsey, *Thinking About Property: From Antiquity to the Age of Revolution* (New York: Cambridge University Press, 2007), 12.

provided as to how the state is to extract this tax from the majority of the populace who are farmers, merchants, and tradesmen. Is an equal amount required from each, or is it assessed in proportion to some base (income, wealth)? Are those wealthier or more able to pay expected to contribute a greater proportion? Is it paid in kind depending on one's trade?[67] Are there exemptions for old age or blindness? Thus, for Plato, as for many people, taxation is a detail, a nuisance akin to taking out the garbage—there is an acknowledged need but little interest in dwelling upon the particulars. Such "particulars," however, I emphasize again, do affect the relation of citizens to each other and to the state. "Without taxes," Piketty contends, "society has no common destiny, and collective action is impossible."[68]

One upshot of this failure to explicitly consider taxation—for Plato and for many utopians—is a reliance on nonpecuniary means for achieving the ends of society. In effect, the functional counterparts of pecuniary taxes—what I term *constructive taxes* (and define in the second part of this chapter)—are assessed and paid in another medium. Examples of constructive taxes (constructive in the sense of *construed*), described in the chapters to follow, include government proscriptions on categories listed in Table 1. This form of taxation explains how utopias—even those that have banned money—still provide traditional governmental functions by replacing pecuniary with nonpecuniary sacrifices.

Defining an ideal tax system—or at least a promising candidate—requires envisioning the full range of possibilities regarding the individual and the general welfare. For this reason, examining utopian thinking on taxation—either explicitly articulated or implicitly portrayed—offers an opportunity for an open hearing on conflicting perspectives. History has already supplied an eclectic sampling of *what* may be taxed, including beards, corn, heads, hearths, salt, slaves, soap, voting, and windows. So any additions to that list by utopians, however strange, may not appear remarkable in historical context; in this case truth has already proved strange enough to require little help from fiction. However, in considering *what* is taxed, it is critical to understand the context of *who* is ultimately taxed and specifically what cost is paid, in what medium, and under what conditions—indicating the underlying view of the general welfare—and the effects the tax system has

---

67. "Ancient governments assessed and collected taxes in kind: grain, animals, and labor services." Carolyn Webber and Aaron Wildavsky, *A History of Taxation and Expenditure in the Western World* (New York: Simon and Schuster, 1986), 17.

68. Piketty, *Capital in the Twenty-First Century*, 493.

Table 1. Utopias Featuring Constructive Tax Policies

Constructive Tax	Primary* Examples	Secondary* Examples	Chapter
Privacy	More, Orwell, Wells, Zamyatin	Hertzka, Huxley, Le Guin, Plato	2
Access to truth	Bacon, Godwin, Orwell, Plato	London	3
Work or occupation (equalizing effort or hours, abolishing useless trades, forced labor)	Bellamy, Campanella, Gilman, Le Guin, More, Nozick, Plato, Saint-Simon, Skinner, Wells	Hertzka, London, Morris	4, 7
Marriage, childrearing (children raised by experts), and eugenics	Bacon, Bellamy, Campanella, Gilman, Owen, Skinner, Wells, Zamyatin	Huxley, More, Plato, Spencer	5
Land proprietorship (common vs. private)	George, Godwin, Harrington, Nozick, Owen, Tolstoy, Wells	Hertzka, Proudhon, Spence, Spencer	6

*Primary and secondary refer only to the extent of coverage the writer receives in this chapter and is unrelated to the extent to which constructive taxes figure in his or her ideal society.

on society, classes or groups within society, and individual lives.[69] As Thoreau quipped, following a controversy about an assessed but unpaid tax, "I did not see why the schoolmaster should be taxed to support the priest, and not the priest the schoolmaster."[70] His simple question reveals the balance of sacrifice society confronts, exposing disparate views of the general welfare. Adam Smith anticipated Thoreau's concern when he warned, "To hurt, in any degree, the interest of any one order of citizens, for no other purpose but to promote that of some other, is evidently contrary to that justice and equality of treatment which the sovereign owes to all the different orders of

---

69. Winfrey notes, "Knowing who writes the check to government does not answer the question of who actually pays. . . . Taxes initially falling on businesses [for example] must all eventually be shifted to individuals." John C. Winfrey, *Social Issues: The Ethics and Economics of Taxes and Public Programs* (Oxford: Oxford University Press, 1998), 56.

70. Henry David Thoreau, *Civil Disobedience* in *Walden and Civil Disobedience* (New York: Barnes and Noble Classics, 2003), 277.

his subjects."[71] Both Thoreau's question and Smith's observation highlight the need, when examining utopian thought, to search for signs of moral discord between the form of taxation proposed (or implied) and the ideal(s) to achieve, especially when that ideal demands treating one class or segment of society as the means to benefit another. Identifying such signs in utopian societies will (presumably) help us recognize problems of misaligned means and ends in our own.

Utopianism is a particularly well-suited medium for exercising the moral imagination. As Godwin observes, "extravagant sallies of mind are the prelude of the highest wisdom."[72] Since few utopias describe their tax systems in any detail and many, as noted, appear to function without taxation, whether there could be an ideal form of taxation, or complete absence of taxes, is a utopian query. Even raising the question will be dismissed as useless by some, while others will recognize in it the hope of improving an institution they find morally inadequate or perhaps morally repugnant.

Part Two:
The Construal of Taxation and of Utopia

THE SINEWS OF TAXATION

Bad taxation is as certain to produce bad government and bad social conditions, as bad food to produce indigestion and decay in the human body.

—Thomas Gaskell Shearman (1834–1900), *Natural Taxation*[73]

---

71. Adam Smith, *Wealth of Nations* (Amherst, NY: Prometheus Books, 1991), bk. 4, chap. 8, 436. Paine echoes this sentiment: "I care not how affluent some may be, provided that none be miserable in consequence of it." Thomas Paine, "Agrarian Justice," https://www.ssa.gov/history/paine4.html (accessed September 15, 2017).

72. Godwin, *Enquiry Concerning Political Justice*, 3rd ed., bk. 6, chap. 3, 576.

73. Thomas Gaskell Shearman, *Natural Taxation* (New York: Doubleday and McClure Co., 1898, repr.), 4.

Most people, I assume, would prefer a utopia without taxation, holding all other things constant. But there is the problem: other things would not remain constant. If no sacrifice is required to maintain society and promote the general welfare—this constituting the central need for taxation—then we have unwittingly or surreptitiously altered the meaning of society or one of the other key terms under examination and thereby entered a new inquiry. Paradoxical to some and intolerable to others, the notion that there must be taxation even in utopia provides a framework for examining the fundamental nature of taxation. In this process, the familiar meanings of the key terms noted earlier (including society, general welfare, government, sacrifice, and taxation) require examination, as adding a new dimension to any one of these concepts may alter the scope of the others.

In their book on the history of taxation, Webber and Wildavsky advise that a nation's taxes are related to its economy, history, and political climate.[74] The same authors argue that the reason we have multiple forms of taxation (including estate tax, excise tax, gift tax, income tax, property tax, sales tax, use tax, value-added tax, and the rest of the list) is that "a multiplicity of tax sources provides a far-reaching redundancy into the nooks and crannies of income otherwise hard to reach."[75] Mill suggests another reason for the multiplicity of taxes. "No tax," he says, "is in itself absolutely just; the justice or injustice of taxes can only be comparative." But even among comparatively just taxes, he admits, "if just in the conception, they are never completely so in the application."[76] For this reason, he conjectures, "it is quite possible that nations may some day be obliged to resort to a moderate tax on all property, as the least unjust mode of raising a part of their revenue."[77]

TAXES IN EDEN

Only with the founding of a state or utopia is there a chance to integrate the system of taxation into the ideals for which that society is to stand. It is only at that time as well that criteria must be established for judging a

---

74. Webber and Wildavsky, *A History of Taxation and Expenditure*, 333.

75. Webber and Wildavsky, 554.

76. John Stuart Mill, "Property and Taxation," in *Essays on Economics and Society*, vol. 5 of *Collected Works of John Stuart Mill* (Toronto: University of Toronto Press, 1967), 701.

77. Mill, 701.

tax as fair or unfair, as this judgment is not independent of the values the society aims at but is an extension and implementation of those values.[78] At that critical time, unless a tax system is devised that supports and enables the society's goals, taxes become a political afterthought that needs retrofitting to an existing system of values and ideals. The resulting tax is a means cut off from the ends of society and will provoke unintended distortions to that system's fundamental moral design. For this reason, when society's original design neglects the question of taxation, multiple forms of taxation may be the only practical way for political leaders to survive. Saint-Simon highlights this fact when he writes that in Europe "the greatest statesman, or at any rate the one who is regarded as the most able, held in the greatest esteem, promoted, and praised highly, is always the man who can find a means of increasing the revenue from taxation without arousing the wrath of the taxpayers."[79]

Benn and Peters address another dimension of this problem, reflecting that until the nineteenth century, taxation was "simply a matter of raising money to cover government expense, as ease of collection counted for a good deal more in the choice of a tax than concern for fair distribution of the tax burden."[80] In discussions of tax policy, ease of collection or convenience is still a commonly voiced justification. From an administrative point of view, a tax relying on the cooperation and honesty of the taxpayer may offer great ease or convenience. But the tax imposed by such systems, Mill asserts, "on whatever principles of equality it may be imposed, is in practice unequal in one of the worst ways, falling heaviest on the most conscientious."[81] And though convenience is one of Adam Smith's canons of taxation, he mentions the convenience of the taxpayer, not that of the tax collector.[82] Although Benn and Peters and others may feel that we have moved beyond "ease of collection" as a driving force in tax policy, it

---

78. Murphy and Nagel argue that "Justice or injustice in taxation can only mean justice or injustice in the system of property rights and entitlements that result from a particular tax regime." Murphy and Nagel, *The Myth of Ownership: Taxes and Justice*, 8.

79. Saint-Simon, *Henri Saint-Simon (1760–1825): Selected Writing on Science, Industry and Social Organization*, trans. and ed. Taylor, 163.

80. S. I. Benn and R. S. Peters, *The Principles of Political Thought* (New York: The Free Press, 1959), 174.

81. John Stuart Mill, *Principles of Political Economy*, abr. J. Laurence Laughlin (New York: Appleton and Company, 1884), 556.

82. Smith, *Wealth of Nations*, bk. 5, chap. 2, 499.

is possible that ease of collection has simply shifted its meaning and now refers to the ease or convenience of legislators seeking to shield themselves from opposition launched by powerful constituencies, whether political or financial, and no longer to the ease or convenience of the taxpayer, or even the tax collectors.[83] As ends become isolated and means become reified, their significance shifts, distortions arise, and Dewey's warning that these "terms denote not a division in reality but a distinction in judgment"[84] is forgotten.

Hayek visits another aspect of the problem of disjointed means and ends: "We are so used to a system under which expenditure is decided upon first and the question of who is to bear the burden considered afterwards, that it is rarely recognized how much this conflicts with the basic principle of limiting all coercion to the enforcement of rules of just conduct."[85] But it is not just the matter of *who* is to bear the burden that is ignored at the outset, but as importantly that of *why* and what impact one system will have on society as opposed to an alternate system. Just as damaging is assuming that economic concerns are the only criteria to evaluate in answering these questions, without considering associated factors that may be historical (custom, tradition), philosophical (justice, personal autonomy), political (democracy, theocracy), psychological (privacy, self-esteem), religious (afterlife, opposition to war), and sociological (equal opportunity, social mobility). What relationship the government assumes with respect to its citizens is as much a result of how it designs and implements its principles of taxation as it is of the specific rights and duties it admits.

At this point, one concern some readers may express is that the very situation I am describing—considering taxation in the initial formation of a government—is itself just another utopian scheme. A critic may rightfully ask: "When will we again be founding a new nation or reforming an old one, where we can benefit from this insight?" But such a framing negatively prejudges the importance (or relevance) of utopian thought. It may be

---

83. In the United States, for example, the notorious complexity of the Internal Revenue Code is proof that the convenience of the taxpayer is not a paramount concern. Judge Learned Hand called the tax law a "fantastic labyrinth" whose words "merely dance before my eyes in a meaningless procession . . . [that] leave in my mind only a confused sense of some vitally important, but successfully concealed, purport, which it is my duty to extract." Eulogy of Thomas Walter Swan, 57 Yale L. J. 167, 169 (1947), quoted in Welder v. United States, 329 F. Supp. at 741–42 (S. D. Tex. 1971).

84. Dewey, *Human Nature and Conduct*, 36.

85. Friedrich A. Hayek, *Law, Legislation and Liberty*, vol. 1 (Chicago: University of Chicago Press, 1979), 137.

perfectly true that we will never be in the position of a nation's founding mothers and fathers, debating the elements of a new constitution.[86] But we will certainly be in the position of debating or merely wondering why taxation seems always to be such a divisive issue.

ECONOMISTS AND TAXES

Taxation is, at its core, an ethical question, as earlier stipulated. Its most contentious features are labeled progressivity, regressivity, and redistribution. A tax is progressive if the ratio of taxes (or sacrifice) to income rises as income (or means) increases. A tax is regressive if the ratio of taxes (or sacrifice) to income rises as income (or means) decreases.[87] Redistribution is the moral feature of taxation aiming at an outcome such as reduction of income or wealth inequality. (Nozick's argument distinguishing two types of redistribution is described in chapter seven.) Paying taxes fosters a moral struggle between the immediate good for the taxpayer and the more remote good for the society the taxpayer is a member and so an indirect beneficiary of. As with ethical questions generally, input from the social sciences—especially economics, political science, psychology, and sociology—is relevant and helpful, but not determinative. As Piketty observes, "the distribution of wealth is too important an issue to be left to economists."[88]

Though economists routinely investigate questions of taxation, their research is generally to determine "what tax system would best achieve explicit objectives under carefully delineated conditions."[89] Such conditions include accepted ethical and political starting points as well as limiting assumptions,

---

86. At the time of the debate in the United States regarding its constitution, Hamilton says of taxes that there is "no part of the administration of government that requires extensive information and a thorough knowledge of the principles of political economy so much as the business of taxation. The man who understands those principles best will be least likely to resort to oppressive expedients, or to sacrifice any particular class of citizens to the procurement of revenue." Alexander Hamilton, *The Federalist Papers* (New York: Penguin Books, 1987), no. 36, 235.

87. A proportional tax applies the same rate on everyone regardless of income or wealth. Proudhon condemns both progressive and proportional taxation as unjust. "If the tax is proportional," he claims, "labor is sacrificed; if progressive, talent." Proudhon, *General Idea of the Revolution in the Nineteenth Century*, 150.

88. Piketty, *Capital in the Twenty-First Century*, 2. For a detailed discussion of this and related topics, see John Broome, *Ethics out of Economics* (Cambridge University Press, 1999).

89. Slemrod and Gillitzer, *Tax Systems*, 4.

for example, "that people understand and react rationally to the tax system."[90] Many economists, says Steuerle, dismiss questions of fairness "as more an issue of aesthetics than of analysis."[91] In an age of compartmentalization, it is natural for a discipline to become associated with a specific kind of problem. In addition, to the extent that modern economics evolved from political economy, which often included unquestioned assumptions about public welfare and human nature, this legacy may still haunt its public perception.[92] As a consequence, many people—including many in government—believe taxation is simply an economic problem and the purview of economists.

When economists venture beyond the scientific determination of the immediate or indirect economic effects of real or proposed tax systems—understood in this limited fiscal sense—and engage in promoting social programs, political ideologies, or the design or defense of ends for government to achieve, their status as economists becomes secondary and their function transforms to that of social or political philosophers, or utopians. Failure to recognize this shift of jurisdiction subjects them to H. G. Wells's criticism that "few earthly economists have been able to disentangle themselves from patriotism and politics," and that, as a result, political economy consists "of a hopeless muddle of social assumptions and preposterous psychology."[93]

PECUNIARY AND NONPECUNIARY TAXES

For most of history taxes were demanded for a given need and often paid in kind, including military service.[94] Adam Smith observes, "War, and the

---

90. Slemrod and Gillitzer, 5.

91. C. Eugene Steuerle, "And Equal (Tax) Justice for All?," in *Tax Justice*, ed. Joseph J. Thorndike and Dennis J. Ventry Jr. (Washington, DC: The Urban Institute Press, 2002), 254.

92. As one economist notes, "economics is rooted in a history of moral and political philosophy that took the matter of people's welfare as a necessarily integral part of the questions that were addressed." Simon Zadek, *An Economics of Utopia* (Brookfield, VT: Ashgate Publishing Company, 1993), 47.

93. H. G. Wells, *A Modern Utopia* (New York: Digireads Publishing, 2011), 35, 37.

94. In the Bible, for example, Samuel warns the people of new nonpecuniary taxes if he appoints a king as they request. "He will take your sons, and appoint *them* for himself. . . . And he will take the tenth of your seed, and of your vineyards . . . [and] the tenth of your sheep." 1 Samuel 8:11–17, KJV. See also Manuel L. Jose and Charles K. Moore, "The Development of Taxation in the Bible: Improvements in Counting, Measurement, and Computation in the Ancient Middle East," *Accounting Historians Journal* 25, no. 2 (December 1998): 63–80.

preparation for war, are the two circumstances which, in modern times, occasion the greater part of the necessary expense of all great states."[95] As taxation has come to be equated exclusively with money, however, the process of collecting revenue into a general fund and the budgeting of the fund's uses have evolved as largely separate, though related, undertakings.[96] Wicksell argues that the problem with this procedure is its tendency to disregard any disparity between what taxpayers pay and what they receive.[97] His utopian recommendation is that "no public expenditures ever be voted upon without simultaneous determination of the means of covering their costs."[98] However, as governments identify ever-increasing needs, they search for new frontiers of revenue and the perennial question becomes: "What else could we tax?" When this occurs it is clear that taxation as a means has been cut off from its ends. In the current political climate there appears little that is safe from taxation; taxing Internet usage, for example, has been a utopian dream for many in government since its inception. But if almost anything may become the object of taxation, what does this say about the reasons for taxing this thing, activity, person, or class rather than another? Thoreau's question noted earlier—"why the schoolmaster should be taxed to support the priest, and not the priest the schoolmaster"[99]—illustrates the scales weighing the sacrifices one segment of society imposes on another.

"The fact that the relationship of the State to its citizens is determined basically by a monetary relationship," declares Simmel, "has its origin primarily in taxation."[100] Coming to view taxation in this narrow light—as a purely pecuniary phenomenon—has eclipsed its broader historical and functional context as a device of political control operating through the imposition of personal sacrifice. When we speak disapprovingly of "throwing money at a problem," we imply that there are other solutions—perhaps better solutions, whether private or governmental—being overlooked and

---

95. Smith, *Wealth of Nations*, bk. 5, chap. 2, 493.

96. Hayek, *Law, Legislation and Liberty*, vol. 1, 137.

97. Thus "taxation according to benefit," he explains, is replaced with "taxation according to ability-to-pay." Knut Wicksell, "A New Principle of Just Taxation," trans. J. M. Buchanan, in *Classics in the Theory of Public Finance*, ed. Richard A. Musgrave and Alan T. Peacock (New York: St Martin's Press, 1967), 74.

98. Wicksell, 91–92.

99. Thoreau, *Civil Disobedience*, 277.

100. Georg Simmel, *The Philosophy of Money*, trans. Tom Bottomore and David Frisby (Boston: Routledge and Kegan Paul, 1978), 316.

not directly connected to revenue. If these solutions compel government to enforce a nonpecuniary sacrifice for the general welfare, they are nonetheless impositions of a tax, albeit constructively levied.

BEYOND REVENUE: DEFINING A TAX

> Am I right in supposing that the effect of your economy is to establish insuperable inequalities among you, and to forbid the hope of the brotherhood which your polity proclaims?
>
> —William Dean Howells (1837–1920), *A Traveler from Altruria*[101]

When construed most broadly, *Black's Law Dictionary* advises the term tax "embraces all governmental impositions on the person, property, privileges, occupations, and enjoyment of the people." And, it continues, "although a tax is often thought of as being pecuniary in nature, it is not necessarily payable in money."[102] It is these nonmonetary forms of taxation that utopias frequently embrace. "Fundamental explanations of a realm"—such as taxation—"are explanations of the realm in other terms," explains Nozick; "they make no use of any of the notions of the realm. Only via such explanations," he continues, "can we explain and hence understand everything about a realm."[103] An explanation of taxation using its own current concepts and jargon would involve terms such as marginal and effective rates, direct, indirect, vertical and horizontal equity, implicit, optimal, and so on. It would also equate taxes with government revenue. On Nozick's reasoning, the depiction of a tax system should occur in a framework that first defines the role of taxation from the vantage of another realm: for

---

101. William Dean Howells, *A Traveler from Altruria* (New York: Sagamore Press, 1957), 65.

102. *Black's Law Dictionary*, 9th ed. (St. Paul MN: West Publishing Co., 2009), 1594. Cummings warns, however, that "It is important to ward off the tendency to seize upon some supposed all-purpose definition of tax that explains all cases: there is none." Jasper L. Cummings Jr., *The Supreme Court, Federal Taxation, and the Constitution* (Washington, DC: American Bar Association, 2013), 83.

103. Nozick, *Anarchy, State, and Utopia*, 19. "Invisible-hand explanations," he stipulates, "minimize the use of notions constituting the phenomena to be explained" (Nozick, 19).

example, the citizens' obligation to the state and the method by which it may be liquidated.

If our goal is to judge (or justify) one tax (or tax system) as morally preferable to another, the definition of tax itself should be morally neutral, not one that begs the question by presupposing a particular ethical stance. Consider the impossibility of objectively evaluating one tax system against another if, for example, we defined taxes, as some writers do, as "forced labor,"[104] "slavery,"[105] or "theft."[106] A definition of tax must allow for a spectrum of moral approval or disapproval; the moral quality of the tax will depend ultimately on the moral justification of the tax system and its implementation—who is taxed, in what medium, and for what purpose in relation to the values upon which the society is predicated.

For this discussion, taxation is defined as a government-required sacrifice for the general welfare. Built into this definition is my assumption that a sacrifice is a potentially *unequal* government-coerced exchange: the value of what one receives—if discernible—is not a function of the value of what one relinquishes; a sacrifice is a moral black hole.[107] This characterization follows the US Supreme Court's understanding of taxes as neither voluntary nor providing any reciprocal benefit and explains why taxes are inherently redistributive.[108] Beginning with this revised (or resurrected) and historically relevant definition of taxation, it is possible by reverse engineering—by deconstructing a state's tax system—to determine its (de facto) conception

---

104. Nozick, *Anarchy, State, and Utopia*, 169.

105. Leo Tolstoy, *The Slavery of our Times* (repr., n.p, Read Books, 2013), 84–85.

106. Murray Rothbard, *The Ethics of Liberty* (New York: New York University Press, 1998), 162.

107. My use of the term *sacrifice* has no connection with the "theory of sacrifice" associated with economists Pigou and Edgeworth, which attempts to justify progressive taxation based on the decreasing marginal utility of the next unit of income.

108. "A tax is not an assessment of benefits. It is . . . a means of distributing the burden of the cost of government. The only benefit to which the taxpayer is constitutionally entitled is that derived from his enjoyment of the privilege of living in an organized society, established and safeguarded by the devotion of taxes to public purposes." Carmichael v. Southern Coal and Coke Co., 301 U.S. 495, 522–23 (1937). Cummings explains that for the Supreme Court, "a tax is neither voluntarily incurred . . . nor does a tax need to produce any identifiable benefit to the payor." Cummings, *The Supreme Court, Federal Taxation, and the Constitution*, 306.

of the general welfare—whatever the possibility of its incoherence. Thus, while ideally a vision of the general welfare should animate the development of a tax system capable of upholding that vision, in practice this is seldom the case, as I previously explained.

Nagel observes that the "problem of utopianism" is that of "discovering the constraints on a well-ordered society."[109] Defining taxation simply as government revenue provides no apparatus for its analysis as a political instrument. Without a more fundamental explanation we are without a rudder in any attempt to change course. Becker observes that the "manipulation of definitions" is an important mode of social and political control.[110] No less important is the interested preservation of a definition that obfuscates underlying problems; acquiescing to a definition of taxation as government revenue has this effect.[111] Defining taxation in terms of unrecompensed sacrifice and coercion rather than revenue directs our attention to its history, conceivable modes, intended targets, and potential for abuse, as well as its vital effects on society.[112]

GENERAL WELFARE

Judge Learned Hand observed that there is "no great difficulty in deciding whether a tax is 'to pay the Debts' of the United States; but at times it is hard to say whether a statute is a tax to 'provide for the . . . general Welfare.' "[113] In this study, the general welfare is not an independent ideal, but a moral placeholder—the result of what each state's laws enforce and the general good each utopia espouses. For this reason, what the citizens must sacrifice is what *that* state demands for its vision of the general welfare. In More's Utopia, for example, the citizens must sacrifice their privacy

109. Nagel, *Equality and Partiality*, 27.

110. Howard Becker, *Outsiders: Studies in the Sociology of Deviance* (New York: The Free Press, 1963), 204–5.

111. Leviner observes that "the extent to which the existing normative tax discourse is based on anecdotes and used to advance self-serving interests rather than a well-defined framework of principles and rationales is striking." Sagit Leviner, "The Normative Underpinnings of Taxation," *Nevada Law Journal* 13, no. 95 (Fall 2012): 1–27, 2.

112. According to D. A. Wells, "Of all the powers conferred upon the Government that of taxation is most liable to abuse." David Ames Wells, *The Theory and Practice of Taxation* (New York: D. Appleton and Company, 1911), 232.

113. Learned Hand, *The Bill of Rights* (New York: Atheneum, 1979), 13.

and private land holdings to ensure the society's somber virtue and the promise of "more than enough of the necessities and even the conveniences of life."[114] In viewing the general welfare in this way, I am not advocating thereby some form of ethical or cultural relativism. My focus is on taxation as a means for achieving the general welfare and as a partial determinant of that end. In particular, I argue that in order to understand a utopia's (or a society's) vision of the general welfare, it is necessary to recognize and understand the impact of its tax system and the form of sacrifice it imposes. Whether the sacrifice is pecuniary or takes some other form, what each person sacrifices, when combined with the sacrifices of others, should—based on the utopia's design—enable the society to function in fulfillment of its ends.

Hayek writes, regarding the general welfare, that it lacks a "sufficiently definite meaning to determine a particular course of action."[115] Of many factors clouding the meaning of general welfare are these questions: How general is general? Who counts as human? What groups (or species) does our conception of general include, exclude, or marginalize? Kant, for example, observes that America as well as the "negro countries," at the time of their discovery, were looked upon as "ownerless territories; for the native inhabitants were counted as nothing."[116] In particular, to what extent does general relate to future or even past generations (ancestors and sacred burial grounds)?[117] For Burke, for example, the general welfare encompasses a contract or partnership "between those who are living, those who are dead, and

---

114. More, *Utopia*, bk. 2, 51.

115. Friedrich A. Hayek, *The Road to Serfdom* (Chicago: Phoenix Books, The University of Chicago Press, 1944), 57.

116. Immanuel Kant, *Perpetual Peace* in *Kant: Political Writings*, trans. H. B. Nisbet (Cambridge: Cambridge University Press, 1970), 106. Regarding the utopian treatment of Indigenous Americans, at least in the late nineteenth century, Roemer explains, "Most [utopian] authors simply could not imagine any place for a race that was supposed to vanish before utopia was realized." Kenneth M. Roemer, *The Obsolete Necessity: America in Utopian Writings, 1888–1900* (The Kent State University Press, 1976), 73.

117. Kaplow explains, "Intergenerational distributive justice involves an additional, intertemporal dimension often presented as the question of whether (and, if so, how much) to discount the lives or utility of future individuals." Louis Kaplow, *The Theory of Taxation and Public Economics* (Princeton, NJ: Princeton University Press, 2008), 382. Rand, for example (discussed in chapter seven), discounts the lives of "future generations" to zero. Ayn Rand, *The Virtue of Selfishness* (New York: Signet Books, 1964), 81.

those who are to be born."[118] In Gilman's *Herland*, by contrast, when asked if her culture esteems the past and their foremothers, Ellador says, "Why, no. . . . Why should we? They are all gone. They knew less than we do."[119] For much of history we know that general welfare calculations omitted (or assigned positions of lower rank to) women, children, slaves, and persons of a different class, language, race, national origin, or religion—their nature being perceived as lacking some essential human feature.[120] There are people in our own time, however, who seek to expand the general welfare's scope to include animals,[121] corporations,[122] human morula,[123] and robots[124] (though not generally the same people). Utopias struggle with the question of inclusion as well. More's Utopia, for example, marginalizes atheists, considering them less than human and denying them the rights of believers.[125] Swift's Country of Houyhnhnms features horses as "the perfection of nature," and the human brutes as merely Yahoos.[126]

---

118. Burke, *Reflections on the Revolution in France*, 96. Against Burke's doctrine of "governing beyond the grave," Paine declares, "There never did, there never will, and there never can exist . . . any generation of men, in any country, possessed of the right or the power of binding and controlling posterity to the 'end of time.'" Thomas Paine, *Rights of Man*, in *Common Sense, Rights of Man, and Other Essential Writings of Thomas Paine* (New York: Signet Classic, 1969), 138.

119. Charlotte Perkins Gilman, *Herland* (Mineola: New York: Dover Publications, 1998), 94.

120. Roemer notes that while the reforms of the late nineteenth-century American utopians "were sincerely proposed on behalf of all mankind," the meaning of "all" was generally restricted "to the size of a full-length mirror." Roemer, *The Obsolete Necessity*, 70.

121. Marks reports, "One significant argument advanced on behalf of human rights for the apes involves their cognitive performance." Jonathan M. Marks, *What it Means to be 98% Chimpanzee: Apes, People, and Their Genes* (Berkeley and Los Angeles: University of California Press, 2002), 189.

122. Citizens United v. Federal Election Commission, 558 U.S. 310 (2010), extends the constitutional right of free speech to independent expenditures by corporations engaging in political speech. The case retained the federal ban on direct contributions from corporations to candidate campaigns or political parties.

123. The human morula is "the development of the zygote from the two-cell stage . . . at approximately 30 hours after fertilization . . . [to] the 12- to 16-cell stage, at approximately 3 days . . . [to] the late morula stage, at approximately 4 days." *Stedman's Medical Dictionary*, 28th ed. (Philadelphia: Lippincott Williams and Wilkins, 2006), 1228.

124. See David J. Gunkel, *Robot Rights* (MIT Press, 2018).

125. More, *Utopia*, bk. 2, 95.

126. Jonathan Swift, *Gulliver's Travels* (New York, Penguin Putnam, 2001), 217.

REQUIRED SACRIFICE

Calling a tax a "required sacrifice" means it matters not whether the sacrifice is made cheerfully, grudgingly, or unwittingly; it is required because government sanctions for noncompliance exist. An "overlord," says Kant, "demands the payment of taxes: he does not demand that they be paid willingly."[127] Thus, each person's reasons for complying are immaterial, though some will do so from a sense of duty and others only from fear of imprisonment or public exposure. Under this broad definition of tax, military conscription—"the mandatory contribution of personal labor to the state"—is a form of taxation[128] and, says Levi, is "just one of many ways democratic governments demonstrate their immense power to tax."[129] Webber and Wildavsky report that conscription (corvée) was, in fact, "the earliest form of taxation for which records exist."[130] Adam Smith traces military conscription as a tax collected in labor to the ancient republics of Greece and Italy where "every citizen was a soldier, and both served, and prepared himself for service, at his own expense."[131] In France, declares de Tocqueville, the conscription "is assuredly the heaviest tax upon the population of that country."[132] When the United States abandoned the military draft in 1973, the greater compensation demanded by volunteers dictated the need for additional tax revenue.[133] The same occurs when a state opts

---

127. Immanuel Kant, "Laws," in *Lectures on Ethics*, trans. Louis Infield (Indianapolis, IN: Hackett Publishing Co., 1963), 35.

128. Webber and Wildavsky, *History of Taxation and Expenditure*, 68.

129. Margaret Levi, *Consent, Dissent, and Patriotism* (Cambridge: Cambridge University Press, 1997), 1.

130. Webber and Wildavsky, *History of Taxation and Expenditure*, 68.

131. Smith also describes the use of conscripted labor (corvée) in the ancient monarchies. "The labor of the country people, for three days before, and for three days after, harvest, was thought a fund sufficient for making and maintaining all the bridges, highways, and other public works." Smith, *Wealth of Nations*, bk. 5, chap. 2, 493–94.

132. de Tocqueville, *Democracy in America*, vol. 1, chap. 13, 185.

133. Calculating the additional tax revenue required for a volunteer military was a prerequisite to eliminating the draft. See John T. Warner and Paul F. Hogan, "Walter Oi and His Contributions to the All-Volunteer Force: Theory, Evidence, Persuasion" (paper presented at the meeting of the American Economic Association, Boston, MA, January 3, 2015).

for a mercenary army.[134] At one time the United States as well as France permitted a conscripted soldier to purchase his replacement.[135] When a pecuniary sacrifice replaces a nonpecuniary sacrifice, such as military conscription, the reason for including both regimes under the single heading of taxation becomes clear. Simmel refers to the transition from required personal services to money payments as a substitute as the "objectification and depersonalization of the [tax] obligation."[136]

CONSTRUCTIVE TAXES

One purpose of this wider—and historically more relevant—construal of taxation is to permit us to recognize its functional role in society by focusing on its overall influence in maintaining social cohesion and other aspects of general welfare. Utopias aside, our own world furnishes examples of nonpecuniary government-required sacrifices justified by the general welfare, including censorship of news, forced labor and slavery, 1920s US prohibition (18th Amendment[137]), war rationing, marriage exclusions (laws forbidding interracial, interfaith, same-sex, or polygamous unions),[138] forced

---

134. In More's *Utopia*, when they go to war on the side of their allies, explains narrator Hythloday, "they take every precaution to avoid having to fight in person, so long as they can use mercenaries to wage war for them." More, *Utopia*, bk. 2, 90. In our own time, says Pincus, "It costs the U.S. government [e.g., taxpayers] a lot more to hire contract employees as security guards in Iraq [Blackwater USA mercenaries (private military contractors), for example] than to use American troops." Walter Pincus, "U.S. Pays Steep Price for Private Security in Iraq," *Washington Post*, October 1, 2007.

135. During the U.S. Civil War (1861–1864), the northern states' military draft permitted a conscripted soldier to "furnish an acceptable substitute to take his place in the draft" by paying him up to $300. "An Act for enrolling and calling out the national Forces, and for other Purposes," Congressional Record, 37th Cong. 3rd Sess., chap. 75, sec. 13, March 3, 1863. When French conscription laws permitted the purchase of replacements, Levi notes, this practice "contributed to the fairly general belief that some, particularly the rich, were escaping altogether." Levi, *Consent, Dissent, and Patriotism*, 46.

136. Simmel, *The Philosophy of Money*, 288.

137. In her autobiography written during this period, Mother (Mary Harris) Jones notes that prohibition was a regressive tax as it required greater sacrifice from the working classes than from the wealthy who had access to private clubs.

138. In the United States, for example, there were laws against interracial marriage until 1967 (Loving v. Virginia, 388 U.S. 1, 12 [1967]) and against same-sex marriage until 2015 (Obergefell v. Hodges, 576 U.S. ___ [2015]).

sterilization of criminals and those living with mental illness,[139] one-child laws,[140] end of life prohibitions,[141] ideologically driven educational curricula,[142] market-biased regulation of the national interest,[143] and ethnic cleansing. Because no single term encompasses these examples (as well as others illustrated in the literature of utopias), in contrast to pecuniary taxes, I refer to these manifestations of government-required sacrifice as *constructive taxes*.[144] In so doing I am using *tax* as a term of art, thereby avoiding its ordinary, imprecise meaning. Note that *constructive* in this context is *not* an evaluative term—not the contrary of destructive—but expresses the legal concept: "that which is established by the mind of the law in its act of *construing* facts."[145] It is in this sense of *construal* that the law speaks of constructive assent, constructive contract, constructive fraud, constructive knowledge, constructive receipt, and Godwin's "constructive treason."[146] Substance takes

---

139. The U.S. Supreme Court, in the 1927 case Buck v. Bell (274 U.S. 200), ruled that a Virginia law permitting the forced sterilization of an institutionalized "imbecile" was constitutional.

140. Though China generally rescinded its 1979 one-child policy in 2015, a one-child per mother policy is found in Charlotte Perkins Gilman's utopia *Herland*.

141. In More's *Utopia* someone "suffering from incurable diseases" and "unequal to any of life's duties, a burden to himself and others," in consultation with a priest, receives encouragement to take his own life. More, *Utopia*, bk. 2, 78.

142. "Hotan, China – On the edge of a desert in far western China, an imposing building sits behind a fence topped with barbed wire. . . . Inside, hundreds of ethnic Uighur Muslims spend their days in a high-pressure indoctrination program, where they are forced to listen to lectures, [and] sing hymns praising the Chinese Communist Party." Chris Buckley, "China Is Detaining Muslims in Vast Numbers. The Goal: 'Transformation,'" *The New York Times*, September 8, 2018.

143. Herman speaks of the "tendency to make 'freedom' synonymous with freedom of markets rather than political (or any other kind of) freedom." Edward S. Herman, "From *Ingsoc* and *Newspeak* to *Amcap*, *Amerigood*, and *Marketspeak*," in *On Nineteen Eighty-Four: Orwell and Our Future*, ed. Abbott Gleason, Jack Goldsmith, and Martha C. Nussbaum, 112–23 (Princeton, NJ: Princeton University Press, 2005), 117.

144. Other terms considered and rejected for this category of nonpecuniary taxes include *implicit taxes*, *indirect taxes*, *hidden taxes*, and *presumptive taxes*. These terms have previously accepted meanings in the tax literature and are thus unavailable.

145. *Black's Law Dictionary*, abridged 6th ed. (St. Paul: MN: West Publishing Co., 1991), 216 (italics in original).

146. William Godwin coined the term *constructive treason* in reference to high treason charges that political activists faced for the implications of their ideas. See Mark Philp, *Godwin's Political Justice* (Ithaca, NY: Cornell University Press, 1986), 117; Don Locke, *A Fantasy of Reason: The Life and Thought of William Godwin* (London: Routledge and Kegan Paul, 1980), 79.

precedence over form. These sacrifices are rooted in the legal requirements of society and thus may be construed as functional substitutes for pecuniary taxes (or the other way around).[147]

Stretching the economic concept of substitution—substituting one good for another based on price changes—the analogy I propose is the substitution of one form of sacrifice for another based on what citizens can be induced to endure. Thus, though we are accustomed to thinking of taxes as a monetary sacrifice, as revenue for the government, in utopias—and more importantly, in "real life"—taxes may involve the legal surrender of diverse facets of personal autonomy.[148] Viewed from this perspective, the struggle for religious freedom; the antislavery movement; the campaign for women's suffrage; 1920s bootlegging; the feminist and anti-draft movements; the pro- and anti-abortion crusades; and the campaigns for civil rights,[149] disability rights, gay rights (including same-sex marriage), and gender recognition rights were—and to the extent they are ongoing, are—each constructive tax-protest movements seeking to right the legally ensconced balance of sacrifice by redefining, through inclusion of a new dimension, the general welfare. In this way, though "nothing could be more mundane than taxes," admit Murphy and Nagel, "they provide a perfect setting for constant moral argument and possible moral progress."[150]

The prospect of constructive taxes should lead us to see pecuniary taxes as only one option for providing order and structure for a functioning society, an option that may camouflage taxation's moral dimensions. It should also lead us to recognize that the societies envisioned by More and Bellamy, for example, were not designed to function without taxation but

---

147. Constructive taxes, like pecuniary taxes, may be conditional or unconditional. This is illustrated in chapter five in connection with marriage prohibitions.

148. Some readers may object that under this definition of tax nearly any law or regulation must qualify as a tax. I believe, however, that reflection on actual examples will dispel this concern. Most laws that affect our daily lives do not require sacrifices in the sense described here. It is easy to see that traffic laws, for example, benefit us as much as the effort necessary to obey them. In paying a traffic fine, therefore, we are not paying a tax.

149. Describing the plight of blacks in the United States preceding the fight for desegregation and the civil rights struggles of the 1960s, Coates exposes their subjection to a mode of double taxation. "In large swaths of the country, blacks paid taxes but could neither attend the best universities nor exercise the right to vote." Ta-Nehisi Coates, *We Were Eight Years in Power* (New York: One World, an imprint of Random House, 2017), 130–31.

150. Murphy and Nagel, *The Myth of Ownership: Taxes and Justice*, 188.

only without pecuniary taxes. It is for this reason that I have chosen sacrifice and coercion as unifying principles, placing taxation in its broadest context, a context that focuses on citizens and their relation to each other and to the state. If sacrifice and coercion are necessary to maintain a society, the moral challenge of taxation is how these burdens may be distributed without harming "the interest of any one order of citizens, for no other purpose but to promote that of some other."[151]

SUMMARIZING THE SINEWS OF TAXATION

Pecuniary taxation evolved out of what I am calling constructive taxation in response to the convenience of a standardized unit of exchange. In the same way, modern commercial transactions evolved out of barter and other rudimentary forms of payment-in-kind. Acknowledging this broader vision of taxation avoids the paradox of tax-free societies, as it elucidates their sinews in terms of sacrifice rather than in terms of revenue. Among the advantages of pecuniary taxation is our ability to quantify the mandatory sacrifice it imposes. Among its disadvantages is our tendency to focus on the relative rates or amounts of a tax rather than on its moral roots and implications for society. As a corollary, our inability to quantify nonpecuniary (constructive) taxes renders their moral evaluation problematic. How do we weigh the effects of marriage restrictions based on race or gender, for example, against constraints on religious freedom or one-child laws? Thus, while states require nonmonetary sacrifices from their citizens, it is enlightening to see these sacrifices as elements of a larger mechanism of control of which pecuniary taxation is only one element.

DEFINING UTOPIA

We dispute whether we must first educate the people and then alter the forms of social life, or first alter the forms of social life; and then we dispute how we are to struggle: by peaceful propaganda or terrorism?

—Leo Tolstoy (1828–1910), *Resurrection*[152]

---

151. Smith, *Wealth of Nations*, bk. 4, chap. 8, 436.

152. Leo Tolstoy, *Resurrection*, trans. Louise Maude (Oxford: Oxford University Press, 1994), 444.

"Utopias as practical political philosophy," explains Stillman, "investigate, compare, and analyze ends, means, and existing conditions in order to encourage and enhance judicious and effective human activity."[153] In *Utopian Thought in the Western World*, Frank and Fritzie Manuel, after sketching the historical development of the term and concept *utopia*, explicitly bypass an attempt at a "rigid definition." They cite as precedent William James "pointedly refusing to define religion" in his lectures on *The Varieties of Religious Experience*, speaking instead of a "religious propensity." In like manner, the Manuels "presuppose the existence of a utopian propensity in man."[154]

The Manuels' historical overview includes the fact that the term *utopia* "could always be used either positively or pejoratively,"[155] and that by the seventeenth century utopia "also came to denote general programs and platforms for ideal societies, codes, and constitutions that dispensed with the fictional apparatus. . . . [Subsequently,] the line between a utopian system and political and social theory often became shadowy."[156] That utopias "are so many and so different from one another," as William James asserts of religions, should be "enough to prove that the word [utopia] . . . cannot stand for any single principle or essence, but is rather a collective name."[157] The "central problem with most approaches to utopianism," adds Sargent, "is the attempt to use a single dimension to explain a multidimensional phenomenon."[158] At most we can retain the goal noted earlier in defining tax that our definition attempt to be morally neutral, thus permitting evaluations from alternative moral perspectives.

In the introduction, I mentioned my desire to avoid labels insofar as practicable. For this investigation it makes little difference whether what

---

153. Peter G. Stillman, " 'Nothing is, but what is not': Utopias as Practical Political Philosophy," in *The Philosophy of Utopia*, ed. Barbara Goodwin, 9–24 (London: Routledge, Taylor and Francis Group, 2001), 20.

154. Frank E. Manuel and Fritzie P. Manuel, *Utopian Thought in the Western World* (Cambridge, MA: The Belknap Press of Harvard University Press, 1979), 5.

155. Manuel and Manuel, 4.

156. Manuel and Manuel, 3–4.

157. William James, *The Varieties of Religious Experience* (London: Collier-Macmillan, 1961), 39.

158. Lyman Tower Sargent, "The Three Faces of Utopianism Revisited," *Utopian Studies* 5, no. 1 (1994):1–37, 3.

I am calling a utopia someone else might call a dystopia or eutopia, or might exclude it from the genre altogether, though it deals with a society that is both nowhere and ideal to *someone*, if only to a fictional character.[159] The meaning of utopia adopted here is therefore operational rather than evaluative. In a dystopia as well as a utopia the tax system should reflect and support the goals of the depicted state (unless its dystopic theme is a state whose tax system is at odds with its ethical ideals). Since I examine taxation—whether constructive or pecuniary—as a means to the ends utopian authors provide, the battle for a definitive definition of utopia may be left for others. Insisting that utopia must refer to an ideal society is only a formal requirement, as noted, and cannot itself settle the question whether Bellamy's *Looking Backward*, for example, is a eutopia or a nightmare.[160] It is in this spirit that Gubar asks: is it "possible that one man's utopia may be one woman's dystopia?"[161] Utopian writers, for my purposes, are those who diagnose society's systemic problems, envisioning solutions for their remediation or reform or delivering dystopic "warnings of future horrors, based on extrapolation and projection of current tendencies or ideas."[162] For this reason, it will not matter whether the author's intent was an imaginary blueprint of an ideal society, a satirical account of an existing society's problems, or a thoughtful social or economic program for reform.

In the following chapters, we will examine the treatment of taxation in a sample of widely cited utopias, with the understanding that we are not committing to a particular definition of utopia but are free to follow William James's advice for gaining a "better understanding of a thing's significance" and consider utopian thinking in "its exaggerations and perversions, its equivalents and substitutes and nearest relatives elsewhere . . . and to have

---

159. Lyman Tower Sargent has compiled an online bibliography of utopian literature in English, from 1516 to the present, including definitions of *utopia, dystopia, critical utopia*, and other related terms at https://openpublishing.psu.edu/utopia/home.

160. With respect to *Looking Backward*, Claeys advises, it "remains unclear as to which side of the utopia/dystopia divide Bellamy belongs." Gregory Claeys, *Dystopia: A Natural History* (Oxford: Oxford University Press, 2017), 321.

161. Susan Gubar, "She in Herland: Feminism as Fantasy," in *Charlotte Perkins Gilman: The Woman and Her Work*, ed. Sheryl L. Meyering (Ann Arbor, MI: UMI Research Press, 1989), 192.

162. Barbara Goodwin and Keith Taylor, *The Politics of Utopia* (Oxford: Peter Lang, 2009), 17.

acquaintance with the whole range of its variations."[163] This will ensure we do not draw an arbitrary line fixing what is or is not utopian and permit our exploration of its shifting frontiers.

The order of topics discussed in chapters two through six is (roughly) based on the scalability of the required sacrifice; to what extent can it be levied by degrees or restricted in its application? While privacy may be invaded selectively, for example, land ownership must be subject to uniform rules. Chapter seven describes two utopias (Rand's and Nozick's) that expressly reject pecuniary taxation or any form of required sacrifice. In the next chapter, we begin our exploration of taxation with utopias that rely on privacy deprivation as a means of control. This form of taxation is administered by Plato, More, Orwell, Wells, and Zamyatin.

---

163. James, *The Varieties of Religious Experience*, 35–36. Among the books banned in Huxley's *Brave New World*, the Controller has in his private library—in a safe—copies of the *Bible*, *The Imitation of Christ* (Thomas à Kempis), and William James's *The Varieties of Religious Experience*. "I've got plenty more," says Mustapha Mond. "A whole collection of pornographic old books. God in the safe and Ford on the shelves." Aldous Huxley, *Brave New World* (New York: Harper Collins 2004), 207–8.

CHAPTER TWO

PRIVACY DEPRIVATION AS TAXATION

THE NATURE AND ROLE OF PRIVACY

> Truth dwells with contemplation. We can seldom make much progress
> in the business of disentangling error and delusion but in sequestered
> privacy.
>
> —William Godwin (1756–1836), *Enquiry*[1]

Government restrictions on privacy act as a control on citizens and as a
constructive tax (constructive in the sense of *construal*). A constructive tax,
recall from chapter one, is a nonpecuniary sacrifice that government imposes
for the general welfare. As a sacrifice, what we receive in return is indeter-
minate. Such restrictions affect the relations of citizens to each other and to
the state. Nissenbaum reports on the "vital role that autonomy is believed
to play in arguments for adequate privacy protection." One perspective,
she says, claims that while we are being "observed, monitored, and possibly
judged," our deliberations and choices are clouded by the voices of others,
and our resulting actions are "not truly voluntary."[2] Social pressure ("mutual

---

1. Godwin, *Enquiry Concerning Political Justice*, 3rd ed., bk. 4, chap. 3, 286.

2. Helen Nissenbaum, *Privacy in Context: Technology, Policy, and the Integrity of Social
Life* (Stanford, CA: Stanford University Press, 2010), 81–82.

control"[3]) and technology are common devices for restricting privacy. Our tendency to underestimate the influence of social pressure, paired with abstract notions of "force of character" and "spirit of self-determination," explains Zimbardo, is a powerful psychological influence. "Paradoxically," he continues, "we, like Winston Smith [in *Nineteen Eighty-Four*], become more vulnerable . . . to the extent that we deceive ourselves into believing we are personally invulnerable."[4]

Since the nineteenth century, technology has played an increasing share in collecting the tax on privacy. In our own time, it has become evident that the proper balance between privacy and transparency—whether in government, business, or in our separate lives—is a worthy topic for an ideal society to address. While maximum privacy may appear desirable to some, Solove warns that privacy reduces society's capacity to uncover illegal conduct, making law enforcement less effective.[5] The challenge is to negotiate a compromise between the privacy individuals desire and the restrictions on privacy required to maintain order and promote the general welfare. Somewhere on this continuum, we assume, there must be an appropriate degree of autonomy for the individual and control for the society. One key to locating the proper mean, according to Solove, is determining society's vested interest in individual privacy.[6] Since there is no "overarching value of privacy in the abstract," he contends, the value of privacy "emerges from the activities that it protects."[7] Central to this nascent debate is the meaning of *privacy*, a term partisans of competing ideologies are eager to capture. For this reason, Nissenbaum advocates "starting with a neutral conception

---

3. Goodwin and Taylor observe that "All utopias rely to some extent on a traditional method of keeping order virtually unknown in modern individualistic society, that of mutual control." Goodwin and Taylor, *The Politics of Utopia*, 59.

4. This influence is referred to as the "Fundamental Attribution Error." The error consists in "overestimating personal power and underestimating situational power." Phillip G. Zimbardo, "Mind Control in Orwell's *Nineteen Eighty-Four*: Fictional Concepts Become Operational Realities in Jim Jones's Jungle Experiment," in *On Nineteen Eighty-Four: Orwell and Our Future*, ed. Abbott Gleason, Jack Goldsmith, and Martha C. Nussbaum, 127–54 (Princeton, NJ: Princeton University Press, 2005), 136–37.

5. Solove, Daniel J., *Understanding Privacy* (Cambridge: Harvard University Press, 2008), 81.

6. Solove, 98.

7. Solove, 98.

of privacy [that] allows one to talk about states of increased and decreased privacy without begging the normative question of whether these states are good or bad."[8]

When utopian writings address privacy as a moral question, it is rarely confronted explicitly. An exception is *A Modern Utopia*, which describes Wells's account of the proper trade-offs between personal privacy and the society's right to know. The other utopians discussed in this chapter approach privacy indirectly; they spur our imaginations to envision a society where the general welfare is promoted through a systemic restriction on privacy—the imposition of a constructive tax. Among these writers are Plato, More, Orwell, and Zamyatin, who each assert the importance of privacy by exploring the effects of its limitation or deprivation.

Rosen observes that privacy is a precondition for friendship, individuality, intimate relationships, and love.[9] Privacy also affects autonomy, creativity, dignity, freedom, human thriving, imagination, psychological well-being, and self-development. But "none of these ends," says Solove, "is furthered by all types of privacy."[10] For this reason, he warns, "Using the general term 'privacy' can result in the conflation of different kinds of problems."[11] Westin identifies four distinct senses of privacy—anonymity, intimacy, reserve, and solitude.[12] The importance of privacy to individuals is, in part, a function of its importance to the government when restrictions on privacy exist to monitor and control citizens' conduct. While citizens seek privacy from one another and from the state, governments also seek privacy, and what they hide from their citizens creates another form of control and required sacrifice (this topic is discussed in chapter three).

In *Why People Obey the Law*, Tyler reports, "Within the general framework of fairness, procedural concerns consistently take precedence over distributive concerns." That is, people judge a legal system's fairness more heavily by the impartiality of its procedures than by the final outcome

---

8. Nissenbaum, *Privacy in Context*, 68.

9. Jeffrey Rosen, *The Unwanted Gaze: The Destruction of Privacy in America* (New York: Vintage Books, 2000), 11.

10. Solove, *Understanding Privacy*, 98.

11. Daniel J. Solove, *Nothing to Hide: The False Tradeoff Between Privacy and Security* (New Haven, CT: Yale University Press, 2011), 46.

12. Alan F. Westin, *Privacy and Freedom* (New York: Atheneum, 1967), 31–32.

of its decisions.[13] Based on this finding, a government's restriction of its citizens' privacy may meet less resistance if applied in a uniform manner, everyone sacrificing alike. Thus, Brin advises, "we must not try to limit the cameras—they are coming anyway. . . . Instead, we must make sure all citizens share the boon—and burden—of sight."[14]

The world of electronic communications has linked privacy and security in complex ways. While Internet security is sought to protect individual privacy, for example, privacy invasion is justified to promote national security. As Bamford reports, the U.S. National Security Agency (NSA) computers search electronic communications for "signals intelligence, or 'sigint.'" These are "particular names, telephone numbers, Internet addresses, and trigger words or phrases."[15] Because the extent of this privacy intrusion is unknown, as well as its benefit to our national security, our sacrifice is inestimable. Our solace, as Tyler suggests, is the hope that this constructive tax is levied impartially and its burdens, therefore, shared equally and so fairly.

Plato's *Republic* features a required sacrifice of privacy for the guardians (the rulers and their auxiliaries). Bloom observes, "this total lack of privacy means that a man cannot have a life of his own."[16] For the guardians this lack of privacy is a function of their communal life. In addition to eating and sleeping in shared facilities, guardians of both sexes exercise together naked.[17] The wider public, however, is not subject to such restrictions. In exchange for "a life of their own," the farmers and merchants support their military and rulers, as we saw in chapter one, providing "sustenance, as much as is needed."[18] Holding everything in common and in the open encourages honesty (or at least discourages fraud and deceit); such, at least, was Plato's expectation. This sacrifice and other constraints on the guard-

13. Tom R. Tyler, *Why People Obey the Law* (Princeton, NJ: Princeton University Press, 2006), 97.

14. David Brin, "The Self-Preventing Prophecy; or How a Dose of Nightmare Can Help Tame Tomorrow's Perils," in *On Nineteen Eighty-Four: Orwell and Our Future*, ed. Abbott Gleason, Jack Goldsmith, and Martha C. Nussbaum, 222–30 (Princeton, NJ: Princeton University Press, 2005), 226n4.

15. James Bamford, "Big Brother is Listening," *The Atlantic Monthly* (April 2006): 66.

16. Allan Bloom, "Interpretive Essay," in *The Republic of Plato*, 2nd ed. (Basic Books, 1968), 379.

17. Plato, *Republic*, bk. 5, 452a–b.

18. Plato, *Republic*, trans. Bloom, bk. 3, 416d–e.

ians' conduct—described in chapter three (taxing access to truth), chapter four (taxation by required work or occupation), and chapter five (taxing the family: marriage, childrearing, and eugenics)—constitute the Republic's constructive tax regime.

THOMAS MORE (1478–1535): NO SPOTS FOR SECRET MEETINGS

> For what objections can be made against a writer who relates only plain facts that happened in such distant countries, where we have not the least interest with respect to either trade or negotiations?
>
> —Jonathan Swift (1667–1745), *Gulliver's Travels*[19]

Thomas More's Utopia, observes Solove, "depicts the idyllic society as one of communal life in which nothing is hidden and social order is paramount."[20] It is memorable for its moneyless economy[21] where they "hold up gold and silver to scorn."[22] Perhaps less memorable, because of its absence, is privacy. As Baker-Smith observes, "it is clear that privacy is not a priority. In fact there are few occasions in Utopia when anyone is out of sight of someone else."[23] "Privacy was something of an innovation in sixteenth-century Europe," the same commentator reports, "but in Utopia this constant exposure to others has its moral function."[24] Unlike the Republic, however, in Utopia this sacrifice affects everyone. This dearth of privacy has nothing to do with technology but everything to do with social control, especially in matters of idleness and adultery. Control results from requiring everyone to live in plain view of her fellow citizens. Large extended families dwell in public housing, where windows are made of glass and doors are never locked. "The double doors, which open easily with the push of a hand . . . let anyone

---

19. Swift, *Gulliver's Travels*, 268.

20. Solove, *Understanding Privacy*, 81.

21. More, *Utopia*, bk. 2, 106.

22. More, 61.

23. Dominic Baker-Smith, *More's Utopia* (London: HarperCollinsAcademic, 1991), 160.

24. Baker-Smith, 160.

come in—so there is nothing private anywhere,"[25] says More's narrator, Raphael Hythloday. Work and leisure are carried out in groups and meals consumed in community dining halls. A central goal of this anti-privacy scheme is deterring those inclined to shirk their work obligations (discussed in chapter four) or engage in illicit sex (discussed in chapter five). As Hythloday explains, "Because they live in the full view of all, they are bound to be either working at their usual trades or enjoying their leisure in a respectable way."[26] What goes on behind closed doors, they assume, is more likely harmful than beneficial to society.

Goodwin and Taylor report that a frequent method of "promoting order, which utopians themselves [historically] considered their most vital innovation, is the prior removal from utopia of all sources of social disruption and temptations to disobedience."[27] In Utopia this method supplants the functions that pecuniary taxes commonly secure by substituting the constructive tax of privacy deprivation. Since there is no private property in Utopia, there are no private homes or buildings to secure privacy. This controlled social environment also affords none of the traditional secret meeting places. As the narrator explains, "nowhere is there any chance to loaf or any pretext for evading work; there are no wine-bars, or ale-houses, or brothels; no chances for corruption; no hiding places; no spots for secret meetings."[28] Living a public existence likewise minimizes the chances for adultery—one of the most serious crimes in Utopia.[29] While privacy does not cause adultery or premarital sex, it is a catalyst for opportunity and so its absence is a deterrent.

Utopia has also established barriers for those seeking privacy through the anonymity of travel. As Hythloday reports, "Any individuals who want to visit friends living in another city . . . can easily obtain permission." This allows further control, however, for they "are given a wagon and a public slave

---

25. More, *Utopia*, bk. 2, 46–47.

26. More, 59.

27. Goodwin and Taylor, *The Politics of Utopia*, 60. As Kenyon notes, however, merely removing sources of social disruption in More's Utopia was insufficient since "Grace and revelation were necessary supplements to reason if the will was to choose the good." T. A. Kenyon, "The Problem of Freedom and Moral Behavior in Thomas More's Utopia," *Journal of the History of Philosophy* 21, no. 3 (July 1983): 349–73, 372.

28. More, *Utopia*, bk. 2, 59.

29. More, 80–81.

to drive the oxen and look after them,"[30] and they must travel in groups. Anyone attempting to thwart these controls by unauthorized travel and is "caught without the governor's letter, is treated with contempt, brought back as a runaway, and severely punished." A second offense is punished with slavery.[31] Slaves are assigned demeaning labor, such as butchering cattle, and are forced to wear gold shackles, a symbol of their moral degradation.[32]

BIG BROTHER'S EYES IN *NINETEEN EIGHTY-FOUR*

"Privacy," said Mr. Charrington, "was a very valuable thing."

—George Orwell (1903–1950), *Nineteen Eighty-Four*[33]

A constructive tax on privacy alters the nature of the society it is imposed on; it is an invisible tax and for that reason more troubling than its pecuniary counterpart, as it may be levied without our knowledge or consent. Unlike a pecuniary tax, there is no way to quantify it and compare its effects to those of other taxes. In *Nineteen Eighty-Four* techniques of electronic technology, psychological disarmament, and a culture of engineered suspicion replace the relatively banal privacy restrictions of More's *Utopia*. The ubiquitous telescreens—two-way flat-screen TV monitors—defend the Party from dissidents by permitting visual dissection of even mundane activities.[34] A party member is subject to inspection whether

> asleep or awake, working or resting, in his bath or in bed. . . . His friendships, his relaxations, his behavior toward his wife and children, the expression of his face when he is alone, the words

---

30. More, 58.

31. More, 58.

32. More, 55, 61.

33. George Orwell, *Nineteen Eighty-Four* (New York: PLUME/Penguin/Harcourt Brace, 1949), 140.

34. By installing millions of CCTV cameras, China has been moving to implement its "social credit system," which, says Greenfield, "has the power to create a generation of compliant subjects both unaware of alternatives and utterly unable to formulate whatever grievances they might hold in a politically potent way." Adam Greenfield, "China's Dystopian Tech Could Be Contagious," *The Atlantic*, February 14, 2018.

he mutters in his sleep, even the characteristic movements of his body, are all jealously scrutinized.[35]

Though the Thought Police monitor the telescreens, "There was of course no way of knowing whether you were being watched at any given moment"[36]—an application of Bentham's principle that "power should be visible and unverifiable."[37]

Winston Smith, Orwell's protagonist, was able to evade the telescreen in his apartment by sitting at a table to its left. Nevertheless, the very presence of a telescreen was not always detectable, as he and his partner Julia discovered. To obtain the privacy they required for a clandestine relationship, Winston and Julia rented a room above Mr. Charrington's antique shop in a rundown Oceania prole neighborhood. On what turned out to be their final visit to that apartment Julia announced to Winston, "I bet that picture's got bugs behind it."[38] She was right, though not in the sense she intended. Not until that fatal day when the picture fell to the floor and a disembodied voice rudely confronted them did they suspect that a telescreen lurked behind the painting of an old church.[39]

When Winston declared, "Nothing was your own except the few cubic centimeters inside your skull,"[40] he may have overestimated. During his interrogation by O'Brien in Room 101, Winston recognizes, "There was no idea that he had ever had, or could have, that O'Brien had not long ago known, examined, and rejected. His mind *contained* Winston's mind," including knowledge of his greatest fear.[41] Since the Thought Police do not

---

35. Orwell, *Nineteen Eighty-Four*, 216.

36. Orwell, 3.

37. Cited by Foucault in a discussion of Bentham's panopticon. Michel Foucault, *Discipline and Punish: The Birth of the Prison*, trans. Alan Sheridan (New York: Penguin Books, 1977), 201.

38. Orwell, *Nineteen Eighty-Four*, 150.

39. Orwell, 227.

40. Orwell, 27.

41. Orwell, 264 (italics in original). O'Brien tells Winston, "The thing that is in Room 101 is the worst thing in the world" (Orwell, 293). Spotting a rat in the apartment above the antique shop, Winston exclaims, "Of all horrors in the world—a rat!" (Orwell, 147). Recounting his experience in the Spanish Civil War (1937), Orwell writes, "The filthy brutes came swarming out of the ground on every side. If there is one thing I hate more than another it is a rat running over me in the darkness." George Orwell,

wear uniforms or badges, no one knows, until it is too late, who they are. A trusted coworker, spouse, or kindly antique dealer may be a member of this feared order. "Always the eyes watching you . . . Asleep or awake, working or eating, indoors or out of doors, in the bath or in bed—no escape."[42] In a totalitarian state, Arendt explains, "the less is known of the existence of an institution, the more powerful it will ultimately turn out to be."[43] Thought Police pose a constant threat to personal privacy, and the mystery of their identity heightens the power of their office. Their effect is evident in the conduct it induces: "Not to let one's feelings appear in one's face was a habit that had acquired the status of an instinct."[44] For a Party member such as Winston, "to do anything that suggested a taste for solitude, even to go for a walk by yourself, was always slightly dangerous."[45]

The privacy deprivation enforced by continuous surveillance in *Nineteen Eighty-Four* is coercive and debilitating.[46] It leads Winston and Julia to forsake caution and risk certain death in exchange for what they hope is a brief span of privacy. In an ideal world the law applies equally to all.

Homage to Catalonia (London: Secker and Warburg, 1938; repr., n.p.: Will Jonson and Dog's Tail Books, n.d.), 63. (Page references are to reprint.)

42. Orwell, *Nineteen Eighty-Four*, 27.

43. Hannah Arendt, *The Origins of Totalitarianism* (Orlando, FL: A Harvest Book – Harcourt, 1968), 403.

44. Orwell, *Nineteen Eighty-Four*, 108.

45. Orwell, 84. In *Brave New World* the desire for privacy is deemed antisocial. "'But people never are alone now,' said Mustapha Mond. 'We make them hate solitude; and we arrange their lives so that it's almost impossible for them ever to have it.'" Huxley, *Brave New World*, 88, 211. Both Orwell and Huxley, says Posner, regard solitude as a "precondition for independent thinking." Richard A. Posner, *Law and Literature*, 3rd ed. (Cambridge, MA: Harvard University Press, 2009), 394.

46. Coercive measures are used against party dissidents to force them to "voluntarily" embrace the teachings of the Party. During one of his electric-shock torture sessions, O'Brien explains to Winston, "We are not content with negative obedience, nor even with the most abject submission. When finally you surrender to us, it must be of your own free will." Orwell, *Nineteen Eighty-Four*, 263. Similarly, in Ayn Rand's utopia *Atlas Shrugged* (discussed in chapter seven), a central character, John Galt, is tortured with electric shocks administered to coax him to "voluntarily" take charge of the nation's economy. Dr. Ferris says, "I don't want him to obey! I want him to *believe*! To *accept*! To *want* to accept! We've got to have him work for us *voluntarily*!" Ayn Rand, *Atlas Shrugged* (New York: Random House, 1957), 1142 (italics in original).

In Oceania there is no law,[47] yet the Party's oppressive assault on privacy is applied consistently; everyone up to the highest ranks of the Inner Party knows they are subject to continual scrutiny; it is no surprise when a friend or coworker suddenly disappears, for each knows anyone might be next. If the procedures restricting privacy are imposed uniformly (everyone sacrificing alike), perhaps those procedures will meet with greater acceptance by appearing fair in the sense of Tyler's research noted earlier. For this reason, when Julia, "realized that she herself was doomed, that sooner or later the Thought Police would catch and kill her,"[48] her concern was *not* whether this was fair.

H. G. WELLS (1866–1946): INDEXING HUMANITY

A person who knows all of another's travels can deduce whether he is a weekly churchgoer, a heavy drinker, a regular at the gym, an unfaithful husband, an outpatient receiving medical treatment, an associate of particular individuals or political groups.

—United States v. Maynard, U.S. Federal Court of Appeals, 2010[49]

In *A Modern Utopia*, the whole world, though not *our* world, is a single unified utopia, a World State. Kumar reports that the "unitary global aspect of Wells's utopianism has always been the part that has evoked the warmest assent and support."[50] This physically distinct world is identical to the earth with the same mountains, oceans, and land masses but existing "beyond the flight of a cannon-ball flying for a billion years."[51] Everyone there speaks a common language, Utopian, and "every race of this planet earth is to be found in the strictest parallelism there, in numbers the same—only . . . with an entirely different set of traditions, ideals, ideas, and purposes, and so

---

47. Orwell, *Nineteen Eighty-Four*, 6. Montesquieu says: "In despotic governments there are no laws, the judge himself is his own rule." Montesquieu, *The Spirit of Laws*, bk. 6, chap. 3, 35.

48. Orwell, *Nineteen Eighty-Four*, 138.

49. U.S. v. Maynard, 615 F. 3d 562 (U.S. Ct. of App., DC Cir., 2010).

50. Krishan Kumar, *Utopia and Anti-Utopia in Modern Times* (Oxford: Basil Blackwell, 1987), 195.

51. Wells, *A Modern Utopia*, 10.

moving under those different skies to an altogether different destiny."[52] Furthermore, says the narrator ("the *Voice*"), there is "universal freedom of exchange and movement."[53] The unified government's ability to maximize personal freedom arises from its authority to control certain activities: those that interfere with the freedom of others. This is an application of Bentham's principle that "all laws creative of liberty, are, as far as they go, abrogative of liberty."[54] Reflecting on this dictum, Wells's narrator says, "Consider how much liberty we gain by the loss of the common liberty to kill."[55]

A RIGHT TO PRIVACY

In the modern Utopia each citizen "limits others by his rights, and is limited by the rights of others, and by considerations affecting the welfare of the community as a whole."[56] One of these rights, in contrast to both More's *Utopia* and Orwell's *Nineteen Eighty-Four*, is the right to privacy, however limited. The modern Utopia features an "extraordinarily higher standard of individual privacy"[57] than on earth. In a modern Utopia, "the private morals of an adult citizen are no concern for the State."[58] Accordingly, Wells's narrator explains, a person's home, whether a sleeping room or a mansion, "must be private" and under his authority and control.[59] But, although the state may not care what you are doing in your home, it will know, nonetheless, when you *are* home.

Though the modern Utopia protects privacy in one's own home, privacy in public is subject to state control and regulation because of its potential effects on the freedom of others and on the welfare of the community.[60] For its citizens, one benefit of this trade-off is the ability to do more things

---

52. Wells, 15.

53. Wells, 14.

54. Bentham, *Anarchical Fallacies*, in *'Nonsense upon Stilts,'* 57.

55. Wells, *A Modern Utopia*, 18.

56. Wells, 18.

57. Wells, 29.

58. Wells, 81. However, the state "must maintain a general decorum, a systematic suppression . . . of the incitations and temptations of the young and inexperienced, and to that extent it will . . . exercise control over morals" (Wells, 82n26).

59. Wells, 21.

60. Wells, 18.

in public, things people formerly were constrained to do in private. On earth, says the narrator, privacy is demanded as a response to those who fail to respect another's right to privacy. In a modern Utopia, however, the increased respect for others (and their privacy) means the demand for privacy in public is correspondingly reduced. This enhancement to the Utopian world's civility is the result of its superior education and manners. Utopian manners, Wells's narrator declares, "will not only be tolerant, but almost universally tolerable.

> In the cultivated State . . . it will be ever so much easier for people to eat in public, rest and amuse themselves in public, and even work in public. Our present need for privacy in many things marks, indeed, a phase of transition from an ease in public in the past due to homogeneity, to an ease in public in the future due to intelligence and good breeding, and in Utopia that transition will be complete.[61]

This means that while communities of the past sought uniformity—the "natural disposition of all peoples, white, black, or brown"[62]—through "common customs and common ceremonies," this disposition to homogeneity is what education in a modern Utopia "seeks to destroy."[63] In place of conformity to one's race and class—enforcing privacy through exclusion and intolerance—education in a modern Utopia seeks diversity by cultivating "more original and enterprising minds."[64] In this way, Kateb observes, "Wells built his Modern Utopia on personal differences."[65]

INDEXING HUMANITY

Despite these guarantees of privacy at home and reductions of the need for privacy in public, infringements on privacy are imposed for social control, as with More and Orwell. In the modern Utopia, to facilitate its unified

---

61. Wells, 21. "Good breeding" in this context includes both manners and eugenic measures; people who prove themselves incorrigible face exile to an island community (Wells, 59).

62. Wells, 20.

63. Wells, 20.

64. Wells, 20.

65. Kateb, *Utopia and Its Enemies*, 220.

government and its techniques of eugenic population management (discussed in chapter five), an intrusive and universal form of privacy invasion is employed. The details of each person's identity form elements of a world-wide database. A thumbmark and number uniquely identify each person in the world and are tied to an ever-mounting collection of personal data. This system of "indexing humanity" is a "scheme by which every person in the world can be promptly and certainly recognized."[66] "Wells' utopians are inveterate world travelers," Manuel observes, "though a meticulous record is kept of their whereabouts."[67] The record, in addition to disclosing health and employment data, reveals "various material facts, such as marriage, parentage, criminal convictions,"[68] and "legally important diseases, offspring, domiciles, public appointments, [and] registered assignments of property."[69] Indexing humanity, Wells clarifies, may be compared to an eye "so sensitive and alert that two strangers cannot appear anywhere upon the planet without discovery."[70] Wells's state-imposed universal human indexing constitutes a required sacrifice for the general welfare and is for that reason a constructive tax.

A TAX ON EXCESS PRIVACY

In addition to these general limitations on privacy in public, a modern Utopia assesses a pecuniary tax on the abuse of privacy at home. Thus, the narrator suggests, "Privacy beyond the house might be made a privilege to be paid for in proportion to the area occupied."[71] This is effected by a tax levied on the proprietor of a tract of land, such as a garden, estate, or private club enclosed by walls that prevent its appreciation by the outside world. The tax is anticipated to deter the excessive enclosure of property that exhibits aesthetic value, including waterfalls and other natural beauty.

---

66. Wells, *A Modern Utopia*, 66.

67. Frank E. Manuel, "Toward a Psychological History of Utopias," in *Utopias and Utopian Thought*, ed. Frank E. Manuel (Boston, MA: Houghton Mifflin Company, 1965), 81.

68. Wells, *A Modern Utopia*, 66.

69. Wells, 77.

70. Wells, 69. In our own time, "The idea behind a new biometric entry-exist system is to add layers of authenticating data—fingerprinting, iris scanning, facial recognition—to verify the identity of a person who is leaving the country, matching records against what was collected upon entry." Adrienne Lafrance, "Biometric Checkpoints in Trump's America," *The Atlantic*, February 14, 2017.

71. Wells, *A Modern Utopia*, 21.

The tax on such walls, explains the narrator, is assessed based on their height and length.[72] To ensure this tax is an effective deterrent, its structure is progressive; the more land a person encloses and the higher the walls, the steeper the tax rate.[73] To prevent whole sections of a city from being walled in, a zoning requirement—a form of constructive tax—sets the maximum area for each square mile of the city that its proprietor may enclose. This measure, explains the narrator, will reduce the "possibility that the poorer townsman will be forced to walk through endless miles of high fenced villa gardens before he may expand in his little scrap of reserved open country."[74]

ZAMYATIN (1884–1937): WHO ARE "THEY" AND WHO ARE "WE"?

Satirical writings are hardly known in despotic governments, where dejection of mind on the one hand, and ignorance on the other, afford neither abilities nor will to write.

—Montesquieu (1689–1755), *The Spirit of Laws*[75]

Perhaps the most extreme deprivation of privacy is found in Yevgeny Zamyatin's *We*, completed in 1921 and banned in his native Russia.[76] The world he depicts exists some thousand years in the future, after the Two-Hundred-Year War of revolution between the city and the countryside[77]—and the con-

---

72. Wells, 22.

73. Goodwin cites progressive taxation as one of the proposals utopians have made that modern Western societies have implemented in their attempt to reduce inequalities. Barbara Goodwin, "Economic and Social Innovation in Utopia," in *Utopias*, ed. Peter Alexander and Roger Gill (London: Duckworth, 1984), 76.

74. Wells, *A Modern Utopia*, 21.

75. Montesquieu, *The Spirit of Laws*, bk. 12, chap. 13, 90.

76. Zamyatin explains: "In 1924 it became clear that, owing to difficulties with the censorship, my novel *We* could not be published in Soviet Russia." Zamyatin, *A Soviet Heretic*, 301.

77. Yevgeny Zamyatin, *We*, trans. Natasha Randall (New York: The Modern Library, 2006), record 5, 20.

struction of the glass Green Wall dividing them. For identifying otherwise homogenous citizens (ciphers), One State uniforms bear a unique number assigned at birth. In summarizing the extent of One State's command over its citizens, protagonist D-503 provides this analogy:

> Take two trays of a weighing scale: put a gram on one, and on the other, put a ton. On one side is the "I," on the other is the "WE," the One State. . . . Assuming that "I" has the same "rights" compared to the State is exactly the same as assuming that a gram can counterbalance a ton. Here is the distribution: a ton has rights, a gram has duties.[78]

The supreme authority, The Benefactor, has ruled continuously, winning forty-eight unanimous unopposed elections.[79] In contrast to Big Brother in *Nineteen Eighty-Four* and the World Controller in *Brave New World*, however, The Benefactor, explains Brown, "does not really have complete control."[80] As with revolutions generally, the defeated party's resistance movement (the MEPHI conspirators) continues its struggle from a position of stealth while its partisans are officially labeled the "enemies of happiness."[81]

THE SPACESHIP AND ITS CARGO

The Benefactor has entrusted D-503, a thirty-two-year-old rocket engineer, with building the *Integral*, a spaceship designed to spread the "beauty and majesty" of One State's culture of rational happiness to other worlds. The Benefactor's vision of the general welfare seeks the bliss of mechanical uniformity and mathematical precision as well as the elimination of chance

---

78. Zamyatin, record 20, 102.

79. Voting is by a public show of hands, not by private ballot, a constructive tax constraining privacy. During the forty-eighth election thousands of MEPHI resistors, including I-330, vote "No." Their votes are considered a "slight disturbance," however, and not counted. Zamyatin, *We*, records 25–26, 126, 130–31.

80. E. J. Brown, *Brave New World, 1984, and We* (Ann Arbor, MI: Ardis, 1976), 46.

81. Shklovsky explains, "The people who oppose the equalization [in One State] call themselves 'Mephi,' an abbreviation of Mephistopheles, because Mephistopheles signifies inequality." Victor Shklovsky, "Evgeny Zamyatin's Ceiling," in *Zamyatin's We: A Collection of Critical Essays*, ed. Gary Kern (Ann Arbor, MI: Ardis Publishers, 1988), 50.

and chaos by extinguishing privacy. The Table of Hours prescribes the exact times for citizens to sleep and wake, to start and end work, and to eat.[82] In support of the *Integral*'s mission, the Benefactor requests a literary cargo of propaganda written by citizens. This is a catalyst for D-503, who initiates his contribution by announcing: "And to you, my unknown planetary readers, we will come to you, to make your life as divinely rational and exact as ours."[83] But, explains Cooke, his inexperience with writing leads him to a genre that is not approved by the state, the "subjective mode" of a personal journal.[84] In his chronicle, D-503 describes One State's ideal as realized in the construction of the *Integral*: "I saw: people below, bending, straightening, turning, like the levers of one enormous machine, on the beat, rhythmically. . . . I saw transparent glass monster cranes slowly gliding . . . like the people, obediently turning, bending, pushing their load into the belly of the *Integral*."[85]

Journalizing his thoughts and experiences provides D-503 with occasions to reflect on the principles of One State and on his evolving role with respect to its political ideals. While his initial relation to the state is one of unquestioned adherence to its machine-like order, his unscheduled encounter with the MEPHI revolutionary I-330 results in his divided loyalty and inaugural experience of sexual jealousy.[86] "As with John the Savage in *Brave New World* and Winston Smith in *1984*," asserts Horan, "D-503's sexual

---

82. Zamyatin, *We*, record 3, 12–13. Zamyatin traces One State's preoccupation with timetables and mathematical precision to industrial efficiency advocate Frederick Winslow Taylor (1856–1915). Foucault observes, however, "The time-table is an old inheritance. The strict model was no doubt suggested by the monastic communities. . . . The rigours of the industrial period long retained a religious air; in the seventeenth century, the regulators of the great manufactories laid down the exercises that would divide up the working day." Foucault, *Discipline and Punish*, 149.

83. Zamyatin, *We*, record 12, 61.

84. Brett Cooke, *Human Nature in Utopia: Zamyatin's We* (Evanston, IL: Northwestern University Press, 2002), 174.

85. Zamyatin, *We*, record 15, 73–74. Machines also represent rationality as a moral ideal in Rand's *Atlas Shrugged* (discussed in chapter seven). Rand expresses this ideal through her heroine, Dagny Taggart. "Why had she always felt that joyous sense of confidence when looking at machines?—she thought. In these giant shapes, two aspects pertaining to the inhuman were radiantly absent: the causeless and the purposeless. Every part of the motors was an embodied answer to 'Why?' and 'What for?' . . . The motors were a moral code cast in steel." Rand, *Atlas Shrugged*, 245–46.

86. Zamyatin, *We*, record 10, 51.

passion awakens his revolutionary impulses."[87] This shift in his personal perspective is revealed in his journal when he writes, "I became glass. I saw into myself, inside. There were two of me."[88] He refers to these two as "my real self" and "my shaggy self." His "shaggy self" is a reference to his hairy hands that his real self resents as atavistic symbols of his connection to the irrational world of nature.[89] He is torn, Vaingurt reports, "between his faith in state orthodoxy and yearning for perfect order, on the one hand, and, on the other, his growing awareness of his own disorderly, irrepressible, idiosyncratic subjectivity."[90] In a telling admission of his conflicted position in the ongoing struggle for political freedom, D-503 admits: "A long time ago I had ceased understanding who 'they' were and who 'we' were."[91] His journal, as a consequence, is transformed from a public declaration extoling the rational happiness of One State to a politically compromising personal confession of his divided loyalty.

Surrounding One State's city that comprises millions of inhabitants is the transparent Green Wall that partitions their civilized and rational society from the irrational forces of nature—the "chaotic world of the trees, birds, animals." In his journal D-503 reports, "Mankind ceased to be wild beast when it built its first wall. Mankind ceased to be savage when we built the Green Wall."[92] In the centuries since the revolution, he explains, none of the city dwellers has gone behind the Green Wall, though later, when I-330 leads him through a passage in the "ancient house," he discovers that travel beyond the Green Wall has always been possible.[93]

THE PRIVACY TAX

The glass of the Green Wall encircling this futuristic city is transparent, as are buildings and the cranes used to build them. The walls and ceilings of

---

87. Thomas Horan, "Revolutions from the Waist Downwards: Desire as Rebellion in Yevgeny Zamyatin's *We*, George Orwell's *1984*, and Aldous Huxley's *Brave New World*," *Extrapolation* 48, no. 2 (2007): 314–39, 319.

88. Zamyatin, *We*, record 10, 50.

89. Zamyatin, record 39, 199. See also record 27, 143.

90. Julia Vaingurt, "Human Machines and the Pains of Penmanship in Yevgeny Zamyatin's *We*," *Cultural Critique* 80 (Winter 2012): 108–29, 108.

91. Zamyatin, *We*, record 27, 142.

92. Zamyatin, record 17, 83.

93. Zamyatin, record 27, 135.

the apartments are clear glass, "woven from the sparkling air."[94] "We have nothing to hide from one another,"[95] explains D-503, and the citizens "live in full view, perpetually awash with light."[96] Eliminating privacy is the "arduous and distinguished task of the Guardians,"[97] the "invisible, ever-present"[98] secret police and public conscience of One State. The glass buildings and public listening devices facilitate their work. The Guardians audit street conversations aided by "concave, pink, quivering . . . membranes"[99] that stretch like eardrums over the avenues of the city.[100]

Despite these extreme privacy restrictions, the actions of I-330 and the MEPHI conspirators threaten the Benefactor's vision of the general welfare. I-330 and her confederates infiltrate the crew of the *Integral*, planning to use the spaceship as a weapon against One State. Though the Guardians on board thwart the hijacking attempt, the MEPHI's subsequent efforts to break through the Green Wall are successful, releasing "chaos, howling, corpses, [and] wild beasts."[101] In the wake of the *Integral*'s compromised maiden flight, the Benefactor summons D-503 to question his complicity in I-330's scheme and express his dismay with D-503's sexual naiveté.[102] Following his excoriation of D-503, the Benefactor shares with him the reason for his disappointment, which stems from his vision for the hap-

---

94. Zamyatin, record 4, 19.

95. Zamyatin, record 4, 19.

96. Zamyatin, record 4, 19. There is also no privacy on the anarchist planet Anarres in Le Guin's *The Dispossessed*. "No doors were locked, few shut," but "sexual privacy was freely available and socially expected; and beyond that privacy was not functional. It was excess, waste." Ursula K. Le Guin, *The Dispossessed* (New York: Harper and Row, Publishers, 1974), 87, 97.

97. Zamyatin, *We*, record 4, 19.

98. Zamyatin, record 28, 147.

99. Zamyatin, record 10, 48.

100. Zamyatin, record 12, 61. The American Civil Liberties Union (ACLU) reports, "Of all of the recent technological developments that have expanded the surveillance capabilities of law enforcement agencies at the expense of individual privacy, perhaps the most powerful is cell phone location tracking. And now . . . this method is widespread and often used without adequate regard for constitutional protections, judicial oversight, or accountability." American Civil Liberties Union, December 23, 2016, https://www.aclu.org/cases/cell-phone-location-tracking-public-records-request (accessed November 18, 2018).

101. Zamyatin, *We*, record 40, 203.

102. Zamyatin, record 36, 188.

piness of One State. The Benefactor equates happiness with the bliss of angels who, "with surgically excised imaginations"[103] are spared the feelings of desire, pity, and love.[104]

In the aftermath of the resurgent revolutionary activity, One State announces its draconian response, a new constructive tax designed to end the revolutionary impulse at "the core of the subversive instinct for freedom."[105] Because One State's scientists have recently discovered the brain center responsible for imagination (in a "pathetic cerebral nodule"), all work is cancelled and everyone is ordered to undergo the "Great Operation"—the offending nodule's X-ray cauterization—a "fantasectomy," says Gottlieb, "the lobotomy of the imagination."[106] Fifteen hundred auditoriums throughout the city are staffed with surgeons and converted into mass-production operating rooms.

Following his audience with the Benefactor, D-503 recounts that "I, and everyone who was with us, were taken . . . and carried off to the nearest auditorium. . . . There, we were bound to tables and subjected to the Great Operation."[107] On the following day, D-503 appears again before the Benefactor and tells him everything that he knows about the MEPHI "enemies of happiness,"[108] then asks himself, "How could this have seemed so hard to do before?"[109]

EXPECTATIONS OF PRIVACY

Pretty harmless, perhaps; but also pretty disquieting. That mania, to start with, for doing things in private. Which meant, in practice, not doing anything at all. For what was there that one could do in private. . . . Yes, what was there?

—Aldous Huxley (1894–1963), *Brave New World*[110]

---

103. Zamyatin, record 36, 188.

104. Zamyatin, record 36, 187.

105. Erika Gottlieb, *Dystopian Fiction East and West: Universe of Terror and Trial* (Montreal: McGill-Queen's University Press, 2001), 59.

106. Gottlieb, 61.

107. Zamyatin, *We*, record 40, 202. The nature of this sacrifice gives new meaning to the term *head tax*.

108. Zamyatin, record 40, 202.

109. Zamyatin, record 40, 202–3.

110. Huxley, *Brave New World*, 88.

Winston Smith, as noted, sat to the left of the telescreen's incessant gaze. "Surveillance can create chilling effects on important activities," warns Solove, "especially ones essential for democracy, such as free speech and free association."[111] The benefits of privacy that Rosen notes are benefits to a society that values friendship, intimacy, and love, not one focused on party loyalty such as Orwell's or rational uniformity like Zamyatin's.

THE OBSERVER EFFECT

The observer effect is an epistemological constraint acknowledging that the measurement of certain phenomena alters the condition being measured.[112] In *Behavior in Public Places* Goffman explains that when a person is being watched and knows the identity of the observer, she may alter her conduct based on that person's anticipated reactions.[113] But, more importantly, he says, "In the asymmetrical case, where a person is being spied upon . . . he may greatly modify his conduct if he suspects he is being observed, even though he does not know the identity of the particular audience." This, he says, "is one of the possibilities celebrated in Orwell's *1984*."[114] It is for this reason that a government using privacy restriction as a tool of hegemony must reconcile itself to the altered form of beings it now controls. In curtailing privacy through surveillance, we are not simply raising the curtain on the actors—like the window of an ant farm—but affecting the emotions, motives, and reasoning directing those actions. People who were once accessible, forthcoming, and honest, for example, may now present themselves as cautious, defiant, and shifty.

PRIVATE COMMUNICATIONS

If privacy is a precondition for friendship and love, the expectation of privacy is a precondition for communications that cultivate and maintain these relationships. The official privacy afforded to personal communications reflects a utopian society's judgment of its importance for the nurture and support of

---

111. Solove, *Understanding Privacy*, 193.

112. For example, checking a tire's air pressure at the valve releases air, reducing the pressure.

113. Erving Goffman, *Behavior in Public Places* (New York: The Free Press, 1963), 16.

114. Goffman, 16.

the general welfare. This appraisal is observed in a "transmission principle," says Nissenbaum, defined as, "a constraint on the flow . . . of information from party to party in a context."[115] In Le Guin's *The Dispossessed*, for example, letters mailed within the anarchist colony on Anarres must remain unsealed, not by law (because there are no laws) but by convention: "you had no right to ask people to carry a message that they couldn't read."[116] Letters in One State in Zamyatin's *We* are read by the Guardians before delivery to the recipient.[117] In our own age, electronic communications have largely supplanted personal letters, and Posner observes, "technology unforeseen by Orwell is overcoming the limitations of human search." Computers now "winnow vast amounts of electronic traffic, flagging the tiny fraction of the intercepted messages suspicious enough to warrant being read or listened to by human intelligence officers,"[118] the "Guardians" of our own age. Orwell's telescreens, Posner continues, "can be imagined morphing into electronic surveillance by the National Security Agency."[119]

TEMPERED EXPECTATIONS

While citizens frequently call for more transparency from their government, they also rely on government to protect the privacy of their personal records, such as medical histories or income tax returns. When a government makes public what was previously assumed to be a citizen's personal business, expectations of privacy are shattered. The government's release or exposure of otherwise private information may serve as a constraining influence over citizens' conduct and as a constructive tax.[120] In Hertzka's *Freeland*, for example, each citizen's personal finances "lie open to the day." For this reason, "all the world knows what everybody has and whence he

---

115. Nissenbaum, *Privacy in Context*, 145.

116. Le Guin, *The Dispossessed*, 220.

117. Zamyatin, *We*, record 10, 45.

118. Posner, *Law and Literature*, 405.

119. Posner, 409.

120. Governments release otherwise private information as a public service. The National Sex Offender Public Website (NSOPW), for example, "provides the public with access to sex offender data nationwide." This form of strategic privacy invasion is a constructive tax with a significant untapped potential for publicizing other matters of public interest, including, for example, child support delinquents, domestic violence perpetrators, DUI offenders, tax cheaters, and children's vaccination records.

gets it."[121] There is no advantage, says Hertzka's narrator, in attempting to look more prosperous than you are because anyone who cares to can look up your earnings. As a result, "No one can deceive either himself or others as to his circumstances."[122] Thus, while More's Utopia abolished money to eliminate ostentation and envy, Freeland pursues the same goal through financial transparency.

In the next chapter we pursue government restrictions on access to truth and the question of government's privacy as a constructive tax, one that restricts citizens' access to its secrets. What is hidden in Plato's *Republic*, Bacon's *New Atlantis*, and Orwell's *Nineteen Eighty-Four* is contrasted with Godwin's prescription for the "euthanasia of government" as the only solution.

---

121. Hertzka, *Freeland*, 249.
122. Hertzka, 249.

CHAPTER THREE

TAXING ACCESS TO TRUTH

Part One:
Plato and Bacon

OPAQUE GOVERNMENT

My friend, the real truth always strikes one as improbable, don't you know that? In order to make truth seem more probable, one must always mix it with some falsehood.

—Fyodor Dostoevsky (1821–1881), *Devils*[1]

When Bacon calls knowledge and power "those twin objects" that "do really meet in one,"[2] he implies an equation: what government subtracts from the citizens' knowledge is likewise a reduction in the citizens' power. When a government's goal is not revenue but control—or maximizing control while conserving revenue—regulating access to truth is a formidable weapon. It is also a constructive tax—a nonpecuniary sacrifice imposed on the citizens in the name of the general welfare. In the preceding chapter we explored the possibility that government restrictions on personal privacy act as a control. But government also seeks privacy, and what it hides from its citizens may

---

1. Fyodor Dostoevsky, *Devils*, trans. Michael R. Katz (Oxford: Oxford University Press, 1999), 226–27.

2. Bacon, "Plan of the Work," *The Great Instauration*, 32.

serve a similar function. Godwin acknowledges the importance of this fact, observing that

> secrets of state will commonly be found to consist of that species of information relative to the interests of a society . . . respecting which the chief anxiety . . . is that it should be concealed from the members of that society.[3]

Censorship, deception, disinformation, lies, propaganda, and suppression of opinion or speech are common forms of political control and state-sponsored roadblocks to discovering truth.[4]

It may be an exaggeration to claim that "opaque government" is redundant, but even the most transparent governments suppress information for reasons of national security. A more sinister picture emerges, however, when the state denies citizens access to information as a tactic of control.[5] The question of free inquiry bleeds into that of free speech. Mill stresses the importance of "the freedom of the expression of opinion"[6] in a society if the goal is to avoid rule by falsehood and superstition. "Truth, in the great practical concerns of life," he declares, is a "question of the reconciling and combining of opposites."[7] For this reason, "All silencing of discussion is an assumption of infallibility,"[8] like that ascribed to the Party in Orwell's *Nineteen Eighty-Four.*

The state's control over access to truth is a vital theme in the utopian writings of Plato, Bacon, Orwell, and Godwin. In part one of this chapter I describe the governmental deception Plato and Bacon advocate in the *Republic* and *New Atlantis*, respectively, and in part two the deception Orwell

---

3. Godwin, *Enquiry Concerning Political Justice*, 3rd ed., bk. 5, chap. 21, 539.

4. Herman observes, "propaganda is a more important means of social control in open societies like the United States than in closed societies like the late Soviet Union." Herman, "From Ingsoc and Newspeak to Amcap, Amerigood, and Marketspeak," 113.

5. See, for example, Dina Fine Maron, "Trump Administration Restricts News from Federal Scientists at USDA, EPA," *Scientific American* (January 24, 2017). https://www.scientificamerican.com/article/trump-administration-restricts-news-from-federal-scientists-at-usda-epa/ (accessed January 30, 2019).

6. John Stuart Mill, *On Liberty* (Chicago: Henry Regnery Company, 1955), 75.

7. Mill, 68.

8. Mill, 25.

depicts in *Nineteen Eighty-Four*. In each case, though in distinctly different ways, these utopian states furtively manage information to manipulate their citizens. In concluding part two I approach the same subject from a contrasting perspective: the utopian ideal of unfettered access to truth, as expressed in the writings of William Godwin. His *Enquiry Concerning Political Justice* examines the stifling effect that government itself—in its many guises—has on our access to truth. He attacks both constructive and pecuniary taxation as antithetical to the general welfare—defined in terms of disinterested reason in search of truth and justice.

PLATO (C. 428–C. 348 BCE): THE REPUBLIC OF LIES

> As for the philosophers, they make imaginary laws for imaginary commonwealths; and their discourses are as the stars, which give little light, because they are so high.
>
> —Francis Bacon (1561–1626), *Of The Advancement of Learning*[9]

Myths, lies, and other deceptions are, for Plato, legitimate tools for molding citizens in his ideal state. To engage citizens in his plan he establishes a connection between their personal lives and the good of the community. This link affirms the citizens' common heritage and explains their assigned position in society. In pondering this scheme, Socrates (Plato's discussion leader) asks if we could "somehow contrive one of those lies that come into being in case of need, . . . [a] noble lie to persuade, in the best case, even the rulers, but if not them, the rest of the city?"[10] His answer is a local creation myth designed to accomplish two goals: one of uniting and the other of dividing the citizens. In recounting the myth, Socrates explains,

> "All of you in the city are certainly brothers," we shall say to them in telling the tale, "but the god, in fashioning those of you who are competent to rule, mixed gold in at their birth; this is

---

9. Francis Bacon, *Of The Advancement of Learning*, in *The Works of Francis Bacon*, ed. James Spedding, Robert Leslie Ellis, and Douglas Denon Heath, vol. 3 (Cambridge: Cambridge University Press, 2011), bk. 2, 475.

10. Plato, *Republic*, trans. Bloom, bk. 3, 414b–c.

why they are most honored; in auxiliaries, silver; and iron and bronze in the farmers and other craftsmen."[11]

The resulting deception (the myth of metals) bonds the citizens while reconciling each to his assigned role in society.[12]

Uniting the citizens is necessary to instill loyalty to their city (state) and implant a belief in their kinship and common heritage.[13] This contrivance, Strauss explains, "demands that the citizens regard themselves as children of one and the same mother and nurse, the earth, and hence as brothers."[14] Bloom adds that the "noble lie was intended . . . to assure that the ruled would be obedient to the rulers, and particularly, to prevent the rulers from abusing their charge."[15] The resulting model community "did not aim at making any one class in the state happy above the rest," explains Socrates, "the happiness was to be in the whole state."[16] In this way his focus aligns with Montesquieu's description of the spirit of a policy that "considers the society rather than the citizen, and the citizen rather than the man."[17]

The second function of the noble lie is dividing the citizens, which is necessary to accommodate Plato's goal (described in chapter four) that each person fulfill a role most beneficial to the general welfare. In announcing Plato's objectives Socrates declares, "our rulers will have to use a throng of lies and deceptions for the benefit of the ruled."[18] As a consequence, one of the principles advanced in the *Republic*, Strauss suggests, is that justice does not always require truth.[19] Though the myths are intended to inform citizens' beliefs, they are not, Socrates claims, *real* or *true lies*, but merely *lies*

---

11. Plato, 415a.

12. "To ensure docility," explains Mumford, "the guardians do not hesitate to feed the community with lies: they form, in fact, an archetypal Central Intelligence Agency within a Platonic Pentagon." Lewis Mumford, "Utopia, the City and the Machine," in *Utopias and Utopian Thought*, ed. Frank E. Manuel (Boston: Houghton Mifflin Company, 1965), 6.

13. Plato, *Republic*, bk. 3, 414d–e.

14. Leo Strauss, *The City and Man* (Chicago: University of Chicago Press, 1964), 102.

15. Bloom, "Interpretive Essay," in *The Republic of Plato*, trans. Bloom, 369.

16. Plato, *Republic*, trans. Benjamin Jowett (New York: Vintage Classics, a division of Random House, 1991), bk. 7, 519e.

17. Montesquieu, *The Spirit of Laws*, bk. 27, chap. 1, 229.

18. Plato, *Republic*, trans. Bloom, bk. 5, 459c.

19. Strauss, *The City and Man*, 68.

in speech. The distinction between true lies and lies in speech is illustrated by the restrictions the Republic's educational curriculum imposes on poetry. This scheme calls for the "supervision" of poets—the redaction or censorship of certain poems. Regarding depictions of Hades that make death sound frightening and loathsome, for example, Socrates says, "We'll beg Homer and the other poets not to be harsh if we strike out these and all similar things."[20] Altering the frightening images, suggests Plato, changes Homer's intent and is in that sense a falsehood, though not a true lie but only a lie in speech. Lies in speech are justified by their context and literary function rather than by their factual content. Amending Homer's words in this case does not alter the facts in the same way, for example, as claiming that the Earth is supported on the back of a turtle.

In her book *Lying*, Bok notes that the "moral question of whether you are lying or not is not *settled* by establishing the truth or falsity of what you say. In order to settle this question, we must know whether you *intend your statement to mislead.*"[21] For this reason, in altering descriptions of Hades or historical accounts where "we don't know where the truth about ancient things lies,"[22] only a lie in speech is possible. In contrast, a *true* or *real lie* is one that is harmful because it produces "ignorance in the soul of the man who has been lied to."[23] As Reeve explains, "a real lie is one that misleads reason, and so prevents the psyche itself from achieving the good."[24]

Though the ruler-philosophers are selected for their commitment to truth and have "no taste for falsehood,"[25] facets of Plato's scheme (e.g., "true lies") are plainly intended to deceive the citizens in a way that the myth of metal-based souls is not. One example is the guardians' breeding ceremony, about which Socrates proclaims: "certain festivals and sacrifices must be established by law at which we'll bring the brides and grooms together."[26] Since such festivals' secret purpose is selective breeding (discussed in chapter five)—to match temporary mates for reproduction—the artifice of a rigged

---

20. Plato, *Republic*, trans. Bloom, bk. 3, 387b.

21. Sissela Bok, *Lying* (New York: Vintage Books, 1978), 6 (italics in original).

22. Plato, *Republic*, trans. Bloom, bk. 2, 382d.

23. Plato, 382b.

24. C. D. C. Reeve, *Philosopher-Kings: The Argument of Plato's Republic* (Princeton, NJ: Princeton University Press, 1988; repr. Hackett Publishing Company), 209.

25. Plato, *Republic*, trans. Bloom, bk. 6, 485c.

26. Plato, bk. 6, 459e–460a.

lottery is employed. These procedures are administered by the older guardians to deceive the younger participants concerning their temporary mates and biological partners of their anticipated children. The very purpose of this device is to mislead reason and impart "ignorance in the soul of the man"[27] or woman whose sexual paring has been subject to the choice of another. This is a *true lie,* and it imposes on the guardians an unwitting sacrifice for the general welfare—a constructive tax.

FRANCIS BACON (1561–1626): THE SACRIFICE TO SCIENCE

The need to seek causes has been put into the soul of man. And the human mind, without grasping in their countlessness and complexity the conditions of phenomena, of which each separately may appear as a cause, takes hold of the first, most comprehensive approximation and says: here is the cause.

—Leo Tolstoy (1828–1910), *War and Peace* [28]

Thomas Hobbes alleges, "Ignorance of natural causes disposeth a man to credulity, so as to believe many times impossibilities: for such know nothing to the contrary, but that they may be true."[29] This describes the plight of ordinary citizens in Francis Bacon's New Atlantis, where the scientists' control over knowledge and its guarded dissemination to the public is a required sacrifice for the general welfare. "His marvelous story is of interest to us today," Suter advises, "because we are [still] concerned about . . . the government control of scientific research."[30] The *New Atlantis* expresses Bacon's vision of the proper role of science in discovering and liberating human potential. It features citizens on the island of Bensalem directed by a secret

---

27. Plato, bk. 2, 382b.

28. Leo Tolstoy, *War and Peace,* trans. Richard Pevear and Larissa Volokhonsky (New York: Vintage Classics, 2008), 987.

29. Thomas Hobbes, *Leviathan: Or the Matter, Forme and Power of a Commonwealth Ecclesiasticall and Civil,* ed. Michael Oakeshott (London: Collier-Macmillan, 1962), first part, chap. 2, 85.

30. Rufus Suter, "Salomon's House: A Study of Francis Bacon," *The Scientific Monthly* 66, no. 1 (January 1948): 62–66, 62. In our own time (August 9, 2001) President George W. Bush, for example, imposed a ban on U.S. federal funding for research on newly created human embryonic stem cell lines.

society of scientists, the members of "Salomon's House" (or the "College of the Six Days Works").[31] *New Atlantis*, notes Eurich, is a testimony of Bacon's belief that "through scientific knowledge man may progress to the utopian world."[32]

Bensalem, says Craig, is a "closed society existing altogether on its own somewhere, unknown to the outside world, where scientific and technological innovation are pursued secretly and under strict regulations."[33] Scientists in Bensalem are charged with uncovering nature's secrets and hidden causes. In this effort, explains Dewey, "Active experimentation must force the apparent facts of nature into forms different to those in which they familiarly present themselves."[34] Bacon believed what passed for science at the end of the sixteenth century was a sterile academic exercise in a closed deductive world incapable of rendering any new insights or discoveries. "We must begin anew," Bacon declares, for it is "idle to expect any great advancement in science from the superinducing and engrafting of new things upon old."[35] The promise of his program is to improve the scientific approach first by beginning from particulars (guided by induction and experimentation[36]) rather than general propositions and second by turning inward to the operations of its primary instrument, the mind.

APPROACHING THE MIND WITH CAUTION

Many misguided notions are traceable, Bacon believes, to our own psychological complacency, our failure to cross-examine our beliefs and their

---

31. Francis Bacon, *New Atlantis*, in *The Works of Francis Bacon*, ed. James Spedding, Robert Leslie Ellis, and Douglas Denon Heath, vol. 3 (Cambridge: Cambridge University Press, 2011), 146, 165.

32. Nell Eurich, *Science in Utopia: A Mighty Design* (Cambridge, MA: Harvard University Press, 1967), 140.

33. Tobin L. Craig, "On the Significance of the Literary Character of Francis Bacon's *New Atlantis* for an Understanding of His Political Thought," *The Review of Politics* 72 (2010): 213–39, 237.

34. John Dewey, *Reconstruction in Philosophy* (Boston, MA: Beacon, 1957), 32.

35. Francis Bacon, *The New Organon*, in *The Works of Francis Bacon*, ed. James Spedding, Robert Leslie Ellis, and Douglas Denon Heath, vol. 4 (Cambridge: Cambridge University Press, 2011), aphorism 31, 52.

36. For Bacon's view of induction see *The New Organon*, aphorism nos. 11–14, 127–45; F. H. Anderson, *The Philosophy of Francis Bacon* (The University of Chicago Press, 1948), 80–90.

origins. Bacon claims human understanding "is of its own nature prone to suppose the existence of more order and regularity in the world than it finds. . . . Hence the fiction that all celestial bodies move in perfect circles."[37] This tendency to impose excessive order gives rise, he observes, to illusions or cognitive distortions confounding the mind's proper scientific operation. He refers to as *idols* the illusions or biases to which our minds naturally tend. These idols are "the deepest fallacies of the human mind," he declares, for they "do not deceive in particulars . . . but by a corrupt and ill-ordered predisposition of the mind, which . . . perverts and infects all the anticipations of the intellect."[38] For this reason the human understanding "is of its own nature prone to abstractions and gives a substance and reality to things which are fleeting."[39] Accordingly, he warns,

> The idols and false notions which are now in possession of the human understanding . . . not only so beset men's minds that truth can hardly find entrance, but even after entrance obtained, they will again in the very instauration of the sciences meet and trouble us, unless men being forewarned . . . fortify themselves . . . against their assaults.[40]

Whitney says Bacon's idols "stand for the limitations of sense, reason, . . . language, and philosophical systems—all made worse by man's idolatrous desire for vain, not useful, knowledge."[41] Furthermore, explains Bacon, the human understanding "receives an infusion from the will and affections"[42] with the result that "what a man had rather were true he more readily believes." Therefore, man rejects

> sober things, because they narrow hope; the deeper things of nature, from superstition; the light of experience, from arrogance

37. Bacon, *The New Organon*, aphorism 45, 55. See also Bacon, *Of The Advancement of Learning*, 395.

38. Francis Bacon, *Of The Dignity and Advancement of Learning*, in *The Works of Francis Bacon*, ed. James Spedding, Robert Leslie Ellis, and Douglas Denon Heath, vol. 4 (Cambridge: Cambridge University Press, 2011), 431.

39. Bacon, *The New Organon*, aphorism 51, 58.

40. Bacon, aphorism 38, 53.

41. Charles Whitney, *Francis Bacon and Modernity* (New Haven, CT: Yale University Press, 1986), 37–38.

42. Bacon, *The New Organon*, aphorism 49, 57.

and pride, lest his mind should seem to be occupied with things mean and transitory.[43]

The doctrine of idols, says Rossi, is, for Bacon, "an integral part of his new logic of science, which deals with the invention of arts, where traditional logic deals with the invention of arguments."[44] Bacon's remedy for the idols is to arm the mind with cognitive weapons. Though he identifies four types of idols, the "false appearances that are imposed upon us by the general nature of the mind" are what he calls Idols of the Tribe.[45] These logical distortions "have their foundation in human nature itself, and in the tribe or race of men."[46] Bacon's insights on the mind's irrational operations have proved a fertile field of research in our own time. Studying certain Idols of the Tribe, for example, psychologists have identified such cognitive biases as availability,[47] framing,[48] and prospect theory (of risk assessment).[49]

---

43. Bacon, aphorism 49, 57.

44. Paolo Rossi, *Francis Bacon: From Magic to Science*, trans. Sacha Rabinovitch (Chicago: The University of Chicago Press, 1968), 160.

45. Bacon, *Of The Advancement of Learning*, 395.

46. Bacon, *The New Organon*, aphorism 41, 54. The Idols of the Tribe, says Anderson, "have their foundation in human nature as such." In contrast, Idols of the Cave arise because "each one is shut within the cave of his own nature with the customs which arise from his peculiar training." Anderson, *The Philosophy of Francis Bacon*, 99, 101.

47. Confirming Bacon's assertion that "what a man had rather were true he more readily believes," Tversky and Kahneman explain that "continued preoccupation with an outcome may increase its availability and hence its perceived likelihood." Amos Tversky and Daniel Kahneman, "Availability: A Heuristic for Judging Frequency and Probability," in *Judgment Under Uncertainty: Heuristics and Biases*, ed. Daniel Kahneman, Paul Slovic, and Amos Tversky (Cambridge: Cambridge University Press, 1982), 178.

48. Framing is the context in which we pose a decision, judgment, or problem. In the "framing phase" of a choice, "the decision maker constructs a representation of the acts, contingencies, and outcomes that are relevant to the decision." Daniel Kahneman and Amos Tversky, "Advances in Prospect Theory: Cumulative Representation of Uncertainty," in *Choices, Values, and Frames*, ed. Daniel Kahneman and Amos Tversky (Russell Sage Foundation, Cambridge University Press, 2000), 46.

49. Prospect theory, pioneered by Tversky and Kahneman, describes people's choices between prospects (prospective outcomes) in terms of framing and valuation (of risk). This theory holds that "Our perceptual apparatus is attuned to the evaluation of changes or differences rather than to the evaluation of absolute magnitudes. . . . A salient characteristic of attitudes to changes in welfare [for example] is that losses loom larger than gains." Daniel Kahneman and Amos Tversky, "Prospect Theory," in *Choices, Values, and Frames*, ed. Daniel Kahneman and Amos Tversky (Russell Sage Foundation, Cambridge University Press, 2000), 32–33.

NEW ATLANTIS

The "very thing which I am preparing and laboring at with all my might," Bacon writes, is "to make the mind of man by help of art a match for the nature of things."[50] In his utopia this paramount art has presumably been discovered, perfected, and used to manage society on a scientific basis. *New Atlantis* is an ostensibly unfinished work of fiction describing the previously unknown culture of an island, Bensalem, that European mariners discover at about the time of Bacon's writing.[51] The civilization has a long-recorded history[52] and its ancient lawgiver, King Solamona, because he "thought nothing wanted," drafted "laws of secrecy touching strangers" nineteen hundred years earlier. These laws restrict travelers to the island and prohibit its own citizens (except certain scientists) from traveling abroad.[53]

The *New Atlantis* portrays an ideal society partitioned between a superior order of scientists and the mass of ordinary, albeit contented and obedient, citizens.[54] Salomon's House, the headquarters of the priestly scientific community, "does not rule officially, says Hale, "but it is closely tied to the governance of the kingdom." In addition, she asserts, "Bacon as a political thinker . . . uses the *New Atlantis* to show his readers what happens when scientists effectively rule."[55] But "what happens" in Bensalem—the daily lives of the citizens and their interaction with the state—is precisely what we don't see. "The mystery of *New Atlantis* culminates in the mystery of who governs."[56] We receive clues both in terms of the orderly conduct of the citizens and Bacon's vision for scientific discovery, but the mechanism by which science produces the citizens'

---

50. Bacon, *Of The Dignity and Advancement of Learning*, 412.

51. Begun in 1624, *New Atlantis* was published posthumously in 1627. White calculates the sailors' landing date as 1612. Howard B. White, *Peace Among the Willows: The Political Philosophy of Francis Bacon* (The Hague: Martinus Nijhoff, 1968), 135.

52. Bacon, *New Atlantis*, 138.

53. Bacon, 140, 144.

54. Blodgett sees *New Atlantis* as Bacon's protest against Campanella's "communistic state [that] does not meet with his approval." She argues that since, "Bacon has centered his interest . . . only upon topics that are included in the *Civitas Solis*," that Bacon's work may have been influenced by Campanella's. Eleanor Dickinson Blodgett, "Bacon's *New Atlantis* and Campanella's *Civitas Solis*: A Study in Relationships," PMLA 46, no. 3 (September 1931): 763–80, 776, 775.

55. Kimberly Hurd Hale, *Francis Bacon's New Atlantis in the Foundation of Modern Political Thought* (New York: Lexington Books, 2013), 97.

56. Robert K. Faulkner, *Francis Bacon and the Project of Progress* (Lanham, MD: Rowman and Littlefield Publishers, 1993), 255.

pervasive civility remains hidden. This is consonant with Bacon's claim that "all governments are obscure and invisible."[57] But, as Weinberger observes, this opacity is a matter of perspective, as the "government is obscure only for the governed toward those who govern, *not* for the governors toward the governed."[58]

What little we learn of the citizens' conduct is not from a picture of their daily lives, for—as in Plato's *Republic*—we see nothing of that. Our primary exposure to the citizens is at official ceremonies where, to some critics, their conduct has seemed unnatural. Faulkner asks, for example, "Are the people drugged or perhaps psychologically conditioned?"[59] Their civil religion, White explains, was proposed, "to make men sheep, subject to the shepherd-political scientist rather than the divine shepherd."[60] Though the compliance of the citizens has a likely connection to the House of Salomon and its scientific discoveries, we cannot determine if the citizens' conduct is a result of scientists sharing their findings with the citizens, thereby informing and enlightening their conduct, or of scientists using these secret findings to produce calculated results on their hapless subjects. Are the citizens acting against their will, or is the control itself such that it regulates the will? In the *Critias*, for example, Plato suggests the gods wield such control. The *Critias*—along with the *Timaeus*—constitutes Plato's brief writings on Atlantis. There, Plato offers a description of how the gods ruled and controlled humans after the apportionment of the earth among the gods.[61] Critias explains,

> they would not coerce body with body in the fashion of shepherds who drive their flocks to pasture with blows; they set the

---

57. Bacon, *Of The Advancement of Learning*, 474. Though Bacon admits that "the government of God over the world is hidden," as is the "government of the Soul in moving the body," he recommends semitransparency for civil government, saying, "contrariwise in the governors toward the governed all things ought, as far as the frailty of man permitteth, to be manifest and revealed" (Bacon, 474).

58. Jerry Weinberger, *Science, Faith, and Politics: Francis Bacon and the Utopian Roots of the Modern Age* (Ithaca, NY: Cornell University Press, 1985), 311 (italics in original).

59. Faulkner, *Francis Bacon and the Project of Progress*, 248.

60. White, *Peace Among the Willows*, 237.

61. Plato's spokesman Critias describes Atlantis as an advanced civilization existing nine thousand years earlier. It is an "island larger than Libya and Asia together." Athens, at the time of Atlantis, was a military power. Written records of the two civilizations were presumably lost in the war between the two states and the earthquakes, tsunamis, and floods that followed. Plato, *Critias*, trans. A. E. Taylor, in *Plato: The Collected Dialogues*, edited by Edith Hamilton and Huntington Cairns (New York: Pantheon Books, 1961), 1213, 108e–110d.

course of the living creature from that part about which it turns most readily, its prow, controlling its soul after their own mind.[62]

This suggests some form of subliminal or telepathic control, with the scientists programming the sheepish citizens, though the text provides no details.[63] "At its worst," says Whitney, "Bacon's utopia and the community of truth-seeking intellectuals at its core . . . represent the blind or the secret will to domination and control that ideologies of both reform and revolution can harbor."[64]

TAXATION IN BENSALEM

The *New Atlantis* is Bacon's utopian vision of a society placing science on a pedestal, where scientists—if not rulers in a traditional sense—are certainly in charge. Though we witness no evidence of pecuniary taxation in Bensalem (except an odd inheritance tax described in chapter five), this may be a product of the island's compliant citizens and its avoidance of war facilitated by its unknown location. The state's major need for public financing appears to be support of the scientists of Salomon's House, though it is possible that the scientists' numerous inventions and discoveries—including submarines and electric lights[65]—serve as a source of royalties for the state as they do, for example, in Wells's *A Modern Utopia*.[66]

---

62. Plato, 1215, 109b–c.

63. Weinberger explains that Renfusa, the name of the city in Bensalem where the sailors land, combines two Greek words that "would be rendered 'sheeplike,' or 'sheep-natured.'" J. Weinberger, "Science and Rule in Bacon's Utopia: An Introduction to the Reading of the *New Atlantis*," *The American Political Science Review* 70, no. 3 (September 1976): 865–85, 876.

64. Whitney, *Francis Bacon and Modernity*, 199.

65. Among the significant inventions are "ships and boats for going under water" and "means . . . of producing light . . . from diverse bodies." Bacon, *New Atlantis*, 157–66. In his Academy of Lagado, which Houston says, "clearly draws upon . . . Salomon's House in Bacon's New Atlantis," Swift parodies the scientists' inventions with, for example, a "project for extracting sunbeams out of cucumbers." Swift, *Gulliver's Travels*, 167; Chlöe Houston, "Utopia, Dystopia or Anti-utopia? Gulliver's Travels and the Utopian Mode of Discourse," *Utopian Studies* 18, no. 3 (2007): 425–42, 428.

66. Wells, *A Modern Utopia*, 107. Wells's modern Utopia staffs a "world-wide House of Saloman." For successful inventions the state pays a royalty that is divided between the inventor and the educational institution that produced her (Wells, 107).

The island's ancient laws of secrecy mean Bensalem is unknown to the rest of the world. Since ordinary citizens are banned from international travel, they know perhaps nothing of the outside realm.[67] The members of the scientific community, however, are accorded superior authority and freedom. "The End of our Foundation," the Father (scientist) from Salomon's House tells a visitor, is the "knowledge of Causes and secret motions of things; and the enlarging of the bounds of Human Empire, to the effecting of all things possible."[68] In addition to their own experiments and discoveries, and to keep abreast of knowledge in the rest of the world, the scientists travel abroad and "know well most part of the habitable world."[69] The scientists' superior knowledge, White emphasizes, means that "the gap between the truth of Salomon's House and the civil religion of the sheep is a chasm of surpassing proportions."[70] While the final quarter of *New Atlantis* is filled with descriptions of flashy experiments, inventions, powers, and procedures, we garner no notion of the moral criteria the scientists use regarding what results they release to the general public (or to the King), though we know there is no intention to be transparent. Since, as Crowther observes, Bacon believed that scientific knowledge "should be under moral and social control,"[71] the Father from Salomon's House tells his guest,

> we have consultations, [regarding] which of the inventions and experiences which we have discovered shall be published, and which not: and take all an oath of secrecy, for the concealing of those which we think fit to keep secret.[72]

This is a tax on access to truth, which the scientists of Salomon's House (the de facto state) levy on the citizens. While we are not privy as to what kind of scientific knowledge is withheld or whether the citizens are told

---

67. Bacon, *New Atlantis*, 136, 145–46.

68. Bacon, 156.

69. Bacon, 136.

70. White, *Peace Among the Willows*, 225.

71. J. G. Crowther, *Francis Bacon: The First Statesman of Science* (London: The Cresset Press, 1960), 56.

72. Bacon, *New Atlantis*, 165. The quote continues, "though some of those we do reveal sometimes to the state, and some not." White refers to this claim as "the most important statement of political power to be found in the work." White, *Peace Among the Willows*, 227.

lies, we are also left to wonder if the conduct of the compliant citizens is a function of a new operation (as in Zamyatin's *We*), operant conditioning (as in Skinner's *Walden Two*), or eugenic breeding (as in Gilman's *Herland*). Spedding suggests a more prosaic explanation, noting Bacon's concern that scientific discoveries might be "misused and mismanaged" if they should fall into "incapable and unfit hands."[73] Ultimately, order and civil harmony might simply be the product of age-old tradition. In Plato's *Laws*, for example, the Athenian says,

> When men have been brought up under any system of laws and that system has, by some happy providence, persisted unchanged for long ages . . . the whole soul is filled with reverence and afraid to make any innovation on what was once established.[74]

Part Two:
Orwell and Godwin

TOTALITARIAN METHODOLOGIES: ORWELL (1903–1950)

The Party told you to reject the evidence of your eyes and ears.

—George Orwell, *Nineteen Eighty-Four*[75]

Privacy deprivation (described in the previous chapter) is only one form of required sacrifice in Orwell's *Nineteen Eighty-Four*. Limiting access to truth is another, and two methods are used in accomplishing this aim. The first consists in a continual revision of history—"Who controls the past . . . controls

---

73. James Spedding, "Notes to Preface to *The Novum Organum*," in *The Works of Francis Bacon*, ed. James Spedding, Robert Leslie Ellis, and Douglas Denon Heath, vol. 1 (Cambridge: Cambridge University Press, 2011), 113.

74. Plato, *Laws*, trans. A. E. Taylor, in *Plato: The Collected Dialogues*, ed. Edith Hamilton and Huntington Cairns (New York: Pantheon Books, 1961), bk. 7, 798.

75. Orwell, *Nineteen Eighty-Four*, 83.

the future."[76] The second involves Newspeak, an engineered language that restricts the quality and nature of thought. Both techniques require sacrifice for the general welfare, albeit welfare seen through the eyes of Big Brother.

HISTORY IS BUNK IN OCEANIA

When current events are placed in their historical contexts, our understanding of both the events and their contexts is enriched. In Oceania consistency of narrative demands the incessant modification of historical events to match the Party-assigned meanings of current events. This requires continual monitoring and revision of "reports and records of all kinds, newspapers, books, pamphlets, films, sound tracks, [and] photographs,"[77] rendering access to original sources impossible. Ideological thinking, explains Arendt, "orders facts into an absolutely logical procedure which starts from an axiomatically accepted premise."[78] The masses who respond to totalitarian propaganda, she reports, "do not trust their eyes and ears but only their imaginations, which may be caught by anything that is at once universal and consistent in itself."[79] The agency responsible for managing history is the Ministry of Truth, which employs Winston Smith. The editing and revision require a painstaking analysis of past news and other documentation to determine what "facts" could benefit from elimination, fabrication, or updating. This systematic and thoroughgoing revision of history ensures that the citizens only comprehend what the government of Oceania desires them to at that time—the imposition of a constructive tax.[80]

NAMING THE PROBLEM

Rational debate about a problem of civic or social interest is jeopardized if an interested party co-opts the language used to frame the debate. "Political language," advises Orwell, "is designed to make lies sound truthful and

---

76. Orwell, 35–36.

77. Orwell, 187.

78. Arendt, *The Origins of Totalitarianism*, 471.

79. Arendt, 351.

80. Gottlieb observes that the denial of the past is a feature *Nineteen Eighty-Four* shares with Huxley's *Brave New World* and Zamyatin's *We*. Gottlieb, *Dystopian Fiction East and West*, 89.

murder respectable."[81] The government's narrowing and limiting language, through the discipline of Newspeak, further restricts citizens' access to truth in Oceania. Guiding thought structures by controlling meanings is a common weapon in the arsenal of political authority. "Superordinate groups," Becker explains, "maintain their power as much by controlling how people define the world, its components, and its possibilities, as by the use of more primitive forms of control." Specifically, "control based on the manipulation of definitions and labels works more smoothly and costs less" than more "primitive" means for establishing order,[82] illustrating the potential substitution of a constructive for a pecuniary tax.

As a practical matter, the effective analysis of a social problem demands a vocabulary of sufficient potency and clarity to characterize it accurately.[83] The recognition of a problem, however, often awaits its naming. This was the case, for example, in the 1960s with the "newly discovered" problem of child abuse. "Despite documentary evidence of child beating throughout the ages," Pfohl advises, "the 'discovery' of child abuse as deviance and its subsequent criminalization are recent phenomena."[84] *Nineteen Eight-Four* employs this insight in reverse. After analyzing the problem of political dissent to determine its causes, the Ministry of Truth identifies the Oldspeak concepts of freedom, justice, and morality, each "with all its vagueness and useless shades of meaning."[85] The initial step in eliminating such causes is eliminating our ability to name them.

Harris describes Newspeak as "a deliberately distorted language, designed to ensure the political enslavement of its speakers."[86] As such, it imposes a constructive tax—a restriction on access to truth. The standard Newspeak dictionary was subject to periodic revision, eliminating words deemed harmful or redundant and narrowing the meaning of others to what was judged

---

81. George Orwell, "Politics and the English Language," in *Why I Write* (New York: Penguin Books, 2004), 120.

82. Becker, *Outsiders*, 204–5.

83. Orwell argues, "The words *democracy, socialism, freedom, patriotic, realistic, justice*, have each of them several different meanings which cannot be reconciled with one another." Orwell, "Politics and the English Language," 109.

84. "In a four-year period beginning in 1962, the legislatures of all fifty states [of the U.S.] passed statutes against the caretaker's abuse of children." Stephen Pfohl, "The 'Discovery' of Child Abuse," *Social Problems* 24, no. 3 (February 1977): 310–23, 310.

85. Orwell, *Nineteen Eighty-Four*, 53.

86. Roy Harris, "The Misunderstanding of Newspeak," in *George Orwell: Modern Critical Views*, ed. Harold Bloom (New York: Chelsea House Publishers, 1987), 114.

essential to the general welfare. "The word *free*," for example, "still existed in Newspeak, but it could only be used in such statements as 'This dog is free from lice.' "[87] The goal of this strategy is to make even thinking about political freedom impossible. As a consequence, people could conceive of political freedom only as something that was forbidden. "All words grouping themselves round the concepts of liberty and equality," we learn, "were contained in the single word *crimethink*."[88] In addition, "other words such as *honor, justice, morality, internationalism, democracy, science*, and *religion* had simply ceased to exist. A few blanket words covered them, and, in covering them, abolished them."[89] Fewer words in a language means sharper lines and distinctions, turning a world to black and white where previously there had been challenging shades of difference.[90] The effect on truth is to narrow the options available for expressing it. Orwell's "reminder of the political importance of truth and of the dependence of complex thought on a rich vocabulary," observes Posner, remains "philosophically interesting and timely."[91]

Syme—a philologist in the Research Department specializing in the retrogression of language—asks Winston, "Do you know that Newspeak is the only language in the world whose vocabulary gets smaller every year?" Winston knew, of course. When Syme then asks if "you see that the whole aim of Newspeak is to narrow the range of thought,"[92] it was a rhetorical question. Other utopias feature idiosyncratic language conventions to mold belief or constrain thought. Swift's Gulliver, for example, after studying the language of the Houyhnhnms, reports that it has no words for lying or falsehood, as that would be to name a *"thing which was not."*[93] Since common ownership is fundamental in Le Guin's *The Dispossessed*, their language, Pravic, extends non-ownership even to oneself. "Little children

87. Orwell, *Nineteen Eighty-Four*, 310 (italics in original).

88. Orwell, 316 (italics in original).

89. Orwell, 316 (italics in original).

90. Gottlieb notes that "an insistent tendency towards polarization, towards splitting the entire world into the opposites of 'them' and 'us,' black and white" is, for Orwell, characteristic of "a mentality he sees as common to both" totalitarianism and religion. Erika Gottlieb, "The Demonic World of Oceania: The Mystical Adulation of the 'Sacred' Leader," in *Bloom's Modern Critical Interpretations: George Orwell's 1984*, updated edition, ed. Harold Bloom (New York: Chelsea House Publishers, 2007), 52.

91. Posner, *Law and Literature*, 409.

92. Orwell, *Nineteen Eighty-Four*, 53–54.

93. Swift, *Gulliver's Travels*, 217 (italics in original).

might say 'my mother,' but very soon they learned to say 'the mother.' "[94] In *Herland*, Gilman's narrator explains, given the fundamental significance of childrearing in their culture, "The language itself they had deliberately clarified, simplified, made easy and beautiful, for the sake of the children."[95]

For Orwell, the government's aim in restricting the Newspeak vocabulary is not simply to limit its range, but also its users' ability to think in a critical, probing, or abstract way. Mastery of Newspeak leads to "not grasping analogies [and] failing to perceive logical errors."[96] Ironically, the outcome of Newspeak mastery suggests the enduring condition of the proles, the "submerged masses"[97] who "without the power of grasping that the world could be other than it is"[98] and "without general ideas . . . could only focus [their discontent] . . . on petty specific grievances."[99] In Emmanuel Goldstein's subversive treatise, Winston learns that in "Newspeak there is no word for 'Science.' " Insofar as access to truth may be gained through scientific inquiry, however, it is not only the word *science* that has been eliminated but the activity of scientific investigation. As it turns out, the "empirical method of thought, on which all the scientific achievements of the past were founded,"[100] is opposed to the Party's most fundamental principles.[101] Scientific inquiry is also banned in Huxley's *Brave New World*, where Mustapha Mond declares, "truth's a menace, science is a public danger."[102]

Orwell did not offer a Newspeak analysis of the words *private* or *privacy*, topics of the previous chapter, but their likely Newspeak treatment is demonstrated by example. We learn that in Newspeak, "A word contains its opposite in itself." "Take 'good' for instance," explains Syme. "If you

---

94. Le Guin, *The Dispossessed*, 51.

95. Gilman, *Herland*, 87. The consequences, if any, of a more child-friendly language on their attempt to "develop two kinds of mind—the critic and inventor" (Gilman, 65)—goes unexplored in *Herland*.

96. Orwell, *Nineteen Eighty-Four*, 217.

97. Orwell, 196.

98. Orwell, 216.

99. Orwell, 74.

100. Orwell, 198.

101. Orwell, 193.

102. Huxley, *Brave New World*, 204. *Brave New World*, notes Horan, "is very like *1984* in that both novels explore the strong bond between thought and language." Horan, "Revolutions from the Waist Downwards," 332.

have a word like 'good,' what need is there for a word like 'bad'? 'Ungood' will do just as well."[103] Following this guidance the Newspeak opposite of *private* might be *social*, making any desire for privacy *antisocial*. Once the word *private* is "suppressed" and replaced with *antisocial*, the elimination of privacy itself is a matter of exploiting the pejorative meaning of *antisocial*. Antisocial conduct, by definition, can never enhance the general welfare. Antisocial behavior becomes anti-state behavior, and the desire for privacy becomes a "thoughtcrime." The process of Newspeak and its contribution to limiting access to truth supports Orwell's warning that "if thought corrupts language, language can also corrupt thought."[104]

WILLIAM GODWIN (1756–1836): ANARCHIST TAX POLICY

> Why should we think? Alexander Nikolayevich, the Emperor, has thought for us, and will think for us on all matters.
>
> —Leo Tolstoy (1828–1910), *Anna Karenina*[105]

William Godwin's opposition to taxation grew out of his disdain for government, and his utopia replaces government with moral autonomy. Each person must exercise independent moral judgment unhampered by government and other institutions and organizations that interfere in self-interested ways. The result is an anarchic society of loosely knit independent thinkers, each seeking justice in what is beneficial to all. The requisite for independent judgment, says Godwin, is access to truth. When government "assumes to deliver us from the trouble of thinking for ourselves," the natural result, he claims, is "torpor and imbecility."[106] For Godwin the general welfare demands an insatiable quest for truth, and "If we would arrive at truth," he says, "each man must be taught to enquire and think for himself."[107]

---

103. Orwell, *Nineteen Eighty-Four*, 52–53.

104. Orwell, "Politics and the English Language," 116.

105. Leo Tolstoy, *Anna Karenina*, trans. Louise and Aylmer Maude (Mineola, NY: Dover Publications, 2004), 725.

106. Godwin, *Enquiry Concerning Political Justice*, 3rd ed., bk. 6, chap. 1, 567.

107. Godwin, 3rd ed., bk. 4, chap. 3, 284.

But the very existence of government—even without Orwell's Ministry of Truth—threatens this pursuit.[108]

Godwin's indictment of government is based on its systemic interference with our access to truth. "Nothing can be more unreasonable," he affirms, "than the attempt to retain men in one common opinion by the dictate of authority."[109] In his *Enquiry Concerning Political Justice*, Godwin explores the debilitating effect on our moral objectivity resulting from government's efforts to divert us from truth. Government, says Godwin, is "an usurpation upon the private judgment and individual conscience of mankind" and a primary reason we do not think for ourselves. "Above all," he declares,

> we should not forget, that government is an evil . . . and that, however we may be obliged to admit it as a necessary evil for the present, it behoves us, as the friends of reason and the human species, to admit as little of it as possible, and carefully to observe whether, in consequence of the gradual illumination of the human mind, that little may not hereafter be diminished.[110]

"The very idea of government," Godwin explains, "is that of an authority superseding judgment."[111] The moral conviction forming the base of Godwin's political philosophy is that "one man can in no case be bound to yield obedience to any other man or set of men upon earth."[112] This he claims

---

108. Godwin summarizes the two principal methods "according to which truth may be investigated." The first, seeking consistency and corroboration, begins from "one or two simple principles," which seem "scarcely to be exposed to the hazard of refutation [appearing self-evident or a priori]" and from these draw out their logical consequences. This, he says, is the method of the *Enquiry Concerning Political Justice*. With this method, he claims, "if all the parts shall thus be brought into agreement with a few principles, and those principles themselves, true, the whole will be found conformable to truth." This method is, however, subject to the "danger, [that] if we are too exclusively anxious about [the] consistency of system . . . we may forget the perpetual attention we owe to experience, the pole-star of truth." The second method, employed in *The Enquirer*, requires "an incessant recurrence to experiment and actual observation." William Godwin, *The Enquirer: Reflections on Education, Manners and Literature* (New York: Augustus M. Kelley Publishers, 1956), v–vi.

109. Godwin, *Enquiry Concerning Political Justice*, 3rd ed., bk. 6, chap. 1, 567.

110. William Godwin, *An Enquiry Concerning Political Justice*, 1st ed. (1793) (Oxford: Oxford University Press, 2013), bk. 5, chap. 1, 204–5.

111. Godwin, 1st ed., bk. 4, chap. 1, 107.

112. Godwin, 1st ed., bk. 3, chap. 6, 96.

not only because all men are fallible but also because, "where I make the voluntary surrender of my understanding, and commit my conscience to another man's keeping . . . I annihilate my individuality as a man."[113]

GROUPTHINK

The difficulties Godwin identifies with government are symptomatic of those he associates with *any* form of cooperative organization. Allegiance to any group, institution, or party diverts us from the search for truth. "Having learned the creed of our party," Godwin declares, "we have no longer any employment for those faculties which might lead us to detect its errors."[114] Each member's "thought is shackled, at every turn, by the fear that his associates may disclaim him."[115] For this reason he warns, "We should avoid such practices as are calculated to melt our opinions into a common mold."[116] In addition to political parties, he sees such appurtenances of government as taxation, public education, lawyers, democracy, and even marriage as suffocating forces restricting access to truth.[117]

PRIVATE JUDGMENT AND PUBLIC DELIBERATION

Godwin's central belief, reports Philp, is that private judgment and public deliberation are the tools for accessing moral truth.[118] These tools are not themselves the standard of right and wrong, Godwin explains, yet they are the means of moral discovery.[119] "From the collision of disagreeing accounts," he maintains, "justice and reason will be produced."[120] The endgame of Godwin's utopian vision features the triumph of individual judgment and

---

113. Godwin, *Enquiry Concerning Political Justice*, 3rd ed., bk. 3, chap. 6, 243.

114. Godwin, 3rd ed., bk. 4, chap. 3, 285.

115. Godwin, 3rd ed., bk. 5, chap. 23, 548. Malthus, a critic of Godwin, claims, "The great error under which Mr Godwin labours throughout his whole work is the attributing almost all the vices and misery that are seen in civil society to human institutions." Malthus, *An Essay on the Principle of Population*, 75.

116. Godwin, *Enquiry Concerning Political Justice*, 3rd ed., bk. 8, chap. 8, 761.

117. Godwin, *An Enquiry Concerning Political Justice*, 1st ed., bk. 5, chap. 14, 261. See also 3rd ed., bk. 5, chap. 14, 487–88 and chap. 23, 547.

118. Philp, *Godwin's Political Justice*, 169.

119. Godwin, *An Enquiry Concerning Political Justice*, 1st ed., bk. 3, chap. 4, 94.

120. Godwin, *Enquiry Concerning Political Justice*, 3rd ed., bk. 6, chap. 6, 598.

a disinterested pursuit of justice that allocates resources—including human talent—based on their benefit for the whole. We hold our person and our property, he believes, "as a trust in behalf of mankind."[121] The sacrifice required for the general welfare in Godwin's ideal society, therefore, is required by justice and not by government.[122]

FALLIBILISM

Resting secure in our beliefs is a temptation we must battle continually. But without the government's support, Godwin asserts, it is doubtful "whether error could ever be formidable or long-lived."[123] Because of (or despite) his emphasis on personal judgment, Godwin is emphatic that judgment is fallible and that any conclusions we reach we must hold provisionally.[124] "A careful enquirer," he affirms, "is always detecting his past errors; each year of his life produces a severe comment upon the opinions of the last; he suspects all his judgments, and is certain of none."[125] Godwin's extensive revisions of the 1793 *Enquiry* published in 1796 and 1798 are testimony to his sincerity.[126] Thus, while promoting the benefits of independent judgment, he recommends the discipline of fallibilism, warning, "we should never consider the book of enquiry as shut."[127]

GODWIN'S ATTACK ON PECUNIARY TAXATION

While it may seem incongruous that an anarchist would have anything substantive to say about tax policy, Godwin's criticisms of taxation provide

---

121. Godwin, 3rd ed., bk. 2, chap. 2, 175.

122. Clark explains that although Godwin does not distinguish clearly between community, country, nation, and society, he "seems to use the term 'society' to refer to all the interrelationships and institutions which arise from the interaction between human beings." John P. Clark, *The Philosophical Anarchism of William Godwin* (Princeton, NJ: Princeton University Press, 1977), 154.

123. Godwin, *An Enquiry Concerning Political Justice*, 1st ed., 1, chap. 4, 26.

124. Godwin, *Enquiry Concerning Political Justice*, 3rd ed., bk. 2, chap. 5, 198.

125. Godwin, 3rd ed., bk. 8, chap. 10, 780.

126. Claeys observes, for example, that as Godwin's philosophy evolved from the first to the third editions of the *Enquiry*, he struggled with seemingly incompatible standards of justice, including need versus merit. Gregory Claeys, "The Effects of Property on Godwin's Theory of Justice," *Journal of the History of Philosophy* 22, no. 1 (January 1984): 81–101.

127. Godwin, *Enquiry Concerning Political Justice*, 3rd ed., bk. 1, chap. 5, 128.

an overview of his views of government, justice, morality, and truth. Though government is frequently "a source of peculiar evils," he explains, "the wise and just man, being unable as yet, to introduce the form of society which his understanding approves, will contribute to the support of so much coercion as is necessary to exclude what is worse, anarchy."[128] If taxes were no more than financial means supporting a necessary evil, Godwin's criticisms of government would make separate condemnations of taxation redundant. But he sees in pecuniary taxation three tributary evils, each with its own damaging effect on society.

Godwin believes that taxes—when they are necessary—should at most be a temporary expedient.[129] For this reason, the first evil he identifies is the tendency for taxation to perpetuate itself and thereby diminish the prospect of eliminating the reach of government. Thus, he asserts that

> every new channel that is opened for the expenditure of the public money, unless it be compensated (which is scarcely ever the case) by an equivalent deduction from the luxuries of the rich, is so much added to the general stock of ignorance, drudgery and hardship.[130]

Government on this basis can only metastasize; it has no motive to check its own spread. Though a tax is initially raised to meet an extraordinary demand (a war or natural disaster, for example), once the emergency has passed, tax collectors and allied occupations retain a vested interest in their livelihood. "If we pay an ample salary to him who is employed in the public service," Godwin asks, "how are we sure that he will not have more regard to the salary than to the public?"[131] In his utopia, where there would be "neither foreign wars nor domestic stipends," he says, "taxation would be almost unknown."[132]

---

128. Godwin, 3rd ed., bk. 7, chap. 5, 667. Godwin says, "The nature of anarchy has never been sufficiently understood. It is undoubtedly a horrible calamity, but it is less horrible than despotism. . . . Anarchy is a short lived mischief, while despotism is all but immortal." Godwin, *An Enquiry Concerning Political Justice*, 1st ed., bk. 5, chap. 20, 291. See also Godwin, *Enquiry Concerning Political Justice*, 3rd ed., bk. 7, chap. 5, 667.

129. Godwin, *Enquiry Concerning Political Justice*, 3rd ed., bk. 5, chap. 1, 409n.

130. Godwin, 3rd ed., bk. 8, chap. 2, 712.

131. Godwin, 3rd ed., bk. 6, chap. 9, 621.

132. Godwin, 3rd ed., bk. 6, chap. 9, 625.

Godwin cites the institution of public education to demonstrate the harm permanent taxation imposes on society.[133] Tax-funded education, he declares, "ought uniformly to be discouraged on account of its obvious alliance with national government."[134] When government wrests control of education, he says, the state "will not fail to employ it to strengthen its hands, and perpetuate its institutions"[135] and thereby limit access to truth. Hobbes expresses an analogous concern with the English universities in respect to the Pope's control over imparting "false doctrines" against the sovereign power of the king. Though "the universities were not authors of those false doctrines," Hobbes explains, "yet they knew not how to plant the true."[136]

DIGRESSION ON CAPITALISM, EDUCATION, AND ACCESS TO TRUTH

Godwin's concern for the corrosive effects of government on tax-funded education is a theme of later utopians Bellamy and London. For these writers, however, the problem had shifted and they feared that the influences of capitalism—including its creed of individualism—had overcome the intellectual independence of university educators.[137] As Bellamy reports, "Each man's line of teaching or preaching was his vested interest—the means of his livelihood." When any new idea is suggested in science, economics, or

> in almost any field of thought, the first question which the
> learned body having charge of that field and making a living out
> of it would ask itself was not whether the idea was good and

---

133. Despite this criticism, Godwin prefers public education for its benefits in socializing students. "The pupil of private education is commonly either awkward and silent," he says, "or pert, presumptuous and pedantical. In either case he is out of his element, embarrassed with himself, and chiefly anxious about how he shall appear. On the contrary, the pupil of public education usually knows himself, and rests upon his proper center . . . [and is not] engrossed by a continual attention to himself." Godwin, *The Enquirer*, 61–62.

134. Godwin, *An Enquiry Concerning Political Justice*, 1st ed., bk. 6, chap. 8, 353.

135. Godwin, 1st ed., bk. 6, chap. 8, 353.

136. Hobbes, *Leviathan*, second part, chap. 30, 253.

137. Tilman says Bellamy is concerned with the "ideological control the capitalist class has over the popular mind. Through its exercise, newspapers, schools, and churches are brought under the capitalist influence and made economically subservient to the vested interests." Rick Tilman, "The Utopian Vision of Edward Bellamy and Thorstein Veblen," *Journal of Economic Issues* 19, no. 4 (December 1985): 879–98, 890.

true . . . but how it would immediately and directly affect the set of doctrines, traditions, and institutions, with the prestige of which their own personal interests were identified.[138]

London's *The Iron Heel* portrays an enfeebled democracy whose assigned role is "to give the stamp of constitutional procedure to the mandates of the Oligarchy."[139] Educators and other professionals who were dependent—directly or indirectly—on government revenue for their livelihood were acknowledged to be levying the subtle and insidious form of constructive tax Godwin had elaborated. In London's vision, the concern that capitalist interests would infect public education was expressed in a professor's seditious book. As the narrator explains,

> This book, "Economics and Education," . . . dealt, in elaborate detail [with] . . . the capitalistic bias of the universities and common schools. It was [an] . . . indictment of the whole system of education that developed in the minds of the students only such ideas as were favorable to the capitalistic regime, to the exclusion of all ideas that were inimical and subversive.[140]

Whether the state employs educators directly or through government grants, Bellamy and London, like Godwin, see these emissaries of the common good as morally compromised agents in the state's conquest over access to truth, and in that sense enforcers of its constructive tax.[141]

---

138. Edward Bellamy, *Equality*, 3rd ed. (New York: D. Appleton and Company, 1897), chap. 27, 228–29.

139. London, *The Iron Heel*, 168.

140. London, 74n51.

141. In our own time, Mayer's *Dark Money* traces efforts by conservative billionaire-reformers to influence higher education through funding programs emphasizing hands-off government and laissez-faire capitalism. It involves, Mayer explains, "a strategy they called the 'beachhead' theory. The aim . . . was to establish conservative cells, or 'beachheads,' " at the most influential schools. Their intention involved funding "private academic centers within colleges and universities [that they believed] were ideal devices by which rich conservatives could replace the faculty's views with their own." (London speaks of "professors who had been broken on the wheel of university subservience to the ruling class." *The Iron Heel*, 56). A "former Cato Institute chairman," Mayer reports, who "had overseen grants to sixty-three colleges . . . required [them] to teach his favorite philosopher . . . Ayn Rand." Jane Mayer, *Dark Money: The Hidden History of the Billionaires Behind the Rise of the Radical Right* (New York: Anchor Books, a division of Penguin Random House, 2016), 126, 446–48.

GOVERNMENT'S HIDDEN EVILS

The second evil Godwin describes occurs when the citizens receiving support from the public fisc abandon the search for truth in favor of an allegiance to their employer. "The most important objection to emoluments flowing from a public revenue," he advises, is their tendency "to corrupt the mind of the receiver."[142] Thus, not only do government workers "have more regard to the salary than to the public,"[143] they have more esteem for the ideas supporting the government and less interest pointing out its defects.

The third evil attendant on permanent taxation is that the wealthy effectively write the laws—including the tax laws. As a general matter, Godwin asserts, "legislation is in almost every country grossly the favourer of the rich against the poor."[144] For this reason, the rich are "directly or indirectly the legislators of the state."[145] The ensuing distortion of justice is a central theme in Godwin's novel *Caleb Williams*. Although Caleb's wealthy master Mr. Falkland had murdered Barnabas Tyrrel, the local magistrates were reticent to trouble him or insult his reputation. "Without causing Mr. Falkland to be apprehended, they sent to desire he would appear before them at one of their meetings."[146] Falkland appeared as requested, but in light of his financial standing and influential reputation, he was quickly acquitted.[147] The law deals harshly with Caleb, however, leading him to reflect: "I am sure things will never be as they ought, till honour and not the law be the dictator of mankind."[148] The rich, affirms Godwin, "are perpetually reducing oppression into a system, and depriving the poor of that little commonage of nature as it were, which might otherwise still have remained to them."[149] As evidence of this process, he cites historical trends for both land taxes, which the rich pay, and consumption taxes, which all

---

142. Godwin, *Enquiry Concerning Political Justice*, 3rd ed., bk. 6, chap. 9, 622.

143. Godwin, 3rd ed., bk. 6, chap. 9, 621.

144. Godwin, 3rd ed., bk. 1, chap. 3, 93.

145. Godwin, *An Enquiry Concerning Political Justice*, 1st ed., bk. 1, chap. 5, 29–30.

146. William Godwin, *Things as They Are or the Adventures of Caleb Williams* (New York: Penguin Books, 1988), 103.

147. Godwin, 103.

148. Godwin, 182.

149. Godwin, *An Enquiry Concerning Political Justice*, 1st ed., bk. 1, chap. 5, 30.

pay, but which fall most heavily on the poor.[150] In England, he reports, the land tax produces "less than it did a century ago, while the taxes on consumption have experienced an addition. . . . This is an attempt," he continues, "to throw the burthen from the rich upon the poor."[151] In light of these facts, he concludes,

> The nature of taxation has perhaps seldom been sufficiently considered. By some persons it has been supposed that the superfluities of the community might be collected, and placed under the disposition of the representative or executive power. But this is a gross mistake. The superfluities of the rich are, for the most part, inaccessible to taxation; the burthen falls, almost exclusively, upon the laborious and the poor.[152]

This problem would be ameliorated in his utopia when individual judgments of justice—rather than government—voluntarily reduce inequalities of income and wealth. (This topic is explored in chapter six.)

THE "EUTHANASIA OF GOVERNMENT"

Godwin's utopian task was the "euthanasia of government,"[153] gradually, and without violent revolution. To this end he recommends only the tools he

---

150. Taxes on consumption (of necessities) are termed *regressive*, as they require a proportionately greater amount of the resources of a lower-income person than of a higher-income person. Hobbes was a proponent of consumption taxes, writing, "when the impositions, are laid upon those things which men consume, every man payeth equally for what he useth." Hobbes, *Leviathan*, chap. 30, 255. Hume concurred. David Hume, "Of Taxes," in *Essays, Moral, Political, and Literary*, ed. Eugene F. Miller (Indianapolis, IN: The Liberty Fund, Inc., 1985), 345.

151. Godwin, *An Enquiry Concerning Political Justice*, bk. 1, chap. 3, 93–94. In our own time a comparable trend has occurred in the United States, as the portion of income taxes paid by corporations (a proxy for the wealthy) has steadily decreased. "The high watermark for corporate taxes as a percent of total governmental receipts was in 1943, when corporate income tax payments amounted to 39.8 percent and individual taxes accounted for 27.1 percent of total tax receipts." By 2011 "only 7.9 percent of federal tax revenues were from corporate income taxes and 47.4 percent were from individual income taxes." Donald Morris, "A Case for Company-Specific Public Disclosure of Corporate Tax Returns," Accounting and the Public Interest 2015, 15:1, 1–21, 1–2.

152. Godwin, *Enquiry Concerning Political Justice*, 3rd ed., bk. 6, chap. 9, 621.

153. Godwin, 3rd ed., bk. 3, chap. 6, 248.

most prizes—independent judgment and public discussion—to slowly and justly dismantle the edifice of government. As government "is a question of force, and not of consent,"[154] Godwin explains, restricting public deliberation serves its interests. Man, he says, "must consult his own reason, draw his own conclusions, and conscientiously conform himself to his ideas of propriety."[155] His guidance for promoting moral progress and "hastening the decline of error, and producing uniformity of judgment, is not by brute force, by laws, or by imitation," he declares, "but, on the contrary, by exciting every man to think for himself."[156] In place of violent action, he recommends not passivity but passionate debate, which, as Kramnick observes, is elevated to "the duty of using free time to inspect and give sincere advice to neighbours."[157] Since this duty is reciprocal, Godwin observes, our neighbor is also "bound to form the best judgement he is able . . . [and] what he thinks, he is bound to declare to others."[158] For Godwin, then, good arguments—not good fences—make good neighbors and ultimately euthanize the state's taxing powers.

Organizing society to optimize its workforce is the focus of the next chapter. Assigning each person the appropriate amount, conditions, or type of work to support the society's view of the general welfare is the basis for this constructive tax, as levied by Plato, More, Bellamy, Gilman, Wells, Skinner, Saint-Simon, and Campanella. In each case, the utopian response to our unequal abilities forms the motive for employing our talents on behalf of the whole.

---

154. Godwin, 3rd ed., bk. 3, chap. 6, 239.

155. Godwin, 3rd ed., bk. 2, chap. 5, 198.

156. Godwin, 3rd ed., bk. 8, chap. 8, Appendix, 758.

157. Isaac Kramnick, introduction to *Enquiry Concerning Political Justice and Its Influence on Modern Morals and Happiness*, by William Godwin, 3rd ed. (New York: Viking Penguin, 1985), 30–31.

158. Godwin, *Enquiry Concerning Political Justice*, 3rd ed., bk. 2, chap. 5, 194. Furthermore, no topic or dispute is off limits. "It is absurd," he says, "to suppose that certain points are especially in my province" (Godwin, 194).

CHAPTER FOUR

TAXATION BY REQUIRED WORK OR OCCUPATION

Part One:
Plato and More

WORK AND INEQUALITY

There is no alternative, but that men must either have their portion of labor assigned them by the society at large, and the produce collected into a common stock; or that each man must be left to exert the portion of industry, and cultivate the habits of economy, to which his mind shall prompt him.

—William Godwin (1756–1836), *The Enquirer*[1]

For many utopians a deliberate and regulated allocation of work across society is crucial to promoting the general welfare. Some writers including More and Skinner focus on equalizing the amount of work or effort. Others including Plato and Saint-Simon believe that the proper distribution of talent will economize society's deployment of its human resources and so promote the general welfare. In this chapter we examine solutions to inequality of ability or effort that require the realignment of work. The solution in each case is the delegation of the appropriate amount, conditions, or type of work to

---

1. Godwin, *The Enquirer*, 168.

each citizen, thereby maximizing the benefits to society. In each instance I will argue that the burden of obligatory work, whether of amount or kind, when performed as a required sacrifice for the general welfare is for that reason a constructive tax (and a device of political control).

Goodwin observes, "there have been utopians who considered that inequality was rooted in human nature to such an extent that the ideal society had to build on it constructively."[2] For these writers the management of inequality—though viewed from diverse perspectives—is a measure of the general welfare. Rousseau in his discourse on that subject distinguishes two forms of inequality, political and natural. Political inequality refers to disparities in privilege, social class, and wealth; natural inequality denotes differences in age, physical strength, and "qualities of mind."[3] Hobbes assumes our natural inequalities are self-cancelling; men are "by nature equal."[4] One man's sagacity, for example, will counterbalance another man's physical strength.[5] On this view society (or the state) has neither an obligation to intercede on behalf of the weak or disadvantaged nor to seek out and promote the gifted; nature *assures* equality of opportunity. Furthermore, claims Adam Smith,

> The difference between the most dissimilar characters, between a philosopher and a common street porter, for example, seems to arise not so much from nature, as from habit, custom, and education.[6]

In consequence, the qualities that distinguish men of different occupations, he asserts, are "not so much the cause, as the effect of the division of labor."[7] For Smith, like Hobbes, the equalization of work (or of opportunity for work) is outside the state's purview; Smith leaves it to the operations of an invisible hand—Hobbes, to chance or Nature.

---

2. Goodwin, "Economic and Social Innovation in Utopia," 71.

3. Jean-Jacques Rousseau, *Discourse on the Origin and Foundations of Inequality Among Men*, in *Rousseau's Political Writings*, trans. Julia Conway Bondanella (New York: Norton, 1988), 8–9. In our own time, Nagel expands the list to five sources of inequality: 1) "hereditary advantage" (political), 2) "variation in natural abilities" (natural), 3) "intentional discrimination," 4) "effort," and 5) "bad luck." Nagel, *Equality and Partiality*, 102–3.

4. Hobbes, *Leviathan*, chap. 13, 98.

5. Hobbes, 98.

6. Smith, *Wealth of Nations*, bk. 1, chap. 2, 21–22.

7. Smith, bk. 1, chap. 2, 21.

MATCHING SPECIALIZED ABILITIES
TO SOCIETY'S NEEDS

So it seems that while all honest work is honored among you, there are
some kinds of honest work that are not honored so much as others.

—William Dean Howells (1837–1920),
A Traveler from Altruria[8]

Utopians from Plato to Saint-Simon have explored the possibility of isolating
and refining each person's unique talents and abilities, creating thereby a
mutual benefit. Beyond the physical strength and sagacity Hobbes suggests
are a vast assortment (and combination) of differences in aptitude, creativity,
and temperament to identify and hone, promising each citizen an optimizing
contribution. This ideal is an expansion of the one-dimensional division of
labor featured in Adam Smith's pin factory, where people are fungible and
labor is divided among workstations on the factory floor—as if by lot. Plato
in particular rejects Smith's claims that differences in natural talents are
insignificant and that only the division of labor distinguishes a "philosopher
and a common street porter." The philosopher in his *Republic* is a unique,
natural kind "born only rarely among human beings."[9]

Economists term as *absolute advantage* the skills, gifts, or talents
that allow us to compete favorably against others in a particular endeavor.
Economists also distinguish between absolute advantage and comparative (or
relative) advantage, when two or more tasks are assigned. When the best
lawyer in the office is also the best typist, for example, her comparative
advantage is as a lawyer, even though she has an absolute advantage in both
legal work and in typing.[10] The dimensions of absolute and comparative
advantage are lacking in Smith's account of a pin factory.[11] Accordingly,
he is not concerned that the best worker on the factory floor might also
have been the best pin salesperson, product engineer, or vice president of
marketing—had her life chances been otherwise.

---

8. Howells, *A Traveler from Altruria*, 11.

9. Plato, *Republic*, trans. Bloom, bk. 6, 491a–b.

10. Paul A. Samuelson and William D. Nordhaus, *Economics*, 14th ed. (New York:
McGraw-Hill, 1992), 663.

11. Smith discusses natural (absolute) and acquired advantage in the context of trade
between nations. Smith, *Wealth of Nations*, bk. 4, chap. 2, 354.

While the task of assessing and organizing employees in a factory based on their absolute or comparative advantages is formidable, doing so in society is an immense undertaking. The responsibility of the state in such a system is to ensure that citizens are educated to know and pursue their individual gifts. Plato characterizes this undertaking as the "practice of minding one's own business."[12] In Bellamy's *Looking Backward*, "The principle on which our industrial army is organized," Dr. Leete explains, "is that a man's natural endowments, mental and physical, determine what he can work at most profitably to the nation and most satisfactorily to himself."[13] Matching specialized abilities to society's requirements enables each person to perform his part for the benefit of the whole.

PLATO (C. 428–C. 348 BCE): THE IDEAL JOB IN THE *REPUBLIC*

The principal task of philosophy has always, in all ages, been to find the necessary connection existing between personal and general interests.

—Leo Tolstoy (1828–1910), *Anna Karenina*[14]

Coercing people into occupations—even into those for which talent and temperament naturally equips them—imposes a constructive tax.[15] Plato's Republic is founded on the belief that "each individual should be put to the use for which nature intended him."[16] Socrates explains, "each of us is naturally not quite like anyone else, but rather differs in his nature; different men are apt for the accomplishment of different jobs."[17] The "foundation of the state," therefore, is that "one man should practice one thing only,

12. Plato, *Republic*, trans. Bloom, bk. 4, 433a.

13. Bellamy, *Looking Backward*, 71.

14. Tolstoy, *Anna Karenina*, 223.

15. To the extent that decisions regarding the assignment of the appropriate type, amount, or conditions of work for each citizen are made for reasons of gender (or race, religion, age, and so on) to maximize the benefits to society, another dimension of constructive taxation is opened. In Gilman's *Herland*, for example, discussed later in this chapter, gender qualifications are confronted directly.

16. Plato, *Republic*, trans. Jowett, bk. 4, 423.

17. Plato, *Republic*, trans. Bloom, bk. 2, 370a–b.

the thing to which his nature was best adapted."[18] This means assignment to one of three classes and that each class "minds its own business."[19] The three classes, based on the myth of metals (see chapter three), are producers (artisans, farmers, and merchants—bronze or iron souls), warrior-athletes (auxiliaries—silver souls), and ruler-philosophers (guardians—gold souls). The dialogue frames this discussion in terms of the city (state) most likely to maximize justice by balancing the three classes, as the three parts of the soul, "like three notes in a harmonic scale, lowest, highest and middle."[20] For, says Socrates, "as the government is, such will be the man."[21]

A city-state emerges, observes Socrates, because none of us is self-sufficient.[22] Permanence (being) and instability (becoming) are important themes for Plato, since "for everything that has come into being there is decay."[23] This includes each system of government; the seeds of its decay, he believes, are present at its founding.[24] To demonstrate his point Plato shows us four imperfect types of government—timocracy, oligarchy, democracy, and tyranny—each exposing a moral imbalance (the seeds of its decay) and incapable of promoting justice.[25]

PLATO'S SOLUTION

Following his description of the imperfect states, Socrates says, "Let me next endeavor to show what is . . . the least change which will enable a state to pass into the truer form."[26] The "least change," however, is immeasurably great, involving assigned occupations for the most capable (silver- and gold-

---

18. Plato, *Republic*, trans. Jowett, bk. 4, 433a.

19. Plato, *Republic*, trans. Bloom, bk. 4, 441d–e.

20. Plato, trans. Bloom, bk. 3, 443d. Socrates explains that "the same classes that are in the city are in the soul" (Plato, trans. Bloom, 441c). In addition, "a man is just in the same manner that a city . . . was just" (Plato, trans. Bloom, 441d).

21. Plato, *Republic*, trans. Jowett, bk. 8, 557.

22. Plato, *Republic*, bk. 2, 369b.

23. Plato, *Republic*, trans. Bloom, bk. 8, 546a.

24. Plato, *Republic*, bk. 8, 546b. This applies to the implementation of Plato's ideal state as well, though not to the ideal itself, which is immutable. See Plato, bk. 8, 546b–d.

25. Plato, *Republic*, bk. 8.

26. Plato, *Republic*, trans. Jowett, bk. 3, 473b.

souled) citizens and a life governed by philosophy.[27] The ruling classes—the guardians and their auxiliaries—are critical to the success of Plato's ideal state. Little notice is taken of the lion's share of citizens: the artisans, farmers, and merchants and their families.[28] While Plato's rulers are largely selected from the guardian class—comprising both men and women—based on a combination of physical and intellectual traits and abilities, plus experience and training, their recruitment extends to the working classes, as Plato did not rule out the possibility of an exceptional child (gold or silver soul) being born to parents of average abilities (bronze souls). In such a case the child would be transferred to the class of warrior-athletes, to rise as high as her abilities would permit.[29] For otherwise, he warns, "those with the best natures become exceptionally bad when they get bad instruction."[30]

RULER SUCCESSION

One of the rulers' responsibilities is overseeing the supply of guardians from whom future rulers will be selected.[31] Since the Republic is premised on the wisdom of its rulers, any problem in securing future guardians will subject the ideal state to the same problem of ruler succession Plato identifies in the defective states. In revamping the process of ruler selection and succession, instead of honor, greed, or ambition, Plato designates wisdom as the defining factor. Only the experienced gold-souled guardians may appoint the new rulers, ensuring (in theory) the integrity of the process. The job of identifying future rulers begins with the young and includes "setting them at tasks . . . labors, pains, and contests."[32] The prospective rulers, he insists,

---

27. Murphy clarifies that for Plato the best life described in the *Republic* "is not the life devoted to philosophy but the life governed by it." N. R. Murphy, *The Interpretation of Plato's Republic* (Oxford: The Clarendon Press, 1951), 54.

28. Reeve observes that "producers seem to have a traditional family-based way of life (4.12). They engage in manufacture and trade, earn money, own their own houses . . . and rear and educate their own children, with the exception of those who turn out to have the potential to be guardians (415c3–5)." Reeve, *Philosopher-Kings*, 184.

29. Plato, *Republic*, bk. 3, 415c; bk. 4, 423c–d.

30. Plato, *Republic*, trans. Bloom, bk. 6, 491d–e. Likewise, of the Alphas, the potential guardians in Huxley's *Brave New World*, we learn, "The greater a man's talents, the greater his power to lead astray." Huxley, *Brave New World*, 137.

31. Plato, *Republic*, bk. 7, 540a–b.

32. Plato, *Republic*, trans. Bloom, bk. 3, 413c–d.

must combine a love of learning, a good memory, "no taste for falsehood,"[33] and the ability "to grasp what is always the same in all respects [being],"[34] as well as to "be philosophic, spirited, swift, and strong."[35] On the difficulty of this assignment, Socrates admits, "such natures are few," for "the parts of the nature that we described as a necessary condition for them are rarely willing to grow together in the same place."[36]

EDUCATING THE GUARDIANS

Socrates identifies as crucial to this state's success the education and discipline of the special class of citizens who will rule but live communally with only the essentials. While initially calling this class the guardians, he subsequently restricts this label to the rulers, while assigning the military branch its own role as auxiliaries.[37] The auxiliaries, chosen for their inborn ability and character, keep order and defend the state from external threats. The guardians, says Strauss, "must be taken from among the elite of the warriors" and receive extensive education and training beyond that of the auxiliaries.[38] This provides an opportunity, says Socrates, "of trying whether, when they are drawn all manner of ways by temptation, they will stand firm or flinch."[39] Central to this education, gained only with great difficulty, is acquaintance with knowledge (the intelligible) and its distinction from belief (appearance).[40]

---

33. Plato, trans. Bloom, bk. 6, 485c–d.

34. Plato, trans. Bloom, bk. 6, 484b.

35. Plato, trans. Bloom, bk. 2, 376c.

36. Plato, trans. Bloom, bk. 6, 491a–b, 503b.

37. Plato, trans. Bloom, bk. 3, 414b.

38. Strauss, *The City and Man*, 101.

39. Plato, *Republic*, trans. Jowett, bk. 8, 539e. Kochin argues that "Plato sought to redefine male excellence because he saw the actual Greek conceptions of masculinity as diseases of the soul, as misalignments of the hierarchy of desires." For this reason, he continues, "Plato understands the exclusion of women and the female from political life as corrupting the ethical development of men." Michael S. Kochin, *Gender and Rhetoric in Plato's Political Thought* (Cambridge: Cambridge University Press, 2002), 21, 8. Bloom provides an illustration of this refinement, arguing that "men must be liberated from their special [paternalistic] concern for women. A man must have no more compunction about killing the advancing female enemy than the male, and he must be no more protective of the heroine fighting on his right side than of the hero on his left." Allan Bloom, *The Closing of the American Mind* (New York: Simon and Schuster, 1987), 103.

40. Plato, *Republic*, bk. 7.

The guardian's soul, explains Socrates, "from youth on" must be "both just and tame,"[41] which is achieved through physical conditioning as well as intellectual training;[42] as gaining command of the body is a prerequisite to disciplining the soul.[43] The state's guardians must also be "magnificent, charming, and a friend and kinsman of truth, justice, courage, and moderation,"[44] with a temperament allowing them to place the good of the state above their own. Based on this resume, when "perfected by education and age," Socrates asks, "wouldn't you turn the city over to them alone?"[45] Plato concedes that only a small cadre of guardian-rulers of both genders will be discovered and developed.[46] One characteristic of these rulers—as opposed to those in the four defective states—is their reticence to assume power, except from duty.[47] As Socrates notes, "each one spends his time in philosophy, but when his turn comes, he drudges in politics and rules for the city's sake, not as though he were doing a thing that is fine, but one that is necessary."[48]

PLATO'S PROGRESSIVE TAX REGIME

The "peacetime revenue of Athens," Hammond reports, "came from the exploitation of trade . . . [including] harbor-dues and tolls, and taxes on metics [resident aliens], slaves, and prostitutes," and only the lower classes were subject to direct taxes. During wartime, however, the "three top classes were liable to pay a capital tax and serve in the forces"[49] (a constructive tax). Like many utopian solutions, the Republic minimizes the need for pecuniary taxation by reducing the sources of civil strife and even war.[50]

Because the ruling caste, the guardians and their auxiliaries, live a Spartan existence—using "common houses and mess, with no one privately

---

41. Plato, *Republic*, trans. Bloom, bk. 6, 486b.

42. Plato, trans. Bloom, bk. 6, 494a.

43. Plato, trans. Bloom, bk. 6, 498b.

44. Plato, trans. Bloom, bk. 6, 487a.

45. Plato, trans. Bloom, bk. 6, 487a.

46. "The birth of one [philosopher], if he has an obedient city, is sufficient for perfecting everything that is now doubted" (Plato, trans. Bloom, bk. 6, 502b).

47. Plato, trans. Bloom, bk. 7, 520d–e.

48. Plato, trans. Bloom, bk. 7, 540a–b.

49. N. G. L. Hammond, *A History of Greece* (Oxford: The Clarendon Press, 1959), 529.

50. Plato, *Republic*, bk. 4, 422a–423a.

possessing anything"[51] and receiving only sustenance from the mass of citizens—their overhead is negligible.[52] Since the guardians, like the citizens of More's Utopia, are banned from possessing money, rather than pecuniary taxes the state imposes a constructive tax requiring the greatest sacrifice from the most able—a progressive tax on the guardians—those who can endure and excel during fifty years of education, training, and testing.[53] These few men and women emerge finally as rulers—as philosopher-kings. Their reward for this arduous journey, however, is additional sacrifice. In their position as rulers they are forbidden to marry or choose their own sexual partners or know their own children[54] (as described in chapter five).

THOMAS MORE (1478–1535):
THE COMMON OBLIGATION OF COMMON DAILY TOIL

> When a traveller gives an account of some distant country, he may impose upon our credulity the most groundless and absurd fiction as the most certain matters of fact.
>
> —Adam Smith (1723–1790), The Theory of Moral Sentiments[55]

In contrasting More's *Utopia* to Plato's *Republic*, Hexter notes that Plato's *Republic* is "by definition a purely imaginative construction," which Plato could furnish with "any customs, laws, and institutions that suited his taste." But, Hexter continues, "because of his literary apparatus More could only ascribe to the Utopians such customs, laws, and institutions as conceivably might prevail on the other side of the world in his own day."[56] Eurich affirms

---

51. Plato, *Republic*, trans. Bloom, bk. 5, 458c. Among the Spartan reforms introduced by Lycurgus (800–730 BCE) was an egalitarian ordinance requiring common dining to discourage ostentation and vanity. As Plutarch notes, "the rich, being obliged to go to the same table with the poor, could not make use of or enjoy their abundance." The common dining convention is employed in the utopias of More, Bellamy, and Skinner.

52. Plato, *Republic*, bk. 4, 420a.

53. See Kenneth Dorter, *The Transformation of Plato's Republic* (Lanham, MD: Lexington Books, 2006), 217.

54. Plato, *Republic*, bk. 5, 464b–c.

55. Adam Smith, *The Theory of Moral Sentiments* (Indianapolis: Liberty Fund, 1976), 314.

56. Hexter, *More's Utopia*, 50.

"More's genuine concern for the solution of practical, economic problems, which reflected the growing secularization of thought in the Renaissance." Among these problems, she observes, "Poverty and taxation, money and the apportionment of wealth, were basic issues requiring answers in *Utopia*."[57] But while More was successful in eliminating money and poverty, in the case of taxation he merely altered its form.

THE ALLOCATION OF GOODS

Referring to Plato, More's narrator Raphael Hythloday says, "Wisest of men, he saw easily that the one and only path to the public welfare lies through equal allocation of goods."[58] At the core of More's *Utopia* is his moral insight that what appear to be shortages or excesses in society are really problems of distribution. After "a barren year of failed harvests," that cost thousands of lives, the barns of the rich, Hythloday observes, will still be filled with enough grain to have "kept all those who died of starvation and disease from even realizing that a shortage ever existed."[59] In our own time, economist Amartya Sen's research confirms More's conviction that famine is a failure of distribution and not, as Malthus supposed, the result of cyclical food shortages ordained by natural laws.[60] Such a failure, says Sen, is at heart a moral problem. "Famines kill millions of people in different countries in the world," he argues, "but they don't kill the rulers. The kings and the presidents, . . . the military leaders and the commanders never are famine victims."[61] Famines are moral problems of allotment and sacrifice and hence of taxation. In More's Utopia, however, there is "not only enough but more than enough" food for all.

More foresees the importance of equitable allotment not only for food but for other necessities, and for work. Any government reallocation, however, comes at a cost—a required sacrifice for the general welfare. As Chambers observes, "the ideal of *Utopia* is discipline, not liberty."[62] The

---

57. Eurich, *Science in Utopia*, 77–78.

58. More, *Utopia*, bk. 1, 37.

59. More, bk. 2, 105.

60. Malthus, *An Essay on the Principle of Population*, 18–19, 57–58, 61.

61. Amartya Sen, *Development as Freedom* (New York: Anchor Books; a division of Random House, 1999), 180.

62. R. W. Chambers, *Thomas More* (Ann Arbor: The University of Michigan Press, 1958), 137.

object of More's redistribution is moderation and necessity, values praised by the Stoics.[63] "The Utopian economy," Hexter informs us, "does not justify itself as modern economies do by claiming to give men the fullest measure of the things they want."[64] Such allocations cause shortages and gluts, while More's apportionment ensures plenty for all.

Utopia's primary necessities are clothing, food, and housing. Clothing is regulated to maximize its durability and minimize its role in bolstering ostentation and pride, problems More sought to stamp out.[65] The work clothes, for this reason, are "unpretentious garments" made to last for seven years.[66] Meals are consumed in each city's neighborhood dining halls. The houses, all the same design, are reallocated among the families every ten years by lot. Though it is public housing, the Utopians are "not only quick to repair deterioration but foresighted in preventing it."[67] Unlike a consumption-based economy featuring planned or unplanned obsolescence, Utopia's economy seeks product minimization and stability. Producing one style of clothing and one type of house eliminates the need for fashion designers, architects, focus groups, and vice presidents of marketing. By making these changes More hopes to put an end to "the crass avarice of a few" with the rich "buying up anything and everything,"[68] resulting always in poverty, famine, and unemployment.

This system, aimed at maintaining the general welfare (understood as egalitarian), allows each person "to live joyfully and peacefully, free from all anxieties, and without worries about making a living." In the end, "where everything belongs to everybody," Hythloday explains, "no one need fear that, so long as the public warehouses are filled, anyone will ever lack for

---

63. More, says Baker-Smith, was especially influenced by Epicurus, Seneca, and Cicero, and the Utopian's ethical system "reconciles Epicurus with the Stoa." Baker-Smith, *More's Utopia*, 171–73. Bloch claims, however, that despite More's theme of "monastic renunciation . . . Epicureanism remains dominant." Ernst Bloch, *The Principle of Hope*, trans. Neville Plaice, Stephen Plaice, and Paul Knight (Cambridge: The MIT Press, 1986), 521.

64. Hexter, *More's Utopia*, 70–71.

65. Hexter, 80.

66. More, *Utopia*, bk. 2, 53.

67. More, bk. 2, 52.

68. More, bk. 1, 20, 38.

anything for his own use."[69] In this economy no money changes hands, as money itself is banned. "For where money is the measure of everything," the narrator relates, "many vain and completely superfluous trades are bound to be carried on simply to satisfy luxury and licentiousness."[70]

THE ALLOTMENT OF LABOR

To ensure the proper allocation of labor, the country's ancient lawgiver Utopus has disbursed the island's population equally among its fifty-four cities. Doing so facilitates planning what to grow or produce and in what quantities. Another facet of his scheme is putting the "crowd of languid idlers," to "productive tasks"[71] to include a useful trade as well as farming. For the workers displaced from "useless trades"—locksmithing, money lending, or practicing law, for example—Utopia rewards them with a shorter workday, job security, and ample if modest health and retirement benefits.[72] In addition, annexing the idlers' labor to the workforce increases the denominator used to calculate the hours needed from each worker, thereby reducing each person's daily burden.[73] "Above all," says Hexter, "idleness, the great emblem of pride in the society of More's time, a sure mark to elevate the aristocrat above the vulgar, is utterly destroyed by the common obligation of common daily toil."[74]

THE SIX-HOUR WORKDAY

In Utopia, once the workload is equally distributed, the required workday is six hours for both women and men.[75] With a mandatory workday no one will sit idle, we are told, and "no one has to be exhausted with endless toil

---

69. More, bk. 2, 104, 103.

70. More, bk. 2, 51.

71. More, *Utopia*, bk. 2, 51.

72. Though More was a lawyer, the practice of law by a "class of men whose trade it is to manipulate cases and multiply quibbles," is one of the "useless trades" banned from Utopia. More, *Utopia*, bk. 2, 82.

73. In a stagnant economy like Utopia's, the necessary hours of work can be calculated in advance as well as how much food will be consumed (More, bk. 2, 44). Three senators (elders elected from each city) meet in the central city of Amaurot to "determine where there are shortages and surpluses, and promptly satisfy one district's shortage with another's surplus" (More, bk. 2, 59). The same principle of food supply planning applies in Gilman's *Herland* because of its strictly regulated population.

74. Hexter, *More's Utopia*, 80.

75. More, *Utopia*, bk. 2, 49–50.

from early morning to late at night."[76] In describing this practice and its rationale, Hythloday explains, "Their working hours are ample to provide not only enough but more than enough of the necessities and even the conveniences of life. You will easily appreciate this," he continues, "if you consider how large a part of the population in other countries lives without doing any work at all."[77]

The proximate means of enforcing Utopia's required work hours is social pressure; as described in chapter two, everyone works in the public eye. When social pressure is inadequate, Utopia employs a class of magistrates called syphogrants, whose chief business is ensuring that everyone works diligently.[78] Officers of Bellamy's industrial army fulfill a similar function in *Looking Backward*. In Utopia the underlying motivation for all proper conduct, however, is religious: "they believe that after this life vices will be punished and virtue rewarded."[79] For this reason, notes Chambers, "so far from doubting the immortality of the soul, they base their whole polity upon it."[80]

OCCUPATIONAL CHOICE

The choice of occupation is left to each person, though women practice the "lighter crafts" while the "heavier jobs are assigned to the men."[81] We are not informed whether exceptions are permitted based on temperament, interest, or ability. Farm labor is on a two-year rotation and everyone must take a shift. Half the farmers change each year and those remaining train the new crop of farmers.[82] Regarding children, Hythloday explains, "Ordinarily, the

---

76. More, bk. 2, 49–50.

77. More, bk. 2, 51.

78. More, bk. 2, 49–50.

79. More, bk. 2, 95. Sargent notes that these "highly rational people act so well only because of the constantly implied threat of punishment." His reference is to punishment "assigned by the senate," however, not punishment promised in the next life. Lyman Tower Sargent, "A Note on the Other Side of Human Nature in the Utopian Novel," *Political Theory* 3, no. 1 (February 1975): 88–97, 90. Kenyon asserts, however, that though "a primary purpose of Utopia was to outline a scheme for the institution of civil society in which people's sinful natures would be brought under control," rationality alone was insufficient. Kenyon, "The Problem of Freedom and Moral Behavior in Thomas More's Utopia," 365, 369, 372.

80. Chambers, *Thomas More*, 135.

81. More, *Utopia*, bk. 2, 49.

82. More, bk. 2, 43–44.

son is trained to his father's craft, for which most feel a natural inclination. But if anyone is attracted to another occupation, he is transferred by adoption into a family practicing that trade."[83] In contrast to Plato's one-career policy, Utopians—through voluntary retraining—may practice up to three, including mandatory farming.[84] Certain jobs, for example, repairing roads or tending the sick, are staffed by volunteers since there are citizens—and "not just a few"—who perform good works with an eye to the afterlife.[85] The most degrading jobs, slaughtering and cleaning animals, for example, are assigned to their slaves.[86]

TAXATION AND SURPLUS LABOR

Thomas More's work, explains Hexter, is "marked by . . . [his] ability to grasp the interconnections of social phenomena, and shrewdness in devising remedies that attack the roots of social ills, as he conceived them."[87] These roots, as we have seen, include pride as well as money and its ill effects. But because money is banned and gold is without value, there can be no pecuniary taxation, and More was left with the choice of a substitute. Though there are slaves in Utopia—potential surrogates for taxation—their role in the economy is minimal.[88] In performing their labors the citizens supply not only their own needs but they generate a surplus—a constructive tax of surplus labor.[89] This surplus funds the twenty-seven thousand workers—including ambassadors, governors, syphogrants, scholars, and priests—excused from their labors (54 cities x 500 workers = 27,000).[90] Their priests, however, "are

---

83. More, bk. 2, 49.

84. More, bk. 2, 49.

85. More, bk. 2, 97.

86. More, bk. 2, 55. "The Utopians feel that slaughtering our fellow creatures gradually destroys the sense of compassion" (More, bk. 2, 55).

87. Hexter, *More's Utopia*, 95.

88. Baker-Smith, *More's Utopia*, 164.

89. Goodwin explains that in "money-less utopias 'tax' in essence consists of labour above and beyond that needed for self-subsistence." She refers to this as *pre-taxation* because the amount of goods produced is diminished by "the amount of goods available for distribution to everyone else." The problem with pre-taxation, she says, is that it is invisible, and invisible taxation is "notoriously hard to challenge or to change." Goodwin, "Taxation in Utopia," 317–18.

90. More, *Utopia*, bk. 2, 52. Of the five hundred, two hundred are syphogrants (More, 47).

of extraordinary holiness," explains Hythloday, "and therefore very few."[91] A scholar must still be productive—publish or perish—or he is "sent packing, to become a workman again."[92]

Marx's concern with surplus labor was in the context of capitalism's "boundless thirst" for production. But, he explains, "Capital has not invented surplus labor," which, in a capitalist economy, each worker "must add to the working time necessary for his own maintenance an extra working time in order to produce the subsistence for the owners of the means of production." But it is clear, he says, that in any

> economic formation of society, where not the exchange value but the use-value of the product predominates, surplus labour will be limited by a given set of wants . . . and . . . no boundless thirst for surplus labour arises from the nature of production itself.[93]

In More's Utopia—as well of those of Bellamy, Morris, Skinner, and others, therefore—surplus labor is self-limiting, since "the use-value of the product predominates," the set of wants is limited, and no surplus labor "arises from the nature of production itself."[94]

When we look in Utopia for the functions taxation commonly funds, we find, for example, a potent military defense network and a thriving public welfare system, including public housing and community dining halls. Since the planned economy relies on a population quota for its fifty-four cities, shuttling residents to homes in neighboring cities prevents shortages and surpluses of food and other goods.[95] Central to its ambitious and potentially profitable foreign policy is an aversion to war and to the cost of a standing army. Utopus, in his founding and design of the land more than seventeen

---

91. More, bk. 2, 98.

92. More, bk. 2, 52.

93. Karl Marx, *Capital*, trans. from 3rd German ed. by Samuel More and Edward Aveling, ed. by Friedrich Engels; revised, with additional trans. from 4th German ed. by Marie Sachey and Herbert Lamm, in *Great Books of the Western World*, ed. by Robert Maynard Hutchins and Mortimer Adler, vol. 50 (Chicago: Encyclopaedia Britannica, 1952), pt. 3, chap. 10, 113.

94. Marx, pt. 3, chap. 10, 113. The *use-value* of a product for Marx expresses a relation between the consumer and what is consumed and contrasts with its *labor-value* or its *market-value* in a capitalist economy.

95. More, *Utopia*, bk. 2, 54.

centuries earlier,[96] partitioned their peninsula from the mainland, creating an island with a crescent-shaped harbor and treacherous rocks defending it.[97] For this reason, the country's most frequent encounters with war, which are seldom, are on the side of an ally where they employ mercenaries with an eye to a profit.[98] Thus while welfare and warfare are two of the greatest triggers of taxation in other societies, Utopia has been so arranged as to avoid their pecuniary demands.

Part Two:
Bellamy, Gilman, Wells, and Skinner

EDWARD BELLAMY (1850–1898): THE INDUSTRIAL ARMY

"Oh yes," said the Altrurian. "At one time, just before we emerged from the competitive conditions, there was much serious question whether capital should not own labor, instead of labor owning capital."

William Dean Howells (1837–1920), *A Traveler from Altruria*[99]

Bellamy's utopia modernizes More's notion of required work, and his solution, like More's, makes pecuniary taxation redundant. Taylor says *Looking Backward* is the first utopia "which both illustrates and humanizes the huge potentialities of the Machine."[100] Pfaelzer observes that in "adding technology to a Social Darwinist scheme of the evolving society, Bellamy built a postindustrial model for human perfection."[101] When Julian West awakens

---

96. More, bk. 2, 46.

97. More, bk. 2, 42.

98. More, bk. 2, 92. The mercenaries are self-funding, paid for from spoils from the defeated nations (More, bk. 2, 88–89, 92).

99. Howells, *A Traveler from Altruria*, 152.

100. Walter Fuller Taylor, *The Economic Novel in America* (Chapel Hill: The University of North Carolina Press, 1942), 187.

101. Jean Pfaelzer, "Immanence, Indeterminance, and the Utopian Pun in Looking Backward," in *Looking Backward 1988–1888*, ed. Daphne Patai (Amherst, MA: The

from his 113-year "mesmeric sleep," in the year 2000, he is informed that a major problem of his day—labor unrest—had been resolved. The nineteenth-century labor problems, West explains, resulted from tensions between the growing power of giant corporations—aggravated by "the absorption of business by ever-larger monopolies"[102]—and reprisals by striking workers. "The workmen claimed they had to organize to get their rights from the big corporations,"[103] and so they formed giant labor organizations. But Dr. Leete, West's host and guide to the twenty-first century, informs him, "The organization of labor and the strikes were an effect, merely, of the concentration of capital in greater masses than had ever been known before."[104]

Before his extended sleep, West lived in Boston in 1887, where labor problems were endemic and any resolution seemed unlikely. Regarding the "frequent episodes of labor-capital violence," O'Donnell reports, "the years 1880–1900 alone witnessed nearly 37,000 strikes."[105] However, West learns from Dr. Leete that the

> movement toward the conduct of business by larger and larger aggregations of capital, the tendency toward monopolies . . . was recognized at last . . . as a process which only needed to complete its logical evolution.[106]

As described by Dr. Leete, the penultimate state to which society had arrived before the bloodless revolution is suggestive of Kurt Vonnegut's *Jailbird*, where one great enterprise—RAMJAC Corporation, a private conglomerate of which other corporations are merely subsidiaries—is believed to own everything in the country.[107] In *Looking Backward*, however, the end state is

---

University of Massachusetts Press, 1988), 60.

102. Bellamy, *Looking Backward*, 64.

103. Bellamy, 63.

104. Bellamy, 63.

105. Edward T. O'Donnell, *Henry George and the Crisis of Inequality* (New York: Columbia University Press, 2015), xix.

106. Bellamy, *Looking Backward*, 65.

107. According to the narrator, "Many people assumed that RAMJAC owned everything in the country. It was something of an anticlimax, then, to discover that it owned only 19 percent of it—not even one-fifth. Still—RAMJAC was enormous when compared with other conglomerates." Kurt Vonnegut, Jr., *Jailbird: A Novel* (New York: Dell Publishing Co., 1979), 271.

not one private corporation owning all businesses but the transformation of a single, privately owned conglomerate into one citizen-owned association. In the natural evolution to this new economic order, the "obvious fact was perceived," explains Dr. Leete, "that no business is so essentially the public business as the industry and commerce on which the people's livelihood depends, and that to entrust it to private persons to be managed for private profit is a folly."[108] The governance of the single conglomerate—"the sole employer, the final monopoly . . . The Great Trust"[109]—is carried out by the most experienced industrial leaders. Since each branch of industry has a guild to represent it, the honorary (retired) members elect a general.[110] In this way, notes Prettyman, Bellamy combines hierarchy and "managerial oversight" with "political and economic inclusiveness," while achieving a "fusion of the mechanical and the living."[111] The hierarchical structure of Bellamy's government, observes Kumar, "breathes the spirit of Saint-Simon throughout."[112]

> In the early years of the twentieth century, Dr. Leete tells West, "the evolution was completed by the final consolidation of the entire capital of the nation." The nation was organized as the one great business corporation . . . in which all previous and lesser monopolies were swallowed up, a monopoly in the profits and economies of which all citizens shared.[113]

In this process no violent revolution was necessary, for as Saint-Simon observes, "in all countries a force exists which is superior to that of governments, and this is the force of public opinion."[114] Thus, Dr. Leete tells West, public opinion had become "fully ripe" for this change.[115] In contrast, Morris's

---

108. Bellamy, *Looking Backward*, 66.

109. Bellamy, 65–66.

110. Bellamy, 144. The top ten (male) generals elect the president from among their ranks.

111. Gib Prettyman, "Gilded Age Utopias of Incorporation," *Utopian Studies* 12, 1 (2001): 19–40, 27–28, 32.

112. Kumar, *Utopia and Anti-Utopia in Modern Times*, 156.

113. Bellamy, *Looking Backward*, 65–66.

114. Henri Saint-Simon, *The Political Thought of Saint-Simon*, ed. Ghita Ionescu (Oxford: Oxford University Press, 1976), 135.

115. Bellamy, *Looking Backward*, 66.

News from Nowhere—written in reaction to *Looking Backward*—depicts the transition from capitalism to communism, "from commercial slavery to freedom," as a "war from beginning to end: bitter war."[116]

REQUIRED LABOR

Under the citizens' common ownership all businesses now operate for the general welfare, and everyone shares the profits equally.[117] The required sacrifice for this outcome, as in More's Utopia, is exacted in labor. The "principle of universal military service" is applied, though wars are presumed a thing of the past.[118] The scope of Bellamy's general welfare comprises protecting "every citizen against hunger, cold, and nakedness, and provid[ing] for all his physical and mental needs."[119] The country's lack of military defense is the theme of a parallel novel by Arthur Vinton. In *Looking Further Backward* (1890), Vinton depicts a one-sided war in which "armed hordes" of Chinese soldiers overrun a defenseless America.[120] "A populace seldom stops long to reason on abstract subjects," explains Vinton's narrator and history

---

116. Morris, *News from Nowhere*, 133. With respect to the transition from a capitalist economy (controlled by a "veiled plutocracy") to a state-organized economy, Dewey says, "it is fairly evident that Bellamy was too much under the influence of the idea of evolution in its Victorian sense." John Dewey, "A Great American Prophet," in *John Dewey: The Later Works, 1925–1953*, vol. 9, ed. Jo Ann Boydston (Carbondale: Southern Illinois University Press, 1989), 103–4. [First published in *Common Sense* 3 (April 1934): 6–7.] Hayek explains Bellamy's nonviolent transition in general terms: "That socialism can be put into practice only by methods which most socialists disapprove is, of course, a lesson learned by many social reformers in the past. The old socialist parties were inhibited by their democratic ideals; they did not possess the ruthlessness required for the performance of their chosen task." Hayek, *The Road to Serfdom*, 137.

117. Mill says, "The objection ordinarily made to a system of community of property and equal distribution of the produce, that each person would be incessantly occupied in evading his fair share of the work, points, undoubtedly, to a real difficulty. But those who urge this objection forget to how great an extent the same difficulty exists under the system on which nine tenths of the business of society is now conducted." Mill, *Principles of Political Economy*, bk. 2, chap. 1, §2, 158.

118. Bellamy, *Looking Backward*, 69.

119. Bellamy, 67.

120. Taylor reports that Vinton's was one of at least fifteen "replies, continuations, and counter-replies" to *Looking Backward* appearing before 1900. Taylor, *The Economic Novel in America*, 206.

professor, Won Lung Li. "Feed it, clothe it, keep it at work and now and then amused, house it decently, and it will remain pacified and content." In Vinton's version, West writes in his diary, "I saw much that compelled me to admire the ingenuity with which our invaders have made the main features of our Nationalistic theory serve the ends of their own government."[121]

In Bellamy's version, industrial service is mandatory for a career of twenty-four years (for men—potentially fewer for women) in the industrial army.[122] This obviates the need for pecuniary taxes.[123] Conscription takes place each year for citizens who have reached age twenty-one and, therefore, completed their schooling. On the same day, citizens who have turned forty-five are released into retirement. While the twenty-four years of work is mandatory, the choice of occupation is left to each citizen "in accordance with his natural aptitude," determined under the scrutiny of the state.[124] For those in the arts community the result is a constructive surtax—a career-choice restriction. Artistic endeavors, though not "useless trades," are nonetheless excluded from the industrial army. For citizens expressing creative inclinations—artists, dancers, musicians, poets, and others in a field of "original genius"—this means a mandatory industrial army ("day job") assignment, with only leisure available for their creative outlet.[125]

Before entering one's chosen occupation, all are required to undergo a three-year boot camp working as common laborers, "assignable to do any work at the discretion of his superiors." Following this indoctrination, Dr. Leete declares, "the young man is allowed to elect a special avocation."[126] The principle on which the industrial army is founded, he continues, is that "a man's natural endowments . . . determine what he can work at most profitably to the nation and most satisfactorily to himself."[127] In providing

---

121. Arthur Dudley Vinton, *Looking Further Backward* (New York: Albany Book Company; repr., n.p., n.d.), 97, 79–80. (Page references are to reprint.)

122. Bellamy, *Looking Backward*, 70.

123. Bellamy, 167.

124. Bellamy, 71.

125. Practitioners may self-finance these endeavors and pursue them in their spare time. The revenue from a successful work creates an offset to the worker's industrial army obligation. Thus, if, for example, an "author's book be moderately successful, he has thus a furlough for several months, a year, two or three years, and if he in the meantime produces other successful work, the remission of service is extended so far as the sale of that may justify." Bellamy, *Looking Backward*, 128–29.

126. Bellamy, 73.

127. Bellamy, 71.

its guidance the state, with "the utmost pains being taken," enables each one "to find out what his natural aptitude really is"[128]—with the notable exceptions of salesman, sculptor, or soldier.

THE WOMEN'S ARMY

Dr. Leete's initial discussion of work relates to men. But when West asks him if, under the new economic conditions, women have been reduced to cultivating "their charms and graces," Dr. Leete replies, "Our women . . . are members of the industrial army, and leave it only when maternal duties claim them."[129] Women, Dr. Leete says, "have quite too much spirit to consent to be mere beneficiaries of society." He then amends his claim of equal membership, noting that women "are under an entirely different discipline . . . and constitute rather an allied force than an integral part of the army of the men."[130] Because women are "inferior in strength to men, and further disqualified industrially, Dr. Leete explains, "under no circumstances is a woman to follow any employment not perfectly adapted, both as to kind and degree of labor, to her sex."[131]

Sargent notes that "Bellamy was severely criticized for these paternalistic sentences and the attitude toward women they represent."[132] In his sequel *Equality*, however, as Sargent indicates, Bellamy had changed his mind and allowed that "there is not a trade or occupation in the whole list . . . in which women do not take part."[133]

INCENTIVE FOR EFFORT

Service in the industrial army—the required sacrifice for the general welfare—while limited to twenty-four years, entails an important qualification. "Effort alone," says Dr. Leete, "is pertinent to the question of desert."[134] Measuring effort, however, is notoriously difficult. "Nothing can be more

---

128. Bellamy, 71.

129. Bellamy, 184.

130. Bellamy, 184–85.

131. Bellamy, 185.

132. Lyman Tower Sargent, "Edward Bellamy's Boston in 2000 from 1888 to 1897: The Evolution of Bellamy's Future Boston from *Looking Backward* Through *Equality*," *Utopian Studies* 27, no. 2 (2016): 152–81, 161, 172.

133. Bellamy, *Equality*, chap. 6, 43. This is Edith Leete's statement.

134. Bellamy, *Looking Backward*, 88.

baffling," says legal scholar Lon Fuller, "than to attempt to measure how vigorously a man intended to do that which he has failed to do."[135] Since (almost) everyone works at the trade of his or her choosing, applying less than one's full effort is a cause for discipline. "The way it strikes people nowadays," explains Dr. Leete, "is that a man who can produce twice as much as another with the same effort, instead of being rewarded for doing so, ought to be punished if he does not do so."[136]

For those who are "able to duty, and persistently refusing"—in contrast to the invisible-hand solution he applies to marriage (discussed in chapter five)—Bellamy relies on the state's heavy hand. Prison awaits those who buck the system by slacking or refusing to work. The sentence of "solitary imprisonment on bread and water" stands until the prisoner submits.[137] To speak of service being "compulsory," Dr. Leete declares, "would be a weak way to state its absolute inevitableness. Our entire social order is so wholly based upon and deducted from it that if it were conceivable that a man could escape it, he would be left no possible way to provide for his existence."[138]

William Morris was critical of *Looking Backward,* especially of Bellamy's treatment of work. He mocked Bellamy, saying that "his only idea of making labour tolerable is to decrease the amount of it by means of . . . fresh developments of machinery." For his part, Morris stressed that the "true incentive to happy and useful labour is . . . pleasure in the work itself."[139] This work involves only occupations that produce personally satisfying products—those well designed to be functional and, when possible, beautiful—or necessary services pleasantly administered, with both products and services directed toward some obviously useful end.[140] Morris's *News from Nowhere,* explains Robertson, offers "an alternative to capitalist modernity, a vision of non-ascetic simplicity."[141]

---

135. Lon Fuller, *The Morality of Law* (New Haven, CT: Yale University, 1964), 43.

136. Bellamy, *Looking Backward,* 88.

137. Bellamy, 107.

138. Bellamy, 69–70.

139. William Morris, "Bellamy's Looking Backward," *Commonweal* 5, no. 8, June 21, 1889. https://www.marxists.org/archive/morris/works/1889/backward.htm (accessed September 6, 2017).

140. William Morris, "Useful Work Versus Useless Toil," in *Political Writings of William Morris,* ed. A. L. Morton (New York: International Publishers, 1973), 86–108.

141. Michael Robertson, *The Last Utopians: Four Late Nineteenth-Century Visionaries and Their Legacy* (Princeton, NJ: Princeton University Press, 2018), 127.

While volunteers for distasteful jobs are induced by shorter terms of duty in Le Guin's *The Dispossessed*,[142] in Bellamy's utopia the daily hours of labor in different trades "differ according to their arduousness."[143] This is an expression of the principle that "no man's work ought to be, on the whole, harder for him than any other man's for him."[144] To attract adequate volunteers for the most distasteful jobs, proclaims Dr. Leete, it might be necessary to reduce the time commitment to ten minutes a day.[145] Thus, though it is otherwise a strictly controlled economy, a market is simulated for occupational choices.

INVALID CORPS

Since a "man's endowments . . . fix the measure of his duty,"[146] accommodation exists for those whose abilities are impaired. For people who are "too deficient in mental or bodily strength to be fairly graded with the main body of workers," explains Dr. Leete, "we have a separate grade . . . a sort of invalid corps, the members of which are provided with a light class of tasks fitted to their strength."[147] These less fortunate citizens, Dr. Leete continues, are still "conceded the full right to live on the produce of [the fully able]."[148] In this way the constructive tax system is redistributive, as the efforts of the able are required in support of those less able or unable. Thus, observes Bellamy, "economic equality, without regard to differences of industrial ability, is necessitated by precisely the same logic which justifies political equality."[149]

---

142. Le Guin, *The Dispossessed*, 131. The extent to which there is "required work" on Anarres is discussed in the last chapter of this book in a digression to Robert Nozick's discussion of forced labor.

143. Bellamy, *Looking Backward*, 72. By contrast, in an aphorism titled "*My utopia*," Nietzsche allocates the most arduous work "to the man who suffers least from it, that is, to the dullest man, and so on step by step upwards to the man who is most sensitive." Friedrich Nietzsche, *Human All Too Human*, trans. Marion Faber and Stephen Lehmann (Lincoln: University of Nebraska Press, 1984), aphorism 462, 220 (italics in original).

144. Bellamy, *Looking Backward*, 72.

145. Bellamy, 72.

146. Bellamy, 88.

147. Bellamy, 109.

148. Bellamy, 111.

149. Edward Bellamy, "How and Why I Wrote Looking Backward," in *America as Utopia*, ed. Kenneth M. Roemer, 22–27 (New York: Burt Franklin and Company, 1981), 26.

As in More's Utopia, in Bellamy's state there is no money and no wages are paid.[150] In their place everyone is allotted an equal slice of the national profit each year. This fund is accessed through a paste board "credit card"—though its function is that of prepaid debit card. Individuals are free to allocate their share in any manner they desire.[151] However, the normal rules of economics apply: more of one thing, like fine clothing, necessarily means less of another, and each person's budgeting skills are put to the test annually.

CHARLOTTE PERKINS GILMAN (1860–1935): HALF THE HUMAN RACE IS DENIED FREE PRODUCTIVE EXPRESSION

"Are credit cards issued to the women just as to the men?" "Certainly," said Dr. Leete.

—Edward Bellamy (1850–1898), *Looking Backward*[152]

"The first duty of a human being," says Gilman, is "to find your real job, and do it."[153] To this point I have described utopian cultures that either stipulate a required amount of work, like in More's or Bellamy's, or assign work based on natural ability, like in Plato's. Latent in both these forms of required work, as I noted, is the question of gender: are women accorded equal opportunities as men?[154] Gilman's 1915 novel *Herland* addresses this question explicitly.[155] Distinctive to her utopia is the absence of men, thereby allowing women full access to the economy and control of the full range of occupations. In light of this change, "required work or occupation" takes on

---

150. Bellamy, *Looking Backward*, 87.

151. Bellamy, 83.

152. Bellamy, 187.

153. Charlotte Perkins Gilman, *The Living of Charlotte Perkins Gilman* (Madison: The University of Wisconsin Press, 1990), 42.

154. Hertzka's *Freeland*, for example, excludes women from working outside the home except as teachers. Hertzka, *Freeland*, 139–41.

155. Claeys and Sargent advise, "Charlotte Perkins Gilman is currently thought to have been the most important American author of the early twentieth-century women's movement." Gregory Claeys and Lyman Tower Sargent, eds. *The Utopian Reader* (New York: New York University Press, 1999), 319.

a new meaning. What she calls "sexuo-economic"[156] barriers are nonexistent in Herland, where everyone is encouraged to find her real job and do it.

The three male explorers in *Herland*, from whose perspectives Gilman describes her "Woman Land," are former college classmates Terry O. Nicholson (a wealthy adventurer), Jeff Margrave (a physician and botanist), and the narrator Vandyck Jennings (a sociologist). The country's management and infrastructure impress the travelers greatly, and they assume it must be the work of other men.[157] When the travelers are eventually captured and discover that all they have been admiring is the work of women, the men, says Gough, "to varying degrees . . . must construct a sense of identity beyond traditional hetero-patriarchal gender roles."[158]

NURTURING VARIETY

Herland depicts a culture that, for the past two thousand years, has successfully operated without men. This country of three million women, we are told, is about the size of Holland. In their economy multiple careers are not uncommon. "Some of us specialize in one line only," says Somel, one of the men's three assigned tutors.[159] "But most take up several," she explains, "some for their regular work, some to grow with. . . . When one settles too close in one kind of work," she advises, "there is a tendency to atrophy in the disused portions of the brain. We like to keep on learning, always."[160] For this reason their educational system encourages girls to explore their true interests and abilities. William Morris also encouraged education for a variety of work,

---

156. Charlotte Perkins Gilman, *Women and Economics* (Mineola, NY: Dover Publications, 1998), 54.

157. Gubar describes the three male explorers as "stereotypical and faintly ludicrous specimens of masculinity, each with his own all too predictable fantasy of what to expect in a country of no men." Gubar, "She in *Herland*: Feminism as Fantasy," 193.

158. Val Gough, "Lesbians and Virgins: The New Motherhood in *Herland*," in *Anticipations: Essays on Early Science Fiction and Its Precursors*, ed. David Seed (Syracuse, NY: Syracuse University Press, 1995), 205.

159. Gilman, *Herland*, 90. Somel is one of the leading female characters and a primary tutor to Vandyck Jennings. The other two tutors are Moadine (Terry Nicholson) and Zava (Jeff Margrave). The men's three love interests are Alima (Terry Nicholson), Celis (Jeff Margrave), and Ellador (Vandyck Jennings). Since the women are all part of one family, none of them has a family name, though some take on a second name, a "descriptive one," according to Moadine. "That is the name we earn" (Gilman, 64).

160. Gilman, 90.

varying "sedentary occupation with outdoor" and work "calling for the exercise of strong bodily energy for work in which the mind had more to do."[161]

SCIENTIFIC APPROACH TO WORK

Of her own childhood education Gilman says, "The one real study which did appeal to me, deeply, was Physics. . . . Here was Law, at last; not authority, not records of questionable truth or solemn tradition, but laws that could be counted on and *Proved*."[162] "Presently," she continues, "I made the observation that these laws had parallels in psychology. . . . Friction i.e., hindrance, interference, produces anger as naturally as heat . . . and oppression produces rebellion."[163]

Women and Economics sets out Gilman's vision of the required work of women. Her underlying observation was that since men control the workforce and the economy (and by implication the government and education), women's labor "has not only been limited in kind, but in degree."[164] Women are crowded out to their detriment, she believes, and to that of the race. Men have assigned themselves what work they desire, leaving few choices for women. Men are adventurers, inventors, miners, and professors while women are left economically stranded. "The female of genus homo," says Gilman, "is economically dependent on the male." "He is her food supply."[165] But, warns Nozick, "If people force you to do certain work . . . they decide what you are to do and what purposes your work is to serve. . . . This process . . . makes them a *part-owner* of you."[166]

Pfaelzer describes Gilman as "the first American social theorist to analyze the origins of patriarchy by tying larger economic patterns to domestic production, evolution, and sexuality."[167] In her autobiography Gilman reports, among her youthful recollections, how deeply she was impressed not only with the injustices inflicted on women but with the negative effects these injustices

---

161. Morris, "Useful Work Versus Useless Toil," 101.

162. Gilman, *The Living of Charlotte Perkins Gilman*, 29 (italics in original).

163. Gilman, 29.

164. Gilman, *Women and Economics*, 34.

165. Gilman, 11.

166. Nozick, *Anarchy, State, and Utopia*, 172 (italics in original).

167. Jean Pfaelzer, *The Utopian Novel in America, 1886–1896: The Politics of Form* (Pittsburgh, PA: University of Pittsburgh Press, 1984), 157.

have had on humankind.[168] Among these is the fact that the benefits women have received from economic progress have always been the provision men have allotted them.[169] Since the prevailing male control of economic activity carries with it the power to define the general welfare—including its legal, economic, and social structures—this system, she asserts, accentuates gender differences and calcifies gender roles.[170] "The highest human attributes are perfectly compatible with the sex-relation," she explains, "but not with the sexuo-economic relation,"[171] which makes economic roles a function of gender.[172] As if citing a principle in physics, she proclaims, "The more widely the sexes are differentiated, the more forcibly they are attracted to each other."[173]

TAX ON GENDER

Herland exposes the constructive tax levied on women that stipulates their required work or occupation. By excluding men from *Herland*, Gilman isolates, contrasts, and underscores the restrictions on women's life and vocational choices—imposed by a male-conceived general welfare. "Half the human race," she declares, "is denied free productive expression, is forced to confine its productive human energies to the same channels as its reproductive sexenergies." In this way, its creative faculty is limited "to the making of clothes and preparing of food." As a result, "No social service is possible."[174] To emphasize the disparity of opportunity in work and economic roles, the

---

168. Gilman, *The Living of Charlotte Perkins Gilman*, 61.

169. Gilman, *Women and Economics*, 5.

170. "For Gilman, the economic dependency of women," says Gubar, "means that . . . a woman . . . identifies herself with sexual function completely, while man is considered the human prototype." Gubar, "She in *Herland*: Feminism as Fantasy," 194.

171. Gilman, *Women and Economics*, 54.

172. Gilman claims, "The sexuo-economic relation . . . began in primeval savagery. It exists in all nations. Each boy and girl is born into it, trained into it, and has to live in it" (Gilman, *Women and Economics*, 40–41).

173. Gilman, 16.

174. Gilman, 59. In our own time Criado-Perez challenges the "male default" model of work that renders "women's work" invisible and unaccounted for. "Women have always worked. They have worked unpaid, underpaid, underappreciated, and invisibly, but they have always worked. . . . The work women do is not an added extra, a bonus that we could do without: women's work, paid and unpaid, is the backbone of our society and our economy." Caroline Criado-Perez, *Invisible Women: Data Bias in a World Designed for Men* (New York: Abrams Press, 2019), 142.

women of Herland perform all spheres of labor, including those traditionally male dominated—forestry, home building, road construction, and stone masonry.[175] In so doing, asserts Gubar, "*Herland* shifts the emphasis onto the multiple 'livings' open to women in a society that no longer opposes reproduction and production."[176]

The reallocation of work is not limited to the reassignment of traditional male roles, however. The women of Herland have also adapted the work required to their specific needs. "Very clear, strong thinkers they were,"[177] observes sociologist Jennings. In planning their work, he reports, the women's focus is on the community and on improving its condition for the centuries to come.[178] Early in their culture, for example, they had selected fruit trees as a primary food source. Trees require less labor than tilling the soil while "bearing a larger amount of food for the same ground space."[179] For fertilizer, says Jennings, the women rely on biodegradation—all the "plant waste from lumber work or textile industry, all the solid matter from the sewage" is restored to the earth.[180] In these ways, Jennings explains, "with their sublimated mother-love" directed toward their national growth, they modified every phase of their work.[181] "Gilman's method of feminism," explains Christensen, "is not to release women from the domestic sphere but to expand the domestic sphere to encompass everything and apply industrial methods and domestic economy across the spectrum."[182]

Gilman saw the oppression of women "as one of the roots of our society and its structures," relates Hall, "and knew that those structures would have

---

175. Gilman, *Herland*, 79.

176. Gubar, "She in *Herland*: Feminism as Fantasy," 194.

177. Gilman, *Herland*, 58.

178. Gilman, 67. Like More's Utopia, Herland's food production requires planning and careful estimates of the number of women their agriculture can support. But while More relies on moving excess population among the cities as well as to neighboring lands, Herland limits its population according to the availability of its food supply (population control is discussed in chapter five). Gilman, 67; More, *Utopia*, bk. 2, 54.

179. Gilman, *Herland*, 67.

180. Gilman, 68.

181. Gilman, 87.

182. Andrew G. Christensen, "Charlotte Perkins Gilman's *Herland* and the Tradition of the Scientific Utopia," *Utopian Studies* 28, no. 2 (2017): 286–304, 290. However, as Robertson observes, "It is not clear how the economy is organized, how goods are produced and distributed, or how people are compensated for their labor." Robertson, *The Last Utopians*, 208.

to change if oppression were to be eliminated."[183] Abolishing the constructive tax on women's obligatory work is the prescription for ending its coercive distortion to the balance of sacrifice founded on gender. Gilman's utopian goal is a "civilized" state, "one in which the citizens live in organic industrial relation. . . . The more perfect the differentiation of labor and exchange of product," she says, "the more perfect is that civilization."[184]

H. G. WELLS (1866–1946): LABOR LAWS AND THE INSULT OF CHARITY

> If we are to have any Utopia at all, we must have a clear common purpose, and a great and steadfast movement of will to override all these incurably egotistical dissentients.
>
> —H. G. Wells (1866–1946), *A Modern Utopia*[185]

"The State is for individuals, the law is for freedoms, the world is for experiment, experience, and change: these are the fundamental beliefs upon which a modern Utopia must go."[186] Instead of hidden in some unexplored corner of the world, Wells's utopia is a worldwide affair on a planet physically identical to our earth, and one where "every man, woman, and child alive has a Utopian parallel."[187] The modern Utopia, he tells us, "will insist upon every citizen being properly housed, well nourished, and in good health, reasonably clean and clothed healthily, and upon that insistence its labor laws will be founded."[188] These laws assume labor is "a delocalized and fluid force"[189] and include a worldwide minimum wage. Wells's worldwide economy and its migratory workforce are facilitated by a sophisticated high-speed rail

---

183. K. Graehme Hall, "Mothers and Children: 'Rising with the Resistless Tide' in *Herland*," in *Charlotte Perkins Gilman: The Woman and Her Work*, ed. Sheryl L. Meyering (Ann Arbor, MI: UMI Research Press, 1989), 169n2.

184. Gilman, *Women and Economics*, 37–38.

185. Wells, *A Modern Utopia*, 53.

186. Wells, 39.

187. Wells, 15.

188. Wells, 57.

189. Wells, 62.

system ("Two hundred miles an hour!"[190]). While More's Utopia is designed to eliminate idleness (but not leisure), Wells's modern Utopia permits idleness, at least when a citizen possesses the financial means.[191] But most citizens must work, and—if they are trained and skilled—work at occupations left to their personal inclinations and ambitions; for, as he notes, "work as a moral obligation is the morality of slaves."[192]

OPPORTUNITY FOR ADVANCEMENT

Since the world government provides education and training, opportunities to advance beyond the minimum wage are abundant. The World State encourages education and research with "great systems of laboratories . . . at which research [is] conducted under the most favourable conditions."[193] Its "world-wide House of Saloman," Wells's "Utopian self" explains, employs "over a million men" engaged in discovery and invention.[194] Unlike Bacon's House of Salomon, however, Wells's scientists include women, since, he specifies, the pronoun " 'He' indeed is to be read as 'He and She.' "[195] To minimize unemployment and to exploit the delocalized and fluid workforce, the modern Utopia employs worldwide labor exchanges that report "the fluctuating pressure of economic demand."[196] It is presumed that a population "largely migratory and emancipated from locality"[197] will relocate once or twice a year, whether locally or globally as the labor exchanges direct.[198] The centralized Divlab computers in Le Guin's *The Dispossessed* perform a similar global labor-allocation function.[199]

---

190. Wells, 94.

191. Wells, 60.

192. Wells, 63.

193. Wells, 107.

194. Wells, 107. For successful inventions the state pays a royalty that is divided between the inventor and her institution.

195. Wells, 75.

196. Wells, 62.

197. Wells, 35.

198. Wells, 61.

199. Le Guin, *The Dispossessed*, 215, 233.

UNSKILLED LABOR TAX

Wells creates two categories for those on the margins of the workforce. The first group is criminals and others detrimental to society. They are exiled to secluded islands (discussed in chapter five). The second group includes workers incapable of establishing themselves in the general workforce—those able to work but unskilled or displaced who are "indecently dressed, or ragged and dirty, or publicly unhealthy."[200] When a citizen comes under state care, Wells says, the state

> will find him work if he can and will work, it will take him to it, it will register him and lend him the money wherewith to lead a comely life until work can be found or made for him, and it will give him credit and shelter him and strengthen him if he is ill. In default of private enterprises it will provide inns for him and food.[201]

Furthermore, he explains, the citizens receive these things "as a shareholder in the common enterprise and not with any insult of charity."[202] Since the state is "the reserve employer,"[203] these citizens are assigned to public works projects—the levy of a constructive tax. "The work publicly provided," says the narrator, "would have to be toilsome, but not cruel or incapacitating."[204] As a consequence of these provisions, Wells's narrator declares, "to be moneyless will be clear evidence of unworthiness."[205] For those who are employed but content with a minimum wage, the state levies an additional constructive tax: a prohibition against adding children to the world (discussed in chapter five).

---

200. Wells, *A Modern Utopia*, 57.

201. Wells, 57.

202. Wells, 58.

203. Wells, 57.

204. Wells, 57.

205. Wells, 61. The worldwide regulated economy is a mixed affair featuring both government enterprises and private businesses and includes subsidies for "commercially unprofitable undertakings as benefit the community as a whole" (Wells, 39).

B. F. SKINNER (1904–1990):
WE HAVE CREATED LEISURE WITHOUT SLAVERY

The life which men praise and regard as successful is but one kind.
Why should we exaggerate any one kind at the expense of others?

—Henry David Thoreau (1817–1862), *Walden*[206]

"Several years ago," recalls Skinner (in 1956), "I spent a pleasant summer writing a novel called *Walden Two*. One of the characters, Frazier, said many things which I was not yet ready to say myself."[207] *Walden Two* embodies Skinner's contention that the goal of social reform is to develop within a culture "a set of contingencies of reinforcement" that both maintain the existing culture and permit its modification in response to changing conditions or emergencies.[208] Some contingencies, he says,

> are part of the physical environment, but they usually work in combination with social contingencies. . . . The social contingencies, or the behaviors they generate, are the "ideas" of a culture; the reinforcers that appear in the contingencies are its "values."[209]

Furthermore, a culture, "like a species, is selected by its adaptation to an environment: to the extent that it helps its members to get what they need and avoid what is dangerous, it helps them to survive and transmit the culture."[210]

---

206. Henry David Thoreau, *Walden*, in *Walden and Civil Disobedience* (New York: Barnes and Noble Classics, 2003), 19. Skinner proclaims, "I am an Emersonian, a Thoreauvian. I want what they wanted. But I want it as part of a successful conception of human behavior." Skinner, *Notebooks*, 69.

207. Skinner, *Cumulative Record*, 123.

208. B. F. Skinner, *Contingencies of Reinforcement: A Theoretical Analysis* (New York: Appleton-Century-Crofts, 1969), 41.

209. B. F. Skinner, *Beyond Freedom and Dignity* (New York: Alfred A. Knopf, 1971), 127–28.

210. Skinner, 129.

THE SOURCES OF CONTROL

"In the long run," Thoreau declares, "men hit only what they aim at. There-fore, though they should fail immediately, they had better aim at something high."[211] *Walden Two* depicts a contemporary U.S. community of a thousand people, managed using the principles of Skinner's behavioral technology. The novel provides a view of the community from the perspective of six visitors who spend a week observing the utopia and peppering (sometimes assailing) its founder and psychologist T. E. Frazier with questions. Castle, the most vocal and antagonistic visitor, embodies Thoreau's objection that "there are nowadays professors of philosophy, but not philosophers."[212] The more sympathetic Burris (Burrhus is Skinner's first name), the narrator, is a former graduate school classmate of Frazier's. Contrary to Castle's accusations, "Frazier does not control the members of Walden Two," says Skinner. "The world which he designed and which they maintain is the controller."[213] The alternatives for Skinner are not between control and freedom but relate to the source of control: whether adventitious or self-chosen. He notes, "we cannot choose a way of life in which there is no control. We can only change the controlling conditions."[214] By doing nothing, he advises, we will "allow a miserable and probably catastrophic future to overtake us." On the other hand, by exploiting our knowledge of human behavior, it is possible to "create a social environment in which we shall live productive and creative lives" without jeopardizing the lives of future generations.[215] "Something like a Walden Two," he says, "would not be a bad start."[216]

REQUIRED WORK TAX

Skinner imposes a universal work requirement as did More and Bellamy. This constructive tax, as Skinner implements it, enhances that of More's Utopia

---

211. Thoreau, *Walden*, 25.

212. Thoreau, 16.

213. Skinner, *Notebooks*, 112.

214. B. F. Skinner, *About Behaviorism* (New York: Alfred A. Knopf, 1974), 190.

215. B. F. Skinner, *Walden Two* (New York: Macmillan Publishing Co., Inc., 1976), xvi.

216. Skinner, xvi.

in three ways. First, Skinner's citizens have reduced the required work from six to an average of four hours a day through innovative efficiencies and technology. Second, they experimentally determine the number of hours required for each job, based on the community's needs. Third, the required work hours are adjusted through a system of work-hour-equivalency credits to accommodate the more distasteful, dangerous, or otherwise unpopular jobs. To entice people to work at less pleasant jobs, "we simply assign different credit values to different kinds of work, and adjust them from time to time on the basis of demand." "Bellamy," says Frazier, "suggested the principle in *Looking Backward*."[217] Thus, cleaning sewers is mentioned as requiring only two hours' work to earn four hours of work credit. And while all goods and services are "free," Frazier says, "each of us pays for what he uses with twelve-hundred labor credits each year."[218] Even visitors are required to earn the equivalent of two labor credits a day to pay for their room and board.[219]

Unlike More's or Bellamy's utopias, the required work in Skinner's utopia is not classified or restricted by gender. "You may have noticed the complete equality of men and women among us," says Frazier. "There are scarcely any types of work which are not shared equally."[220] "Anyone born into Walden Two has a right to any place among us for which he can demonstrate the necessary talent or ability."[221] Utopias, Frazier claims, "usually spring from a rejection of modern life. . . . We look ahead, not backwards, for a better version."[222] "When we're not being imposed on," he continues, "when we choose our work freely, then we *want* to work. . . . William Morris, you remember, tried to make that state of affairs plausible in *News from Nowhere*, but without success, I think. Imagine our surprise to find we had made him a true prophet!"[223]

---

217. Skinner, 46.

218. Skinner, 45.

219. Skinner, 58.

220. Skinner, 123.

221. Skinner, 218. Hertzka's *Freeland* makes a similar claim, but only for its men. Women are relegated to propagation and "beautifying and refining life." Hertzka, *Freeland*, 139–41.

222. Skinner, *Walden Two*, 68.

223. Skinner, 147 (italics in original).

Part Three:
Saint-Simon and Campanella

HENRI SAINT-SIMON (1760–1825):
THE HUMAN SPIRIT FOLLOWS
A PREDETERMINED COURSE

Work is the source of all virtues; the most useful work should be the most highly esteemed.

—Henri Saint-Simon, *The Political Thought of Saint-Simon*[224]

The utopias we have examined to this point have largely ignored pecuniary taxes. With Saint-Simon, however, the administration and reduction of taxes is a significant concern. In particular, his proposals shift the authority to tax to those most responsible for payment—the industrials ("*industriels*"[225])—while reducing reliance on taxation by remedying problems toward which it traditionally goes (idle classes, poverty, strife, unemployment, war). Though More avoided pecuniary taxes by limiting privacy and personal choice and imposing a universal work obligation, Saint-Simon foretold a political order with increased liberty that reduced pecuniary taxes to a minimum. Though this sounds like a libertarian utopia, it is not.[226] In contrast to personal freedom, the liberty he foresaw was that of the social order and a function

---

224. Saint-Simon, *The Political Thought of Saint-Simon*, 187.

225. Manuel explains, when Saint-Simon "invented a new word such as *industriel*, he did not use it consistently." Although he "sometimes used the term industrial to mean industrialists in the narrow sense, that is, entrepreneurs of manufactures, in his writing from 1815 through 1817 . . . he applied it to the whole class of those who worked as distinguished from the idlers." Frank E. Manuel, *The New World of Henri Saint-Simon* (Cambridge, MA: Harvard University Press, 1956), 4, 250.

226. "At first sight," says Markham, "Saint-Simon's views . . . appear to be the purest economic laissez-faire, as taught by the classical economists; government should be reduced to the minimum, and the economic system will flourish automatically." F. M. H. Markham, introduction, *Henri Comte De Saint-Simon (1760–1825): Selected Writings*, ed. and trans. F. M. H. Markham (New York: The MacMillan Company, 1952), xxvi.

of the state of civilization.[227] Establishing a new economic order necessitates a change in political control, the catalyst for which, he believes, is scientific innovation—the vanguard of progress—empowering industry, weakening the feudal sinews, and liberating the forces of social change. "Our intention," writes Saint-Simon, "is simply to promote and explain a development which is inevitable."[228] Thus, a reordered society and its ensuing benefits are the natural outcome of historical progress, which itself is stimulated by scientific advancement.[229]

POLITICS AND SCIENCE

Born to a Parisian family of some nobility—a "descendant of Charlemagne"[230]—Saint-Simon was a political scientist, social reformer, and visionary who, at least to his own satisfaction, based his utopian recommendations on historical and scientific evidence. During his career he enjoyed wealth and endured poverty and was imprisoned on more than one occasion. Of his writing style Manuel says, "He was a conversationalist who could not learn how to write."[231] For this reason, none of his works provides "an orderly presentation of his thought."[232] In spite of this, "Saint-Simon really had a *doctrine*," says Manuel, elaborated in his "haphazard publication[s] from 1802 to 1825."[233]

One element of this doctrine is that since progress is a function of scientific advancement, politics itself must be converted into a science, which means divorcing it from both religion and political economy.[234] One aim

---

227. Manuel, *The New World of Henri Saint-Simon*, 268.

228. Henri Saint-Simon, *Henri Comte De Saint-Simon (1760–1825): Selected Writings*, ed. and trans. F. M. H. Markham (New York: The Macmillan Company, 1952), 70.

229. See Manuel, *The New World of Henri Saint-Simon*, especially chapters 13 and 19.

230. Bloch, *The Principle of Hope*, 565. But see Manuel, *The New World of Henri Saint-Simon*, 9.

231. Manuel, *The New World of Henri Saint-Simon*, 118.

232. Manuel, 5.

233. Manuel, 5.

234. Mannheim contends that the difficulties of establishing a science of politics "arise from the fact that we are not dealing . . . with rigid, objective entities but with tendencies and strivings in a constant state of flux." Karl Mannheim, *Ideology and Utopia: An Introduction to the Sociology of Knowledge*, trans. Luis Wirth and Edward Shils (San Diego, CA: A Harvest Book, Harcourt, 1936), 116.

of this process, says Saint-Simon, is "to replace metaphysical reasoning with facts."[235] A second is to extract politics—"the science of the organization of societies"—from political economy, "which teaches how wealth is formed, distributed, and consumed."[236] Saint-Simon's rationale for this change—citing economist Jean-Baptiste Say—is that a well-administered state can prosper under any form of government.[237] Based on this assumption, politics should not be saddled with an economic bias, such as seeking to maximize wealth, which presents only one possible goal. Disentangling the science of politics from political economy liberates politics to establish its own criteria for achieving Saint-Simon's ambitious mission: to discover if there is a form of government whose very nature is good, and which is "founded on certain, absolute, universal principles, independent of time and place."[238] In the judgment of Markham, "no other political and social thinker of the nineteenth century surpasses him in originality of approach to these problems, or in boldness and breadth of view."[239]

Saint-Simon was an "organicist," observes Ionescu, "particularly interested in the biology of societies, in the way . . . [they] form and animate a common body."[240] Accordingly, Saint-Simon framed his ideal society in biological rather than mechanical terms. Viewing society as an organism permits him to analyze the origins of social progress in ways that a mechanical model would not, including the appraisal of a society's relative health. The most prominent example of this organic model, he believes, is industry, where there "is but one single, vast body, all of whose limbs respond

235. Saint-Simon, *Henri Saint-Simon (1760–1825): Selected Writings*, ed. and trans. Taylor, 250.

236. Jean-Baptiste Say, qtd. in *Henri Saint-Simon (1760–1825): Selected Writings*, ed. and trans. Taylor, 166.

237. Say's original statement: "Wealth . . . is essentially independent of political organization. Under every form of government, a state, whose affairs are well administered, may prosper. Nations have risen to opulence under absolute monarchs, and have been ruined by popular councils." Jean-Baptiste Say, *A Treatise on Political Economy*, 4th French ed., trans. C. R. Prinsep (New Brunswick, NJ: Transaction Publishers, Rutgers, 2001), 15.

238. Saint-Simon, *Henri Comte De Saint-Simon (1760–1825): Selected Writings*, ed. and trans. Markham, 39.

239. Markham, introduction, *Henri Saint-Simon (1760–1825)*, xx.

240. Ghita Ionescu, introduction, *The Political Thought of Saint-Simon*, ed. Ghita Ionescu (Oxford: Oxford University Press, 1976), 30.

to each other. . . . Always it has just one interest, one need, one life."[241] Saint-Simon's objective, notes Ionescu, is "to provide the *scientific analysis* of the interrelation and the functioning of the entire *industrial system* . . . and to grasp the ultimate reality of modern and future mankind as transformed by industry."[242] The sciences, while affording leadership for industry in this transition, were themselves to be integrated by synthesizing their discoveries and methods. "He wanted . . . to reveal the common elements in the sciences and their dependence upon one another."[243] The resulting society, Saint-Simon argues, would place the most qualified and capable class of individuals—the eminent scientists and captains of industry—in positions of political leadership.

PROGRESS

"In the development of the sciences and arts," Saint-Simon believes, "the human spirit follows a predetermined course which is superior to the greatest intellectual forces."[244] In *The Idea of Progress*, Van Doren notes that for Saint-Simon, progress "is a natural phenomenon; it consists in advance toward a society that is based on, and congruent to, what is natural to man."[245] For Saint-Simon this ascent includes the elimination of the idle classes (a vestige of feudal society), who use "force to live off the work of the rest,"[246] and the establishment of "useful work"[247]—made possible by scientists and implemented by industrials—as society's foundation. "The object of my enterprise," he says, "is to free those men who are engaged in work of the most positive and most direct utility from the domination exercised over

---

241. Saint-Simon, *Henri Saint-Simon (1760–1825): Selected Writings*, ed. and trans. Taylor, 161.

242. Ionescu, introduction, *The Political Thought of Saint-Simon*, 30 (italics in original).

243. Manuel, *The New World of Henri Saint-Simon*, 131.

244. Henri Saint-Simon, qtd. in Manuel, *The New World of Henri Saint-Simon*, 151.

245. Charles Van Doren, *The Idea of Progress* (New York: Frederick A. Praeger Publishers, 1967), 400–401.

246. Saint-Simon, *Henri Saint-Simon (1760–1825): Selected Writings*, ed. and trans. Taylor, 158.

247. Among the useful occupations, Saint-Simon includes physicists, chemists, physiologists, mathematicians, poets, painters, sculptors, musicians, writers, and farmers. Saint-Simon, *Henri Comte De Saint-Simon (1760–1825): Selected Writings*, ed. and trans. Markham, 72.

them hitherto by the clergy, the nobility, and the judicial order, as well as by the property owners who are not industrials."[248] He envisions this change occurring naturally and without the need for violent revolution. Unlike Marx and Engels who stressed "the inevitability of conflict between capitalists and proletariat," says Taylor, "Saint-Simon believed that these two groups shared a common interest in production, and that consequently . . . relations between them should be . . . friendly and cooperative."[249] Insurrection as a tactic for social change, explains Saint-Simon, "is first of all the most inadequate of all methods; and second, it runs absolutely contrary to the interests of *industry*."[250] Without such threats in the future, he predicts, the need for large standing armies will dissolve, along with their continual demand for tax revenue.[251]

IMPROVEMENT OF CIVILIZATION

Government must be in the hands of those whose interests align most directly with progress—not the idle classes (clergy, nobles, and nonindustrial landowners), but the scientists and masters of industry. The role Saint-Simon assigns to the scientists—arguably comparable to their position in Bacon's *New Atlantis*[252]—permits them to guide society with discoveries that improve the work of the members of the industrial division ("artisans, manufacturers, merchants, entrepreneurs of land and sea transport"[253]). The industrials (or industrialists), he says, "will form the leading class in society" and "decide

---

248. Saint-Simon, 217.

249. Keith Taylor, *The Political Ideas of the Utopian Socialists* (London: Frank Cass and Company, 1982), 66.

250. Saint-Simon, *The Political Thought of Saint-Simon*, 124 (italics in original).

251. Saint-Simon, *Henri Comte De Saint-Simon (1760–1825): Selected Writings*, ed. and trans. Markham, 78.

252. Manuel notes the influence of Bacon's *New Atlantis* in appointing the scientists as his spiritual leaders. Manuel, *The New World of Henri Saint-Simon*, 124.

253. Saint-Simon, *Henri Saint-Simon (1760–1825): Selected Writings*, ed. and trans. Taylor, 190. In his later writing, according to Taylor, Saint-Simon gave preference to the " 'practical' classes, i.e. in particular the farmers, manufacturers, merchants, and bankers. . . . The scientists and artists were excluded and regarded henceforth as 'non-industrials,' although they were still considered to be useful 'theoretical' workers." Taylor, *The Political Ideas of the Utopian Socialists*, 65.

the positions that the other classes shall occupy."[254] The industrials enforce their leadership not by coercion but through an understanding of the organic nature of industry and its operations.

COLLECTIVE LIBERTY

"Men engaged in industry," Saint-Simon declares, "whose association forms the true society, have only one need: liberty. Liberty for them is to be unrestricted in productive work, to be allowed free enjoyment of what they produce."[255] He emphasizes the importance of liberty in scientific terms with his deterministic claim that "industrial activity declines at a rate which is an exact function of the restrictions to which it is subject."[256] Though his call for noninterference with industry is reminiscent of modern fiscal conservatives (including Hayek[257] and Rand), the freedom Saint-Simon stresses is not individual but collective. If the "vague and metaphysical idea of liberty current today continued to be taken as the basis of political doctrines," Saint-Simon argues, it would undermine the scientific development of civilization.[258] Observe, he says, "Men do not associate in order to be free. Savages associate to hunt, to make war, but certainly not to produce liberty."[259] Saint-Simon, notes Adler, rejects the freedom "to do as one pleases under circumstances that permit the individual to realize his own desires."[260] On the contrary, he advocates a "freedom which the human race will enjoy collectively in the future when it has achieved the ideal mode of association that is the goal of mankind's historical development."[261]

---

254. Saint-Simon, *The Political Thought of Saint-Simon*, 187.

255. Saint-Simon, *Henri Saint-Simon (1760–1825): Selected Writings*, ed. and trans. Taylor, 158.

256. Saint-Simon, 159.

257. "The aim of interference," says Hayek, "is always to bring about a particular result which is different from that which would have been produced if the mechanism had been allowed unaided to follow its inherent principles." Hayek, *Law, Legislation and Liberty*, vol. 2, 129.

258. Saint-Simon, *Henri Saint-Simon (1760–1825): Selected Writings*, ed. and trans. Taylor, 229.

259. Saint-Simon, 229.

260. Mortimer J. Adler, *The Idea of Freedom: A Dialectical Examination of the Conceptions of Freedom*, vol. 1 (Garden City, NY: Doubleday and Company, 1958), 370.

261. Adler, 370–71.

In the past, Saint-Simon reports, the control of workers was in the hands of those who owned the land and capital. Industrialization has changed the nature of work and produced a corresponding shift in its control. The industrials, he asserts, "appeared with a new character: from the beginning of their political existence they did not seek to command and did not wish to obey."[262] Instead, they "introduced a system based on private contract between themselves and their superiors or inferiors. The only masters they recognized were the calculations which reconciled the interests of the contracting parties."[263] The industrious man, he says, "is really subject to only one law: that of his self-interest."[264] In a claim prescient of Shevek's in Le Guin's *The Dispossessed*, Saint-Simon asserts the only useful actions that people can perform are actions on things and not actions on other people.[265] The action of one person on another, he observes, is always "harmful to the species because of the twofold waste of energy which it entails."[266] Applying Newton's law of the conservation of energy to society, he explains, "The energy which had previously been wasted upon the exercise of power over men would be channeled in another direction, toward the ever more intensive exploitation of nature."[267]

EXTOLLING INEQUALITY

In calling for the political ascendency of industrials and scientists, Saint-Simon seeks to capitalize on natural inequality. "He envisioned the society of the future not as a classless society," observes Manuel, "but as an ideal order based on natural classes, determined by capacity, with each capacity finding its proper and essential place in the great national workshop."[268] For the purpose of governing, Saint-Simon believes, classes based on natural ability—rather than social or economic factors—produce organically unified components, distinct yet complementary. Saint-Simon regarded inequality,

---

262. Saint-Simon, *Henri Saint-Simon (1760–1825): Selected Writings*, ed. and trans. Taylor, 247.

263. Saint-Simon, 247.

264. Saint-Simon, 158.

265. Saint-Simon, qtd. in Manuel and Manuel, *Utopian Thought in the Western World*, 604. Shevek says of the Odonian centralized labor administration (Divlab), "They do not govern persons; they administer production." Le Guin, *The Dispossessed*, 67.

266. Saint-Simon, qtd. in Manuel and Manuel, *Utopian Thought in the Western World*, 604.

267. Saint-Simon, 604.

268. Manuel, *The New World of Henri Saint-Simon*, 245.

Hertzler asserts, as "the very basis of association, as the indispensable condition of social order."[269] Like Plato, says Nisbet, Saint-Simon "wished only to make it possible for the best, irrespective of origin, to rise as quickly as possible to leadership and participation in absolute power over the nation; absolute power based, of course, upon the laws of science."[270] Thus, rather than social or economic equality, Saint-Simon sought only equality of opportunity, allowing men of "transcendent talent to rise to the first rank, no matter in what position the chance of birth may have placed them."[271]

THE STRUCTURE OF GOVERNMENT

Though Saint-Simon's views shifted, in his 1825 *Fragments on Social Organization* he identifies the three forces or functions to balance as invention (artists), examination (scientists), and execution (industrials),[272] each with one of the three chambers of parliament representing it. The Chamber of Examination (scientists) critically evaluates the suggestions from the Chamber of Invention (artists). The Executive Chamber comprises those "chosen from the most important heads of industrial houses," working without salary because they "should all be rich."[273]

One of Saint-Simon's critics is economist F. A. Hayek, who argues that government-centered economic planning is too often planning against competition—that is, collectivism or planning that displaces the possibility of competition.[274] Accordingly, Hayek says, "planning and competition can be combined only by planning for competition but not by planning against competition."[275] By inserting the captains of industry into the executive role,

---

269. Joyce Oramel Hertzler, *The History of Utopian Thought* (New York: The Macmillan Company, 1926; repr.), 196. (Page references same as original.)

270. Robert Nisbet, *History of the Idea of Progress* (New York: Basic Books Publishers, 1980), 248.

271. Saint-Simon, qtd. in Manuel, *The New World of Henri Saint-Simon*, 309–10.

272. Saint-Simon, *Henri Saint-Simon (1760–1825): Selected Writings*, ed. and trans. Taylor, 267.

273. Saint-Simon, 205.

274. Hayek refers to Saint-Simon disparagingly as "the first of modern planners" and as one of the founders of socialism who believed that freedom of thought was "the root-evil of nineteenth-century society." Hayek, *The Road to Serfdom*, 24.

275. Hayek, 42. In a review of Hayek's *The Road to Serfdom*, Orwell observes, "In the negative part of Professor Hayek's thesis there is a great deal of truth. It cannot be said too often—at any rate, it is not being said nearly often enough—that collectivism is not

however, Saint-Simon (unwittingly?) envisions the champions of competition (or at least those who have proven themselves the most successful business competitors, since they "should all be rich"[276]) as executing his organic central planning. The result is an intriguing utopian paradox.

THE POWER TO TAX

"The greatest, most important power entrusted to the Government," Saint-Simon declares, "is the power to tax the citizens. All its other powers spring from this right."[277] How effectively government uses this power, he believes, can be judged from the relative portions of public revenue that go to support what is useful in contrast to what is destructive, idle, or unproductive. As he explains,

> there is surrounding society, there circulates in its bosom a throng of parasites who, although they have the same needs and desires as the others, have not been able to overcome the natural laziness common to all men, and who, although they produce nothing, consume or seek to consume as though they did produce.[278]

Taylor reports that the portion of public revenue subsidizing this "throng of parasites" is, for Saint-Simon, "being squandered on the army, police, courts, and aristocracy," rather than being "invested in science and industry so as to promote social welfare, develop transport and communications, and provide useful employment for all men."[279] Once the industrials control and properly direct the flow of public revenue, this will "reduce poverty, idleness, and ignorance, the chief sources of public disorder," thereby eliminating the need for most governmental functions.[280]

---

inherently democratic, but, on the contrary, gives to a tyrannical minority such powers as the Spanish Inquisitors never dreamed of." George Orwell, review, "*The Road to Serfdom* by F. A. Hayek," *Observer* 9, April 1944. https://thomasgwyndunbar.wordpress.com/2008/10/09/george-orwell-review/ (accessed February 16, 2019).

276. Saint-Simon, *Henri Saint-Simon (1760–1825): Selected Writings*, ed. and trans. Taylor, 205.

277. Saint-Simon, 189.

278. Saint-Simon, 158.

279. Taylor, *The Political Ideas of the Utopian Socialists*, 56.

280. Manuel and Manuel, *Utopian Thought in the Western World*, 608.

Saint-Simon is not opposed to taxation, only to wasteful tax policy. Since governmental activity "may be deemed a service which is useful to society," he advises, "society should consent to pay for this service."[281] But, he adds, "Industry needs to be governed as little as possible, and this can only be done if it is governed as cheaply as possible."[282] To this end, the functions of government "should be limited to maintaining public order,"[283] by which he means the provision of education and jobs, not the legalized exercise of force. It is work, he claims, "which eliminates every tendency toward disorder."[284] The priority in state expenditure, therefore, should be ensuring everyone's ability to work by providing education and "spreading throughout the proletarian class a knowledge of positive science."[285] Tax revenues that "idlers, that is, thieves"[286] had formerly raised and spent on large standing armies would no longer be required.

Where tax laws come from, who proposes them, and on what basis are important considerations for political philosophy. In contrast to most utopians, Saint-Simon stresses the importance of these questions while supplying his own unconventional answers. Since the industrials pay what pecuniary taxes there are, he argues, they should also design and implement tax policy.[287] To parliament's Executive Chamber he assigns "the control of taxation and expenditure."[288] Under such a system, tax revenue "will be supplied by voluntary subscription," says Saint-Simon, "and the subscribers will themselves supervise the spending and administration of their own money."[289] Accordingly, his anticipated transformation of society—including defunding the idle classes—is destined to result, he claims, "in a large increase

---

281. Saint-Simon, *Henri Saint-Simon (1760–1825): Selected Writings*, ed. and trans. Taylor, 159.

282. Saint-Simon, 159.

283. Saint-Simon, *Henri Comte De Saint-Simon (1760–1825): Selected Writings*, ed. and trans. Markham, 79.

284. Saint-Simon, *Henri Saint-Simon (1760–1825): Selected Writings*, ed. and trans. Taylor, 265.

285. Saint-Simon, *Henri Comte De Saint-Simon (1760–1825): Selected Writings*, ed. and trans. Markham, 77.

286. Saint-Simon, *Henri Saint-Simon (1760–1825): Selected Writings*, ed. and trans. Taylor, 158.

287. Saint-Simon, 172.

288. Hertzler, *The History of Utopian Thought*, 194.

289. Saint-Simon, *Henri Comte De Saint-Simon (1760–1825): Selected Writings*, ed. and trans. Markham, 71.

in national income and a large decrease in expenditure."[290] By emphasizing science and hierarchical society, Saint-Simon's utopia, says Bloch, "is considerably closer to Campanella than to More."[291]

TOMMASO CAMPANELLA (1568–1639): ASSIGNED LABOR IN *THE CITY OF THE SUN*

> There is no special faculty of administration in a state which a woman has because she is a woman, or which a man has by virtue of his sex, but the gifts of nature are alike diffused in both.
>
> —Plato (c. 428–c. 348 BCE), *Republic*[292]

I conclude this chapter by returning to the early seventeenth century to emphasize one aspect of the required-work regime largely ignored to this point. *The City of the Sun* was written in 1602 while Campanella was imprisoned in Naples for heresy and sedition. In the same year, explains Donno, "the Inquisition sentenced him to life imprisonment without hope of reprieve."[293] Though a Dominican by training, Campanella took issue, as did Bacon later in the century, with the stultifying influence of Aristotle on scientific progress. Genoese, Campanella's seafaring narrator, explains that in the more enlightened City of the Sun, wisdom resides in an integrated knowledge of all things and not, as in their country, in "servile" mastery of Aristotle's grammar or logic, which "deprives the mind of vitality" because it requires meditation "upon books instead of things."[294] The Solarians (as they are called) "are enemies of Aristotle," he proclaims, "and call him a pedant."[295] Campanella turned instead to Plato for inspiration, and—while

---

290. Saint-Simon, *Henri Saint-Simon (1760–1825): Selected Writings*, ed. and trans. Taylor, 174.

291. Bloch, *The Principle of Hope*, 568.

292. Plato, *Republic*, trans. Jowett, bk. 5, 455.

293. Daniel J. Donno, Introduction to *The City of the Sun*, by Tommaso Campanella, trans. Daniel J. Donno (Berkeley: University of California Press, 1981), 10.

294. Tommaso Campanella, *The City of the Sun*, trans. Daniel J. Donno (Berkeley: University of California Press, 1981), 45.

295. Campanella, 109. Campanella argues, "one would have to be insane to think that Aristotle has established the truth about the heavens and that there is nothing more to be investigated." Thomas Campanella, *A Defense of Galileo*, trans. Richard J. Blackwell (Notre Dame, IN: University of Notre Dame Press, 1994), 60.

diverging from the *Republic* on key points—was largely in agreement regarding the distribution of work for the benefit of all. In the City of the Sun, for example, "Men and women perform the same tasks, whether of a mental or a mechanical nature,"[296] and "each individual is assigned to the work he has the greatest aptitude for."[297] Their life, observes Bloch, is "like clockwork in a military monarchic fashion."[298]

SCIENTIFIC EDUCATION FOR WORK

In *Science in Utopia*, Eurich notes, *The City of the Sun* was "the first utopia to give a leading role to natural sciences and base its structure on a scientific foundation."[299] Campanella's ideal society reveres science, but, contrary to Bacon's House of Salomon, it extends scientific education to all. Preparation for a life of work is grounded in a scientifically oriented general education. This is evidenced by the city's public display of scientific exhibits; the "entire city is their schoolroom,"[300] explains Blodgett. The city's seven concentric walls serve as a learning resource center, with each wall's sides featuring a discrete theme, including displays of minerals and metals, maps, plant and animal species, languages, mathematical figures, and mechanical arts and their inventors.[301] In this way, observes Donno, "students may be in contact with real things, which are the best teachers, rather than with mere pictures and models."[302] Thus, "without effort," boasts the narrator, "merely while playing, their children come to know all the sciences."[303]

Among their forms of work, both sexes are "trained in all pursuits,"[304] though tasks that are "the least fatiguing are given to women."[305] This begins with their common education at age three, where children "learn their

---

296. Campanella, *The City of the Sun*, 49.

297. Campanella, 81.

298. Bloch, *The Principle of Hope*, 524.

299. Eurich, *Science in Utopia*, 120.

300. Blodgett, "The 'New Atlantis' and Campanella's '*Civitas Solis*,'" 772.

301. Campanella, *The City of the Sun*, 33, 35.

302. Donno, Introduction to *The City of the Sun*, 18.

303. Campanella, *The City of the Sun*, 37.

304. Campanella, 41.

305. Campanella, 81.

alphabet and language, which are inscribed on the walls."[306] "Then at the age of ten," explains Genoese, "they all study mathematics, medicine, and other sciences."[307] Their aptitudes for the various kinds of work are assessed, though all join in military service and "work in the fields and pastures." "They regard these activities as the noblest," and "they consider the noblest man to be the one who has mastered the greatest number of skills."[308]

ENABLING THE WORKFORCE

Though written more than four hundred years ago, Campanella's utopia displays a flash of modernity in its allocation of required work. It is one of the few utopias (if there are others) to offer special consideration to disabled workers—matching them with suitable yet necessary work. Bellamy, for example, acknowledges the "lame and blind and crippled"[309] but puts them to work in his invalid corps, like our sheltered workshops, where they "are provided with a light class of tasks fitted to their strength."[310] Wells addresses "the endless variety of men, their endless gradation of quality" and relegates the disabled and "inferior types" to government jobs as a public service.[311] Other utopians ignore the disabled altogether or plot against their reproduction (with eugenic measures described in chapter five). In the City of the Sun, however, "no physical defect justifies a man's being idle except the decrepitude of age, at which time of life he is still useful as an adviser." Rather than "make-work" as a concession to their limitations, their strengths are recognized and engaged.

> If a man is lame, his eyes make him useful as a sentinel; if he is blind, he may still card wool or pluck down from feathers to stuff mattresses; if he has lost his hands, he can still serve some purpose. If he has but one sound limb remaining, he gives service with that.[312]

---

306. Campanella, 41.

307. Campanella, 43.

308. Campanella, 81.

309. Bellamy, *Looking Backward*, 109. These citizens receive the same income as everyone else though their work expectations are less.

310. Bellamy, 109.

311. Wells, *A Modern Utopia*, 56–57. These citizens receive the minimum wage, making them ineligible to reproduce.

312. Campanella, *The City of the Sun*, 67.

The City of the Sun's exploitation of each person's unique abilities and its focus only on life's necessities means its requirement of four hours of daily work from every citizen—regardless of gender and without exceptions or excuses[313]—comes without the surplus labor found in the utopias of More and Bellamy. Thus the constructive tax imposed (as by Plato) is that of assigned occupations. The "particular inclination of each person is seen in his birth," explains the narrator, "and in the division of labor no one is assigned to things that are destructive to his individuality but rather to things that preserve it."[314] Citizens "are selected for their tasks in infancy according to the constellation that was visible at their birth."[315] In this way, explains the narrator, "each citizen, working according to the inclination of his nature, does his work happily and well because it is natural to him."[316]

A society's control over marriage affords a direct link to its future. Within one generation China's one-child policy, for example, affected its workforce, demand for education, eldercare, and gender balance. The next chapter addresses constructive tax systems devised to regulate marriage (Plato, More, Bacon, and Wells as well as Le Guin's contrasting anarchic society), structured childrearing (Owen, Gilman, Skinner), and eugenic procedures (Campanella, Bellamy, Zamyatin, Huxley). While restrictions on privacy or access to truth affect existing generations, constraints on the family may prove lasting devices of political control.

---

313. Campanella, 67.

314. Campanella, 81.

315. Campanella, 79. "Campanella reinstated astrology, that fantastic pseudo-science of absolutism, as the guiding principle of his *City of the Sun*." Darko Suvin, *Metamorphoses of Science Fiction* (New Haven: Yale University Press, 1979), 100.

316. Campanella, *The City of the Sun*, 79.

CHAPTER FIVE

TAXING THE FAMILY

Marriage, Childrearing, and Eugenics

Part One:
Plato, More, Bacon, Wells, and Le Guin

MARRIAGE RESTRICTIONS

The welfare of society depends upon marriage, the family, and population more than upon anything else. . . . If the state machinery can
be used for any selected purpose, it should first of all be employed
upon these three.

—William Graham Sumner (1840–1910), "Modern Marriage"[1]

Cicero observes that "the first bond of union is between husband and
wife; the next, that between parents and children."[2] Assuming we would
rather choose our own mate(s) (including his or her age, gender, race, and

---

1. William Graham Sumner, "Modern Marriage," in *Essays of William Graham Sumner*
(Hamden, CT: Archon Books, 1969), 277.

2. Cicero, *On Duties* (*De Officiis*), trans. W. Miller (Cambridge, MA: Harvard University
Press, Loeb Classical Library (LCL 30), 1913), bk. 1, §17, 57.

religion) and whether to have and how best to raise our own children, the state's regulation of these choices is a constructive tax—a required sacrifice for the general welfare.[3] In the United States, for example, there were state laws prohibiting interracial marriage until 1967 and same-sex marriage until 2015.[4] Like the law Anatole France cites, which "prohibits the wealthy as well as the poor from sleeping under the bridges, from begging in the streets, and from stealing bread,"[5] the constructive tax embodying these marriage proscriptions was imposed equally on all but collected from citizens denied their chosen mate by law.[6]

"The family," says Aristotle, "is the association established by nature for the supply of men's everyday wants. . . . But when several families are united, and the association aims at something more than the supply of daily needs, the first society to be formed is the village." If Aristotle is right that the state or political community "aims at good in a greater degree than any other, and at the highest good,"[7] its regulation of marriage, procreation, and childrearing must contribute to such a good. When the state formalizes who may have children, it may be promulgating preexisting religious convictions,

---

3. Concerning marriage in utopia, Goodwin says, "even today we still display the same conservative reluctance as most earlier utopians to abandon the institution despite increasingly conclusive evidence (*vide* the divorce rate) that lifelong monogamy is an unattainable ideal, and maybe no ideal at all." Goodwin, "Economic and Social Innovation in Utopia," 80.

4. In Loving v. Virginia, 388 U.S. 1, 12 (1967), the U.S. Supreme Court invalidated bans on interracial unions. In later holding that the states must permit same-sex marriage, the same court said, "The nature of injustice is that we may not always see it in our own times." Obergefell v. Hodges, 576 U.S. ___ (2015). To the extent that required sacrifices regarding marriage and childrearing depend on male-dominated lawmaking, even in utopias, the result is a constructive tax falling most heavily on women. Coverture laws, for example, prescribe that upon marriage, the wife cannot "own property free from the husband's claim or control." *Black's Law Dictionary*, abr. 6th ed., 254.

5. Anatole France, *The Red Lily* (repr., n.p, Dodo Press, n.d.), 65.

6. Of the two types of constructive taxes, conditional taxes such as marriage restrictions affect only those who fit the conditions of their imposition. An income tax collected only from people with an income above a certain threshold is an example of a conditional pecuniary tax. A head tax is an example of an unconditional pecuniary tax, imposed on and collected from all. A constructive tax restricting privacy, like that imposed by the Thought Police in Orwell's *Nineteen Eighty-Four*, is levied on and collected from everyone, including those in the Inner Party.

7. Aristotle, *Politics*, trans. Benjamin Jowett (New York: The Modern Library, 1943), bk. 1, chap. 2, 1252a–b.

attitudes about property rights, or what is believed most advantageous for the general welfare (or the ruling class). It may also be engaging in eugenics—and the imposition of a constructive tax.

This chapter's opening discussion concerns marriage restrictions imposed on citizens in Plato's *Republic*, More's *Utopia*, Bacon's *New Atlantis*, and Wells's *A Modern Utopia* as a device of political control. It also explores the absence of marriage restrictions in Le Guin's *The Dispossessed*. This is followed by an examination of writers emphasizing state-required childrearing practices as a means of reforming society. Included are the views of Owen, Gilman (including her views on eugenics), and Skinner. The chapter concludes with an overview of the eugenic procedures outlined in Campanella's *City of the Sun*, Bellamy's *Looking Backward*, Zamyatin's *We*, and Huxley's *Brave New World*. Providing context for that discussion is a brief introduction to Herbert Spencer's utopian views on eugenics, views that permeated the political discourse of the late nineteenth and early twentieth centuries.

PLATO (C. 428–C. 348 BCE): THE EUGENIC TAX ON BREEDING

"Plato's only radical innovation in the *Republic*," claims Mumford, "is the rational control of human breeding through communal marriage."[8] Far from the all-out eugenics of Huxley's *Brave New World*, however, the *Republic's* program is restricted to a minority of the population, breeding society's best as frequently as permissible. For the guardians in Plato's Republic—the smallest but most essential class in society—Plato's scheme permits "marriage" only under the direction of the state and solely for reproduction. The system of pairing mates by rigged lot drawing and the guardians' state-prescribed education were described in chapters three and four of this book. Rather than guardians selecting their own sexual partners, the elder rulers arrange special hymeneal festivals during which the right to sexual intercourse is awarded.[9] Following each festival, marriage rights are terminated and participants must remain celibate. The system's goal is to permit the most able guardians to reproduce most often (positive eugenics) while removing those

---

8. Mumford, "Utopia, the City and the Machine," 6.

9. In the *Laws*, written after the *Republic*, Plato claims monogamy to be the ideal and does away with the rigged lottery. He does maintain, however, that "a man should 'court the tie' that is for the city's good, not that which most takes his own fancy." Plato, *Laws*, trans. Taylor, bk. 6, 773b.

least promising from the reproductive pool (negative eugenics).[10] Though critical to the state's success, the precise timing of the mating ceremonies is subject to human error. As Socrates explains, the guardians "will at some time beget children when they should not."[11] Ultimately, he predicts, the guardians will choose from among "unworthy" successors, planting the seeds of the state's decay, and faction will enter their ranks.[12]

The guardians' children are raised in common, not knowing the identity of their biological parents. From the time she gives birth, a guardian-mother is forbidden to know which of the babies in the nursery is hers.[13] If a child of "slight ability were born of the guardians," explains Socrates, "he would have to be sent off to the others"[14] (a reference to the working classes). But if a child is born deformed, he continues, they will hide him away in an "unspeakable and unseen place."[15] These required sacrifices, plus those discussed in chapters three and four—cloaked in noble lies and administrative mendacity—embody Plato's system of constructive taxation.[16]

THOMAS MORE (1478–1535): "CONFINEMENT TO A SINGLE PARTNER"

With regard to marriage, More's narrator Hythloday explains, the Utopians had "extra reason . . . to be careful, because in that part of the world they

---

10. Plato, *Republic*, bk. 5, 459d.

11. Plato, *Republic*, trans. Bloom, bk. 8, 546b. The "guardians from ignorance . . . [will] cause grooms to live with brides out of season" (Plato, trans. Bloom, 546d). The text provides Plato's enigmatic description of the mathematical principles for calculating the nuptial number (Plato, trans. Bloom, 546b–c), about which Bloom says it is "one of darkest passages in Plato's works. . . . Its interpretation has been a subject of dispute since antiquity." Bloom, Notes to Plato, *Republic*, trans. Bloom, bk. 8, note 5, 467. See also Popper, *The Open Society and Its Enemies*, 78.

12. Plato, *Republic*, trans. Bloom, bk. 8, 546a–d.

13. Plato, trans. Bloom, bk. 5, 460c–d.

14. Plato, trans. Bloom, bk. 4, 423c.

15. Plato, trans. Bloom, bk. 5, 460c.

16. D. Galton (not Francis) confirms the scientific legitimacy of Plato's plan: "Different choices of partners at serial marriage festivals amongst a selected elite of the population would be expected to lead to an optimal spread of abilities for their offspring." David J. Galton, "Greek Theories on Eugenics," *Journal of Medical Ethics* 24, no. 4 (August 1988): 263–67, 266.

are the only people who practice monogamy, and because their marriages are seldom terminated except by death."[17] "Clandestine premarital intercourse, if discovered and proved," results in the couple's permanent loss of eligibility to marry anyone (unless pardoned by the governor).[18] The reason for this harsh penalty, says Hythloday, is their belief that few people would trouble with marriage and its "confinement to a single partner and all the petty annoyances that married life involves" unless they were barred from alternative sexual outlets.[19] Three conditions that Utopus, the ancient founder of Utopia, had enacted signal this emphasis on the longevity of marriage to a single partner—a sacrifice required for the general welfare. The first is a minimum age requirement: for women eighteen and for men twenty-two. The second, reminiscent of Plato's stipulation in the *Laws*, is their tradition of permitting the prospective couple to view each other naked in the presence of a chaperon.[20] Though Bacon criticizes this practice as insensitive,[21] it serves as a precaution, says More's narrator, against "a deformity [that] may lurk under clothing, serious enough to alienate a man's mind from his wife when his body can no longer lawfully be separated from her."[22] The third condition imposes deterrents to infidelity "and comparable crimes against society" when such acts, says Baker-Smith, seem to be "a public declaration of [the Utopian's] inner slavery to passion and unreason."[23] Brothels are outlawed as are wine bars, ale houses, and other secret meeting places (chapter two describes such sacrifices of privacy). When such deterrents prove insufficient and the constructive tax of confinement to a single partner is evaded, violators are punished with the "strictest form of slavery."[24]

---

17. More, *Utopia*, bk. 2, 80. Maine observes the irony that while many ancient societies evolved from polygamy to monogamy to facilitate the "liberty of divorce," that the "license of divorce" was subsequently banned by Christian morality. Henry Sumner Maine, *Lectures on the Early History of Institutions* (New York: Henry Holt and Company, 1888), 60.

18. More, *Utopia*, bk. 2, 79.

19. More, bk. 2, 79.

20. More, bk. 2, 79–80. Plato suggests that the prospective couple, through ceremonial dances, should take "the opportunity . . . of seeing and being seen in undress." *Laws*, trans. Taylor, bk. 6, 772a.

21. Bacon's narrator says, "This they dislike; for they think it a scorn to give a refusal after so familiar knowledge." Bacon, *New Atlantis*, 154.

22. More, *Utopia*, bk. 2, 80.

23. Baker-Smith, *More's Utopia*, 164.

24. More, *Utopia*, bk. 2, 80.

FRANCIS BACON (1561–1626):
MARRIAGE EXCEPT FOR THE WISE

All extraordinary men are not good men: that seems to be a lottery, dependent on circumstances apparently the most trivial.

—William Godwin (1756–1836), *Caleb Williams*[25]

Though some of what goes on in Bensalem in Bacon's *New Atlantis* is secretive (as described in chapter three), what is not secret is often left to the imagination. "We learn virtually nothing," says Bruce, of their "courts, nothing of their warehouses, markets, or executions."[26] Albanese adds, "the *New Atlantis* never elucidates its civil hierarchy, never gives articulation to its structure of power."[27] Marriage, however, is one aspect of civil life about which we are informed. Marriage is encouraged for the production of children. A father with at least thirty (legitimate) descendants above the age of three is distinguished with the title "Tirsan" and described as a *"well-beloved friend and creditor"* of the king who is "debtor to no man, but for the propagation of his subjects."[28] In recognition of the Tirsan's distinction the state honors him with a ceremony, the "Feast of the Family," giving him "many privileges, exemptions, and points of honor" as well as revenue.[29] At the feast a scroll from the king is read listing the benefits for the Tirsan that are, it is stipulated, different for each family, according to its "number and dignity."[30] The scroll, Wortham explains, "simultaneously rewards and regulates generation, since breeding, it is suggested, is mainly a means to achieve financial security."[31] In addition, the governor of the city validates the proclamations of the Tirsan with respect to his extended

---

25. Godwin, *Caleb Williams*, 320.

26. Susan Bruce, ed., *Three Early Modern Utopias* (Oxford: Oxford University Press, 1999), xxxii.

27. Denise Albanese, "The New Atlantis and the Uses of Utopia," ELH 57, no. 3 (Autumn 1990): 503–28, 515.

28. Bacon, *New Atlantis*, 149 (italics in original).

29. Bacon, 149.

30. Bacon, 149.

31. Simon Wortham, "Censorship and the Institution of Knowledge," in *Francis Bacon's New Atlantis*, ed. Bronwen Price (New York: Manchester University Press, 2002), 195.

family and in that sense gives them the force of law.[32] For this reason, Aughterson observes, Bacon "inverts the relationship between family and national political authority."[33]

LAWS TOUCHING MARRIAGE

Joabin, a spokesman, informs the visiting sailors that in Bensalem there are "many wise and excellent laws touching marriage."[34] Marriage is regulated by certain prohibitions and, to some undetermined extent, by an odd inheritance tax. Bacon's explanation of this tax is specific as to its rate and the conditions for its imposition, but not as to its ultimate justification. Though this tax (or penalty) is not connected to a plan to equalize estates, as found (for example) in Harrington's *Oceana*, it is still likely related to promoting an orderly society. It is an incentive encouraging couples to obtain their parents' prior approval for marriage. Heirs who fail to obtain consent or marry against their parents' wishes are subject to the forfeiture of two-thirds of the bequest they would otherwise have received.[35]

Commentators are at odds in explaining the role of this rather arbitrary-sounding tax. Faulkner, for example, plays down its importance, calling it "minor."[36] Hale says of the tax that it "would not likely serve as a strong deterrent."[37] Bacon implies a different explanation in his essay "Of Love," in

---

32. Bacon, *New Atlantis*, 148.

33. Kate Aughterson, "'Strange Things So Probably Told': Gender, Sexual Difference and Knowledge in Bacon's *New Atlantis*," in *Francis Bacon's New Atlantis*, ed. Bronwen Price (New York: Manchester University Press, 2002), 165.

34. Bacon, *New Atlantis*, 153.

35. Bacon, 153–54. Bacon's proposal is reminiscent of ancient Roman law that Montesquieu says, punished violations of marriage laws by limiting an inheritance by up to one-tenth. Montesquieu, *The Spirit of Laws*, bk. 23, chap. 21, 195. Some commentators term it a penalty rather than a tax, no doubt because Bacon says "they mulct it in the inheritors," where *mulct* generally refers to a penalty. However, it is stipulated that "marriage without consent of parents they do not make void." Bacon, *New Atlantis*, 153–54. On the question, when is it appropriate to prohibit an action rather than taxing it, D. Wells answers: "To impose taxes upon an evil in any degree short of its prohibition is in effect to recognize and license this evil." D. A. Wells, *The Theory and Practice of Taxation*, 254.

36. Faulkner, *Francis Bacon and the Project of Progress*, 241.

37. Hale, *Francis Bacon's New Atlantis in the Foundation of Modern Political Thought*, 90.

which he approvingly cites the proposition, "it is impossible to love and to be wise," and observes, "it is a strange thing to note the excess of this passion, and how it braves the nature and value of things."[38] This suggests trepidation about marrying for the wrong reason—purely for love—and accords with his general mistrust of human judgment. Alluding to the Idols of the Tribe, he warns, "Numberless . . . are the ways, and sometimes imperceptible, in which the affections color and infect the understanding."[39] As a precaution Bacon recommends seeking counsel for significant decisions.[40] In his essay "Of Counsel," for example, he warns that if decisions "be not tossed upon the arguments of counsel, they will be tossed upon the waves of fortune."[41]

Other laws "touching marriage" include prohibitions against polygamy as well as against prostitutes. Societies that permit brothels, says Joabin, are antagonistic to marriage; prostitutes are seen as a "tax" on marriage itself, he explains, since they are believed to reduce the incentive to marry and, as in More's Utopia, encourage its betrayal.[42] These prohibitions are constructive taxes in the sense I have described—required sacrifices for the general welfare.

EUGENIC PARADOX OF MARRIAGE

In his essay "Of Marriage and Single Life," Bacon declares that "the best works, and of greatest merit for the public, have proceeded from the unmarried or childless men; which both in affection and means have married and endowed the public."[43] This supports Sessions's assumption that the Fathers (scientists) of Salomon's House are celibate and operating in a "sexless world that generates not children but inventions."[44] Given Bacon's mandate for unlocking nature's secrets, however, it seems curious that he would have

---

38. Francis Bacon, "Of Love," in *The Essays or Counsels Civil and Moral*, ed. Brian Vickers (Oxford: Oxford University Press, 1999), 22, 23.

39. Bacon, *The New Organon*, aphorism 49, 57–58.

40. At the Festival of the Family, the Tirsan mediates problems between family members, including direction "given touching marriage." In addition to marriage counseling, this presumably includes advice to prospective spouses. Bacon, *New Atlantis*, 148.

41. Francis Bacon, "Of Counsel," in *The Essays or Counsels Civil and Moral*, ed. Brian Vickers (Oxford: Oxford University Press, 1999), 47.

42. Bacon, *New Atlantis*, 153.

43. Francis Bacon, "Of Marriage and Single Life," in *The Essays or Counsels Civil and Moral*, ed. Brian Vickers (Oxford: Oxford University Press, 1999), 16.

44. W. A. Sessions, *Francis Bacon Revisited* (New York: Twayne Publishers, 1996), 158.

paid no heed to Plato's call for eugenic breeding for the guardians of his state—the scientists—to improve and replenish their order for future generations.[45] White observes that Bacon, "deliberately, does not tell us very much about what it takes to be a member of Salomon's House."[46] In the end, perhaps the scientists' solution to the eugenic paradox of marriage—whether "the offspring of the celibate scientists"[47] is limited to scientific discoveries by Fathers who have "married and endowed the public"[48] or includes (as in the Republic) breeding society's best—is one of the secrets they choose not to share.

H. G. WELLS (1866–1946): MOTHERHOOD AS A SERVICE TO THE STATE

But here's what: unnecessary people should never be born. First remake the world so they won't be unnecessary, then give birth to them.

—Fyodor Dostoevsky (1821–1881), *Devils*[49]

In *A Modern Utopia*, the World State's interest in marriage is exclusively with respect to the future of society, and thus with its children. Accordingly, it "intervenes between the sexes only because of the coming generation."[50] Like Bacon's Bensalem, the state boasts "wise marriage laws."[51] However, marriage is not restricted to couples but may include polygamous or, as in Plato's Republic, sequential mates. The "modern Utopia," says Wells's narrator, "should not refuse a grouped marriage to three or more freely consenting persons."[52] There is no restriction against interracial marriage;

---

45. While the scientists experiment on people, these experiments do not aim at altering the genetic stock. In the case of animals, however, Bacon's narrator says, "We find means to make commixtures and copulations of different kinds; which have produced many new kinds." Bacon, *New Atlantis*, 158–59.

46. White, *Peace Among the Willows*, 235.

47. Sessions, *Francis Bacon Revisited*, 158.

48. Bacon, "Of Marriage and Single Life," 16.

49. Dostoevsky, *Devils*, 665.

50. Wells, *A Modern Utopia*, 78.

51. Wells, 62; Bacon, *New Atlantis*, 153.

52. Wells, *A Modern Utopia*, 83.

same-sex marriage is not addressed but would depend on the question of children. A modern Utopia, says Wells, "is a Utopia as wide as Christian charity, and white and black, brown, red and yellow, all tints of skin, all types of body and character, will be there . . . [though functioning under] an entirely different set of traditions, ideals, ideas, and purposes."[53] As in Bacon's *New Atlantis*, the marriage license imposes a waiting period allowing either party to withdraw.[54]

From the perspective of the state and its view of the general welfare, there is little reason for a couple to marry if they do not intend to have children. For this reason, marriages that fail to produce a child lapse, though the spouses may renew their vows.[55] The state sees children as its ultimate responsibility and pays for each legitimate child's nutrition, education, and health care. "When a child comes in, the future of the species comes in; and the state comes in as the guardian of interests wider than the individual's."[56]

The general welfare requires that future generations benefit, rather than suffer, from the actions and policies of past generations. For this reason, though citizens may choose "any sort of union" they desire, they may not produce illegitimate offspring. The penalty for begetting unauthorized children is "to make the parents chargeable with every duty, with maintenance, education, and so forth, that in the normal course of things would fall to the State."[57] This is because "Utopia will hold that sound childbearing and rearing is a service done, not to a particular man," says Wells's narrator, "but to the whole community."[58]

MARRIAGE LICENSE

Obtaining a marriage license is a process imposing a constructive tax on both (or all) parties. It is also the first phase of the modern Utopia's eugenics program, for without the license reproduction is illegal. The marriage license

---

53. Wells, 15.

54. Wells, 77; Bacon, *New Atlantis*, 153.

55. Wells, *A Modern Utopia*, 78. The same rule applies to the ruling order called samurai who Wells compares to Plato's guardians (Wells, 107, 115). Women samurai are permitted to marry men who are "outside the Rule" but not vice versa (Wells, 116).

56. Wells, 77.

57. Wells, 77.

58. Wells, 76.

policy is an implementation of Wells's utopian vision for a society where "every human being shall live in a state of reasonable physical and mental comfort, without the reproduction of inferior types."[59] As an enhancement to the schemes of More and Bacon to foreclose premarital deceptions, each partner in a modern Utopia receives a copy of the official record of the intended spouse. This dossier (as described in chapter two) includes "previous marriages, legally important diseases, offspring, [and] . . . criminal convictions."[60] In addition, the "contracting parties must be in health and condition, free from specific transmissible taints."[61] They must also be "sufficiently intelligent and energetic to have acquired a minimum education." Finally, "The man at least must be in receipt of a net income above the minimum wage"[62]—"holding a position of solvency and independence in the world."[63] These provisions preclude marriage, and so reproduction, by society's "congenital invalids, its idiots and madmen, its drunkards and men of vicious mind, its cruel and furtive souls, its stupid people, too stupid to be of use to the community, its lumpish, unteachable and unimaginative people,"[64] as well as any others lacking the "minimum of physical development."[65] Like marriage-related taxes noted earlier, this constructive tax—though levied equally on all—is collected from those the state deems unworthy to reproduce.[66]

In a modern Utopia the state supports children, and "motherhood is a service to the State and a legitimate claim to a living." Accordingly, as in Bellamy's *Looking Backward*, a woman "who is, or is becoming, a mother, is . . . entitled to . . . support, to freedom, and to respect and dignity."[67] In

---

59. Wells, 56.

60. Wells, 66.

61. Wells, 77. In Gilman's utopian novel, *Moving the Mountain*, "it was held a crime to poison another human being with syphilis," and a marriage license required a "clean bill of health." Charlotte Perkins Gilman, *Moving the Mountain* (1911) (repr., n.p, n.d.), chap. 5, 34, 36.

62. Wells, *A Modern Utopia*, 77.

63. Wells, 74.

64. Wells, 56.

65. Wells, 74.

66. Holland notes that Wells's samurai oversee and enforce the state's eugenics policy. Owen Holland, "Spectatorship and Entanglement in Thoreau, Hawthorne, Morris, and Wells," *Utopian Studies* 27, no. 1 (2016): 28–52, 44.

67. Wells, *A Modern Utopia*, 75, 79. Bellamy, *Looking Backward*, 188.

the case of illegitimate children, however, the narrator advises the offender that she is under a debt to the state

> that has in the last resort your liberty as a security, and, more-over, if this thing happens a second time, or if it is a disease or imbecility you have multiplied, we will take an absolutely effectual guarantee that neither you nor your partner offend again in this matter.[68]

The "absolutely effectual guarantee" is a reference to the constructive tax of forced sterilization. Wells explains, in a discussion of Francis Galton's views on eugenics, "It is in the sterilization of failures, and not in the selection of successes for breeding, that the possibility of an improvement for the human stock lies."[69]

---

68. Wells, *A Modern Utopia*, 74.

69. H. G. Wells, "Discussion," in Francis Galton, "Eugenics: Its Definition, Scope, and Aims," *The American Journal of Sociology* 10, no. 1 (July 1904): 1–25, 11. Bloomfield observes, Wells was "the first Utopian familiar with Darwin and Galton. He laid down that a couple not licensed—because not eugenically fully qualified—to produce children would be liable to sterilization after the birth of a *second* defective child." Paul Bloomfield, "The Eugenics of the Utopians: The Utopia of the Eugenists," *The Eugenics Review* 40 (21 new series), (April 1948–January 1949): 191–98, 193 (italics in original). Hofstadter reports, "The ideas of the [eugenic] movement began to receive practical application [in the U.S.] in 1907, when Indiana became the first state to adopt a sterilization law; by 1915 twelve states had passed similar measures." Richard Hofstadter, *Social Darwinism in American Thought*, rev. ed. (Boston: Beacon Press, 1944), 162. The U.S. Supreme Court, in a 1927 case Buck v. Bell (274 U.S. 200), ruled that a Virginia law permitting the forced sterilization of an institutionalized "imbecile" was constitutional. As the court notes, "the health of the patient and the welfare of society may be promoted in certain cases by the sterilization of mental defectives." The court's opinion, written by Oliver Wendell Holmes Jr., states, "We have seen more than once that the public welfare may call upon the best citizens for their lives. It would be strange if it could not call upon those who already sap the strength of the State for these lesser sacrifices." It is in the same opinion that Holmes proclaims, "three generations of imbeciles are enough." Thus, we glimpse Holmes's view of a "civilized society" for which he says, "taxes are what we pay." Compania General De Tabacos De Filipinas v. Collector of Internal Revenue, 275 U.S. 87, 100 (1927). Stern reports that by 1932, twenty-seven states had legalized forced sterilization and that by the mid-1970s roughly 60,000 such procedures had been carried out in the United States. In addition, the constructive tax of forced sterilization was collected primarily from "the foreign born, the working class, and young women

MARGINALIZED CITIZENS

Wells proposes another form of constructive taxation for those at the margins of society—the dull and the base.[70] While the state will take measures (described in chapter four) to remediate any of these individuals that it can, the ones who prove themselves incurable or incorrigible face exile to an island community.[71] The primary goal of this isolation is eugenic. "So soon as there can be no doubt of the disease or baseness of the individual," the narrator explains, "so soon as the insanity or other disease is assured, or the crime repeated a third time . . . so soon must he or she pass out of the common ways of men."[72] Separate islands are assigned for each form of misfit, outcast, or scofflaw—including, for example, "the Island of Incurable Cheats." Though not arranged in descending circles as in Dante's *Inferno*, each island's unfortunates are left to deal only with their own kind (and their own gender)—"a company of kindred souls."[73] The dual goal of this series of islands is to segregate, but not to punish, the inhabitants, and so to prevent them from reproducing. "You must seclude," says Wells's narrator, "but why should you torment?"[74] This is a constructive tax and not a penalty because those so secluded are not blamed for their unproductive conduct: "Crime and bad lives are the measure of a State's failure, all crime in the end is the crime of the community."[75]

Progress, claims the narrator, "depends essentially on competitive selection"[76]—"there must be a competition in life of some sort to determine who are to be pushed to the edge, and who are to prevail and multiply,"[77]—and

---

deemed 'unfit.' " Alexandra Minna Stern, "STERILIZED in the Name of Public Health: Race, Immigration, and Reproductive Control in Modern California," *American Journal of Public Health* 95, 7 (2005):1128–38, 1128, 1132, 1136. Published online: October 10, 2011, http://doi.org/10.2105/AJPH.2004.041608.

70. Wells, *A Modern Utopia*, 105.

71. Wells, 59.

72. Wells, 58.

73. Wells, 59.

74. Wells, 60.

75. Wells, 59. The same sentiment appears in Bellamy, *Equality*, chap. 37, 363.

76. Wells, *A Modern Utopia*, 73.

77. Wells, 56–57.

this requires "a kind of social surgery."[78] On the continuum of "the endless variety of men" and "their endless gradation of quality," Wells stipulates, "the people of exceptional quality must be ascendant. The better sort of people . . . must have the fullest freedom of public service, and the fullest opportunity of parentage."[79]

LE GUIN (1929–2018): ANARCHISM AND THE TAX-FREE FAMILY IN *THE DISPOSSESSED*

Man has not evolved as an ethical or moral animal. He has evolved to the point at which he has constructed an ethical or moral culture.

—B. F. Skinner (1904–1990), *Beyond Freedom and Dignity*[80]

It is not unusual for an anarchist's spirit to inform her view of marriage. Emma Goldman, for example, writes that "marriage and love have nothing in common . . . [they are] antagonistic to each other."[81] Though twice married, Godwin asserted, "it is absurd to expect the inclinations and wishes of two human beings to coincide, through any long period of time. . . . In almost every instance they find themselves deceived."[82] In Ursula K. Le Guin's *The*

---

78. Wells, 58. Parrinder asserts, "The fictive world of *A Modern Utopia* is one in which human 'culture' has been changed at will, without in the least altering human 'nature.'" Patrick Parrinder, "Utopia and Meta-Utopia in H. G. Wells," *Utopian Studies* 1 (1987): 79–97, 86. However, the purpose of Wells's eugenic policy is, presumably, to alter human nature by ridding it of "its cruel and furtive souls, its stupid people . . . its lumpish, unteachable and unimaginative people," to the extent these traits are genetically transmitted. In the modern Utopia this process has been underway for "several hundred years." Wells, *A Modern Utopia*, 102.

79. Wells, 56.

80. Skinner, *Beyond Freedom and Dignity*, 175.

81. Emma Goldman, *Anarchism and Other Essays* (New York: Dover Publications, Inc., 1969), 227.

82. Godwin, *Enquiry Concerning Political Justice*, 3rd ed., 761–62. His first wife, Mary Wollstonecraft, saw marriage as a salvageable institution that was currently impaired by the educational and economic inequality of women. "If marriage be the cement of society, mankind should all be educated after the same model, or the intercourse of the sexes will never deserve the name of fellowship, nor will women ever fulfil the peculiar duties of their sex, till they become enlightened citizens, till they become free, by being enabled to earn their own subsistence, independent of men." Mary Wollstonecraft, *Vindication*

Dispossessed, the extent to which there is a government on Anarres—where anarchist exiles from Urras founded a colony seven generations earlier—is negligible. It is a cooperative anarchy adhering to principles established by its inspirational leader, Odo, modified by tradition and public opinion. The Odonians subscribe to their leader's organic and decentralized view of society. Neither laws nor personal property exist and what administration is needed, we are told, is that of production rather than of people.[83]

ANARCHY—RESPONSIBILITY AS FREEDOM

Confronting the question of the planet's organizational structure, Shevek, a physicist and Le Guin's protagonist, asks his friends, rhetorically: "Are we kept here by force? What force—what laws, governments, police? None."[84] What keeps the people of Anarres faithful to their planet, he continues, is their "common nature to be Odonians, responsible to one another. And that responsibility is our freedom."[85] Each person, explains Shevek's physics supervisor Sabul, "should know not only his cellular function but his organic function—what his optimum role in the social organism is."[86] Critical to Odonian "anarchist communism," argues Sabia, is the "interdependence of individual and society in a constantly changing natural and human environment."[87] Rogers notes, "Le Guin provides the reader with a working model for utopia as evolution—not a place, but a process of becoming."[88]

---

of the Rights of Woman (repr., n.p., n.d.), chap. 12, 175. Wollstonecraft died in the year of their marriage, 1797, following the birth of their daughter Mary Shelley. Godwin's second wife was his widowed neighbor, Mary Jane Clairmont.

83. Le Guin, *The Dispossessed*, 67.

84. Le Guin, 39–40.

85. Le Guin, 40. *The Dispossessed* contrasts two worlds, neither of which its protagonist Shevek views as utopian.

86. Le Guin, 231. The Odonians' "primary social problem," notes Moylan, "is the danger of centralization of power in an élite group and the reduction of the ideas of the revolution into a dogmatic ideology." Tom Moylan, *Demand the Impossible: Science Fiction and the Utopian Imagination*, ed. Raffaella Baccolini (Oxford: Peter Lang, 2014), 95.

87. Dan Sabia, "Individual and Community in Le Guin's *The Dispossessed*," in *The New Utopian Politics of Ursula K. Le Guin's The Dispossessed*, ed. Laurence Davis and Peter Stillman, 111–28 (Lanham, MD: Lexington Books, 2005), 113.

88. Jennifer Rogers, "Fulfillment as a Function of Time, or the Ambiguous Process of Utopia," in *The New Utopian Politics of Ursula K. Le Guin's The Dispossessed*, ed. Laurence Davis and Peter Stillman, 181–94 (Lanham, MD: Lexington Books, 2005), 181.

In his speech to the working classes of Urras (the planet from which the Odonians were exiled), Shevek says,

> We have no law but the single principle of mutual aid between individuals. We have no government but the single principle of free association. We have no states, no nations, no presidents, no premiers, no chiefs, no generals, no bosses, no bankers, no landlords, no wages, no charity, no police, no soldiers, no wars. . . . We are sharers, not owners.[89]

PARTNERSHIPS

Applied to sexual relations, this kind of interdependence means, "No law, no limit, no penalty, no punishment, no disapproval applied to any sexual practice of any kind."[90] This sexual latitude does not extend to rape, however, which vengeful neighbors spontaneously punish unless the rapist obtains asylum in a "therapy center."[91] In place of traditional marriage (on Earth or Urras), the narrator discloses, an Odonian undertakes "partnership" (monogamy), a "voluntarily constituted federation,"[92] as she might undertake a "joint enterprise in production."[93] "So long as it worked, it worked, and if it didn't work it stopped being"[94]—with or without children. Morris's *News from Nowhere* reflects a comparable conjugal convention.[95]

Partnership, an application of Odonian social theory, is a shared convention rather than an institution. Its only sanction, explains the narrator, is "private conscience."[96] "The validity of the promise, even promise of indefinite

---

89. Le Guin, *The Dispossessed*, 261–62.

90. Le Guin, 215.

91. Le Guin, 215.

92. Le Guin, 214.

93. Le Guin, 214.

94. Le Guin, 214.

95. Marriage in *News from Nowhere* is a personal commitment with no state involvement because there is no state. Hammond explains that while marriages are sometimes dissolved by either party, divorce is no longer necessary. Legal divorce proceedings were only required to establish and enforce property rights that have since been abolished. Morris, *News from Nowhere*, 90–93.

96. Le Guin, *The Dispossessed*, 214.

term, was deep in the grain of Odo's thinking." A promise, she advised, "is a direction taken, a self-limitation of choice. . . . So Odo came to see the promise, the pledge, the ideas of fidelity, as essential in the complexity of freedom."[97] On the other hand, the narrator explains,

> those who undertook to form and keep a partnership, whether homosexual or heterosexual, met with problems unknown to those content with sex wherever they found it. They must face not only jealousy and possessiveness and other diseases of passion for which monogamous union provides such a fine medium of growth, but also the external pressures of social organization.[98]

These external pressures meant that a couple who undertook partnership was reconciled to potential separation at any time by "the exigencies of labor distribution."[99] "To survive, to make a go of life," declares the narrator, "an Anarresti knew he had to be ready to go where he was needed and do the work that needed doing."[100] ("Labor drafts" as required work are discussed in chapter seven.)

"What is special about belonging to their community that would justify individual sacrifices?" asks Tunick.[101] In one sense all cooperative actions in this anarchist society are required sacrifices for the general welfare; in another sense they are all free.[102] Odonians chastise each other for lapses into either "egoizing" or altruism.[103] "Between altruism and self-interest," notes Sabia, "lies a proper or enlightened sense of self-interest."[104] The tension of their

---

97. Le Guin, 214.

98. Le Guin, 215.

99. Le Guin, 215.

100. Le Guin, 215.

101. Mark Tunick, "The Need for Walls: Privacy, Community, and Freedom in *The Dispossessed*," in *The New Utopian Politics of Ursula K. Le Guin's The Dispossessed*, ed. Laurence Davis and Peter Stillman, 129–47 (Lanham, MD: Lexington Books, 2005), 132.

102. Aggravating this tension, notes Sargent, their society "has allowed freedom to be eroded, in part by equality." Sargent, "Authority and Utopia: Utopianism in Political Thought," 573.

103. Le Guin, *The Dispossessed*, 26, 232.

104. Sabia, "Individual and Community in Le Guin's *The Dispossessed*," 120.

moral motivation and their ambiguous anarchy—neither altruist nor egoist—is grounded in a self-imposed commitment to Odo's teaching on the organic collaboration between individual and society. Though the principles of "partnership" place the group's survival above the couple's, these "marriage" restrictions are unenforceable and so fail to reach the prominence of a constructive tax.

Part Two:
Owen and Gilman

ROBERT OWEN (1771–1858):
THE TAX ON CHILDREARING

The pride of philosophy has taught us to treat man as an individual. He is no such thing. He holds necessarily, indispensably, to his species.

—William Godwin (1756–1836), *Caleb Williams*[105]

Assessment of character is a prelude to predicting conduct. Convinced of the importance of this fact, Mill declares, "given the motives which are present to an individual's mind, and given likewise the character and disposition of the individual, the manner in which he will act might be unerringly inferred."[106] In law the significance of character has long received recognition, as have its limitations.[107] Psychological research has illuminated the reasons

---

105. Godwin, *Caleb Williams*, 313.

106. John Stuart Mill, *A System of Logic Ratiocinative and Inductive* (Honolulu, HI: University Press of the Pacific, 2002), bk. 6, chap. 2, §2, 547.

107. "In evidence law, 'character' means the type of person someone is—honest, dishonest, generous, selfish, friendly, nasty, careless, cautious, hot-headed, or calm. A basic rule (with some exceptions) is that evidence of a person's character may not be introduced to support an inference that the person acted on a specific occasion in conformity with that character." Arthur Best, *Evidence* (Boston: Little, Brown, 1994), 29.

for certain of these limitations in an asymmetry between people's views of their own characters and their views of character in others.[108]

At a time when the nature–nurture controversy was expected to yield to an unequivocal solution, Owen proclaimed that character is formed in early childhood, not as a result of a person's own efforts but through exposure to external factors of training and education. In support of what he calls his "discovery," Owen offers the following proclamation: " 'That the character is formed *for* and not *by* the individual,' is a truth to which every fact connected with man's history bears testimony."[109] Based on this seminal conviction, he developed a plan to reform society and spent his life refining and promoting his utopian program.

Employing the monetary meaning of taxes, Owen was a proponent of radical tax reform. "Law and taxation," he says, "as these are now necessarily administered, are evils of the greatest magnitude."[110] Misconduct, misfortune, and military exploits are three of the greatest costs consuming taxes. Taxes, he believes (like Godwin), are a curse on society, because they perpetuate the problems they were designed to remediate. His plan to minimize pecuniary taxes involves educational reform aimed at abolishing the societal problems that traditionally deplete tax resources (including crime, ignorance, poverty, unemployment, and war). His reform requires compulsory standardized education for all children from an early age using a new psychological model for character formation. "Among the protagonists for popular education in the early part of the [nineteenth] century," Boyd observes, Owen "was the

---

108. Attribution theory asserts that "we attribute others' behavior largely to personality factors and our own behavior largely to situational factors to which we respond." Robyn M. Dawes, *Rational Choice in an Uncertain World* (New York: Harcourt Brace Jovanovich, 1988), 29.

109. Robert Owen, *A New View of Society and Other Writings* (New York: Penguin Classics, 1991), 305. While Owen speaks of "his discovery," Godwin had argued (in 1798) that "the characters of men are determined in all their most essential circumstances by education," by which he meant "every incident that produces an idea in the mind, and can give birth to a train of reflections." Godwin, *Enquiry Concerning Political Justice*, 3rd ed., bk. 1, chap. 4, 111. Claeys refers to Godwin as Owen's mentor who he met with on numerous occasions. Gregory Claeys, *Citizens and Saints: Politics and Anti-Politics in Early British Socialism* (Cambridge: Cambridge University Press, 1989), 122.

110. Owen, *A New View of Society and Other Writings*, 201.

most outstanding figure."[111] To this Morton adds, Owen "played a decisive part in the beginnings of almost every valuable development of the age."[112]

OWEN AND CHARACTER FORMATION

Owen was an influential industrialist born in North Wales. His life mission to reform society grew out of insights he gained during the thirty years he spent managing cotton mills where he saw, on a limited scale, the effects and causes of human friction. The distinctiveness of his discovery was the purported simplicity of his solution and his claim to have experimentally verified its efficacy. The false premise and prevailing view against which he tirelessly argues is this proposition: "each individual man forms his own character, and . . . therefore he is accountable for all his sentiments and habits, and consequently merits reward for some and punishment for others."[113] This is the conception that, with respect to character, free will is omnipotent. This "evil principle," Owen explains, "will ever produce, the same unwelcome harvest of evil passions—hatred, revenge, and all uncharitableness, and the innumerable crimes and miseries to which they have given birth."[114] On the contrary, he insists, "*Man . . . never did, nor is it possible he ever can, form his own character*."[115] It was Owen's conviction that costly and needless government institutions follow in the wake of the erroneous belief in self-caused character. "It fills prisons, and aids to fill lunatic asylums; stands in the way, often, of great general public improvements; and increases the expenses of society, to protect itself."[116] "*But while man remains individualized*," he warns, taxes "*must continue*" and "must unavoidably still increase in magnitude of evil."[117] Based on his initial experience at Manchester, England, and its subsequent confirmation at New Lanark, Scotland, Owen believed he had uncovered the principles

---

111. William Boyd, *The History of Western Education*, 8th ed. (New York: Barnes Noble, 1961), 369.

112. A. L. Morton, *The English Utopia* (London: Lawrence and Wishart, 1952; repr., Berlin: Seven Seas Books, 1968), 170. (Page references are to reprint.)

113. Owen, *A New View of Society and Other Writings*, 43.

114. Owen, 305.

115. Owen, 43 (italics in original).

116. Robert Owen, *The Revolution in the Mind and Practice of the Human Race* (London: Effingham Wilson, Publisher, 1849; Nabu Public Domain Reprints), 112. (Page references same as original.)

117. Owen, *A New View of Society and Other Writings*, 201 (italics in original).

of character formation and tested these principles in practice. The result, he claims, is that it is possible to create "any general human character, good, bad, or indifferent,"[118] in any population—but especially in children[119]—"yet preserving always the organic peculiarities of each individual."[120] In asserting this, Claeys specifies, "Owen never implied that any character could be 'given' to every individual, only that groups could be educated to share certain characteristics in common."[121] It was to the formation of such communities of like-minded workers that Owen applied his efforts. When he assumed the management of the mill at New Lanark, he announced,

> I had now to commence . . . the great experiment which was to prove to me, by practice, the truth or error of the principles . . . from which all great and permanent good practice must proceed—to commence the most important experiment for the happiness of the human race that had yet been instituted at any time in any part of the world.[122]

To the end of spreading his reform, Owen spoke and wrote passionately, says Heilbroner, "in endless tracts endlessly the same."[123]

---

118. Owen, *The Revolution in the Mind*, 22.

119. Owen, *A New View of Society and Other Writings*, 19.

120. Owen, *The Revolution in the Mind*, 22.

121. Gregory Claeys, Introduction to *A New View of Society and Other Writings,* by Robert Owen (New York: Penguin Classics, 1991), xxiv.

122. Robert Owen, *The Life of Robert Owen Written by Himself* (New York: Augustus M. Kelley Publishers 1967), 59–60.

123. Robert L. Heilbroner, *The Worldly Philosophers*, 3rd ed. (New York: Simon and Schuster, 1953), 106. Owen lobbied British government officials in unstinting pursuit of his vision and established an experimental community in the United States near the southern tip of Indiana in New Harmony. The Owenite community of about one thousand members inhabited the former Harmony Society village, founded by George Rapp's followers. Though Owen's New Harmony only lasted from 1825–1827, its notoriety continued to attract influential visitors. During that time, according to Claeys, "the community was the most important cultural outpost on the American frontier." Claeys, Introduction to *A New View of Society and Other Writings,* by Robert Owen, xvi. Among its notable inhabitants was Owen's youngest son, Richard Dale Owen, who trained as a scientist at the University of Strathclyde in Glasgow and served as the first president of Purdue University. The town now features a museum, the Atheneum, commemorating its early utopian heritage. See the University of Southern Indiana website: http://www.usi.edu/hnh.

REDIRECTING SOCIETY

The "evil principle" Owen identifies—that "each individual man forms his own character,"[124]—confounds our will's influence on our character with our character's influence on our will. According to Owen's unnamed opponents, "*infants, children, and men, are agents governed by a will formed by themselves and fashioned after their own choice.*"[125] This is the view Skinner later called *autonomous man*—"an initiating, creative agent"[126] whose behavior is uncaused by external forces.[127] Owen's view implies that character is more fundamental than will, which merely carries out the character's propensities. Believing our will forms our character, however, would mean that our character traits—our dispositions and inclinations, including ambition, adaptability, courage, honesty, humility, integrity, patience, and self-control—result from our conscious choice. Such a belief—which Nietzsche calls "a sort of rape and perversion of logic"[128]—presumes that our individual freedom (free will) is of the most profound and unlimited variety.

In *The Idea of Freedom*, Adler analyzes and classifies the historical array of philosophical views on free will. In so doing, he offers a description that corresponds to the opinion Owen calls erroneous. This view, that Adler terms *natural freedom of self-determination*,[129] holds that

> It is within everyone's power, by the choices he freely makes, to acquire virtue, perfect himself, and grow in moral stature. . . . Even the vicious or corrupt man can, by his power of self-determination, bring about his own reformation.[130]

This radical form of free will disparages the importance of early childhood experience and education as well as genetic influences in forming a person's character. Adler cites Kant and Rousseau, among others, as exponents of

---

124. Owen, *A New View of Society and Other Writings*, 43.
125. Owen, 289 (italics in original).
126. Skinner, *About Behaviorism*, 189.
127. Skinner, *Beyond Freedom and Dignity*, 19, 200.
128. Nietzsche, *Beyond Good and Evil*, 28.
129. Adler, *The Idea of Freedom*, vol. 1, 400.
130. Owen, 563.

this view. Kant, for example, writes of the "freedom of the will" as a "power of *spontaneously* beginning a series of successive things or states,"[131] and he says, "What man is or ought to be in a moral sense he must make or must have made *himself*. Both must be the effect of his free elective will, otherwise it could not be imputed to him, and, consequently, he would be *morally* neither good nor bad."[132]

One effect of the belief in this brand of free will, Owen supposes, is society's wrongly rewarding or condemning people for actions presumed to be the product of their self-formed characters. When we realize that prevailing economic, political, religious, and social institutions form people's characters, he argues, we should acknowledge important limits to personal responsibility.[133] Within utopian literature, Ayn Rand's *Atlas Shrugged* (discussed in chapter seven) exemplifies this "natural freedom of self-determination," the antithesis of Owen's conception of character. John Galt, Rand's spokesman, declares that free will "is your mind's freedom to think or not" and that your will's freedom "controls all the choices you make and determines your life and your character."[134] Rand emphasizes that volition with respect to consciousness implies choosing one's own character, and that a child can "shape his own soul."[135] Though Owen derides this brand of free will, he characteristically failed to make any attribution of its origins[136] or explain why he thinks it is universally held, though he claims its promoters and enablers

---

131. Immanuel Kant, *Critique of Pure Reason*, trans. Norman Kemp Smith (London: Macmillan and Co., 1964), (B476), 412 (italics in original). He admits that for philosophy, "there are insurmountable difficulties in the way of admitting any such type of unconditioned causality" (Kant, 412).

132. Immanuel Kant, *First Part of the Philosophical Theory of Religion*, 4th ed., trans. Thomas Kingsmill Abbott (repr., n.p., n.d.), 28 (italics in original).

133. Saint-Simon's opposition to this brand of free will is described in chapter four.

134. Rand, *Atlas Shrugged*, 1017.

135. Ayn Rand, *The Romantic Manifesto* (New York: Signet Books, 1971), 99, 101, 139–40.

136. Harrison says, "Owen seldom quoted any other author, since he was convinced that his views sprang entirely from his own experience in Manchester and, more particularly, at New Lanark." John F. C. Harrison, *Utopianism and Education* (New York: Teachers College Press, Teachers College, Columbia University, 1968), 13. Owen's son Dale vouched that his father rarely read books and that he dismissed most authors as making the same errors he sought to remedy. "He was not, in any true sense of the word, a student." Robert Dale Owen, *Threading My Way* (London: Turner and Co., 1874; repr. Forgotten Books, 2012), 67. (Page references same as original.)

are the government, religious leaders, and political economists[137]—"without," however, "in the slightest degree attributing blame" to anyone.[138] "I blame not the governors, priests, statesmen, political economist, legislators, and men of great business," he explains, "they, like all other men, are the creatures of the circumstances in which they have, by necessity, been placed."[139]

EXPERIMENTAL EVIDENCE

Owen's views on poverty, explains Morton, "were directly contrary to the orthodox thinking of his time and class. It was for them an article of faith that the masses were poor because they were idle, vicious, intemperate and ignorant."[140] Owen believed transforming his workers' character and their productivity was a function of the changes he had introduced in their work environment.[141] He experimented with measures to promote civility and cooperation wherein he attempted to rid his employees of their vices and

---

137. Owen speaks of "the *government* and *church*, unitedly, adopting a system to govern by force and fraud, through the ignorance of the people and mystification of all classes." Robert Owen, *The Book of the New Moral World* (New York: Augustus M. Kelley Publishers, 1970), fifth part, chap. 4, 44 (italics in original). Owen censured political economists as a group for promoting individualism, which he believed had its basis in the notion of a self-caused character. Owen, *A New View of Society and Other Writings*, 276. Claeys notes that the political economists' criticisms of Owen's economic plans helped him "to see not only that the political economists were his most powerful opponents, but also that to some extent he would have to accept some part of their language, claims and intellectual strategy if his own plans were to appear legitimate." Gregory Claeys, *Machinery, Money and the Millennium: From Moral Economy to Socialism, 1815–1860* (Princeton, NJ: Princeton University Press, 1987), 49.

138. Owen, *Lectures on an Entire New State of Society*, 28.

139. Robert Owen, *A Development of the Principles and Plans on Which to Establish Self-Supporting Home Colonies* (London: Home Colonization Society, 1841; repr., Kessinger), 17. (Page references same as original.)

140. A. L. Morton, *The Life and Ideas of Robert Owen* (London: Lawrence and Wishart, 1962), 20–21.

141. Marx reports, "Robert Owen, soon after 1810, not only maintained the necessity of a limitation of the working day in theory, but actually introduced the 10 hours' day into his factory at New Lanark. This was laughed at as a communistic Utopia; so were his 'Combination of children's education with productive labor and the Co-operative Societies of Workingmen,' first called into being by him. To-day, the first Utopia is a Factory Act, the second figures as an official phrase in all Factory Acts, the third is already being used as a cloak for reactionary humbug." Marx, *Capital*, pt. 3, chap. 10, 145n2.

other "pernicious habits." With the workers' children, however, he sought to thwart these vices before they took root.

Of his social investigations, Owen writes, "Seeing that the most injurious circumstance was the very defective and false character given by ignorant workpeople to their children, I commenced building an establishment for forming their characters from as early a period as I could obtain the control of them from their parents."[142] In 1816, in conjunction with the cotton mills, he opened the Institution for the Formation of Character.[143] In his *Address to the Inhabitants of New Lanark*, he explains, "the Institution has been devised to afford the means of receiving your children at an early age, as soon almost as they can walk,"[144] and thereby "to effect a complete and thorough improvement in the *internal* as well as *external* character of the whole village."[145] In this effort, his son Dale observes, he brought together "upwards of a hundred children, from one to six years of age, under two guardians."[146] The teachers were trained to "deal kindly"[147] with children while providing instruction in the "rudiments of common learning."[148] For the parents, it meant less care and anxiety about their children and consequently more productive work in the mill. Owen's work, report Lawson and Silver, "gave rise to an infant-school movement."[149]

---

142. Owen, *The Revolution in the Mind*, 13.

143. Owen, 34.

144. Owen, *A New View of Society and Other Writings*, 110.

145. Owen, 110 (italics in original).

146. R. D. Owen, *Threading My Way*, 90.

147. Harold Silver, *Robert Owen on Education* (Cambridge: Cambridge University Press, 1969), 28.

148. Owen, *A New View of Society and Other Writings*, 111. In response to the concerns of his business partners over the added cost of his educational efforts, Owen reports, "pecuniary profits . . . during these thirty years [1799–1829]," after covering these additional expenses, "and allowing five per cent per annum for the use of the capital employed, were upwards of three hundred thousand pounds. . . . This statement of profits," he hoped, would "satisfy the ignorant and vulgar commercial mind." Owen, *The Revolution in the Mind*, 34. Morton observes, "It was not till his third partnership, formed in 1813, and consisting largely of Quakers, but including also . . . Jeremy Bentham, that he had partners who were content with a fixed return of 5 per cent on their capital and were prepared to give him a fairly free hand." Morton, *The Life and Ideas of Robert Owen*, 23–24.

149. John Lawson and Harold Silver, *A Social History of Education in England* (London: Methuen and Co., 1973), 247.

Owen's goal was to transform education, employing specially trained instructors teaching a universal curriculum, including the proper view of character formation. "The child who from infancy has been rationally instructed in these principles," he observes, "will readily discover and trace *whence* the opinions and habits of his associates have arisen, and *why* they possess them."[150] During each child's education, he "will have acquired reason sufficient to exhibit to him forcibly the irrationality of being angry with an individual for possessing qualities which . . . he had not the means of preventing."[151] A critical element of Owen's educational philosophy is the elimination of both punishments and rewards. Accordingly, he says, "in a thoroughly well-constituted society both would be forever unknown."[152]

Education, notes Harrison, "was to be the lever, first for dealing with the problem of the poor, but soon for effecting change throughout the whole of society."[153] The aim of Owen's infant school was to break the chain of causation by altering the process through which parents replicate their own malformed characters in their children. On the success of his experimental arrangement, Owen claims, a "new character was formed for the children of these workpeople, superior to any ever given the working class." In fact, he says, "The character of the whole population was gradually greatly changed for the better, physically, mentally, morally, and practically."[154]

A NEW SOCIAL ORDER

Owen's plan for disseminating the transformative education involves estab-lishing communities (variously called townships, nuclei, or home colonies) of roughly 2,000–2,500 people, comprising workers and their families living and working together. This was the size he determined most effective during his experiments with the mill in New Lanark. For his scheme, it is critical that each township "should be devised to be self-educating, self-employing, self-supporting, and self-governing."[155] Accordingly, he advises, each nucleus

---

150. Owen, *A New View of Society and Other Writings*, 20 (italics in original).

151. Owen, 20.

152. Owen, *The Revolution in the Mind*, 32.

153. Harrison, *Utopianism and Education*, 33.

154. Owen, *The Revolution in the Mind*, 32.

155. Owen, 43.

or township must encompass sufficient land for farming and manufacture to permit its population to be self-sufficient.[156] Though each community operates autonomously, they will all "be governed in a like manner by the same laws."[157] These laws, Owen claims, are "deduced from, and in unison with, the ascertained *laws of nature*." As such, they "are plain and simple, and will be readily understood by every one made rational from birth."[158]

OWEN'S CONSTRUCTIVE TAX SYSTEM

Owen describes his constructive tax system as a sacrifice that will obviate the need for most government services that pecuniary taxes commonly pay for. The sacrifice derives from the first of his six laws:

> Every human being, male and female, shall be as well trained and educated from birth, physically, mentally, morally, and practically, as the knowledge of well-forming the human character possessed at the time will admit.[159]

Hertzler observes, this education "was to be universal and compulsory, and no child . . . was to be excluded from its benefits."[160]

Demonstrating his fervor for equality, especially between genders—and the wider sense of freedom this implies—Owen proclaims: "Both sexes shall have equal education, rights, privileges, and personal liberty." To this end a mandate places all children under the care of the township of their birth.[161] "The single family arrangements will be broken up, and every thing connected with them."[162] However, he clarifies, although the children are under the continuous control of their teachers, the parents are always

---

156. Owen, *The Book of the New Moral World*, fifth part, chap. 6, 58; Owen, *The Revolution in the Mind*, 118.

157. Owen, *The Revolution in the Mind*, 125.

158. Owen, *The Book of the New Moral World*, sixth part, chap. 6, 82 (italics in original).

159. Owen, third part, chap. 12, 77.

160. Hertzler, *The History of Utopian Thought*, 217. In *Walden Two*, Skinner's character Frazier explains, "All of our ethical training is completed by the age of six." Skinner, *Walden Two*, 98.

161. Owen, *The Revolution in the Mind*, 61.

162. Owen, *Lectures on an Entire New State of Society*, 141.

welcome to oversee their progress.[163] The physical removal of the children is necessary, he explains, because their parents' affections for them are "too strong for their judgments."[164] Owen's rationale for this sacrifice is that the township, "as the general parental authority," has a more enduring interest in the proper formation of each child's character than do her biological parents.[165] In an echo of Plato and Campanella, Owen advises, "All children in the same Township shall be trained and educated together, as children of the same family."[166]

REVOLUTIONIZING THE PECUNIARY TAX SYSTEM

Owen "was not an economist," writes Heilbroner, but "he was an economic innovator who reshaped the raw data with which economists have to deal."[167] At the center of his economic innovation is the possibility of reducing pecuniary taxes to a minimum. "Those who have reflected on the nature of public revenue," Owen explains, "know that revenue has but one legitimate source—that it is derived directly or indirectly from the labor of man." As such, people face taxes "in proportion to their strength, industry, and capacity."[168] Given this fact, he asks: "can that system be right, which compels the industrious, temperate, and comparatively virtuous, to support the ignorant, the idle, and the comparatively vicious?"[169] Owen's solution substitutes land for labor as the basis of pecuniary taxation. "Governments should gradually purchase the land . . . and thus make it public property . . . from which alone the public revenue should be derived."[170] In a foreshadowing of Henry George (discussed in chapter six), Claeys reports, "When proposing himself as a member of parliament in 1832 . . . Owen

---

163. Owen, *A Development of the Principles and Plans on Which to Establish Self-Supporting Home Colonies*, 70; Owen, *The Revolution in the Mind*, 61, 79.

164. Owen, *The Revolution in the Mind*, 78.

165. Owen, 79. At one time Bellamy shared a similar view. Edward Bellamy, "The Economy of Happiness," in Arthur E. Morgan, *The Philosophy of Edward Bellamy* (New York, King's Crown Press, 1945), 75.

166. Owen, *The Revolution in the Mind*, 80.

167. Heilbroner, *The Worldly Philosophers*, 106.

168. Owen, *A New View of Society and Other Writings*, 68.

169. Owen, 69.

170. Owen, *The Revolution in the Mind*, 42.

offered . . . a graduated property tax equal to the national expenditure [and] the abolition of all other taxes."[171]

CHARLOTTE PERKINS GILMAN (1860–1935): MOTHERHOOD AND EUGENICS IN *HERLAND*

These people will have to be in the descendant phase, the species must be engaged in eliminating them. . . . No longer will it be that failures must suffer and perish lest their breed increase, but the breed of failures must not increase, lest they suffer and perish, and the race with them.

—H. G. Wells, *A Modern Utopia*[172]

Robert Owen's emphasis on early childhood development has not gone without analog in later utopias. Notably, Gilman in *Herland* and Skinner in *Walden Two* focus on removing children from their parents' misguided management. "*Herland* is not a feminist blueprint for the future," says Gough, "but a fantasy of what would happen if motherhood was conceived otherwise than in hetero-patriarchal terms."[173]

The constructive taxes falling on motherhood and on childrearing in Herland grew out of that country's historical and geological past. Though only women now occupy the country, "at about the time of the Christian era," explains narrator Vandyck Jennings, they comprised a "bi-sexual race."[174] "They had ships," he continues, "an army, a king," and commerce with the "best civilization of the old world."[175] However, in what the narrator calls "a succession of historic misfortunes,"[176] a "volcanic outburst" sealed off the mountain pass affording sole access to their land.[177] "Instead of a passage, a

---

171. Claeys, *Citizens and Saints*, 74.
172. Wells, *A Modern Utopia*, 56.
173. Gough, "Lesbians and Virgins," 197.
174. Gilman, *Herland*, 46.
175. Gilman, 46.
176. Gilman, 46.
177. Gilman, 47.

new ridge, sheer and high, stood between them and the sea."[178] The women now had "no way up or down or out;"[179] the men, away engaged in battle, were lost. Facing an uncertain future, the women deliberated their options. "For five or ten years they worked together, growing stronger and wiser and more and more mutually attached, and then the miracle happened,"[180] explains Jennings: "They developed this virgin birth capacity."[181] When "one of these young women bore a child," he continues, "they decided it must be a direct gift from the gods, and placed the proud mother in the Temple of Maaia—their Goddess of Motherhood." And there, he reports, "this wonder-woman bore child after child, five of them—all girls." Each daughter of this first mother—also through parthenogenesis—"bore five daughters," and each of these gave birth to five more.[182] This population expansion continued for five hundred years, after which it became apparent that their ability to produce enough food for any larger population—even with all the efficiencies and land-saving measures they had introduced—was exhausted. "Here was this dreadful period," Jennings recounts, "when they got far too thick, and decided to limit the population."[183] Henceforward each woman would restrict her maternal output as the state would direct (generally to one child)—a required sacrifice for the general welfare—and the first of three (or possibly four) constructive tax regimes.

In summarizing their maternal practices, Jennings declares, "you make Motherhood the highest social service—a sacrament, really; that it is only undertaken once, by the majority of the population;[184] that those held unfit are not allowed even that."[185] Elaborating on this sacrifice Somel explains, "almost every woman values her maternity above everything else. Each girl holds it close and dear, an exquisite joy, a crowning honor, the most intimate, most personal, most precious thing."[186]

---

178. Gilman, 47.

179. Gilman, 47.

180. Gilman, 48.

181. Gilman, 57.

182. Gilman, 48.

183. Gilman, 59.

184. The minority of the population encouraged to bear more than one child are the "Over Mothers" (Gilman, 59).

185. Gilman, 59.

186. Gilman, 70.

MOTHERHOOD AS THE HIGHEST SERVICE

A second sacrifice involves the rearing and education of the girls. In what Krieg calls "an all-female welfare state," the "highest welfare," she says, "is that of its future citizens."[187] "The care of babies," explains Somel, "involves education, and is entrusted only to the most fit."[188] For that reason, "child-rearing has come to be with us a culture so profoundly studied . . . that the more we love our children the less we are willing to trust that process to unskilled hands—even our own."[189] Accordingly, she continues, education "is our highest art, only allowed to our highest artists."[190] In an essay on education for motherhood, Gilman holds that every child is entitled to social care on a level exceeding what the family is able to provide[191]—where children are "heavily loved and violently cared for."[192] Children are "born into the arms of an endless succession of untrained mothers," she declares, "who bring to the care and teaching of their children neither education . . . nor experience therein."[193] The ability to deliver the required level of professional care, however, is not inborn but must be learned and "can never be learned until serious, life-long, study and practice is given to it."[194] The result in Herland recalls Owen's infant schools and prefigures Skinner's nurseries: biological mothers relinquish their central position to experts who educate the girls for the benefit of society. In Herland, however, before surrendering her daughter, "Each mother had her year of glory; the time to love and learn, living closely with her child, nursing it proudly."[195]

---

187. Joann P. Krieg, "Charlotte Perkins Gilman and the Whitman Connection," in *Charlotte Perkins Gilman: The Woman and Her Work*, ed. Sheryl L. Meyering (Ann Arbor, MI: UMI Research Press, 1989), 147.

188. Gilman, *Herland*, 70.

189. Gilman, 70. Hertzka takes the contrary approach in *Freeland* where "the earliest education is the special duty of the mother. A Freeland wife seldom needs to be taught how this duty can be best fulfilled." Hertzka, *Freeland*, 230–31.

190. Gilman, *Herland*, 70.

191. Charlotte Perkins Gilman, "Education for Motherhood," in *Charlotte Perkins Gilman: A Nonfiction Reader*, ed. Larry Ceplair (New York: Columbia University Press, 1991), 246.

192. Gilman, *Women and Economics*, 142.

193. Gilman, 96–97.

194. Gilman, "Education for Motherhood," 246.

195. Gilman, *Herland*, 88.

In *Women and Economics*, Gilman provides the moral justification for this constructive tax. "Maternal love is an enormous force," she says, "but force needs direction. Simply to love the child does not serve him unless specific acts of service express this love. What these acts of service are and how they are performed make or mar his life forever."[196] Gilman, explains Gough, "did not simply seek the professionalization and collectivization of motherhood; she sought to revolutionize its fundamental purpose."[197] This includes venerating those with the ability to develop in the girls recognition of what Gilman claims is the evolutionary, cooperative, and organic nature of society. From the experts the children learn the traits Gilman believes most important: exercising self-control and being "kind, gentle, strong, wise, brave, courteous, cheerful, true."[198] "Self-control," writes Gilman, "is one of the first essentials in the practice of ethics" and—she continues, sounding remarkably like Skinner[199]—"can be taught a child by gently graduated exercises."[200]

THE OBSOLESCENCE OF EGOISM

Gilman sees humankind evolving socially and morally as well as physically. But modes of thought that antedate society linger and obstruct social progress. This atavistic tendency means our minds are "still darkened by the beast-concept of Egoism."[201] All social evolution, she says, is the "development and improvement of the connective tissues of Society . . . and that connection is by every test organic."[202] Social evolution, she elaborates, "tends to an increasing specialization in structure and function, and to an

---

196. Gilman, *Women and Economics*, 96–97.

197. Gough, "Lesbians and Virgins: The New Motherhood in *Herland*," 201.

198. Gilman, *Women and Economics*, 161.

199. In *Walden Two* Frazier explains, "We had to *design* a series of adversities, so that the child would develop the greatest possible self-control." Skinner, *Walden Two*, 105 (italics in original).

200. Charlotte Perkins Gilman, *Concerning Children* (Project Gutenberg, 2012) http://www.gutenberg.org/files/40481/40481-h/40481-h.htm (accessed February 2, 2019). Originally published London: G. P. Putnam's Sons, 1903.

201. Charlotte Perkins Gilman, *Human Work* (Lanham, MD: AltaMira Press, A Division of Roman and Littlefield Publishers, 2005), 119.

202. Gilman, *Human Work*, 112–13.

increasing interdependence of the component parts."[203] As society develops and differentiates, Gilman argues, men are "of increasing use to one another, no longer competitors in any legitimate sense."[204]

EUGENIC SACRIFICE OF EGOISM

In *Herland* a third form of constructive tax falls on women for whom egoism is a dominant trait, namely on those seeking motherhood at the expense of the general welfare. As Somel explains, "We have, of course, made it our first business to train out, to breed out, when possible, the lowest types."[205] In this way, says Hudak, "they choose not only how many people to 'make' but what *kinds* of people to make."[206] Eugenics is at the "center of Gilman's progressive feminist program of reform," observes Robertson.[207] Beginning with the first mother, Somel advises, "we inherited the characteristics of a long race-record behind her. And they cropped out from time to time—alarmingly. But it is . . . six hundred years since we have had what you call a 'criminal.' "[208] "If the girl showing the bad qualities had still the power to appreciate social duty," she continues,

> we appealed to her, by that, to renounce motherhood. Some of the few worst types were, fortunately, unable to reproduce. But if the fault was in a disproportionate egotism—then the girl was sure she had the right to have children, even that hers would be better than others.[209]

---

203. Gilman, *Women and Economics*, 52.

204. Gilman, *Human Work*, 112.

205. Gilman, *Herland*, 70.

206. Jennifer Hudak, "The 'Social Inventor': Charlotte Perkins Gilman and the (Re) Production of Perfection," *Women's Studies* 32 (2003): 455–77, 470 (italics in original).

207. Robertson, *The Last Utopians*, 215.

208. Gilman, *Herland*, 70. Given Herland's emphasis on teaching self-control and its absence of criminals, it is noteworthy that a lack of self-control is the single temperamental trait that criminologists Gotfredson and Hershi say is necessary for explaining criminal behavior. In summarizing their research, the authors observe that "people who lack self-control will tend to be impulsive, insensitive, physical (as opposed to mental), risk-taking, short-sighted, and nonverbal, and they will tend therefore to engage in criminal and analogous acts." Michael R. Gottfredson and Travis Hirschi, *A General Theory of Crime* (Stanford, CA: Stanford University Press, 1990), 89–90.

209. Gilman, *Herland*, 70.

That, declares Somel, "we never allowed."[210]

EUGENICS AND ACCESS TO TRUTH

The goal of negative eugenics is to prevent "undesirable" people—"those who already sap the strength of the State"[211]—from reproducing. For Gilman's utopian contemporaries, Bellamy and Wells, this was a sufficient objective. Plato's *Republic*, by contrast, added positive eugenics—encouraging the best guardians to breed as frequently as possible. The extent to which either negative or positive eugenics is expected to alter human nature (and in what ways) is a utopian query.[212] *Herland's* eugenic program features both negative and positive strategies; the positive permitting its Over Mothers (the hereditary ruling order; "the nearest approach to an aristocracy") to produce more than one daughter.[213] This fact suggested to at least one commentator a utopian refinement of positive eugenics. Hudak observes, "it becomes clear throughout the novel that only the best 'types' of women can participate in society."[214] The best "types" she refers to constitute a race of like-minded women, resulting from Herland's eugenic agenda, for whom "the beliefs of individuals would coincide . . . with the needs of the social whole."[215] Thus,

---

210. Gilman, *Herland*, 70. Gilman, says Robertson, "gives little sense of the regime of social control that enforces these eugenic programs . . . but it is clear that Herland lacks the programs of forced sterilization that many U.S. progressives enthusiastically supported." Robertson, *The Last Utopians*, 213. In Gilman's earlier utopian novel, *Moving the Mountain*, however, "A large class of perverts were incapacitated for parentage." Gilman, *Moving the Mountain*, chap. 7, 51. Gilman's extra-utopian (and social Darwinian) stance on eugenics focused on maintaining discrete races and encouraging birth control for the poor. On the "race question," she says, "it is physically possible for all races to interbreed, but not therefore desirable." Charlotte Perkins Gilman, "Is America Too Hospitable?" in *Charlotte Perkins Gilman: A Nonfiction Reader*, ed. Larry Ceplair (New York: Columbia University Press, 1991), 291.

211. Oliver Wendell Holmes Jr., U.S. Supreme Court, Buck v. Bell (274 U.S. 200), 1927.

212. Darwin reports, "it is notorious that breeders of cattle, horses and various fancy animals, cannot positively tell, until some time after birth, what will be the merits and demerits of their young animals." Charles Darwin, *The Origin of Species*, 6th ed. (1876), in the *Works of Charles Darwin*, vol. 16, ed. Paul H. Barrett and R. B. Freeman (New York University Press, 1988), 407.

213. Gilman, *Herland*, 59.

214. Hudak, "The 'Social Inventor': Charlotte Perkins Gilman," 457.

215. Hudak, 472.

while Plato bred guardians to be "philosophic, spirited, swift, and strong,"[216] Gilman breeds women to embrace her organic vision of moral progress.

The objective of the women's cohesion of conviction in Herland has potential implications for accessing truth. "Unanimity of a certain sort," explains Godwin, "is the result to which perfect freedom of inquiry is calculated to conduct us."[217] He warns, however, that we should "avoid such practices as are calculated to melt our opinions into a common mold."[218] In Herland, explains Hudak, "By containing and 'curing' those with dissident views, and by 'preventing' others from being born, the Herlanders ensure that the only women who remain exist in perfect agreement with each other."[219] Perfect agreement, however, is no guarantee of veracity, and the question is: agreement to what? Are they breeding a race of conformity-seeking sycophants, like the Deltas in Huxley's *Brave New World*,[220] or one engaged in reason that "strikes you with immediate conviction" like Swift's Houyhnhnms?[221]

Part Three:
Skinner, Eugenic Tax Procedures

B. F. SKINNER (1904–1990): ELIMINATING THE MEANER EMOTIONS IN *WALDEN TWO*

We see but a part, and being thus unable to generalise human conduct, except very roughly, we deny that it is subject to any fixed laws at all, and ascribe much both of a man's character and actions to chance, or luck, or fortune.

—Samuel Butler (1835–1902), *Erewhon*[222]

---

216. Plato, *Republic*, trans. Bloom, bk. 2, 376c.

217. Godwin, *Enquiry Concerning Political Justice*, 3rd ed., bk. 5, chap. 23, 548.

218. Godwin, bk. 8, chap. 8, 761–62.

219. Hudak, "The 'Social Inventor': Charlotte Perkins Gilman," 473.

220. The Deltas could not understand liberty. Huxley, *Brave New World*, 199.

221. Swift, *Gulliver's Travels*, 246.

222. Samuel Butler, *Erewhon* (Mineola, NY: Dover Publications, Inc., 2002), 130–31.

Central to Skinner's philosophy of behaviorism[223] is his observation that "we cannot choose a way of life in which there is no control. We can only change the controlling conditions."[224] Doing so requires choosing or altering the environment in which we operate based on experimental design. Since our behavior is responsive to the consequences it elicits in the environment, understanding the sources of those consequences is crucial to controlling behavior. "A scientific analysis of behavior," explains Skinner, "must assume that a person's behavior is controlled by his genetic and environmental histories rather than by the person himself as an initiating, creative agent."[225]

He rejects the idea that a utopia, or even modest social reform, must obey a blueprint. For this reason, says Kumar, *Walden Two* "is a utopia of means, not ends."[226] Skinner "presents an impeccable example of utopian activity," write Goodwin and Taylor. "He discovers an idea which seems to point to a fundamental truth about human nature and existence, and goes on to elaborate logically how a new model of the Good Life can be constructed round this discovery."[227]

Like Owen, Skinner believes the proper approach for reorganizing our culture includes creating and then replicating small communities based on sound psychological foundations.[228] "Walden Two works," he says, "because it is small."[229] Like Owen's home colonies, each community's population size is capped to ensure the efficacy of its experimental design. Rather than a master plan, Skinner holds that " 'nibbling' at cultural practices in general—as in education, therapy and so on,"[230] is the most effective means

---

223. "Behaviorism is not the science of human behavior; it is the philosophy of that science." Skinner, *About Behaviorism*, 3. Goodwin and Taylor refer to behaviorism as a "quasi-scientific theory." Goodwin and Taylor, *The Politics of Utopia*, 4–5.

224. Skinner, *About Behaviorism*, 190.

225. Skinner, 189.

226. Kumar, *Utopia and Anti-Utopia in Modern Times*, 349.

227. Goodwin and Taylor, *The Politics of Utopia*, 51.

228. Because of its growth, Walden Two began developing a second community. Skinner, *Walden Two*, 208–9. The Twin Oaks Community in Louisa, Virginia, was founded in 1967 following the principles of Skinner's *Walden Two*. Though the community is still in operation, it is no longer a behaviorist community.

229. B. F. Skinner, "News from Nowhere, 1984," *The Behavior Analyst* 8, no. 1 (Spring 1985): 5–14, 11.

230. B. F. Skinner to Donald Morris, October 13, 1977. Skinner collections, Harvard University Archives, Pusey Library.

for achieving experimentally tested improvements. This provides the entry point for altering a culture—not all at once, but through incremental steps. On this point, says Skinner,

> men have designed their cultures largely by guesswork, including some very lucky hits; but we are not far from a state of knowledge in which this can be changed. The change does not require that we be able to describe some distant state of mankind toward which we are moving or 'deciding' to move. Early physical technology could not have foreseen the modern world, though it led to it. Progress and improvement are local changes. We better ourselves and our world as we go.[231]

TURNING A BLIND EYE TO CONTROL OF HUMAN BEHAVIOR

However, as Skinner also observes, "When a science of behavior reaches the point of dealing with lawful relationships, it meets the resistance of those who give their allegiance to prescientific or extrascientific conceptions."[232] A designed society is synonymous, for many, with a state marked by oppression and lack of freedom, and critics, note Goodwin and Taylor, "have not been slow to draw the sinister pro-totalitarian conclusions of his arguments."[233] Krutch, for example, characterizes Walden Two as a model of totalitarianism.[234] Concerning the general opposition to his approach, Skinner stresses, "men have suffered long enough from that strange quirk in their behavior which keeps them from applying the methods of natural science to their own lives."[235] Furthermore, he explains, "The first step in a defense against tyranny is the fullest possible exposure to controlling techniques."

> The danger of the misuse of power is possibly greater than ever. . . . We cannot make wise decisions if we continue to

---

231. Skinner, *Cumulative Record*, 49.

232. B. F. Skinner, *Science and Human Behavior* (New York: Macmillan Company, 1953), 17.

233. Goodwin and Taylor, *The Politics of Utopia*, 51.

234. Joseph Wood Krutch, *The Measure of Man* (New York: Grosset and Dunlap, 1953), 71.

235. B. F. Skinner, "The Problem of Consciousness—A Debate," *Philosophical and Phenomenological Research* 27, 3 (March 1967): 317–37, 332 (with B. Blanshard).

pretend that human behavior is not controlled, or if we refuse to engage in control when valuable results might be forthcoming. Such measures weaken only ourselves leaving the strength of science to others.[236]

Knowing your enemy in this case means knowing the behavioral technology they use against you. "No theory changes what it is a theory about," he emphasizes. "What does change is our chance of doing something about the subject of a theory."[237]

Skinner's answer to questions such as Krutch's—about who will control the controllers in a controlled environment, and who in turn will control them—is that they are not such profound questions as they may first appear.[238] This is the case for two reasons. First it is possible, as in the fictional Walden Two community, to arrange the contingencies used to control behavior so that they also control the behavior of the controllers. The second point concerns the nature of the control Skinner employs and the fact that it is not aversive. The control that he stresses as most effective is that which avoids punishment, though this may not be the form of control those who raise this question have "in mind."[239] Though despotic

---

236. Skinner, *Cumulative Record*, 11.

237. Skinner, *Beyond Freedom and Dignity*, 213.

238. Krutch speaks of the "second generation of dictators to whom the dictator of Walden Two expects to pass on the control of affairs [and who] will be conditioners who have themselves been conditioned." Krutch, *The Measure of Man*, 66. Krutch's attack on Skinner includes repeated references to the "scientific ability to control men's thoughts with precision," which are not Skinner's words but those of MIT dean John Ely Burchard. MIT's Mid-Century Convocation, March 31, 1949, as quoted by Winston Churchill on that occasion. https://libraries.mit.edu/archives/exhibits/midcentury/midcent-churchill.html (accessed January 15, 2019).

239. Ayn Rand (discussed in chapter seven) takes Skinner to task in a review of *Beyond Freedom and Dignity*. She says that one implication of his argument is that "slave-driving and wage-paying are both 'techniques of control,'" and that for Skinner, "every human relationship, every instance of men dealing with one another, is a form of *control*." Ayn Rand, *Philosophy: Who Needs It* (New York: Signet, 1984), 190 (italics in original). Skinner would not disagree with this assessment in general, though what Rand means by *control* is obviously quite different than what Skinner is talking about. Thus, he says, for example, "The slave controls the master as completely as the master the slave, in the sense that the techniques of punishment employed by the master have been selected by the slave's behavior in submitting to them." Skinner, *Cumulative Record*, 45.

governments rely on aversive controls, Skinner explains, "there could be difficult problems concerning the control of behavior by potential despots even though positive techniques are used."[240] In contrast to *Walden Two*, Skinner explains, "*1984* is a picture of immediate aversive control for vicious selfish purposes. The founder of Walden Two, on the other hand, built a community in which neither he nor any person exerts *current* control. His achievement lay in his original *plan*."[241]

BEHAVIORAL TECHNOLOGY USING OPERANT CONDITIONING

In Huxley's utopia, *Island*, we learn that "all the gods are homemade, and that it's we who pull their strings and so give them the power to pull ours."[242] The behavioral technology of Walden Two involves operant conditioning, "not to be confused with the conditioned reflexes of Pavlov."[243] Operant behavior is characterized by the organism's *operating* on the environment and the environment's replying in some way. Operant behavior is that class of actions (called operants) that tend to increase or decrease in probability depending on the consequences they elicit from the environment. Operant behavior begins with an operant (a gesture, for example, or a movement, sound, or other "original 'spontaneous' activity") produced by the organism and followed by an environmental answer. As the environmental consequences tend to increase or decrease the probability (relative frequency) of the operant reoccurring, operant conditioning is said to take place. Operant behavior is originally "*emitted*, rather than *elicited*," explains Skinner. "It must have this property," he asserts, "if the notion of probability of response is to make sense."[244] A common misconception regarding operant conditioning is that an organism performs an act or refrains from so doing because of

---

240. Skinner to Morris, October 13, 1977. Skinner collections, Harvard University Archives, Pusey Library. Despite this fact and their claim that "critics tend to approach utopians with preconceived ideas," Negley and Patrick assume control in *Walden Two* is by dictatorship, declaring, "Of all the dictatorships espoused by utopists [Skinner's] is the most profound." Negley and Patrick, *The Quest for Utopia*, 308, 583.

241. Skinner, *Cumulative Record*, 37 (italics in original).

242. Aldous Huxley, *Island* (New York: HarperCollins, 1962), 246.

243. B. F. Skinner, *The Technology of Teaching* (New York: Meredith Corporation, 1968), 62.

244. Skinner, *Science and Human Behavior*, 107 (italics in original).

the expected consequences. Accordingly, Skinner says, "Instead of saying that a man behaves because of the consequences which *are* to follow his behavior, we simply say that he behaves because of the consequences which *have* followed similar behavior in the past."[245]

An environmental event that follows an operant (gesture, movement, sound) and tends to increase its probability is called a reinforcer. "We observe the frequency of a selected response," explains Skinner, "then make an event contingent upon it and observe any change in frequency. If there is a[n] [increasing] change, we classify the event as reinforcing to the organism under the existing conditions."[246] Reinforcers are of two kinds: positive and negative. Positive reinforcers add some stimulus to the environment such as food or sexual contact. Negative reinforcers, he says, remove something—for example, a loud noise or electric shock—from the environment.[247] "In both cases the effect of reinforcement is the same—the probability of response is increased."[248]

ABANDONING PUNISHMENT

Skinner observes that "organized agencies or institutions, such as governments . . . exert a powerful and often troublesome control. It is exerted in ways which most effectively reinforce those who exert it, and unfortunately," he explains, "this usually means in ways which are . . . aversive to those controlled."[249] He notes, "Hobbes's use of 'war' to represent interpersonal relations makes clear the ubiquity of aversive control in daily life."[250] But those controlled by aversion take action, he submits, "They escape from the controller—moving out of range if he is an individual, or defecting from a government."[251] In this respect he was anticipated by Owen, who said, "punishment is not only useless, but very pernicious, and injurious to

---

245. Skinner, 87 (italics in original).

246. Skinner, 73. Skinner explains, "There is nothing circular about classifying events in terms of their effects; the criterion is both empirical and objective. It would be circular, however, if we then went on to assert that a given event strengthens an operant because it is reinforcing" (Skinner, 73).

247. Skinner, 73.

248. Skinner, 73.

249. Skinner, *About Behaviorism*, 190.

250. Skinner, *Notebooks*, 26.

251. Skinner, *About Behaviorism*, 190.

the punisher and punished."[252] Walden Two founder, Frazier, explains that since they now understand how reinforcement works and why punishment does not, it is possible to be "more deliberate, and hence more successful" in applying behavioral technology to cultural design.[253]

As earlier mentioned, Skinner finds disturbing the extent to which people living in a scientific age have carefully resisted the application of scientific principles to their own behavior. For this reason, he claims, "It is not surprising to encounter the proposal that science should be abandoned, at least for the time being." But such an approach, he remarks, "resembles the decision of the citizens of Samuel Butler's *Erewhon*, where the instruments and products of science were put into museums."[254] "Is it not safer," the Erewhonians asked, "to nip the mischief in the bud?"[255]

AUTONOMOUS MAN

Belief in an outdated psychology is, for Skinner, belief in what he calls *autonomous man*. Man is thought to be autonomous, he says, "in the sense that his behavior is uncaused."[256] Autonomous man, accordingly, "is a device used to explain what we cannot explain in any other way."[257] In that sense man is supposed "free" and "can be held responsible for what he does and justly punished if he offends."[258] Owen questioned this conception of unlim-

---

252. Owen, *The Life of Robert Owen Written by Himself*, 11.

253. Skinner, *Walden Two*, 246. "We don't punish," says Frazier. "We never administer an unpleasantness in the hope of repressing or eliminating undesirable behavior" (Skinner, 104). In light of Skinner's explanation of positive and negative reinforcement in *Science and Human Behavior* (73, 185), Frazier's statement in *Walden Two*, "Now that we know how positive reinforcement works and why negative doesn't" (Skinner, 246), should be understood as paraphrased here in terms of reinforcement vs. punishment rather than positive vs. negative reinforcement.

254. Skinner, *Science and Human Behavior*, 5.

255. Butler, *Erewhon*, 119. The citizens were convinced that "machines were ultimately destined to supplant the race of man" as they developed their own consciousness (Butler, 44).

256. Skinner, *Beyond Freedom and Dignity*, 19.

257. Skinner, 200.

258. Skinner, 19. Fuller argues that Skinner's position encourages "an attitude of indifference toward the decay of the concept of responsibility implicit in many developments in the law." Fuller, *The Morality of Law*, 164. Since ought implies can, however, Fuller's complaint ignores the law's responsibility to keep pace with the science of human behavior and developments in psychology that redefine our nature and capacities.

ited free will, as earlier noted. Only by "dispossessing" autonomous man, argues Skinner, "can we turn to the real causes of human behavior."[259] A person controls himself, stresses Skinner, "precisely as he would control the behavior of anyone else—through the manipulation of variables of which behavior is a function."[260]

CULTURE AND EDUCATION IN WALDEN TWO

Skinner's spokesman Frazier gloats that Walden Two "is an environment in which people just naturally do the things they need to do to maintain themselves (with something to spare for the future) and treat each other well."[261] Because of their limited work hours (discussed in chapter four) and extensive leisure time, he continues, the members "just naturally do a hundred other things they enjoy doing because they do not have to do them." The things people just naturally do are positively reinforcing, in contrast to "unnecessary labor forced upon people by a poorly designed environment."[262]

Walden Two is a nearly self-sufficient communal society that values leisure and the pursuit of personal interests. "We have created leisure without slavery, a society which neither sponges nor makes war."[263] It is the only utopia with which I am familiar that expressly promotes the benefits of a sense of humor.[264] Concerning this utopia's political and economic structures, Skinner explains that

> Walden Two is state ownership without a state. Its members [work but] are not employed because there is no employer. They come into direct contact with the world, as people did before there were governments. . . . They . . . behave in ways which

---

259. Skinner, *Beyond Freedom and Dignity*, 201.

260. Skinner, *Science and Human Behavior*, 228.

261. Skinner, "News from Nowhere, 1984," 9.

262. Skinner, 9. "When we choose our work freely, then we *want* to work," claims Frazier. "William Morris, you remember, tried to make that state of affairs plausible in *News from Nowhere*" (Skinner, *Walden Two*, 147).

263. Skinner, *Walden Two*, 69.

264. Skinner, 100.

not only support their way of life but give them the sense of satisfaction that comes from effective action.[265]

"The task of the cultural designer," explains Skinner, "is to accelerate the development of practices which bring the remote consequences of behavior into play."[266] The childhood education that occurs in Walden Two is effected through direct experience with the environment, as in *News from Nowhere*.[267] The role of the specially trained teachers in this process is to guide what experiences the children encounter and to "arrange special contingencies which expedite learning."[268] For this reason, asserts Frazier, "A much better education would cost less if society were better organized."[269] This arrangement of contingencies, says Skinner, while accelerating the learning process also ensures the acquisition of specific behaviors that "might otherwise never occur."[270]

THE CONSTRUCTIVE TAXATION OF CONTROL

Skinner's strategy for altering society—like Owen's and Gilman's—requires taking charge of children at the earliest age and averting possibly irreversible damage to their ability to deal effectively with the world. "Taking charge" in this context refers to controlling and scheduling the consequences of their behavior, increasing the likelihood of repeating certain behaviors and decreasing the prospect of others. For this reason, children are segregated from their parents—a constructive tax—for trained childcare workers to raise them using agreed-upon procedures of behavioral technology. One of Frazier's goals in designing Walden Two was to avoid another generation of citizens burdened by useless and counterproductive emotions including,

---

265. Skinner, "News from Nowhere, 1984," 7.

266. Skinner, *Beyond Freedom and Dignity*, 143.

267. Morris's spokesman Dick explains, "our children learn, whether they go through a 'system of teaching' or not. . . . They all of them know how to cook; the bigger lads can mow; many can thatch. . . . I can tell you they know plenty of things." Morris, *News from Nowhere*, 66.

268. Skinner, *The Technology of Teaching*, 65.

269. Skinner, *Walden Two*, 109.

270. Skinner, *The Technology of Teaching*, 65.

for example, envy, jealousy, self-pity,[271] and wounded pride.[272] According to Frazier, "sorrow and hate—and high-voltage excitements of anger, fear and rage—are out of proportion with the needs of modern life, and they're wasteful and dangerous."[273] The "meaner and more annoying" emotions, those that breed unhappiness, Frazier continues, "are almost unknown here, like unhappiness itself."[274] The elimination of these futile emotions is undertaken along two dimensions, one of child training and the other of restructuring the family.

CHILD TRAINING

The focus of Walden Two's behavioral engineering is this question: "What's the best behavior for the individual so far as the group is concerned? And, how can the individual be induced to behave in that way?"[275] The answer for Skinner always lies in the child's environment. The younger the child the easier it is to control this environment.[276] "When a baby graduates from our Lower Nursery," Frazier explains, "it knows nothing of frustration, anxiety

---

271. Skinner, *Notebooks*, 295.

272. Skinner, *Walden Two*, 131.

273. Skinner, 92.

274. Skinner, 92.

275. Skinner, 95.

276. Claeys lists the foundation of Skinner's educational system as one of four common "'dystopian' charges" directed against *Walden Two*. Claeys describes these critics' focus as "the system of behavioural stimulus-response with which children are educated." Claeys, *Dystopia: A Natural History*, 451–52. Skinner, however, is not promoting stimulus-response (respondent) conditioning—which applies only to a small percentage of human behavior—but operant conditioning, as earlier explained. According to Skinner, "The stimulus-response model was never very convincing . . . and it did not solve the basic problem because something like an inner man had to be invented to convert the stimulus into a response." Skinner, *Beyond Freedom and* Dignity, 18. Regarding stimulus-response, Kumar points out that it is "Pavlovian, not Skinnerian, conditioning that is satirized by Huxley in *Brave New World*. Hence it is wrong to assume that *Walden Two* simply presents in a positive and rosier light the techniques so witheringly attacked by Huxley. The two utopias employ different types of conditioning." Kumar, *Utopia and Anti-Utopia in Modern Times*, 354. Thus, training exercises in *Brave New World* result in behavioral responses "almost as automatic and inevitable as blinking." Huxley, *Brave New World*, 80. Carter illustrates the critics' confusion when he speaks of "the ubiquitous operant conditioning" in *Brave New World*. Steven Carter, "The Masks of Passion," in *George Orwell's 1984*, Bloom's Modern Critical Interpretations, updated ed., ed. Harold Bloom (New York: Chelsea House Publishers, 2007), 129.

or fear. It never cries except when sick, which is very seldom, and it has a lively interest in everything."[277]

All procedures are experimentally tested and modified as needed. For the young children, Frazier observes, an environment was designed that exposes them to "gradually increasing annoyances and frustrations" in otherwise peaceful surroundings. The purpose of these adversities (as it was for Gilman) is to help the children develop "the greatest possible self-control."[278] This way, he says, the children are able to build a "tolerance for frustration."[279] "We control adversity," he assures them, "to build strength."[280] If self-adjustment is not forthcoming the schedule is altered. In consequence of these trials, what a child achieves

> is escape from the petty emotions which eat the heart out of the unprepared. They get the satisfaction of pleasant and profitable social relations on a scale almost undreamed of in the world at large. They get immeasurably increased efficiency, because they can stick to a job without suffering the aches and pains which soon beset most of us. They get new horizons, for they are spared the emotions characteristic of frustrations and failure.[281]

The living arrangements and schedules of the older children furnish a "particularly good example of behavioral engineering," notes Burris. They allow a child to emulate children "slightly older than himself." Ultimately, he continues, "control of the physical and social environment" is "progressively relaxed" and "transferred from the authorities to the child himself."[282] At age thirteen, he concludes, adult supervision of the "young members" is terminated.[283] At age sixteen the "young members" are eligible for marriage.

RESTRUCTURING THE FAMILY: THE CONSTRUCTIVE TAX

Walden Two's social environment is designed to root out the causes of unproductive emotions, noted earlier, in three related ways: communal property,

---

277. Skinner, *Walden Two*, 88.

278. Skinner, 105 (italics in original); Gilman, *Concerning Children*.

279. Skinner, *Walden Two*, 88–89.

280. Skinner, 105 (italics in original).

281. Skinner, 102.

282. Skinner, 107.

283. Skinner, 108.

segregating children from their parents, and the Walden Code. Communal ownership eradicates the cause of envy by eliminating competition for goods. In dealing with jealousy—understood as analogous to envy but directed to personal relations rather than to things—Walden Two's culture is so arranged that it can hardly arise. "In a cooperative society," Frazier declares, "there's no jealousy because there's no need for jealousy."[284] "For one thing," he says, "we encourage simple friendship between the sexes. The world at large all but forbids it."[285] Although the average age for marriage is seventeen,[286] there are "no hasty marriages among us,"[287] he explains, as there are no social or economic pressures to encourage it (there being universal childcare and health care, and no overanxious parents, social classes, or unemployment).

Establishing a cooperative society involves restructuring the family to facilitate proper child training—levying a constructive tax.[288] In effecting this restructuring, Frazier asserts, "We have to attenuate the child-parent relation."[289] Children are separated from their biological parents at birth and raised with their peers. "Group care," Frazier claims, "is better than parental care."[290] Walden Two, he stipulates, "replaces the family, not only as an economic unit, but to some extent as a social and psychological unit as well."[291] Suggestive again of Owen and Gilman, Frazier declares: "The control of behavior is an intricate science, into which the average mother could not be initiated without years

---

284. Skinner, 93. Walden Two's system also buffers children from discord in their parents' relationship, should it arise. Thus, Frazier advises, "When divorce cannot be avoided, the children are not embarrassed by severe changes in their way of life or their behavior toward their parents" (Skinner, 133). To reduce the likelihood of divorce, married couples are advised to sleep in separate bedrooms. "We don't insist on it," Frazier explains, "but in the long run there's a more satisfactory relation when a single room isn't shared" (Skinner, 128). Owen anticipated Skinner in this recommendation, noting that "every adult, male and female, will have two convenient apartments to themselves, a bed room and a sitting room" (with separate heat controls) to provide each spouse with "the personal liberty which this arrangement will afford." Owen, *Lectures on An Entire New State of Society*, 141.

285. Skinner, *Walden Two*, 129.

286. Skinner, 119.

287. Skinner, 124.

288. An additional constructive tax is imposed on all residents in the form of required medical checkups and preventative medical practices (e.g., vaccines) (Skinner, 176–77).

289. Skinner, 131.

290. Skinner, 131.

291. Skinner, 128.

of training."[292] In contrast to Plato's Republic, however, the parents of Walden Two may still know and interact with their own children, but they may not dote on them, as they must give equal attention to their children's friends. For this reason, says Frazier, "we have made it bad taste to single out one's own child for special favors."[293] In this way the lines of family demarcation are intentionally blurred and "blood relationships can be happily forgotten."[294] "Our goal," Frazier continues—in an echo of Plato's guardians—"is to have every adult member of Walden Two regard all our children as his own, and to have every child think of every adult as his parent."[295]

GOVERNMENT AND THE WALDEN CODE

In Walden Two, Frazier reports, "Our only government is a Board of Planners."[296] At the grassroots level there are also Community Managers to whom everyone has access. When asked if the Planners and Managers function on a democratic basis, Frazier's answer mirrors Plato's: "Democracy is the spawn of despotism."[297] "The will of the people is carefully ascertained," explains Frazier, but—in a paraphrase of Godwin—there are no "election campaigns to falsify issues or obscure them with emotional appeals."[298] "Insofar as the Planners rule at all," Frazier affirms, "they do so through positive reinforcement."[299] Membership in the experimental community is contingent upon

---

292. Skinner, 132. Though Skinner, by his phrasing, implies that it is the mother's role to raise children, in Walden Two's childrearing facility instructors are both men and women. Frazier reports, "Many parents are glad to be relieved of the awful responsibility of being a child's only source of affection and help" (Skinner, 133).

293. Skinner, 132.

294. Skinner, 133.

295. Skinner, 132; Plato, *Republic*, bk. 5, 461, 466. However, Frazier clarifies, "It's true he may not call anyone 'Mother' or 'Father,' but we discourage this anyway, in favor of given names" (Skinner, 132).

296. Skinner, *Walden Two*, 48.

297. Skinner, 252; Plato, *Republic*, bk. 8, 564a; bk. 9, 578b. In addition, declares Frazier, "the triumph of democracy doesn't mean it's the best government. . . . It isn't, and can't be, the best form of government, because it's based on a scientifically invalid conception of man." Skinner, *Walden Two*, 257.

298. Skinner, *Walden Two*, 253. Godwin advises, "Observe the practices of a popular election, where the great mass are purchased by obsequiousness, by intemperance and bribery, or driven by unmanly threats of poverty and persecution." Godwin, *Enquiry Concerning Political Justice*, 3rd ed., bk. 8, chap. 3, 726.

299. Skinner, *Walden Two*, 256.

acceptance of the Walden Code, ensuring "a share in the wealth and life of the community."[300] In Walden Two, there is no money and so no pecuniary tax system and hence the need for constructive taxation.[301] As far as political organization is concerned, Frazier clarifies that while they are not anarchists, they are opposed to all the existing forms of government, as none of them is based on the science of human behavior.

EUGENIC TAX PROCEDURES: CAMPANELLA, BELLAMY, ZAMYATIN, HUXLEY

> Electricity minus heavy industry plus birth control equals democracy and plenty. Electricity plus heavy industry minus birth control equals misery, totalitarianism and war.
>
> —Aldous Huxley (1894–1963), *Island*[302]

A common criticism of utopias is that they do not deal with people as they really are but as the author hopes they could be. The counterargument is that once social conditions change, we will finally see people "as they really are." In utopias that rely on eugenic measures to alter (and presumably to improve) who people "really are," the assumption is that human nature is fundamentally flawed and that altering social and economic conditions will not be sufficient. As Sargent explains, eugenic legislation may be "the ultimate in the expres-

---

300. Skinner, 150.

301. "The community was not . . . completely self-sufficient. It needed certain materials and equipment and had to buy power and pay taxes" (Skinner, 72). The community, as owner of its land, pays property taxes to the county, but since it has no money, Frazier explains, "we keep [the county roads] in repair by way of working out our county taxes" (Skinner, 17). Castle challenges Frazier on Walden Two's alleged self-sufficiency with respect to national defense and other functions federal income taxes pay for. Frazier's answer, that "we pay for these services exactly like other taxpayers" (Skinner, 188), indicates his level of tax naiveté. By U.S. law, each member's income is based on the value of the goods and services she receives in exchange for her labor. This income (from barter) must be reported annually to the federal government. Unless these procedures were followed and any tax due paid (in dollars), they have not paid for "these services exactly like other taxpayers." 26 CFR 1.61-2; IRS *Reg.* Sec. 1.61-2(d)(1).

302. Huxley, *Island*, 176. Birth control on Huxley's island of Pala is supplemented by artificial insemination from donors with superior abilities. "Give us another century, and our average IQ will be up to a hundred and fifteen" (Huxley, 232).

sion of a distrust of people as they are now constituted."[303] When the state administers a eugenic strategy, it imposes an unrecompensed sacrifice on one segment of society (or future society) for the benefit of another; the result is a constructive tax. "The aim of eugenics," says Francis Galton, is "to cause the useful classes in the community to contribute more than their proportion to the next generation."[304] This may be undertaken affirmatively or by imposing strategies of benign neglect on the less useful classes.[305]

THE CITY OF THE SUN

The guardians are the most valuable class in Plato's Republic, and his eugenic plan was unambiguous as to its purpose and methods. Campanella was acquainted with Plato's views and Genoese, his sea captain narrator, upon returning from the City of the Sun, tells his inquisitor, "They laugh at us because we are careful about the breeding of dogs and horses while we pay no attention to our own breeding."[306] "Care in mating, therefore, is a matter of major concern."[307] Furthermore, he explains, their "rules governing procreation are religiously observed for public, not for private ends."[308] In contrast to Plato's *Republic*, says Parrinder, their eugenic provisions "may be described as comparatively liberal," in that "the priests . . . decide whether or not a couple can marry [mate]."[309] As with the guardians of the Republic, the Solarians regulate their conception schedules but do so by reference to the stars (their reliance on astrology is addressed in chapter four).[310] Contrary to Plato's concern with reproducing the best guardians, Campanella's eugenic tax touches the whole population in an effort to combat extremes of temperament and physique. Accordingly, "Men who have a flighty, capricious disposition," for

---

303. Sargent, "A Note on the Other Side of Human Nature in the Utopian Novel," 93.

304. Francis Galton, "Eugenics: Its Definition, Scope, and Aims," *The American Journal of Sociology* 10, no. 1 (July 1904): 1–25, 3.

305. Limited access to medical care and education, for example, ensure higher infant mortality rates and unemployment.

306. Campanella, *The City of the Sun*, 37.

307. Campanella, 57–59.

308. Campanella, 61.

309. Patrick Parrinder, "Eugenics and Utopia: Sexual Selection from Galton to Morris," *Utopian Studies* 8, no. 2 (1997): 1–12, 3.

310. Campanella, *The City of the Sun*, 39, 55.

example, "are matched with women who are fat, even-tempered, and gentle."[311] In this effort, "Love," one of three priestly officials, selects sexual pairings in consultation with the chief physician, the astrologer, and the teachers.[312]

> Since both males and females, in the manner of the ancient Greeks, are completely naked when they engage in wrestling exercises, their teachers may readily distinguish those who are able to have intercourse from those who are not and can determine whose sexual organs may best be matched with whose.[313]

Campanella recaps his judgment on eugenic policy in a poem on natural faith.

> But blame and punishment fall to the country and kingdom
> that does not ensure that the time, place, and person
> of the parents provide a worthy seed.[314]

HERBERT SPENCER

An obligatory government eugenics policy affects living citizens by restricting their marriage and childrearing choices—a constructive tax.[315] Though eugenics was not a nineteenth-century innovation, it garnered new significance with the popularization of social Darwinism, encouraged by the writings of Herbert Spencer and William Graham Sumner, among others. Sumner, for example, writes, "It is a strange thing that we . . . should think men the

---

311. Campanella, 57.

312. Campanella, 55. In Campanella's hierarchy of priests, Power, Wisdom, and Love are under the direction of the Prince Prelate, "whom they call Sun" (Campanella, 31, 95, 101).

313. Campanella, 55.

314. Tommaso Campanella, *Selected Philosophical Poems of Tommaso Campanella*, trans. and ed. by Sherry Roush (Chicago: University of Chicago Press, 2011), 47.

315. In "Eugenics and Utopia," Smith distinguishes three categories of eugenic procedures—"selectionist eugenics, transformationist eugenics, and biological engineering." Of the utopias described here, those discussed before Huxley (including Plato, Campanella, Bellamy, Gilman, Wells, and Zamyatin) all deal with selectionist eugenics, which Smith says "is the application to ourselves of the techniques which . . . we have been applying in the breeding of our domestic animals." John Maynard Smith, "Eugenics and Utopia," in *Utopias and Utopian Thought*, ed. Frank E. Manuel, 150–68 (Boston: Houghton Mifflin Company, 1965), 150. None of the writers I discuss employ the direct manipulation of genes for the creation of specific types of individuals, such as "cancer resistant" or "able to run a three-minute mile."

only organisms which it is not worthwhile to breed."[316] In *Social Darwinism in American Thought*, Hofstadter identifies eugenics as the most "enduring fact of social Darwinism."[317] In Spencer's 1850 *Social Statics*, he argues that helping those whom nature has disadvantaged is retarding the natural process by which the race is evolving toward perfection.[318]

Spencer divides his social philosophy into two components, one for the study of the ends society seeks and the other for the study of the means. The first, which he calls *statics*, is the study of the "equilibrium of a perfect society."[319] The second, *dynamics*, is the study of "the forces by which society is advanced towards perfection."[320] It was a hands-off (or invisible hand) passive-aggressive approach that permitted nature to take what Spencer saw as its course without human interference, especially interference through governmental action on behalf of the poor.[321] "The poverty of the incapable, the distresses that come upon the imprudent, the starvation of the idle," he argues, "are the decrees of a large, far-seeing benevolence"[322] that demands "discipline which is pitiless in the working out of good."[323]

GENDER EQUALITY AND EUGENICS IN BELLAMY'S *LOOKING BACKWARD*

In *Walden Two* Burris, after an initial tour of the facility, says to Frazier, "I can understand why a builder of Utopias would choose to have only

---

316. Sumner, "Modern Marriage," in *Essays of William Graham Sumner*, 277.

317. Hofstadter, *Social Darwinism in American Thought*, 161.

318. For Darwin, however, perfection was relative and not absolute. "Natural selection tends only to make each organic being as perfect as, or slightly more perfect than the other inhabitants of the same country with which it comes into competition." Darwin, *The Origin of Species*, 171.

319. Herbert Spencer, *Social Statics* (1850) (repr., New York: D. Appleton and Company, 1865), 447. (Page references are to reprint.)

320. Spencer, 447.

321. During the ninetieth century, Marks reports, "evolution was commonly seen as a single-dimensional process, with healthy adult European Christian men at a pinnacle, and non-Europeans, non-Christians, non-men, non-adults, and non-healthy people somewhere below them. In essence, the other categories of people comprised humans who were not fully developed." Marks, *What it Means to be 98% Chimpanzee*, 189.

322. Spencer, *Social Statics*, 353–54.

323. Spencer, 353.

beautiful women about him . . . but I'm amazed at your success."[324] Though Morris's *News from Nowhere* and Bellamy's *Looking Backward* are otherwise antithetical, especially regarding work's role in society, like *Walden Two* they emphasize the improved physical appearance of a "new" population. Morris's William Guest, for example, declares, "I could hardly have believed that there could be so many good looking people in any civilized country."[325] And Bellamy's Julian West (in the sequel *Equality*) remarks on the "strong and beautiful" bodies of the youth and on women's "splendid chests and shoulders."[326] Unlike Plato's *Republic*, however, neither *News from Nowhere* nor *Looking Backward* reveals state-regulated marriages.[327] Morris stresses the physical beauty and youthful appearance that results from performing desirable work rather than drudgery.[328] In *Equality* Bellamy links healthier bodies to exercise and recreation enabled by economic equality and resulting changes in women's fashion that permitted escape from a "complicated system of bondage."[329]

"A central issue for utopia," Sargent observes, "is whether a better social order allows people to become better," or the eugenic alternative—only "better people [can] create a better social order."[330] William Morris accepts the former. The improved appearance and conduct of the people in *News from Nowhere*, as noted, is a function of their restructured society. By a circuitous route, Bellamy arrived at the same conclusion. Lipow traces the evolution of Bellamy's utopian vision, noting that in his earlier writings, "human nature itself had to be altered" for social and political change to occur. This could be accomplished either "at the level of biology or of character" by "an external force . . . brought to bear upon the recalcitrant

---

324. Skinner, *Walden Two*, 28.

325. Morris, *News from Nowhere*, 96.

326. Bellamy, *Equality*, chap. 21, 145–46.

327. Parrinder observes that while Morris's romantic writings, such as *The Roots of the Mountains*, were "steeped in the discourse of eugenics," *News from Nowhere* reflects only "mildly eugenic measures," "libertarian," or "inadvertent eugenic policy," and, I note, no government-coerced sacrifices, ex hypothesi. Parrinder, "Eugenics and Utopia: From Galton to Morris," 1, 6–7.

328. Morris, *News from Nowhere*, 159.

329. Bellamy, *Equality*, chap. 21, 144–45.

330. Lyman Tower Sargent, *Utopianism: A Very Short Introduction* (Oxford: Oxford University Press, 2010), 111.

human material."[331] In *Looking Backward*, however, Dr. Leete replies to West's question, whether human nature has changed: "Not at all . . . but the conditions of human life have changed, and with them the motives of human action."[332] The old life conditions and related motives of action that "repel" human nature—industrial competition ("a battlefield as wide as the world"[333]) and "the instinct of selfishness"[334] it fosters—were supplanted by financial equality. Equality, "met head-on with competition," observes Roemer, and the "'cutthroat' competition of free enterprise was banned from most of the [late nineteenth century] utopias."[335]

Changes in the conditions of life and the motives of action include the circumstances of marriage and the state's eugenics agenda. Resulting from these social and economic shifts, "the unlovely in human nature," says Taylor, "will be gradually eliminated,"[336] while the "attributes that human nature admires"—the "gifts of person, mind, and disposition"—"are sure of transmission to posterity."[337] Marriage was "an institution deformed by late-nineteenth-century capitalistic culture," says Tilman, "in which women were little more than slaves."[338] The new conditions of marriage resulting from a woman's economically uncoerced selection of a breeding partner are reflected in Dr. Leete's observation: "The necessities of poverty, the need of

---

331. Arthur Lipow, *Authoritarian Socialism in America: Edward Bellamy and the Nationalist Movement* (Berkeley, CA: The University of California Press, 1982), 52.

332. Bellamy, *Looking Backward*, 68. On this point Hansot argues, "if Bellamy is to be taken seriously . . . then what is left as a permanent part of human nature are only those traits that were thwarted in the old capitalistic system but are fully expressed in the new economic organization." Elisabeth Hansot, *Perfection and Progress: Two Modes of Utopian Thought* (Cambridge, MA: The MIT Press, 1974), 123–24 (see also 120, 134). Lorenzo argues that while Bellamy assumes that humans are "hardwired" for competition, "one does not attempt to undo the wiring that makes humans competitive; one merely changes the prizes of competition." David J. Lorenzo, *Cities at the End of the World* (New York: Bloomsbury, 2014), 88.

333. Bellamy, *Looking Backward*, 169.

334. Bellamy, 178.

335. Kenneth M. Roemer, "Utopia and Victorian Culture: 1888–99," in *America as Utopia*, ed. Kenneth M. Roemer, 305–32 (New York: Burt Franklin and Company, 1981), 318. Henry George was a notable exception, viewing competition as necessary for economic life. Hofstadter, *Social Darwinism in American Thought*, 110.

336. Taylor, *The Economic Novel in America*, 197.

337. Bellamy, *Looking Backward*, 191.

338. Tilman, "The Utopian Vision of Edward Bellamy and Thorstein Veblen," 891.

having a home no longer tempt women to accept as the fathers of their children men whom they neither can love nor respect."[339] This shift in the circumstances of marriage prompts Dr. Leete to make what sounds like a eugenic proclamation:

> For the first time in human history the principle of sexual selection, with its tendency to preserve and transmit the better types of the race, and let the inferior types drop out, has unhindered operation. . . . Every generation is sifted through a little finer mesh than the last.[340]

But since there is no state regulation in the choice of a partner, there is no required eugenic sacrifice, and thus no constructive tax.

BELLAMY'S CONSTRUCTIVE TAX ON INHERITED DEPRAVITY

Bellamy's overt eugenic proposal results in a constructive tax on criminals and those who refuse or are unable to work. With the organization of the industrial army, work is now available at an equal living wage, rendering the criminal alternatives to unemployment less attractive.[341] Those who from disability or illness are truly unable to work are still comrades in Bellamy's "brotherhood of man" and as such receive an equal allocation of the nation's prosperity, not as charity but as a right (see chapter four).[342] As in Wells's *A Modern Utopia*, Bellamy's new society sequesters the "large residuum too hopelessly perverted, too congenitally deformed, to have the power of leading a good life, however assisted."[343] Toward this population, "the new society, strong in the perfect justice of its attitude, proceed[s] with merciful

---

339. Bellamy, *Looking Backward*, 191. "In believing that economic factors alone were responsible for women's equality," Pfaelzer asserts, "Bellamy perpetuated patriarchal images of natural female inferiority and created socialist female characters who . . . were pure, pious, domestic, and submissive." Pfaelzer, *The Utopian Novel*, 36. Also see Roemer, *The Obsolete Necessity*, 132.

340. Bellamy, *Looking Backward*, 191.

341. Bellamy, *Equality*, chap. 37, 363.

342. Bellamy, *Looking Backward*, 111.

343. Bellamy, *Equality*, chap. 37, 363.

firmness."[344] The incorrigible criminals and the "morally insane," explains Dr. Leete, are segregated with "a good conscience," not as punishment but to ensure their inability to reproduce.[345] In these ways, he advises, society was able to rid itself of "a load of inherited depravity" within one generation following the brief bloodless Revolution."[346]

QUALITY CONTROL IN ZAMYATIN'S *WE*

In its quest to make the citizens of Zamyatin's One State more rational, society had first overcome hunger and then, three hundred years ago, turned to taming sex ("love"). "Finally, even this natural force was conquered, i.e. organized and mathematicised," through the proclamation that "each cipher [person] has a right to any other cipher as sexual product."[347] As in *Nineteen Eighty-Four*, One State's goal is to minimize emotional attachments arising from sexual union. Unlike Orwell's system, however, its aim is not to transform sexual activity into a "slightly disgusting minor operation"[348] but to facilitate routine sexual activity as part of a lifestyle of rational bliss. Cooke explains that One State's goal in conquering love is to "suppress sexual envy."[349] However, when D-503 realizes he is sharing I-330 with his friend R-13, he exclaims, "you—you also? With her?" and asks himself (his "real" self): "Can it be that all that craziness (love, jealousy, etc.) isn't only the stuff of idiotic ancient books?"[350]

In the drive toward industrial standardization as a measure of rational progress, breeding for physical uniformity is One State's logical response. However, as Vaingurt observes, "Eugenics laws have been in operation for hundreds of years, and yet the goal of physical standardization has not been

---

344. Bellamy, chap. 37, 363.

345. Bellamy, chap. 37, 364.

346. Bellamy, chap. 37, 364.

347. Zamyatin, *We*, record 5, 21.

348. Orwell, *Nineteen Eighty-Four*, 67.

349. Cooke, *Human Nature in Utopia: Zamyatin's We*, 136. The principle of avoiding permanent attachments is comparable to that in *Brave New World*, where "individual love and the satisfaction of the sexual urge are kept separate. Individual love, tending as it does to create independent social cells within a greater social body, is considered especially dangerous." Gerber, *Utopian Fantasy*, 71.

350. Zamyatin, *We*, record 11, 56–57.

achieved."[351] To this Cooke responds, "the clear physical contrast between the citizens of the city with the hairy people living beyond the Wall suggests how much change has been wrought."[352]

Central to One State's eugenic control is its strict regulation of all sexual encounters through registration with the Guardians and the issuance of pink tickets used to schedule each tryst.[353] In this way I-330 selects D-503 as part of her plan to hijack the spaceship *Integral.* One State's goal with respect to controlling reproduction is uniformity,[354] which it implements by testing sex hormones and ensuring conformity to standardized parental norms.[355] O-90, one of D-503's sexual partners, was adjudged too short ("about ten centimeters below the Maternal Norm"[356]) and is therefore denied a chance at motherhood—the levy of a constructive tax. The sanction for giving birth to unauthorized children is death. Despite this threat O-90 becomes pregnant, with the reluctant help of D-503.[357]

Zamyatin "resembles Morris," claims Lorenzo, "in viewing science and its accompanying language of mathematical reason as problematic with respect to a truly human existence."[358] But while Morris's vision of a truly human existence lies in creative engagement with one's work (in an otherwise static world), Zamyatin sees the human ideal not in the Benefactor's conception of rational bliss but in I-330's dynamic infinite revolution.[359] For this reason,

---

351. Vaingurt, "Human Machines and the Pains of Penmanship in Yevgeny Zamyatin's *We,*" 120.

352. Cooke, *Human Nature in Utopia: Zamyatin's We,* 142.

353. Zamyatin, *We,* record 5, 21.

354. Zamyatin's narrator muses (echoing Campanella), "Isn't it funny to know crop breeding, poultry breeding, fish breeding . . . and not to be able to get to the top rung of that logical ladder: child breeding?" (Zamyatin, record 3, 14).

355. The right to have sex with another person (cipher) begins with an examination in the "Bureau of Sex" where "they generate a corresponding Table of Sex Days for you" (Zamyatin, record 5, 21).

356. Zamyatin, record 2, 6.

357. Zamyatin, record 19, 99; record 20, 102.

358. Lorenzo, *Cities at the End of the World,* 130.

359. Zamyatin, *We,* record 30, 153. Wegner observes, "it is through I-330 that Zamyatin reveals the dialectical nature of his concept of infinite revolution." Phillip E. Wegner, "On Zamyatin's *We*: A Critical Map of Utopia's 'Possible Worlds,'" *Utopian Studies* 4, no. 2 (1993): 94–116, 109.

affirms Suvin, "the basic values of *We* imply a stubborn revolutionary vision of a classless new moral world free from all social alienations."[360] As a consequence, in contrast to *Nineteen Eighty-Four* and *Looking Backward*, argues Wegner, *We* "does not configure any *singular* monolithic future world."[361] In the end, the success of the Benefactor's "Great Operation" (surgically excised imaginations) may decide the contest between the objective of rational bliss and the aims of the MEPHI revolutionaries—the "enemies of happiness."

HUXLEY'S BRAVE NEW FAMILY

Hamlet asks: "What is a man, if his chief good and market of his time be but to sleep and feed?"[362] In Huxley's *Brave New World* Mustapha Mond, the World Controller, tells John the New Mexico Savage, "People are happy; they get what they want, and they never want what they can't get."[363] Instead of Gilman's "find your real job, and do it"[364] (see chapter four), one's real job, in Huxley's London, is the basis of one's embryo's development. "We also predestine and condition," explains Mr. Foster, the hatchery technician. "We decant our babies as socialized human beings, as Alphas or Epsilons."[365] Reproduction is carried out in laboratories using the Bokanovsky Process of egg division,[366] with the aid of Podsnap's Technique,[367] and the imposition of graduated oxygen deprivation to the embryos.[368] In this way the state is able to produce citizens with the capacities appropriate to perform society's work at any one of five levels (or fifteen, when augmented with plusses and minuses): Alphas, Betas, Gammas, Deltas, and Epsilons. This constructive tax fulfills Galton's aim for eugenics, "to represent each class

---

360. Suvin, *Metamorphoses of Science Fiction*, 257.

361. Wegner, "On Zamyatin's *We*," 96.

362. William Shakespeare, *Hamlet*, in *The Complete Works*, comp. ed. (653–90) (Oxford: Clarendon Press, 1988), act 4, scene 4.

363. Huxley, *Brave New World*, 198 (italics in original).

364. Gilman, *The Living of Charlotte Perkins Gilman*, 42.

365. Huxley, *Brave New World*, 23.

366. Huxley, 17.

367. Huxley, 19.

368. " 'The lower the caste,' said Mr. Foster, 'the shorter the oxygen.' The first organ affected was the brain" (Huxley, 24).

or sect by its best specimens."[369] The state raises children in warehouse-style nurseries and socializes them with hypnopaedia (hypnosis during sleep), the "greatest moralizing and socializing force of all time."[370] In this process each citizen "is so conditioned that he will feel happy in this future role, and would be unhappy if any other kind of occupation and life were assigned to him."[371] Unlike *Nineteen Eighty-Four*, sex is openly encouraged with multiple partners—"Orgy-porgy"—though never with the goal of reproduction.[372] Marriage has no purpose and, therefore, no role in Huxley's vision—"Every one belongs to every one else."[373]

> When John asks Bernard: " 'Are you married to [Lenina]?'
> Bernard replies, 'Am I what?' . . . 'Ford no!' Bernard couldn't help laughing.
> John also laughed, but for another reason. . . . 'O brave new world, that has such people in it.' "[374]

What John calls "such people" are the product of the state's regulation of marriage, childrearing, and eugenics. While manipulating our privacy, access to truth, and work assignments provide state control in the present, manipulating the types of people who get reproduced is critical to shaping the society of the future.

In the next chapter we examine the utopian treatment of land proprietorship and the disparate societies projected to result from land's ownership as either a private commodity or a common resource. In either case a sacrifice is levied on one segment of society, resulting in a constructive tax. Proponents of a worldview favoring land's common ownership are Owen, George, Tolstoy, and Wells, while those favoring private ownership include Harrington, Godwin, and Nozick.

---

369. F. Galton, "Eugenics: Its Definition, Scope, and Aims," 2.

370. Huxley, *Brave New World*, 36.

371. Gerber, *Utopian Fantasy*, 71.

372. Women are responsible for contraceptive practices. For Lenina, says Huxley's narrator, "Years of intensive hypnopaedia and, from twelve to seventeen, Malthusian drill three times a week had made the taking of these precautions almost as automatic and inevitable as blinking" (Huxley, 80).

373. Huxley, 52.

374. Huxley, 130.

CHAPTER SIX

TAXATION AND LAND PROPRIETORSHIP

Part One:
Harrington, Godwin, and Owen

THE LAND QUESTION

The hopes of mankind, in relation to their future progress depend upon their observing the genuine effects of erroneous institutions.

—William Godwin (1756–1836),
Enquiry Concerning Political Justice[1]

In Tolstoy's story, "How Much Land Does a Man Need?" the central character, Pahom, spends his life in an insatiable pursuit of land; the more he owns, the more he wants. The story ends with Pahom's death and the digging of his grave—as well as the answer to the titular question: "Six feet from his head to his heels was all he needed."[2] Two prominent themes of

---

1. Godwin, *Enquiry Concerning Political Justice*, 3rd ed., bk. 7, chap. 8, 690.

2. Leo Tolstoy, *How Much Land Does a Man Need? And Other Stories*, trans. Louise and Aylmer Maude (repr., n.p. digireads.com, n.d.), 52.

utopian thought are the division of labor and the division of land. Either division, when under state control and imposing a sacrifice for the general welfare, results in a constructive tax. Aspects of the division of labor were discussed in chapter four. This chapter examines selected utopias that address the division and proprietorship of land.

A significant question for utopian theory, raised by Thomas Paine, is the extent to which each generation's life opportunities should include equal access to land.[3] "Persons are born into a world in which property is already attached to states, individuals and collectivities," observes Reeve, "and the question is what makes it legitimate to require these new arrivals to respect a division of property about which they were not consulted."[4] Land's moral status, its just distribution and control, as well as its characterization either as property subject to private ownership or as our common inheritance, are elements of what came to be called "the land question." Herbert Spencer articulates the parameters of the land question in the 1850 publication of his *Social Statics*: "Either men *have* a right to make the soil private property, or they *have not*. . . . There can be no half-and-half opinion."[5]

In *The Politics of Utopia*, Goodwin and Taylor write: "The major cause of social evil, utopians almost unanimously agree, is private property, which produces a variety of disruptive sentiments and desires."[6] Barring unanimity are certain libertarian utopians, including Ayn Rand and Robert Nozick (discussed in this and the next chapter), who see private ownership of land as essential to an ideal society. "Without property rights," declares Rand, "no other rights are possible,"[7] and hence no political freedom and no human flourishing. Anticipating this argument, Spencer counters that "an exclusive possession of the soil necessitates an infringement of the law of equal freedom. For, men who cannot 'live and move and have their being'

---

3. Paine recommends countries establish funds to compensate citizens for the loss of their "natural inheritance, by the introduction of the system of landed property." Paine, *Agrarian Justice*.

4. Andrew Reeve, *Property* (Atlantic Highlands, NJ: Humanities Press International, 1986), 178.

5. Spencer, *Social Statics*, 139 (italics in original).

6. Goodwin and Taylor, *The Politics of Utopia*, 60; see also 136–37.

7. Rand, *The Virtue of Selfishness*, 33. Rand says, "no rights can exist without the right to translate one's right into reality—to think, to work and to keep the results—which means: the right of property." Rand, *Atlas Shrugged*, 1062.

without the leave of others, cannot be equally free with those others."[8] This result, he believes, necessitates two classes—landlords and trespassers.[9] In his later career, when he had become a prominent and influential writer and public figure, Spencer (or perhaps because of his prominence) reversed his view on the land question in favor of private landholding. For some of his admirers—Leo Tolstoy in particular—Spencer's earlier views retained their logical force;[10] for Henry George, however, Spencer's capitulation was inexplicable: "Here, with one flash of synthetic logic, the horse chestnut becomes a chestnut horse!"[11]

Whether land can be owned, or is like air and water our common heritage of the earth, is not a legal or scientific question of empirical fact but

---

8. Spencer, *Social Statics*, 132. Spencer's "law of equal freedom" stipulates that in a just society everyone's freedom must be equal. This is implemented by the "law of right social relationships," which states, "*Every man has freedom to do all that he wills, provided he infringes not the equal freedom of any other man*" (Spencer, 106, 121; italics in original). Magner notes that Spencer struggled with the extent to which the law of equal freedom applied to women, as it was only men who "had the obligation to defend the state through military service." Lois N. Magner, "Darwinism and the Woman Question: The Evolving Views of Charlotte Perkins Gilman," in *Critical Essays on Charlotte Perkins Gilman*, ed. Joanne B. Karpinski, 115–28 (New York: G. K. Hall and Co., 1992), 118.

9. Spencer, *Social Statics*, 132.

10. In Tolstoy's novel *Resurrection*, the principal character Nekhlyudov "was specially struck by the position taken up by Spencer in *Social Statics*, that justice forbids private land-holding . . . a brilliant corroboration of which he . . . later . . . found in the works of Henry George." Tolstoy, *Resurrection*, 18–19.

11. George, *A Perplexed Philosopher*, 208; see also 204–5. George reports of Spencer, "the times had changed since he wrote 'Social Statics.' From an unknown man, printing with difficulty an unsalable book, he had become a popular philosopher . . . and in the United States . . . hailed as a thinker beside whom Newton and Aristotle were to be mentioned only to point his superiority" (George, 84–85). "Ostensibly his reason for attacking Spencer," says Thomas, "was the Englishman's supposed cowardice in selling out to the landlords. . . . But George's real target was not the act of betrayal but the original Synthetic Philosophy itself." John L. Thomas, *Alternative America: Henry George, Edward Bellamy, Henry Demarest Lloyd and the Adversary Tradition* (Cambridge, MA: The Belknap Press of Harvard University Press, 1983), 324. It is thus that George says, "in his effort to smooth away the monstrous injustice of private property in land, Mr. Spencer does violence to his own theories—not alone to the theories which he held when he wrote 'Social Statics,' but to theories of his Synthetic Philosophy." George, *A Perplexed Philosopher*, 204–5.

a moral question whose answer forms a worldview's foundation.[12] "Property is controversial," observes Macpherson, "because it subserves some more general purposes of a whole society, or the dominant classes of a society."[13] Moreover, "to see property as a right does not imply approving any particular system of property as morally right."[14] Concurring, Nozick adds, "it is not only persons favoring *private* property who need a theory of how property rights legitimately originate. Those advocating collective property . . . also must provide a theory of how such property rights arise."[15]

RIVAL WORLDVIEWS

Broome, in a chapter on fairness and the distribution of goods, discusses cases where "the good to be distributed is indivisible, and . . . all the candidates have equal claims." Whether land is an indivisible good to which we all have equal claims is the question spawning the two worldviews.[16] The moral dimension of land proprietorship is the question of which group to sacrifice and why—not as between landowners and non-landowners, but as between the proponents of the two opposing worldviews: those pursuing the general welfare through common ownership of land and those seeking it through private land ownership. By *worldview* I mean the broad organizing context of our fundamental convictions, some of which may be so familiar that we remain unaware of them until they contrast with someone else's opposing view.[17] Thus, Shevek, in *The Dispossessed*, says, "We've . . . built

---

12. It is not only utopians who raise moral questions about private land ownership. Mill argues, "No Man made the land. It is the original inheritance of the whole species. Its appropriation is wholly a question of general expediency. When private property in land is not expedient, it is unjust." Mill, *Principles of Political Economy*, bk. 2, chap. 1, §6, 173. See also Alan Ryan, *Property and Political Theory* (Oxford: Basil Blackwell, 1984), 154.

13. C. B. Macpherson, *Property* (Toronto: University of Toronto Press, 1978), 11.

14. Macpherson, 3.

15. Nozick, *Anarchy, State, and Utopia*, 178.

16. His focus is on organ transplants, rather than land, where he supports distribution by lottery. John Broome, *Ethics out of Economics* (Cambridge University Press, 1999), 119–20.

17. By contrast, "ideologies," according to Mannheim, are "ideas transcending the existing order . . . and harmoniously integrated into the world-view characteristic of the period." Mannheim, *Ideology and Utopia*, 193. The difference between a worldview and what Pepper calls a world hypothesis is the fact that a world hypothesis cannot reject anything as irrelevant. It is a metaphysical system designed to organize our understanding based on a "root-metaphor." Examples include organicism and mechanism. Thus, a worldview may

walls all around ourselves, and we can't see them, because they're part of our thinking."[18] In *Ideology and Utopia*, Mannheim asks, "how it is possible that the identical human thought-processes concerned with the same world produce divergent conceptions of that world."[19] The answer posed by Lakoff is that they are not "identical human thought-processes" if they are framed in morally distinct language.[20] The two opposing worldviews discussed here—one requiring private ownership of land and the other proscribing it—have inspired utopians to commend the moral necessity of one and to censure the ignominy of the other.

PRIVATE PROPERTY

In *A Modern Utopia* Wells emphasizes one aspect of the controversy regarding private ownership of land when he warns: "Very speedily, under terrestrial conditions, the property of a man may reach such proportions that his freedom oppresses the freedom of others."[21] George illustrates this point with a thought experiment. "Place one hundred men on an island from which there is no escape, and whether you make one of these men the absolute owner of the other ninety-nine, or the absolute owner of the soil of the island, will make no difference either to him or to them."[22] Wells also suggests that a landowner's power to control the lives and freedom of others is a matter of scale and may reach a point of diminishing influence. In *When the Sleeper Wakes,* Graham, the central character, is the owner of half of the earth, yet what this permits him to do is in question. Ostrog (Graham's rival for power) tells him, "You are Owner perhaps of half the property in the world. But you are not Master."[23]

---

comprise a world hypothesis but need not do so. Stephen C. Pepper, *World Hypothesis* (Berkeley: University of California Press, 1942).

18. Le Guin, *The Dispossessed*, 288.

19. Mannheim, *Ideology and Utopia*, 9.

20. George Lakoff, *Don't Think of an Elephant!* (White River Junction, VT: Chelsea Green Publishing, 2014), xi–xii.

21. Wells, *A Modern Utopia*, 40. On the same point, see Macpherson, *Property*, 12.

22. Henry George, *Progress and Poverty* (New York: Robert Schalkenbach Foundation 1953), 347.

23. H. G. Wells, *When the Sleeper Wakes, in Three Prophetic Novels of H. G. Wells* (New York: Dover Publications, Inc., 1960), 161.

Kant observes, "no-one originally has any greater right than anyone else to occupy any particular portion of the earth."[24] One of the greatest chasms in utopian literature and arguably the most fundamental question of political philosophy—and hence of tax policy, as George was at pains to illustrate—is the ownership of land. "The ownership of land," he proclaims, "is the great fundamental fact which ultimately determines the social, the political, and consequently the intellectual and moral condition of a people."[25] In this context, perhaps more than others, the importance of general welfare considerations on future generations is paramount. In a dramatic illustration of this fact Kavka says, "given how much the absence of the private property system would have changed world history, it is likely that no presently existing individual would have existed if the private property system had not."[26] In this discussion my aim is not to defend one worldview against the other but to highlight the prospect—illustrated in utopian literature—that either position, in imposing an unrequited sacrifice on one segment of society by the other, levies a constructive tax.

PRIVATE VS. COMMON OWNERSHIP

My concern in this chapter is with the proprietorship of land, whether private or non-private. While I refer to non-private land ownership as *common ownership*, I acknowledge the distinctions others have drawn between common, collective, and communal ownership.[27] Since my focus is on the fact that some utopians (for example, Rand and Nozick) hold that the institution of private land ownership (and private property generally) is essential to the general welfare while others (for example, George and Tolstoy) see this same institution as the major impediment to the general welfare, using "common ownership" as the contrary of private ownership is primarily for ease of expression. Standing in the way of a clear exposition

---

24. Kant, *Perpetual Peace*, 106.

25. George, *Progress and Poverty*, 295.

26. Gregory S. Kavka, "An Internal Critique of Nozick's Entitlement Theory," in *Equality and Liberty: Analyzing Rawls and Nozick*, ed. J. Angelo Corlett, 298–310 (Houndsmills, UK: Macmillan, 1991), 308.

27. See Jeremy Waldron, *The Right to Private Property* (Oxford: Clarendon Press, 1988), 40–41. Robert Owen and Henry George speak of *public property* as the alternative to private property.

of this topic, however, is the fact that the single term *property*, especially *private property*, refers to both land and non-land (realty and personality). Consequently, some writers, when speaking of property, fail to specify their meaning or distinguish land from other property.[28] Rand and Nozick, discussed in this and the next chapter, are examples. But what may be true of property generally may not be true of land in particular, and the other way around. This verbal imprecision can lead to invalid inferences, some of which may be inadvertent.[29]

THE DISPUTANTS

The goal of this chapter is to explore a sample of utopian writers who recognize that the laws society adopts with respect to land proprietorship are critical in producing a balance of required sacrifice. Drawing attention to the difficulties inherent in this issue, Milton Friedman asserts, "the notion of property, as it has developed over centuries and as it is embodied in our legal codes," involves "complex social creations rather than self-evident propositions."[30] At least some disputants, however (Spencer and Rand were noted earlier), hold their positions as self-evident, that is, as a priori moral bedrock. Rand, for example, says the protection of rights (including property rights) and hence freedom is the only "moral purpose of a government,"[31] since "no human rights can exist without property rights."[32] Rand subscribes to what Macpherson calls the "perennial justification" of the institution of private property: "that property ought to be an enforceable claim because

---

28. Some writers, to their credit, are explicit on this point. Spence, for example, says, "The right of property is that which belongs to every citizen to enjoy and dispose of according to his pleasure, property, revenues, labor, and industry. Here his property in land is excepted, which, being inseparably incorporated with that of his fellow parishioners, is inalienable." Thomas Spence, *The Constitution of Spensonia* in *Pig's Meat: Selected Writings of Thomas Spence, Radical and Pioneer Land Reformer* (Nottingham: Spokesman, 1982), 168.

29. George accuses Spencer of using this tactic in his later writings. George, *A Perplexed Philosopher*, 248.

30. Milton Friedman, *Capitalism and Freedom* (Chicago: The University of Chicago Press, 2002), 26.

31. Rand, *The Virtue of Selfishness*, 33.

32. Rand, 91.

property is necessary for the realization of man's fundamental nature, or because it is a natural right."[33] This, says Tolstoy, was "the usual argument in favor of private ownership of land, supposed to be irrefutable."[34] In opposition to Rand and the "perennial justification," Cohen argues: "the familiar idea that private property and freedom are conceptually connected is an ideological illusion."[35] Waldron concurs, affirming that no system of property can legitimately claim an advantage in the provision of liberty.[36] Jonathan Wolff elaborates this point, maintaining:

> We should not take it for granted that libertarian property rights best promote secure enjoyment of valuable liberty. . . . An observation of Bentham puts the point well; "How is property given? By restraining liberty; that is, by taking it away as far as necessary for the purpose. . . . Thus all property arrangements deny some liberty or other.[37]

Bentham generalizes this principle: "But as against the coercion applicable by individual to individual, no liberty can be given to one man but in proportion as it is taken from another."[38]

More, Owen, Tolstoy, and others offer common ownership of land as a means for eliminating poverty and other social ills. A political system supporting private land ownership requires a sacrifice from those who, such as Proudhon, believe land, like the air, is a common element of our environment.[39] When the state supports a system of private land ownership, as

---

33. Macpherson, *Property*, 3. Burke supplies a variation of this argument in speaking of the intergenerational transmission of landed property as central to the conservation and perpetuation of society. In his view land forms the basis for linking generations within families, maintaining order and class hierarchy and ensuring the form of government that maintains these institutions. Burke, *Reflections on the Revolution in France*, 51.

34. Tolstoy, *Resurrection*, 348.

35. Cohen, *Self-Ownership, Freedom, and Equality*, 89. On the relation between freedom and property, see Reeve, *Property*, 77–111.

36. Waldron, *The Right to Private Property*, 293–94.

37. Jonathan Wolff, *Robert Nozick: Property, Justice and the Minimal State* (Stanford, CA: Stanford University Press, 1991), 97–98.

38. Bentham, *Anarchical Fallacies*, in '*Nonsense upon Stilts*,' 57.

39. According to Proudhon, "water, air, and light are common things, not because they are inexhaustible, but because they are indispensable. . . . Similarly, the land is

George observes, the government imposes its will by enforcing a monopoly of one of the "natural elements which human exertion can neither produce nor increase."[40] In this sense, government enforcing private land monopolies is no less coercive than its favoring a business with a monopoly on the sale of an essential product or service. In either case the state imposes a privileged monopoly through its legalized use of force. The problems resulting from this monopoly are, George believes, practical and far-reaching. For George, writes Dewey, "the fact that a few have monopolized the land . . . [means] they have the power to dictate to others access to the land and to its products—which include waterpower, electricity, coal, iron and all minerals, as well as the foods that sustain life."[41] Moreover, explains George, "Whoever, under our laws, acquires ownership in land *may* deprive others of light, air, running water, etc." The owner of land *is* the owner of these natural legacies, "not merely virtually, but formally and legally."[42] For those opposing private ownership of land, the general welfare is best served when land is owned in common. Enforcement of either worldview requires a sacrifice to the enforcer's vision of the general welfare and for that reason the payment of a constructive tax.[43]

The remainder of this chapter highlights seven utopians—Harrington, Godwin, Owen, George, Tolstoy, Wells, and Nozick—who recognize the significance of land proprietorship as an instrument of the general welfare (or, in Nozick's case, individual autonomy as a surrogate for the general welfare). Except for Godwin and Nozick, each in his own way devises a

---

indispensable to our existence, thus a common thing, consequently insusceptible of appropriation; but land is much scarcer than the other elements." Pierre-Joseph Proudhon, *What Is Property?* ed. and trans. Donald R. Kelley and Bonnie G. Smith (Cambridge: Cambridge University Press, 1994), 73.

40. Specifically, George speaks of land rent as "the price of monopoly, arising from the reduction to individual ownership of natural elements which human exertion can neither produce nor increase." George, *Progress and Poverty*, 167.

41. John Dewey, "Steps to Economic Recovery," in *John Dewey: The Later Works, 1925–1934*, vol. 9, ed. Jo Ann Boydston (Carbondale, IL: Southern Illinois Press, 1986), 63.

42. George, *A Perplexed Philosopher*, 195–96 (italics in original).

43. Murphy and Nagel expose another dimension of the land question that adds to its complexity. "Private property," they explain, "is a legal convention, defined in part by the tax system; therefore, the tax system cannot be evaluated by looking at its impact on private property, conceived as something that has independent existence and validity." Murphy and Nagel, *The Myth of Ownership: Taxes and Justice*, 8.

means for legally altering the institution of landholdings to improve the balance of required sacrifice.

JAMES HARRINGTON (1611–1677): INHERITANCE TAX IN *OCEANA*

The beginning of reform is not so much to equalize property as to train the nobler sort of natures not to desire more, and to prevent the lower from getting more; that is to say, they must be kept down, but not ill-treated.

—Aristotle (384–322 BCE), *Politics*[44]

Inheritance law seeks to balance the desires of the dead against the wishes of the living and the needs of the unborn. "When framed in a particular manner," argues de Tocqueville, inheritance law "unites, draws together, and vests property and power in a few hands."[45] Harrington was concerned with preventing the concentration of power and sought to reform inheritance law as one means.[46] His *Commonwealth of Oceana* (1656), says Claeys, was "by far the most important political utopia" of its time.[47] The "main question," asserts Harrington, is "how a commonwealth comes to be an empire of laws and not of men?"[48] His suggested reforms include the secret ballot,

---

44. Aristotle, *Politics*, trans. Jowett, bk. 2, chap. 7, 1267b.

45. de Tocqueville, *Democracy in America*, vol. 1, chap. 3, 43.

46. Hertzler observes that *Oceana* "stripped of its allegorical trappings is little more than a magnified written constitution." It was written "to solve the needs of its country at a very critical time in its history . . . during the days of Cromwell." Hertzler, *The History of Utopian Thought*, 169, 168. When Cromwell is referred to in *Oceana* he is called Olphaus Megaletor who, Pocock says, is "occupying a fictional and ideal moment at which a potentiality ascribed to the real man—that of acting as a legislator—is seen being actualized." J. G. A. Pocock, historical introduction, *The Political Works of James Harrington* (Cambridge: Cambridge University Press, 1977), 50. While England is referred to as Oceana, Scotland is called Marpesia ("being of the northern part of the same island") and Ireland Panopea ("a neighbor island anciently subjected by the arms of Oceana").

47. Gregory Claeys, *Searching for Utopia: The History of an Idea* (London: Thames and Hudson, 2011), 100.

48. James Harrington, *The Commonwealth of Oceana* (1656) in *The Political Works of James Harrington*, ed. J. G. A. Pocock (Cambridge: Cambridge University Press, 1977), 171.

term limits, and a two-chamber legislative system[49] (separating debating and voting powers).[50] But a critical component is the *agrarian law* that restricts the value of inherited landholdings.[51] "An equal agrarian," says Lord Archon, his spokesman,

> is a perpetual law, establishing and preserving the balance of dominion by such a distribution, that no one man or number of men, within the compass of the few or aristocracy, can come to overpower the whole people by their possessions in lands.[52]

Concerning the agrarian law Macpherson observes: "The argument essentially is that the commonwealth could not be overthrown as long as the agrarian law held, and that the agrarian law would hold because no class strong enough to alter it would have an interest in doing so."[53] Indeed, Harrington argues, "without an agrarian [law], government, whether monarchical, aristocratical, or popular, has no long lease."[54] Harrington was one of the first utopians, says H. F. Russell Smith, "to give to economic considerations the prominence that they deserve and to bring them into connection with the science of politics."[55]

Harrington's insight, important for this chapter, was to see land as an independent variable for the law to manipulate in distributing its mandatory

---

49. Hertzler, *The History of Utopian Thought*, 172–73.

50. Harrington, *Oceana*, 172–73.

51. Montesquieu warns: "It is not sufficient in a well-regulated democracy that the divisions of land be equal; they ought also to be small, as was customary among the Romans." Montesquieu, *The Spirit of Laws*, bk. 5, chap. 6, 21. Adam Smith observes, however, that "Rome, like most of the other ancient republics, was originally founded upon an agrarian law, which divided the public territory, in a certain proportion, among the different citizens who composed the state. The course of human affairs . . . necessarily deranged this original division, and frequently threw the lands . . . into the possession of a single person." Smith, *Wealth of Nations*, bk. 4, chap. 7, 415.

52. Harrington, *Oceana*, 181.

53. C. B. Macpherson, *The Political Theory of Possessive Individualism Hobbes to Locke* (Oxford: Oxford University Press, 2011), 182.

54. Harrington, *Oceana*, 164.

55. H. F. Russell Smith, *Harrington and His Oceana: A Study of a 17th Century Utopia and its Influence in America* (Cambridge: At the University Press, 1914; republished by Leopold Classic Library), 36.

sacrifices.[56] In recognizing this principle, he understood it is possible to shift the sacrifices land ownership imposes—as with other tax burdens—in support of society's ideals.[57] The specific restrictions of his agrarian law limit a son's inheritance to no more land than would produce a yearly revenue of 2000 pounds (£456,361 in 2018).[58] Harrington explains that "every man who is at present possessed . . . of an estate in land exceeding the revenue of five thousand pounds a year, and having more than one son, shall leave his lands [with qualifications and restrictions] . . . equally divided among them."[59] Over the span of an undetermined number of generations, this utopian solution, Harrington assumes, will stabilize land ownership (at least among those families who already possess land), providing stability to government. While Harrington's political reforms were taken seriously, his crucial means for effecting economic balance, the mandatory intergenerational redistribution of landholdings—a form of constructive taxation—was not. Though perhaps unworkable as designed,[60] Harrington's agrarian law in *Oceana* illustrates an ideal society willing to consider the consequences of its land policies on the welfare of future generations.

---

56. Morton observes, "Harrington's scheme was based on the appreciation of a great truth, whose clear enunciation gives him an important place in the development of the conception of historical materialism. The character of a society will depend, he believed, upon the distribution of property among the classes within it. By property he meant landed property." Morton, *The English Utopia*, 98.

57. "By keeping power in the hands of the steadier section of the community, which is engaged in agriculture," says Smith, Harrington "hoped to avoid the extreme form of democracy." Smith, *Harrington and His Oceana*, 36.

58. £2000 in 1656 adjusted for inflation. https://www.bankofengland.co.uk/monetary-policy/inflation/inflation-calculator (accessed February 4, 2019).

59. Harrington, *Oceana*, 231. Under this system, explains Pocock, "no one of them can inherit land worth more than that figure, unless the proportion of the number of sons to the value of the estate renders division at a lower figure impossible." Pocock, *The Political Works of James Harrington*, 62. Harrington's agrarian scheme thus would abolish primogeniture by dividing the estate to be inherited as equally as possible among all the sons.

60. Hume was skeptical of Harrington's agrarian proposal, calling it "impracticable." "Men will soon learn the art which was practised in ancient Rome," he says, "of concealing their possessions under other people's name." Hume, "Idea of a Perfect Commonwealth," 515.

WILLIAM GODWIN (1756–1836):
ANARCHY AND PRIVATE PROPERTY

All men, even the most stupid and unthinking, abhor fraud, perfidy, and injustice, and delight to see them punished. But few men have reflected upon the necessity of justice to the existence of society.

—Adam Smith (1723–1790), *The Theory of Moral Sentiments*[61]

The basis of Godwin's land policy is separating the question of land ownership from that of land use. Perhaps surprising for an anarchist, he defends private property for the same reason Henry George defends common property: it is the form of proprietorship that facilitates land's application for the benefit of the whole.[62] In chapter three I described Godwin's central teachings on seeking truth in the pursuit of justice, in which he says, "I should contribute every thing in my power to the benefit of the whole."[63]

Applying his conception of justice to property in general and land in particular, Godwin declares, "We have in reality nothing that is strictly speaking our own. We have nothing that has not a destination prescribed to it by the immutable voice of reason and justice."[64] Suppose one person, he says, through his own work or by inheritance, owns a greater portion of property than another. Despite the method of acquisition, he explains, justice "obliges him to regard this property as a trust, and calls upon him maturely to consider in what manner it may be employed for the increase of liberty, knowledge and virtue."[65] In expressing this view he does not advocate the elimination of private landholdings. According to Godwin, "the idea of property . . . will remain, but no man will have the least desire, for purposes of ostentation or luxury, to possess more than his neighbors."[66] Each of us, he argues, has a moral obligation to place what property we own, including

---

61. Smith, *The Theory of Moral Sentiments*, 89.

62. George, *Progress and Poverty*, 401.

63. Godwin, *An Enquiry Concerning Political Justice*, 1st ed., bk. 2, chap. 2, 52.

64. Godwin, *Enquiry Concerning Political Justice*, 3rd ed., bk. 2, chap. 5, 194.

65. Godwin, 175.

66. Godwin, 199. Ryan argues, "It is evident that Godwin's view amounts to the denial of anything one can call property rights at all." Ryan, *Property and Political Theory*, 93.

land, at the disposal of our neighbor if she can produce from our property "a much higher degree of benefit and pleasure" for society.[67]

"Few things have contributed more to undermine the energy and virtue of the human species," he insists, "than the supposition that we have a right . . . to do what we will with our own."[68] It is not the right to own land that Godwin disputes, but the right to ignore justice, reason, and the plight of humankind in considering the use to which land should be assigned. In carrying out the commands of justice, Godwin asks, "how much am I bound to do for the general weal, that is, for the benefit of the individuals of whom the whole is composed?" He answers himself: "Everything in my power."[69] He acknowledges, however, that "a long period of time must probably elapse before [his plan] can be brought entirely into practice."[70]

ROBERT OWEN (1771–1858): PEACEFUL REVOLUTION

> Every real advance in England on behalf of the workers, links itself onto the name of Robert Owen.
>
> —Frederick Engels (1820–1895), *Socialism: Utopian and Scientific*[71]

In the previous chapter I set out Owen's program for compulsory early childhood education as his solution to the problem of character formation and the catalyst for sweeping social revolution. This change, Owen explains, "must be effected in the same manner in which all other general changes

---

67. Godwin, *Enquiry Concerning Political Justice*, 3rd ed., bk. 8, chap. 5, 740.

68. Godwin, bk. 2, chap. 5, 194. Claeys discusses the distinction between "rights enjoining restraint" and "rights permitting activity" that allows Godwin to both admit private property and yet to disavow property rights enlisted in defense of holding property in an individualistic sense ("a right . . . to do what we will with our own"). Claeys, "The Effects of Property on Godwin's Theory of Justice," 95–96. That one has a right to "choose what to do with what one has" is characteristic of Nozick's libertarian position on property, discussed later in this chapter. Nozick, *Anarchy, State, and Utopia*, 167.

69. Godwin, *An Enquiry Concerning Political Justice*, 1st ed., bk. 2, chap. 2, 56.

70. Godwin, *Enquiry Concerning Political Justice*, 3rd ed., bk. 8, chap. 5, 740.

71. Frederic Engels, *Socialism: Utopian and Scientific* (New York: Pathfinder, 1972), 37.

have been accomplished; that is, by making it appear, first to the few, and then to the many, that the principle to be abandoned"—the false view of self-caused character—"is producing great evil, and that the one to be adopted, will produce great good."[72]

Owen's utopian plan is one of devolution, as is Skinner's in *Walden Two*. Rather than dealing with a country's problems at a national level, Owen argues, "the large accumulated masses of poverty, vice, crime, misery, and pernicious habits, must be gradually separated, divided into manageable portions, and distributed over the country."[73] News of his success in New Lanark, he believed, had set in motion the momentum for a social transformation. "A new state of society for Europe has . . . become an immediate, irresistible necessity."[74] To facilitate these changes, he explains, "a rational government is required to gradually supersede those governments which experience has proved to be most irrational and injurious in practice."[75] The result, he predicted, would be a "change of the most extensive magnitude . . . accomplished without violence or confusion, or any very apparent opposition."[76]

"The land became permanent individual private property," Owen claims, "through oppression and gross injustice. It has, however, through succeeding events, become the private possession of individuals."[77] Private property in general, he believes, is "a never-failing source of deception and fraud between man and man" and the cause of endless evils.[78] Under his reform, however, land will return, gradually and peacefully, to the public domain. To accomplish this goal, Owen recommends the government purchase property from landowners at its fair market price and "make it the

---

72. Owen, *A Development of the Principles and Plans on Which to Establish Self-Supporting Home Colonies*, 31.

73. Owen, *A New View of Society and Other Writings*, 174.

74. Owen, *The Revolution in the Mind*, 138. Claeys reports, "Owen suffered a lifetime of disappointments as a result of his desire to introduce reforms through existing governments." Claeys, *Citizens and Saints*, 102. Owen thus faced Gandhi's hard lesson that "it is the reformer who is anxious for the reform, and not society, from which he should expect nothing better than opposition, abhorrence, and even mortal persecution." Gandhi, *An Autobiography*, 200.

75. Owen, *The Revolution in the Mind*, 138.

76. Owen, *A New View of Society and Other Writings*, 225.

77. Owen, *The Revolution in the Mind*, 121.

78. Owen, *The Book of the New Moral World*, sixth part, chap. 4, 41.

public property of each succeeding generation."[79] The public reappropriation of the land will *not* constitute a tax, however, as there is no sacrifice resulting, for example, from government expropriation or condemnation, merely a voluntary exchange of one asset for another of equal value. As his plan unfolds, Owen foresees a succession of uniform communities featuring a standardized layout and architecture.[80] As a consequence of his educational reforms, Owen believed the home colonies would gradually develop and spread throughout England, then Europe, and eventually worldwide.[81] In this way, Claeys explains, "Owen envisioned a world government built upon a federal structure, with communities as the basic units of organization."[82]

Part Two:
George, Tolstoy, Wells, and Nozick

HENRY GEORGE (1839–1897):
PROGRESS, LAND, AND POVERTY

In my opinion the least bad tax is the property tax on the unimproved value of land, the Henry George argument of many years ago.

—Milton Friedman (1912–2006), *Human Events*[83]

---

79. Owen, *The Revolution in the Mind*, 121; see also 42. It is not clear how to determine the "fair market price" under such conditions as there would be only one buyer, the government.

80. Each township's square will enclose "an area of about sixty-five acres," within an estate of "about 2,000 or 3,000 acres" (2,560 acres is four square miles). Owen, *A Development of the Principles and Plans on Which to Establish Self-Supporting Home Colonies*, 38.

81. Owen, *The Revolution in the Mind*, 120. My father, reports his son Dale, was at that time, "engrossed by the exciting delusion that he was about suddenly to revolutionize society and reform the world." R. D. Owen, *Threading My Way*, 23.

82. Claeys, *Citizens and Saints*, 99. Claeys advises, "The key issue for Owen was . . . the provision of employment for those whose labour was being displaced by machinery, and Owen's planned villages became his solution both to the general immorality of the factory system—the problem of 'character'—and the more immediately pressing threat of distress." Claeys, *Machinery, Money and the Millennium*, 39–40.

83. Milton Friedman, interview in *Human Events*, November 19, 1979. Qtd. in Richard Fisher, "Henry George: Antiprotectionist Giant of American Economics," *Economic*

In his foreword to *The Philosophy of Henry George*, Dewey writes, "The 'science' of political economy was to [George] a body of principles to provide the basis of policies to be executed, measures to be carried out, not just ideas to be intellectually entertained."[84] In *Progress and Poverty* George claims he has established a connection between increasing poverty and increasing wealth (and increasing wealth inequality). "The great cause of inequality in the distribution of wealth," he asserts, "is inequality in the ownership of land."[85] The problem George undertakes to explain, says Geiger, is that while the production of wealth had increased, "the distribution of wealth had increased only the disparity between those who had and those who had not."[86] More than a "squalid, unaesthetic sight," Geiger continues, poverty was, for George, "a conditioning element of much of our social life, the background against which were formed so many of man's habits."[87] George claims that private ownership of land is so commonplace and so thoroughly embedded in our laws and customs that the majority of people, rather than questioning it, see it as a practical necessity.[88] Accordingly, the unquestioned acceptance of land as individual property obscures from debate the constructive tax it imposes.[89] When land is subject to private ownership, he explains, "The strongest and most cunning easily acquire a superior share . . . and in becoming lords of the land they become necessarily lords of their fellow-men."[90] George's self-appointed mission was to pull back the curtain, proclaiming: "There is on earth no power which can

---

Insights, Federal Reserve Bank of Dallas, 10, no. 2 (2005). http://www.dallasfed.org/assets/documents/research/ei/ei0502.pdf (accessed November 23, 2016).

84. Dewey, foreword to George Raymond Geiger, *The Philosophy of Henry George* (repr., New York: The Macmillan Company, 1933), x.

85. George, *Progress and Poverty*, 295.

86. George Raymond Geiger, *The Philosophy of Henry George* (repr., New York: The Macmillan Company, 1933), 15.

87. Geiger, 7.

88. George, *Progress and Poverty*, 368.

89. Like Proudhon, George holds that private property in land is theft. He says, it is "not merely a robbery in the past; it is a robbery in the present—a robbery that deprives of their birthright the infants that are now coming into the world!" George, *Progress and Poverty*, 365. Proudhon claims that property is theft in the same way that slavery is murder, not directly but indirectly in terms of its effects on people's lives. Proudhon, *What Is Property?*, 13.

90. George, *Progress and Poverty*, 350.

rightfully make a grant of exclusive ownership in land."[91] The moral object of this claim, suggestive of Proudhon and Spence, is that "the equal right of all men to the use of land is as clear as their equal right to breathe the air—it is a right proclaimed by the fact of their existence."[92]

WHY PROGRESS PRODUCES POVERTY

The association of poverty with progress, George decrees, is the "riddle which the Sphinx of Fate put to our civilization."[93] Unraveling the link between increasing wealth and worsening poverty, he says, is the key to resolving the "industrial, social, and political difficulties that perplex the world."[94] His aim is to explain why industrial progress, while raising the standard of living for some and making others wealthy, leaves the working poor no better off. In so doing George struggled against Malthus's pervasive theory that the poor are and will remain poor by the interaction of natural laws. Natural cycles or "oscillations," Malthus claims, increase "the number of people before the means of subsistence are increased."[95] A swelling population also means a surplus of laborers relative to the available work. During this phase, the price of labor will decrease while the price of food rises.[96] And since, as he believes, the population is capable of exponential growth while the food supply can only increase arithmetically, the increasing price of food relative to the wages of the increasing number of workers will ensure that the poor

---

91. George, 339. George defines land to include "not merely the surface of the earth as distinguished from the water and the air, but the whole material universe outside of man himself." Qtd. in Charles R. McCann Jr., "Apprehending the Social Philosophy of Henry George," *American Journal of Economics and Sociology* 67, no. 1 (January 2008): 67–88, 79.

92. George, *Progress and Poverty*, 338. Proudhon, *What is Property?*, 73. Spence argued that "there is no living but on land and its productions, consequently, what we cannot live without we have the same property in as our lives." Thomas Spence, "The Rights of Man" (1793), in *Pig's Meat: Selected Writings of Thomas Spence, Radical and Pioneer Land Reformer* (Nottingham: Spokesman, 1982), 60. This argument may be taken to imply a logical link between what *is* and what *ought* to be (the *is-ought* problem). Ayn Rand's opposing *is-ought* claim that human existence justifies private ownership of land is described in the next chapter.

93. George, *Progress and Poverty*, 10.

94. George, 10.

95. Malthus, *An Essay on the Principle of Population*, 19.

96. Malthus, 19.

remain poor.[97] George finds Malthus's theory preposterous, since it makes "poverty, want, and starvation . . . the inevitable results of universal laws." The "Malthusian doctrine," he argues, also "parries the demand for reform, and shelters selfishness from question."[98] As a consequence, social reforms such as George's, "which would interfere with the interests of any powerful class," are "discouraged as hopeless."[99]

CAUSES OF INCREASING LAND RENTS

The three factors of production for George are labor, capital, and land. The reason for his insistence that land is separate from capital follows upon his view of production; as production derives from labor, capital, and land, so produce is divided among "the laborer, the capitalist, and the land owner." The term *rent* thus applies exclusively to payments for the use of land.[100] "If, with an increase of production," he says, "the laborer gets no more and the capitalist no more, it is a necessary inference that the land owner reaps the whole gain."[101] A number of factors cause the value of land, and hence its rental rate, to increase. Each cause, he maintains, produces a corresponding reduction in wages.[102] The problem George's analysis reveals, says Wasserman, "lies in the privilege granted to landowners to share in the rewards of production without themselves having contributed to that process."[103]

The most valuable land is not the richest farmland but the land of cities on which the greatest concentration of people live and work.[104] Increasing land values are a function of increasing population density, George advises. He advances three reasons for greater population concentrations: (1) population growth, (2) improvements in industrial production resulting from advances in technology, new inventions, and specialized labor, and (3) enhancements in education and the dissemination of knowledge which

---

97. Malthus, 19.

98. George, *Progress and Poverty*, 99.

99. George, 99.

100. George, 165.

101. George, 222.

102. George, 223.

103. Louis Wasserman, "The Essential Henry George," in *Critics of Henry George*, ed. Robert V. Andelson (Malden, MA: Blackwell Publishing, 2003), 28.

104. George, *Progress and Poverty*, 242.

lead to further developments in production and "increase the power of producing wealth."[105] But it is not simply population growth or concentration that drives up land value, Dewey explains. George stresses "that the desire to share in the higher values which the community brings is a decisive factor in raising the rental value of land."[106]

ENDING PRIVATE LAND OWNERSHIP

George claims to have traced the unequal distribution of wealth to the institution of private property in land.[107] As a consequence, any future advances in industrial production, he asserts, will not only fail to benefit the poor but may serve "further to depress their condition."[108] Only by substituting common ownership of land for private ownership can we "extirpate poverty," he argues, and "make wages what justice commands they should be, the full earnings of the laborer."[109] Answering the familiar charge that without private ownership of land people will be sapped of their incentive to work,[110] George states, "What is necessary for the use of land is not its private ownership, but the security of improvements,"[111] that is, security in the private ownership of what a person produces. Regarding land as private property, he insists, "stands in the way of its proper use."

> Were land treated as public property it would be used and improved as soon as there was need for its use and improvement, but being treated as private property, the individual owner is

---

105. George, 228.

106. John Dewey, "An Appreciation of Henry George," in *John Dewey: The Later Works, 1925–1953*, vol. 3, ed. Jo Ann Boydston (Carbondale: Southern Illinois Press, 1984), 360. First published in *Significant Paragraphs from Progress and Poverty*, ed. Harry Gunnison Brown (Garden City, NY: Published for the Robert Schalkenback Foundation by Doubleday, Doran and Co., 1928), 1–3.

107. George, *Progress and Poverty*, 328–29.

108. George, 328.

109. George, 328.

110. In Tolstoy's novel *Resurrection* (discussed in the next section), Nekhlyudov's brother-in-law Rogozhinsky says, "The rights of property are inborn in man; without them there would be no incentive to the cultivation of the land." Tolstoy, *Resurrection*, 348.

111. George, *Progress and Poverty*, 398.

permitted to prevent others from using or improving what he cannot or will not use or improve himself.[112]

According to George, the solution, though not practical at the time, would be for the government to control land as a common resource and lease it to individuals and corporations.[113] However, procuring government control over land poses overwhelming problems. For this reason, says McCann, "George finally seems to acquiesce, to allow that, after all, it may be possible to continue to tolerate private ownership of land, as long as the fruits of that ownership are distributed in such a manner as they would were the land taken as common property."[114] "What I, therefore, propose," George declares,

> as the simple yet sovereign remedy, which will raise wages, increase the earnings of capital, extirpate pauperism, abolish poverty, give remunerative employment to whoever wishes it, afford free scope to human powers, lessen crime, elevate morals, and taste, and intelligence, purify government and carry civilization to yet nobler heights, is—*to appropriate rent by taxation.*[115]

Thus, while he lobbied against private land ownership, he saw the peaceful resolution to the question as arising in a simple land tax rather than, for example, the state's expropriation of land or a full-fledged revolution. In this sense his reasoning concurs with that of Mill,[116] who invites us to consider this scenario:

> Suppose that there is a kind of income that constantly tends to increase, without any exertion or sacrifice on the part of the

---

112. George, 401. See Mill's related argument in *Principles of Political Economy*, bk. 2, chap. 1, §6, 172–73.

113. George, *Progress and Poverty*, 403–4. This was the approach adopted in Wells's *A Modern Utopia.*

114. McCann, "Apprehending the Social Philosophy of Henry George," 74.

115. George, *Progress and Poverty*, 405–6 (italics in original).

116. For a discussion of economic influences on George, including David Ricardo and John Stuart Mill, see Harold M. Groves, *Tax Philosophers: Two Hundred Years of Thought in Great Britain and the United States*, ed. Donald J. Curran (Madison, WI: University of Wisconsin Press, 1974), 123–26.

owners. . . . In such a case it would be no violation of the principles on which private property is founded if the state should appropriate this increase in wealth. . . . This would not properly be taking anything from anybody; it would merely be applying an accession of wealth, created by circumstances, to the benefit of society, instead of allowing it to become an unearned appendage to the riches of a particular class.[117]

In determining the most practical method to "appropriate this increase in wealth," George settled on a single tax on the unimproved value of land for practical as well as moral and economic reasons. On the practical side, he notes that local governments already engage the machinery for assessing and collecting this tax and that the land's "value can be readily ascertained." Furthermore, unlike other sources of tax revenue, land cannot be "hidden or carried off."[118]

SINGLE TAX ON LAND RENTS

George believes it is possible to shift the total source of tax revenue to land rents because, as Groves explains, "land is socially a costless asset; we would still have its services if all rent were appropriated by government."[119] George proclaims the tax on land as "the most just and equal of all taxes. It falls only upon those who receive from society a peculiar and valuable benefit, and upon them in proportion to the benefit they receive."[120] Under George's vision, says Fisher, "Labor and capital—so often burdened by the patchwork of taxes on labor, savings and entrepreneurs—would be unleashed because none of these would be taxed."[121] Dewey attributes the failure of George's

---

117. Mill, *Principles of Political Economy*, bk. 5, chap. 1, 546–47.

118. George, *Progress and Poverty*, 414.

119. Groves, *Tax Philosophers*, 130.

120. George, *Progress and Poverty*, 421. In this he follows Spence (1750–1814) who called for "one simple Tax which is the Land-tax" to support government. Thomas Spence, *The Restorer of Society to its Natural State*, in *Pig's Meat: Selected Writings of Thomas Spence, Radical and Pioneer Land Reformer* (Nottingham: Spokesman, 1982), 148.

121. Richard Fisher, "Henry George: Antiprotectionist Giant of American Economics," *Economic Insights*, Federal Reserve Bank of Dallas 10, no. 2 (2005). http://www.dallasfed.org/assets/documents/research/ei/ei0502.pdf (accessed February 2, 2019).

tax reform plan to gain traction with lawmakers and academics to the fact that George "thought, wrote, and worked" outside the academy. This placed him, Dewey says, in direct opposition to the "force of tremendous vested interests [that] depreciated his intellectual claims in order to strengthen opposition to his practical measures."[122]

ECONOMIC REFORMER

In *The Worldly Philosophers*, Heilbroner explains that for George, "the injustice of rents not only robbed the capitalist of his honest profit but weighed on the shoulders of the working man as well."[123] Despite calling for an end to private land ownership, George stands as a defender of competition and capitalism, touting the economic neutrality of his system, which taxes neither capital nor labor.[124] George considered himself a "purifier of capitalism," writes Andelson, rather than its enemy.[125] George's goal, he continues, was to make free enterprise "truly free" by eliminating "the monopolistic hobbles which prevent its effective operation."[126]

> George believed in competition, in the free market, in the unrestricted operation of the laws of supply and demand. He distrusted government and despised bureaucracy. He was no egalitarian leveler; the only equality he sought was equal freedom of opportunity.[127]

For these reasons, George explains, "the doctrine that all men are equally entitled to the use of land does not involve communism or socialism, and

---

122. Dewey, "An Appreciation of Henry George," 359.

123. Heilbroner, *The Worldly Philosophers*, 170.

124. Hofstadter notes that while both George and Bellamy engaged in "refuting the conservative arguments of evolutionary sociology . . . George differed from other dissenting ideologists in his acceptance of competition as the necessary way of economic life." Hofstadter, *Social Darwinism in American Thought*, 110.

125. Robert V. Andelson, "Henry George and The Reconstruction of Capitalism," Robert Schalkenbach Foundation, http://schalkenbach.org/on-line-library/works-by-robert-v-andelson/henry-george-and-the-reconstruction-of-capitalism/ (accessed November 24, 2016).

126. Andelson.

127. Andelson.

need cause no serious change in existing arrangements."[128] George took issue with those who assert that capitalism demands private ownership of land, says McCann, and railed against the government-granted monopoly in private land ownership that distorts what might otherwise constitute a "true" capitalist economy. "Thus does George appear not so much the utopian *socialist* as the utopian *capitalist*."[129]

TOLSTOY (1828–1910): A LANDOWNER'S STRUGGLE WITH THE LAND PROBLEM

> An equal distribution of land is impossible, and anything short of that would be only a mitigation, not a cure, and a mitigation that would prevent the adoption of a cure.
>
> —Henry George (1839–1897), *Progress and Poverty*[130]

In *What Shall We Do Then?* Tolstoy proclaims, "Property is the root of all evil; and the whole world is busy dividing and protecting property." Ownership of land, he continues, "is only a means for using the labor of others."[131] Though a landowner himself, Tolstoy was concerned with the moral questions Henry George had raised. "The more I know of him," Tolstoy wrote in 1894, "the more I esteem him."[132] In a letter to George, Tolstoy says, "The reading of every one of your books makes clear to me things which were not so before, and confirms me more and more in the truth and practicability of your system."[133] As Tolstoy became increasingly aware of the fate of the poor—both those in the cities and the peasants on his estates—he recognized that the origin of their problems, as George

---

128. George, *A Perplexed Philosopher*, 27, 244.

129. McCann, "Apprehending the Social Philosophy of Henry George," 80 (italics in original).

130. George, *Progress and Poverty*, 327.

131. Count Lev N. Tolstoy, *What Shall We Do Then?*, trans. Leo Wiener (repr., Boston: Dana Estes and Company, 1904), 319.

132. Tolstoy to Ernest Crosby, November 24, 1894, in *Tolstoy's Letters*, vol. 2, trans. R. F. Christian (New York: Charles Scribner's Sons, 1978), letter no. 402, 512.

133. Tolstoy to George, March 20, 1896, in *Tolstoy's Letters*, vol. 2, letter no. 423, 537.

claimed, was in the institution of private land ownership. The question of economic science, says Tolstoy, is why men who own land and capital "are able to enslave those who have no land and no capital?"[134] What science must determine, he declares, is the cause that "produces the alienation of the land and of the tools of labor from those who work the land and employ the tools."[135] George's solution, Tolstoy says, is "that all the land be regarded as the property of the state" and that all other forms of tax be replaced with a single tax on ground rent; in this way, "every man who makes use of the land shall pay to the state the value of its rent."[136]

RESURRECTION

Tolstoy's last novel, *Resurrection*, is a statement of his utopian-reformist views—especially on poverty, the decay of institutional religion, justice and prison conditions, the military, and the land question. Prince Nekhlyudov, the central figure and an advocate of George's land argument, says, "The land is common to all. All have the same right to it."[137] Nekhlyudov's similarities with Tolstoy include his noble birth and acquiescence to his class's values during the first half of his life, followed by a moral awakening regarding the miserable fate of the peasants. This awakening resulted in his desire to uncover the causes of the status quo, which led to his conflicted attempts to set matters straight both in his own life and in the wider Russian society. Wenzer observes, "Nekhlyudov (as Tolstoy) reappears as the repentant noble who eschews his peers for the salvation of people."[138] While *Progress and Poverty* stimulated him, Tolstoy undertook his own study of poverty that he recounts in *What Shall We Do Then?* In a letter to George, Tolstoy writes, "Though the paths we go by are different, I do not think that we differ in the foundation of our thoughts."[139] The difference of emphasis

---

134. Tolstoy, *What Shall We Do Then?*, 108.

135. Tolstoy, 109.

136. Tolstoy, 157.

137. Tolstoy, *Resurrection*, 252.

138. Kenneth C. Wenzer, "Tolstoy's Georgist Spiritual Political Economy (1897–1919): Anarchism and Land Reform," *American Journal of Economics and Sociology* 56, no. 4 (October 1997): 639–67, 641.

139. Tolstoy to George, March 27/April 8, 1896, in *Tolstoy's Letters*, vol. 2, letter no. 423, 537.

between the two writers is not the economic connection between private land ownership and poverty, but Tolstoy's additional linking (at least in Russia) of land ownership and poverty with state-sanctioned injustice. In *Resurrection* he depicts the government's class-bound administration of the poor, especially through the courts, the police, and the prison system. In this way he expands the scope of George's economic analysis to include the state's institutionalization of poverty on behalf of the landed class.

STRUGGLING WITH THE LAND PROBLEM

Though Tolstoy accepted George's diagnosis of the land problem, he wavered on the solution. "Every now and then," says Wenzer, "Tolstoy still had hesitations about the single tax but he was an inveterate questioner and reexaminer of everything."[140] He recognized in George's plan "a transitional stage towards an anarchist utopia."[141] In *The Slavery of Our Times*, Tolstoy expresses his reservations about George's compromise solution of a land tax and explains,

> Those who, like Henry George . . . would abolish the laws making private property of land propose new laws imposing an obligatory rent on the land. And this obligatory land rent will necessarily create a new form of slavery, because a man compelled to pay rent, or the single tax, may at any failure of the crops or other misfortune have to borrow money . . . and he will again lapse into slavery.[142]

As Godwin had, Tolstoy recognized that the operations of government, including taxation, were incompatible with his view of humanity. The doubts he expresses regarding George's proposal of a single tax on land rents are in consequence of his biblically inspired anarchist inclinations.[143]

---

140. Wenzer, "Tolstoy's Georgist Spiritual Political Economy (1897–1919): Anarchism and Land Reform," 655.

141. Kenneth C. Wenzer, "The Influence of Henry George's Philosophy on Lev Nikolaevich Tolstoy: The Period of Developing Economic Thought (1881–1897)," *Pennsylvania History* 63, no. 2 (April 1996): 232–52, 233.

142. Tolstoy, *The Slavery of our Times*, 85.

143. Commentators' references to Tolstoy as a Christian anarchist are misleading without further delineation of the sense in which he was a Christian and an anarchist. His anarchism consisted in the conviction that government, insofar as it establishes

On the one hand the land tax requires government enforcement. On the other hand, in *Resurrection* Nekhlyudov tells the peasants, "The earth is no man's; it is God's."[144]

In *A Confession*, Tolstoy (like Nekhlyudov) takes stock of his life and asks: "What had I done during the whole thirty years of my responsible life? . . . I lived as a parasite, and on asking myself, what is the use of my life? I got the reply: 'No use.'"[145] In 1881, at the onset of his thirty-year utopian struggle, Tolstoy confided his moral uncertainty to a friend. "I see now that I knew all about the evil and the mass of temptations among which people live, but I didn't believe them and couldn't imagine them. . . . And [now] the mass of evil overwhelms me, depresses me and makes me incredulous."[146] "And yet," observes Christian, "there is no hopelessness in Tolstoy's work, only an endless seeking which provides that quality of ambiguity and lack of finality so important to a work of art."[147]

In his 1886 *What Shall We Do Then?* Tolstoy explores the lives of the poor and his recognition of their problem's magnitude. He sees that his class's expected response of supplying charity is worse than inadequate

---

and defends the institutions of private land ownership and taxation, enables slavery, allowing some to control the lives of others. His classification as a Christian is based on his personal understanding of Christ's teachings in the gospels, though he studied other religions as well. He was a harsh critic of the organized Christian religion that had excommunicated him. The church's strict regulation of Christian teachings and its connection to the government had, he believed, eroded the personal nature of the religious experience. A scene in *Resurrection* (the church service in chapter 39) shows his (or at least Nekhlyudov's) Christian faith to be analogous to that of Kierkegaard—who distinguished the official Christendom of the masses and church officials from Christianity. "Christendom," says Kierkegaard, "has slyly done away with Christianity by the affirmation that we are all Christians." In Christendom, he continues, "where one naturally has no presentment of what Christianity is, and where it could never occur to anyone . . . that Christianity has been *abolished* by *expansion*, by these millions of name-Christians, the number of which is surely meant to conceal the fact that there is not one Christian, that Christianity simply does not exist." Søren Kierkegaard, *Attack Upon "Christendom,"* trans. Walter Lowrie (Princeton, NJ: Princeton University Press, 1944), 127 (italics in original).

144. Tolstoy, *Resurrection*, 252.

145. Leo Tolstoy, *A Confession*, trans. Aylmer Maude (Mineola, NY: Dover Publications, 2005), 56.

146. Tolstoy to V. I. Alexeyev, November 1881, in *Tolstoy's Letters*, vol. 2, letter no. 264, 353–54.

147. R. F. Christian, *Tolstoy: A Critical Introduction* (Cambridge: Cambridge University Press, 1969), 217.

since it only serves to mask and perpetuate the underlying conditions while providing moral cover for those who, like himself, are the source of the problem. It was not simply that he was rich and they were poor, but that the circumstance of his wealth was the cause of their being poor.

> I am sitting on a man's neck, choking him, and demanding that he carry me, and, without getting off him, I assure myself and others that I am very sorry for him and want to alleviate his condition by all possible means except by getting off his neck.[148]

"Tolstoy was plagued by the difficulty of reconciling reason and faith, science and the masses," says Wenzer. "But he preferred the childlike faith of the people and their closeness to the soil."[149]

RESOLVING THE LAND PROBLEM

In *Resurrection* Tolstoy portrays the struggles of Nekhlyudov, showing the intransigence of the moral problems he confronted. During his first thirty years, Nekhlyudov had been emotionally insulated from the daily lives of the poor and knew them only in their roles as maids and servants or as peasants working the land on his two estates. The catalyst for his moral awakening occurs when he is summoned for jury duty and confronts the defendant, twenty-six-year-old Katyusha Maslova. She is his aunts' former maid and seven years earlier had been the object of his outrageous, class-inspired sexual degradation. "The recollection of what had passed [between them] burnt his conscience. In . . . the very depths of his soul—he had acted in a base, cruel, cowardly manner."[150] Maslova's subsequent pregnancy led to her dismissal by Nekhlyudov's aunts and ultimately to her life as a prostitute. Her trial was for theft and murder by poisoning, though the charges were of questionable veracity.

The failure of an officer of the court to properly instruct the jury marred their deliberations. At a crucial point in his instructions the officer failed to explain that their answer to either charge could be qualified by

---

148. Tolstoy, *What Shall We Do Then?*, 97. Bellamy's comparison of society to a "prodigious coach" makes a similar point. Bellamy, *Looking Backward*, 39.

149. Wenzer, "The Influence of Henry George's Philosophy on Lev Nikolaevich Tolstoy," 240.

150. Tolstoy, *Resurrection*, 71.

the phrase "without intent." Thus when the jury answered that Maslova was guilty of murder, they neglected to add "without intent to take life." The resulting sentence of hard labor in Siberia shocked both the jurors and the court.[151] To pay for his guilt, Nekhlyudov dedicates his life to serving Maslova and working on judicial and social reforms to benefit the poor. He also determines to rid himself of his two landed estates. "Concerning money matters, he resolved to arrange them in accord with his conviction that the holding of landed property was unlawful."[152] For this reason Nekhlyudov decides that even "if he should not be strong enough to give up everything, he would still do what he could, not deceiving himself or others."[153]

At the first estate Kusminsky, Nekhlyudov determines to quit his farming operation and to rent the land to the peasants at thirty percent less than the prevailing rate. This, he says, will "enable them to cultivate it without depending on a landlord."[154] In light of his goals with respect to the land question, Nekhlyudov admits this "was not a solution of the problem, but it was a step towards the solution; it was a movement towards a less rude form of slavery."[155] He leaves Kusminsky satisfied that the reduced rent will be sufficient for his needs but dissatisfied with himself for not accomplishing his moral goal. At the second estate, Panovo, he announces, "I have come here because I no longer wish to possess any land, and now we must consider the best way of dividing it."[156] Here Nekhlyudov offers to give up his land to the peasants for them to own in common. Under this plan the peasants will continue to work the land, enjoy its fruits, and pay rent. But the rent, in an amount for the peasants to regulate, will go into "a communal fund for their own use."[157] In their discussions with Nekhlyudov and among themselves, the peasants convey their mistrust and the concern that any change in the current arrangements will inevitably benefit the landlord and make their situation worse.[158] After three days of debate an agreement emerges, and the peasants acquiesce to the experiment of a communal arrangement. When he leaves the second estate, Nekhlyudov feels "nothing but unceasing

---

151. Tolstoy, 91.
152. Tolstoy, 127.
153. Tolstoy, 127.
154. Tolstoy, 217.
155. Tolstoy, 217.
156. Tolstoy, 250.
157. Tolstoy, 242.
158. Tolstoy, 242.

joy at the deliverance, and a sensation of newness, something like a traveler must experience when discovering new lands."[159]

Though Nekhlyudov embraces George's assessment of the land problem, in *Resurrection* he is incapable of instituting his solution, saying of the arrangements for the two estates that "This, of course, was not the single-tax system, still it was as near an approach to it as could be made in the existing circumstances."[160] George's system, Tolstoy acknowledges, requires specific action from the government. In an 1894 letter to a social reformer, he says, "If the new Tsar were to ask me what I would advise him to do, I would say to him: use your autocratic power to abolish the land property in Russia and to introduce the single tax system; and then give up your power and [give] the people a liberal constitution."[161] However, Tolstoy was not convinced of the morality of *any* tax system. In *What Shall We Do Then?* he argues that George's solution was insufficient since it still involved government as the administrator of the single tax. Tolstoy had analyzed what he called "slavery" and isolated its practice into three methods: "militarism, taxation of land . . . and the tribute which is imposed on all the inhabitants by means of direct and indirect taxes."[162] Under George's system, as he understood it, even if the peasants were to own the land in common, the land tax payable to the government would remain an enduring form of slavery.

For both Tolstoy and Nekhlyudov, the optimal solution to the land question remained elusive. This was in part due to the fact that Tolstoy's moral concern was not simply with the means of resolving the problem but also with the purity of his motives. Nekhlyudov asks himself regarding his plans for disposing of his land, "are you really acting according to your conscience, or are you doing it in order to show off?"[163] This was the same problem Tolstoy acknowledged in *Father Sergius* and challenged himself with in *A Confession.*[164]

---

159. Tolstoy, 254.

160. Tolstoy, 239.

161. Tolstoy to Ernest Crosby, November 24, 1894, in *Tolstoy's Letters*, vol. 2, letter no. 402, 512.

162. Tolstoy, *What Shall We Do Then?*, 156. Tolstoy claims, "The slavery of our times results from three sets of laws: those about land, taxes, and property." Tolstoy, *The Slavery of Our Times*, 84.

163. Tolstoy, *Resurrection*, 220.

164. Christian says, "Tolstoy's *A Confession*, completed in 1882 but not allowed to be published in Russia, is the best introduction to the spiritual struggle he was to wage for

In a 1906 letter, Tolstoy addresses the accusation that while he wrote and talked extensively about the land question and advocated release of the land to the peasants, yet he himself was a wealthy landowner.

> My attitude not only to landed property but to any property at all is this, that no Christian should consider anything his own and so should not defend . . . by force, land to which all people have equal rights. . . . In order to rid myself of landed property which was reckoned to be mine, I decided to act as though I were dead. . . . The fact is that about 20 years ago my heirs each took what was due to him by law, and I kept nothing myself, and since then I have neither owned nor had control of any property except my own clothes.[165]

In the end, like his character Pahom, all the land that Tolstoy required was "six feet from his head to his heels."[166]

WELLS (1866–1946): THE LAND QUESTION IN *A MODERN UTOPIA*

> The State is to be progressive, it is no longer to be static, and this alters the general condition of the Utopian problem profoundly; we have to provide not only for food and clothing, for order and health, but for initiative.
>
> —H. G. Wells, *A Modern Utopia*[167]

In the spirit of Thomas More, Wells's narrator declares: "Now we need not argue here to prove that the resources of the world and the energy of

---

the remaining thirty years of his life and which was to have such profound repercussions on his art." Christian, ed., *Tolstoy's Letters*, vol. 2, 337.

165. Tolstoy to A. S. Marov, March 22, 1906, in *Tolstoy's Letters*, vol. 2, letter no. 532, 656.

166. Tolstoy, *How Much Land Does a Man Need?*, 52. Tolstoy was buried at the family estate at Yasnaya Polyana, Russia.

167. Wells, *A Modern Utopia*, 38.

mankind, were they organized sanely, are amply sufficient to supply every material need of every living human being."[168] The result of this proposition is a World State that owns and controls all its planet's land and resources.[169] The implementation of this system means that while the World State is the "sole landowner," the local governments it comprises function as its landlords, collecting rent for the use of the land and royalties for its resources.[170] "Within this scheme," Wells explains, the State is the "source of all energy, and the final legatee." In its capacity as sole landowner, the State "will pour out this energy by assignment and lease . . . upon its individual citizens." The energy-producing resources—including "the exploitation of coal and electric power, and the powers of wind and wave and water"[171]—are a revenue tributary of the modern Utopia's tax structure. License fees and transfer taxes supplement the revenue it receives from land leases, royalties, and the reclamation of business assets in the settlement of estates.[172]

OWNERSHIP FOR INITIATIVE

Though land may be leased but not owned, in a modern Utopia this does not preclude the personal ownership of homes, buildings, or other business- or personal-use assets. In explaining the importance of ownership for the World State's citizens, Wells's narrator ("the *Voice*") declares that "a man without some negotiable property is a man without freedom, and the extent of his property is very largely the measure of his freedom."[173] But land itself is not the source of this freedom; rather, it is "the values his toil

---

168. Wells, 56.

169. Wells, 41. Morton says, "*A Modern Utopia* . . . describes a mixed economy based largely on the ideas of Hertzka's *Freeland*, an economy in which private enterprise still operates in a framework of the public ownership of land." Morton, *The English Utopia*, 243. In *Freeland*, however, Hertzka's narrator explains, "With us, the land—so far as it is used as a means of production and not as sites for dwelling-houses—is absolutely masterless, free as air; it belongs neither to one nor to many: everyone who wishes to cultivate the soil is at liberty to do so where he pleases, and to appropriate his part of the produce." Hertzka, *Freeland*, 93, 257.

170. Wells, *A Modern Utopia*, 39.

171. Wells, 39.

172. Wells, 39.

173. Wells, 39.

or skill or foresight and courage have brought into being."[174] In this way the modern Utopia applies George's principle that "whatever your labor or capital produces on this land shall be yours."[175] In its encouragement of ownership, says Wells, the World State's goal is to create initiative and individuality ("individuality is the method of initiative").[176] The origin of this initiative, he stresses, is not found in the ownership of land but in the guarantee to the producer that he will own what he produces.

Property is divided into three categories: 1) land, all of which is owned by the state; 2) privately owned business-use or investment property; and 3) private or personal-use property. Land, explains the narrator, "will be leased out to companies or individuals, but—in view of the unknown necessities of the future—never for a longer period than . . . fifty years."[177] The ownership and accumulation of all other property—its purchase or sale, and the uses to which it may go—is under the control of the individual or her business.

At death an estate tax applies, primarily to business and investment assets (excepting savings for a child's education). The government takes the lion's share, says the narrator, of the things that the deceased used to make his living.[178] These include the business assets of a proprietor—machinery and equipment—and the ownership rights in a corporation or partnership. But an individual's personal belongings, her residence, furniture, books, and jewelry, pass as designated to the heirs.[179]

LAND ZONING

The modern Utopia imposes land zoning (a constructive tax) for health and aesthetic reasons. It segregates residential from industrial land to prevent the familiar pattern of slums encircling factories, refineries, and mines. The problem Wells attacks is one afflicting the working poor primarily, seeing a solution in Utopia's high-speed rail transportation system. "On our own poor haphazard earth," Wells explains, "wherever men work, wherever there are

---

174. Wells, 40.

175. George, *Progress and Poverty*, 398.

176. Wells, *A Modern Utopia*, 38.

177. Wells, 41.

178. Wells, 41. This is an estate tax rather than an inheritance tax, because it is levied on the estate's assets and not on what the beneficiaries receive.

179. Wells, *A Modern Utopia*, 40.

things to be grown, minerals to be won, power to be used, there, regardless of all the joys and decencies of life, the households needs must cluster." "But in Utopia," he continues, there will be wide stretches of cheerless or unhealthy or toilsome or dangerous land with never a household;"[180]

> there will be regions of mining and smelting, black, with the smoke of furnaces and gashed and desolated by mines, with a sort of weird inhospitable grandeur of industrial desolation, and the men will come thither and work for a spell and return to civilization again, washing and changing their attire in the swift gliding train.[181]

An extension of the modern Utopia's land-zoning policy reinforces its position on childrearing (discussed in chapter five). In a modern Utopia, the *Voice* explains, "there will be beautiful regions of the earth specially set apart and favored for children." Families choosing these aesthetic sanctuaries benefit from tax breaks, while a tax penalty awaits parents subjecting their children to the unsavory, "less wholesome places"—those "black, with the smoke of furnaces and gashed and desolated by mines."[182]

ROBERT NOZICK (1938–2002): ENTITLEMENT THEORY

> But it often happens, that the title of the first possession becomes obscure thro' time; and that 'tis impossible to determine many controversies, which may arise concerning it.
>
> —David Hume (1711–1776), *A Treatise on Human Nature*[183]

---

180. Wells, 24. Modern zoning laws, reports Criado-Perez, have "woven a male bias into the fabric of cities around the world," a constructive tax on women. They are based on and prioritize the needs of "a bread-winning heterosexual married man who goes off to work in the morning, and comes home . . . to relax at night." Criado-Perez, *Invisible Women*, 39–40.

181. Wells, 24.

182. Wells, 24.

183. David Hume, *A Treatise of Human Nature*, ed. L. A. Selby-Bigge (Oxford: Clarendon Press, 1967), bk. 3, pt. 2, iii, 507–8.

Moral philosophy, Nozick proclaims, "sets the background for, and boundaries of, political philosophy."[184] For this reason he believes, as Locke did, that property rights arise outside a system of law,[185] and government's only function, therefore, is to protect rights people already possess.[186] On this he is in direct opposition to Bentham, for example, who argues, "The rights of the governed and the rights of the government spring up together;—the same cause which creates the one creates the other."[187] For Nozick private land ownership is a moral right.[188] "The libertarian conception of property as a prepolitical moral notion," write Murphy and Nagel, "is based not on the idea of moral desert but rather on the idea of moral entitlement."[189] Moreover, says Cohen, for Nozick freedom is conceptually connected to this right since what Nozick means by freedom, Cohen claims, is "the freedom of private property owners to do as they wish with their private property."[190]

A private landowner's moral right to her holding, Nozick argues, is historically evidenced. The determinative factor is the moral process by which the given portion of the earth's surface came to rest in its current owner's possession.[191] The historical ownership tracing begins with a just initial acquisition of an unowned tract of land.[192] In this way he defends the status of private land ownership without (as in Locke) an appeal to

184. Nozick, *Anarchy, State, and Utopia*, 6.

185. John Locke, *Second Treatise of Government*, ed. C. B. Macpherson (Cambridge: Hackett Publishing Company, 1980), §31, 20–21.

186. Locke, §124, 66.

187. Jeremy Bentham and C. K. Ogden, *Bentham's Theory of Fictions* (Paterson, NJ: Littlefield, Adams, 1959), 121.

188. J. W. Singer asserts that libertarians adopt "some version of the castle model of property as an organizing paradigm. They start from an image of the rights of the owner. Because they generally have expansive views of property rights, they are likely to identify any claim to control valued resources as a property right deserving strong legal protection." Joseph William Singer, "How Property Norms Construct the Externalities of Ownership," in *Property and Community* 57–79, ed. Gregory S. Alexander and Eduardo M. Peñalver (Oxford: Oxford University Press, 2010), 63.

189. Murphy and Nagel, *The Myth of Ownership: Taxes and Justice*, 66.

190. Cohen, *Self-Ownership, Freedom, and Equality*, 90.

191. Nozick's preference for "process" solutions over "end state" solutions is further illustrated in chapter seven.

192. Nozick, *Anarchy, State, and Utopia*, 152.

God, Natural Law, or a social contract.[193] While Locke's theory of ownership requires mixing one's labor with the land, Nozick asks, "why isn't mixing what I own with what I don't own a way of losing what I own rather than a way of gaining what I don't?"[194]

ENTITLEMENT THEORY

In *Thinking About Property*, Garnsey says: "Proudhon saw that the argument over first acquisition was going nowhere and that there could be no resolution."[195] In *Anarchy, State, and Utopia*, however, Nozick revives the argument. He seeks to justify land ownership (and private ownership generally) with his entitlement theory designed to resolve moral questions about current property holdings in terms of their original acquisition and subsequent transfers.[196] "If the world were wholly just," he explains, "the following inductive definition would exhaustively cover the subject of justice in holdings."[197]

1. A person who acquires a holding in accordance with the principles of justice in acquisition is entitled to that holding.

2. A person who acquires a holding in accordance with the principle of justice in transfer, from someone else entitled to the holding, is entitled to the holding.

---

193. Waldron asserts, "Even if a private property economy is against the general interest, even if it can be shown that it does not generate the economic prosperity that is often claimed for it, even if the possession of . . . private property does not in the end maximize individual liberty—still, Nozick claims, it must be upheld and protected." Waldron, *The Right to Private Property*, 128.

194. Nozick, *Anarchy, State, and Utopia*, 174–75.

195. Garnsey, *Thinking about Property*, 236.

196. Nozick recognizes as a limitation of this approach the fact that "any theory which gets to a process must start with something which is not itself justified by being the outcome of a process." Nozick, *Anarchy, State, and Utopia*, 207. It is in the application of his entitlement theory to land that Nozick escapes the force of Okin's argument that his "extreme property rights-based libertarianism fails to be able to take women into account." Okin states, "by all canons of Nozick's entitlement theory of justice, children are the property of those who made them." Susan Moller Okin, *Justice, Gender and the Family* (n.p.: Basic Books, 1989), 85–87.

197. Nozick, *Anarchy, State, and Utopia*, 151.

3. No one is entitled to a holding except by (repeated) applications of 1 and 2.[198]

Nozick's transitivity analysis dictates that private property holdings are morally justified only if the property acquired was justly transferred from someone whose title resulted from a prior just transfer or who was the original just acquirer.[199] In this way, he claims, a tract of land or landed estate with a just pedigree is justly owned.[200] Justice for Nozick is a derivative condition, a function of individual rights. Justice in acquisition thus means acquisition without violating someone's property rights.[201] This contrasts with Godwin, for example, who took justice to be fundamental and cared more for duty than for rights.[202] On the futility of Nozick's project, George reports, "In California our land titles go back to the Supreme Government of Mexico, who took from the Spanish King, who took from the Pope, when he by a stroke of the pen divided lands yet to be discovered between the Spanish or Portuguese—or if you please they rest upon conquest."[203]

Waldron objects to Nozick's line of reasoning, saying that " 'Who had it first?' may be a natural enough way of resolving disputes about the ownership of a resource once we have established that it is a good idea that resources should be privately owned."[204] But, he contends, it does not itself justify the

---

198. Nozick, 151.

199. Nozick, 153. See also Robert Nozick, *Philosophical Explanations* (Cambridge: The Belknap Press of Harvard University Press, 1981), 48.

200. Nozick, *Anarchy, State, and Utopia*, 207.

201. Goodwin claims that Nozick's entitlement theory of justice measures justice in acquisition or in transfer "according to the laws at the time of the transaction." Goodwin, "Taxation in Utopia," 325. But this requires a determination that the laws at the time of the transaction were themselves just—that they did not violate individuals' preexisting moral property rights.

202. Claeys notes that Godwin rejected the notion of rights that entails the possibility of conflicting rights or "rights and duties hostile to each other." Claeys, "The Effects of Property on Godwin's Theory of Justice," 95.

203. George, *Progress and Poverty*, 342.

204. Waldron, *The Right to Private Property*, 285. Maine reports, "It is only when the rights of property have gained a sanction from long practical inviolability and when the vast majority of the objects of enjoyment have been subjected to private ownership, that mere possession is allowed to invest the first possessor with dominion over commodities in which no prior proprietorship has been asserted." Henry Sumner Maine, *Ancient Law* (repr., n.p.: Nu Vision Publications, 2009), 126.

institution of private property as opposed to other possible types of property systems.[205] One of the issues regarding private land ownership is what, exactly, is owned. As Waldron explains, "land is identified with the location—a region of three-dimensional space."[206] Nozick's argument assumes that the earth's landmasses are fixed in their configuration and not subject, for example, to continental drift or the formation of a new Pangaea. Thus, today's owner of a beachfront villa may be tomorrow's sealord for algae and mollusks.[207]

Nozick's opponents are on the one hand anarchists (as he understands them) and on the other hand those who believe that the state should orchestrate the just distribution of property in adherence to a specified end or preconceived (what Nozick calls "patterned") outcome—for example, equality, desert, or the total happiness of society or of the ruling class (or any consequentialist ideals). While he holds that "almost every" suggested principle of distributive justice is patterned, he specifies that his entitlement theory is not.[208] But the logic of his historical-process methodology—like the turtle supporting the earth on its back—requires just entitlement "all the way down."[209] He acknowledges this limitation, asking, "If past injustice has shaped present holdings in various ways . . . what now, if anything, ought to be done to rectify these injustices?"[210]

RECTIFICATION AND COMPENSATION

Nozick's answer is a *principle of rectification* offering compensation (reparations) to those whose rights past unjust property transfers had violated (for instance, fraudulent or coercive transfers by prior owners).[211] In evaluating the prospect

---

205. Waldron, *The Right to Private Property*, 285. On this point Kavka advises, "after a number of generations, those without significant inheritances will likely find that there is not 'enough and as good' available for them to use." Kavka, "An Internal Critique of Nozick's Entitlement Theory," 300.

206. Waldron, *The Right to Private Property*, 36.

207. For a discussion of this issue in relation to the land question, see George, *A Perplexed Philosopher*, 192–97.

208. Nozick, *Anarchy, State, and Utopia*, 156–57.

209. In contrast to entitlement, Nozick claims, "It needn't be that the foundations underlying desert are themselves deserved, *all the way down*." Nozick, 225 (italics in original).

210. Nozick, 152; see also 230–31.

211. Nozick, 230–31. In "The Case for Reparations," Coates reports, "the Associated Press published [in 2001] a[n] . . . investigation into the theft of black-owned land stretching

of this rectification, he admits, "past injustices might be so great as to make necessary in the short run a more extensive state in order to rectify them."[212] A more extensive state does more than the libertarian maximum of protecting citizens' moral rights to life, liberty, and property by, for example, taxing some people to provide benefits to others.[213] But, he protests, "to introduce socialism as the punishment for our sins would be to go too far."[214] J. Wolff objects to the principle of rectification, arguing that "if Nozick's view is that we should remedy all wrongs which, according to entitlement theory, have occurred, then the prospect is mind-boggling."[215] Since there is no moral reason to stop before the first such injustice—because for Nozick people are ends and not merely means—it is a curious utopian speculation whether, in the end, Nozick's principle of rectification might not lead to a Henry George–style land tax as the nearest approximation for rectifying past ownership injustices.[216]

In the next chapter I deal more fully with Nozick's minimal state and utopia. That discussion is preceded by recounting the utopias Ayn Rand explores in *Atlas Shrugged*. The significance of Rand and Nozick in this context is their libertarian opposition to taxation. Their success in eliminating taxation can be judged by the extent to which their utopias maintain some degree of "society," though no apparent sacrifice is demanded from the citizens. Their challenge was identified by Piketty, as noted earlier: "Without taxes, society has no common destiny, and collective action is impossible."[217]

---

back to the antebellum period. The series documented some 406 victims and 24,000 acres of land valued at tens of millions of dollars. The land was taken through means ranging from legal chicanery to terrorism." Ta-Nehisi Coates, "The Case for Reparations," *The Atlantic*, June 2014; republished in Coates, *We Were Eight Years in Power*, 165.

212. Nozick, *Anarchy, State, and Utopia*, 231.

213. Nozick, says Macey, argues that "the state is not justified in engaging in the redistribution of wealth, so long as the initial allocation of property rights against which the state is acting was originally established through just transfer or just acquisition of property." Jonathan R. Macey, "Government as Investor: Tax Policy and the State," *Social Philosophy and Policy* 23, no. 2 (2006): 255–86, 260.

214. Nozick, *Anarchy, State, and Utopia*, 231.

215. Wolff, *Robert Nozick: Property, Justice and the Minimal State*, 115.

216. In his 1797 essay *Agrarian Justice*, as noted, Paine recommends reparations for people's loss of their "natural inheritance, by the introduction of the system of landed property."

217. Piketty, *Capital in the Twenty-First Century*, 493.

CHAPTER SEVEN

TAXATION PURGED FROM UTOPIA

Part One:
Ayn Rand (1905–1982): *Atlas Shrugged*

DISPARATE SOCIAL SYSTEMS

The plot may be developed by one of two methods—inductive or deductive. . . . [Using the deductive method] the writer first concerns himself with an abstract idea and then embodies it in images, events, characters. . . . This method is used in works of a didactic nature and . . . it is dangerous, for the resulting plots seldom achieve faultless literary form.

—Yevgeny Zamyatin (1884–1937), *A Soviet Heretic*[1]

"I saw the root of the world's tragedy, the key to it and the solution. I saw what had to be done. I went out to do it."[2] Robert Owen might have

---

1. Zamyatin, *A Soviet Heretic: Essays by Yevgeny Zamaytin*, 166–67.
2. Rand, *Atlas Shrugged*, 745.

spoken these words, but they are the words of John Galt, a central figure in Ayn Rand's utopian novel *Atlas Shrugged*.[3] The root of the world's tragedy, as Galt identifies it, is the moral code of altruism making *need* the preeminent value. "When need is the standard," Galt explains, "every man is both victim and parasite. As a victim, he must labor to fill the needs of others, leaving himself in the position of a parasite whose needs must be filled by others."[4] "In the U.S. today," observes Sargent, "most anarcho-capitalism and libertarianism stems from Ayn Rand, whose novels . . . and many essays became the most popular expression of these positions."[5] Lewis compares Rand, a Russian-born émigré,[6] with Bellamy in terms of writing ability, classifying both as "competent." Both utopians, Lewis asserts, "have presented proposals by means of a story that interests the reader largely through identification with the hero." And while Bellamy's Nationalist movement brought about "major reforms" in America, he says, Rand's system, "continues to attract large numbers of followers."[7]

---

3. Owen's vision of the world's tragedy—the belief in self-formed character—is described in chapter five. Peikoff writes, "Rand is the first moralist to say no to the dogma of self-sacrifice. . . . She is thus the first to identify in completely rational terms what that dogma is doing to the human race and what the alternative to it is." Leonard Peikoff, *Objectivism: The Philosophy of Ayn Rand* (New York: Meridian, a division of Penguin Books USA, 1991), 249.

4. Rand, *Atlas Shrugged*, 1033. For Rand's definition of a moral code, see Ayn Rand, *Introduction to Objectivist Epistemology*, exp. 2nd ed. (New York: Meridian, a division of Penguin Books USA, 1990), 33.

5. Lyman Tower Sargent, *Contemporary Political Ideologies: A Comparative Analysis*, 14th ed. (Belmont, CA: Wadsworth, 2009), 215. In our own time Paul Ryan, former Speaker of the U.S. House of Representatives, says it was *Atlas Shrugged* that first interested him in economics, and that he gives it as a Christmas gift and makes his interns read. Rachael Weiner, "Paul Ryan and Ayn Rand," *Washington Post*, August 13, 2012. The extent to which Rand is properly called libertarian is discussed by Douglas J. Den Uyl and Douglas B. Rasmussen in *The Philosophic Thought of Ayn Rand*, ed. Douglas J. Den Uyl and Douglas B. Rasmussen (Urbana: University of Illinois Press, 1984), 225.

6. Ayn Rand was born Alissa Zinoviena Rosenbaum in St. Petersburg. She immigrated to the United States in 1926. Anne C. Heller, *Ayn Rand and the World She Made* (New York: Doubleday, 2009), 1, 52–53.

7. Arthur O. Lewis, "The Utopian Hero," in *America as Utopia*, ed. Kenneth M. Roemer, 133–47 (New York: Burt Franklin and Company, 1981), 145.

Atlas Shrugged presents disparate utopias and contrasting tax systems.[8] Rand's stated purpose is to exhibit the ideal man, which she says requires also presenting "the kind of social system that makes it possible for ideal men to exist and function."[9] Novelist Philip Roth warns that looking for a "writer's thinking in the words and thoughts of his characters is looking in the wrong direction."[10] Rand is an exception; both she and her commentators cite the speeches of her protagonists as statements of her own beliefs.[11] Published in 1957, *Atlas Shrugged* portrays the United States at a political and economic tipping point. The country is polarized, with a small minority of productive individualists[12]—those Rand calls "prime

---

8. According to Sargent, while "an argument can be made for the existence of a free market utopianism, the explicit position of those advocating a free market is anti-utopian . . . they are inheritors of a long tradition." Sargent, "The Three Faces of Utopianism Revisited," 21. Applying Mannheim's distinction, what make's Rand's position utopian rather than ideological is not its free market stance, but its "break[ing] the bonds of the existing order" and expressing "revolutionary possibilities"—specifically, the absence of required sacrifice and hence of taxation. Mannheim, *Ideology and Utopia*, 192–93.

9. Rand, *The Romantic Manifesto*, 156–57. Rand's definition of social system does not mean society but a social-political-economic arrangement such as capitalism, altruism, feudalism, absolute monarchy, socialism, or fascism. Ayn Rand, *Capitalism: The Unknown Ideal* (New York: Signet Books, 1967), 341. Rand claims, "there is no such entity as 'society,' since society is only a number of individual men." Rand, *The Virtue of Selfishness*, 14–15. Claeys explains that historically, "liberalism has often promised that the good life consisted of maximizing individual liberty, autonomy and independence, and trumpeted the pursuit of greed or selfishness as the means of achieving them. As such it has often denigrated 'society,' or the existence of any common or public good." Claeys, *Searching for Utopia*, 10.

10. Philip Roth, "My Life as a Writer," interview by Daniel Sandstrom, *New York Times Book Review*, March 2, 2014.

11. Rand says, for example, "Since I am to speak on the Objectivist Ethics, I shall begin by quoting its best representative—John Galt, in *Atlas Shrugged*." Rand, *The Virtue of Selfishness*, 13.

12. Branden, long-term Rand protégé, defines an individualist as "a man who lives for his own sake and by his own mind; he neither sacrifices himself to others nor sacrifices others to himself." Nathaniel Branden, "Counterfeit Individualism," in Rand, *The Virtue of Selfishness*, 136 (italics in original). Hofstadter provides historical context for this form of "atomistic individualism" and its enabling "social system." He says that society, according to the "formalistic thought of the nineteenth century . . . was a loose collection of individual agents; social advance depended upon improvements in the personal qualities of these individuals, their increased energy and frugality; among these individuals the strongest and best rose to the top and gave leadership to the rest." Hofstadter, *Social Darwinism in American Thought*, 168.

movers"[13]—living by the moral ideals of egoism, while the rest of the country, managed by government officials professing a moral code championing sacrifice for the needs of others, wallows in altruism.[14] Younkins claims Rand's story "is an apocalyptic vision of the last stages of a conflict between two classes of humanity.[15] As the government's policies demand increasingly unsustainable sacrifices—first from successful businesses and then from the general public—the country and its leaders plunge into an economic morass of self-destruction. As Galt observes, "a cannibal society . . . exists for a while by devouring its best and collapses like a cancerous body, when the healthy have been eaten by the diseased, when the rational have been consumed by the irrational."[16]

RAND'S FOUR UTOPIAS

> Reason has discovered the struggle for existence and the law that I must throttle all those who hinder the satisfaction of my desires. That is the deduction reason makes. But the law of loving others could not be discovered by reason, because it is unreasonable.
>
> —Leo Tolstoy (1828–1910), *Anna Karenina*[17]

The utopian evolution set forth in *Atlas Shrugged* comprises four interacting components—one past, two present, one future—illustrating Claeys's assessment that the "concept of utopia in every age is some variation on an ideal present, an ideal past and an ideal future, and the relation between the

---

13. Ayn Rand, *Journals of Ayn Rand*, ed. David Harriman (New York: The Penguin Group, 1997), 392.

14. According to Rand, "Altruism declares that any action taken for the benefit of others is good, and any action taken for one's own benefit is evil." Rand, *The Virtue of Selfishness*, viii. This is a strawman, however. Egoism—altruism's contrary—does not claim that any action taken that benefits others (secondary beneficiaries) is bad nor that any action that benefit oneself (license) is good (Rand, 58).

15. Edward W. Younkins, "Rand's Philosophical and Literary Masterpiece," in *Ayn Rand's Atlas Shrugged*, ed. Edward W. Younkins (Burlington, VT: Ashgate Publishing Company, 2007), 10.

16. Rand, *Atlas Shrugged*, 1062.

17. Tolstoy, *Anna Karenina*, 716–17.

three."[18] The first utopia is the age preceding the novel's action. It is fancied as a golden age in the United States when, during the country's first one hundred years, "an ideal social system had . . . been almost within men's reach."[19] During this period, that Rand elsewhere extends to one hundred and fifty years, she says, America "came close" to achieving a political system where "the government's function was changed from the role of ruler to the role of servant."[20] The nineteenth century, Rand stresses, "looks like a fiction-Utopia."[21] In contrast to most of human history, she explains, it was "like a blinding burst of sunlight" exhibiting creative energy, abundance, and wealth. Economically it raised the standard of living for "every level of the population."[22]

In that age of economic liberation, she asserts, capitalism was largely laissez-faire and free trade "liberated the world."[23] During this era the nation's great industrial cornerstones arose, including giant banks, steel mills, and railroads. In *Atlas Shrugged* this included the Taggart Transcontinental Railroad that Nathanial Taggart had built during the golden age.[24] This company is a primary focus of the novel, which begins its narrative at a time in the twentieth century when his descendants, James Taggart and Dagny Taggart (brother and sister), own and manage the railway.[25]

---

18. Claeys, *Searching for Utopia*, 7.

19. Rand, *Capitalism: The Unknown Ideal*, viii. Heller reports that Rand "wanted to be the architect of an American utopia that looked backward to the gilded age of American industrial titans." Heller, *Ayn Rand and the World She Made*, xiii.

20. Rand, *The Virtue of Selfishness*, 95.

21. Rand, *Philosophy: Who Needs It*, 89.

22. Rand, 89.

23. Rand, *Capitalism: The Unknown Ideal*, 35.

24. "In his lifetime, the name 'Nat Taggart' was not famous, but notorious. . . . and if anyone admired him, it was as one admires a successful bandit." Rand, *Atlas Shrugged*, 60.

25. An entertaining contrast to this golden age of capitalism is described in Orwell's *Nineteen Eighty-Four*. There, a children's history book claims: "Children no older than you had to work twelve hours a day for cruel masters, who flogged them with whips if they worked too slowly and fed them on nothing but stale bread crusts and water. But in among all this terrible poverty there were just a few great big beautiful houses that were lived in by rich men who had as many as thirty servants to look after them. These rich men were called capitalists. They were fat, ugly men with wicked faces. . . . The capitalists owned everything in the world, and everyone else was their slave." Orwell, *Nineteen Eighty-Four*, 75.

THE UTOPIA OF NEED

The bulk of the novel encompasses the second utopia (utopia from the point of view of certain government and business leaders). This is the altruistic utopia of need whose inevitable collapse constitutes the thrust of the novel's action and focus of its dialogue.[26] What Bellamy describes as a smooth, natural evolution from capitalism to the nationalization of industry in *Looking Backward,* Rand frames as the fateful triumph of myopic ineptitude. The growing intrusiveness of government and its futile attempts to satisfy escalating declarations of need is the catalyst for a small group of productive individualists mounting a strike.[27] While the country is slipping into a crushing depression and resultant state of smoldering anarchy, the productive minority—that of the prime movers, the striking individualists—abandons the larger society and forms a private colony in a valley in the Colorado mountains. This colony is the novel's penultimate utopia, effectively a staging area for the glorious return of the strikers to the larger economy as the final utopia. In Colorado the strikers wait out the impending economic catastrophe and plan the country's rebirth under sounder economic and moral leadership. In a sixty-page secular sermon marking the beginning of the end for the need-based society, Galt declares: "A country's political system is based on its code of morality."[28] The collapsing political system in *Atlas Shrugged* is based on the utopian belief that deep pockets have no bottom. Expressing the prevailing but

---

26. By need Rand implies a cluster of characteristics including sloth, an inability or unwillingness to think or think rationally and act decisively, and a resulting repudiation of responsibility. It represents what she calls a "sense of life," in this case, one that is unproductive and irrational. Rand, *The Romantic Manifesto,* 14–15. Rand's "need" resembles what psychologists term learned helplessness, an unwarranted passivity and resulting moral inertia. See Christopher Peterson, Steven F. Maier, and Martin E. P. Seligman, *Learned Helplessness* (Oxford: Oxford University Press, 1993).

27. Rand believes, "Capitalism and altruism are incompatible; they are philosophical opposites; they cannot co-exist in the same man or in the same society." Ayn Rand, *For the New Intellectual* (New York: Signet Books, 1963), 54.

28. Rand, *Atlas Shrugged,* 1061. Rand would take issue with Lewis's assertion that "throughout the speech, as throughout the book, it is not the rightness of his beliefs but the force of his personality that brings to Galt's side those whom he needs in his conquest of society." Lewis, "The Utopian Hero," 140.

faltering social philosophy, one character explains, "in order to be placed above rights, above principles, above morality . . . all a man has to do is to be in need."[29]

CONSTRUCTIVE TAXES IN THE COLLAPSING UTOPIA OF NEED

The tax system underlying the utopia of need is multifaceted, heavy-handed, and self-defeating. In addition to pecuniary taxation, the government imposes increasingly burdensome economic sacrifices in its attempt to placate need, especially that of less-fortunate businesses. Wesley Mouch, the Top Coordinator of the Bureau of Economic Planning and National Resources, issues a series of directives, each imposing a new constructive tax. Directive 10-289, for example, establishes the Unification Board, enforces an employment freeze, and commands that all business establishments "shall . . . remain in operation," and the owners "shall not quit nor leave nor retire."[30]

The required sacrifices assume many guises: "in hidden taxes, in regulations, in wasted time, in lost effort, [and] in energy spent to overcome artificial obstacles."[31] In a series of strategic maneuvers the government assumes control over the oil industry and establishes oil rationing;[32] it nationalizes railroads and steel mills and dictates that companies hire unqualified employees as its Unification Board directs.[33] Electricity usage is limited,[34] and copper and the special *Rearden Metal* are also subject to regulation.[35] In keeping with the government's interpretation of the general welfare, all directives intended to alleviate need incorporate need-based exceptions. These constructive taxes, expected to overcome the growing scarcity of goods and

---

29. Rand, *Atlas Shrugged*, 577. The utopian novel *A Traveler from Altruria* explores an "altruistic commonwealth" where "it is not human nature to hoard and grudge, but . . . to give and to help generously." Howells, *A Traveler from Altruria*, 196, 198.

30. Rand, *Atlas Shrugged*, 538–39.

31. Rand, 579.

32. Rand, 344.

33. Rand, 603–4.

34. Rand, 1158, 498.

35. Rand, 926.

services, cause even greater shortages.[36] The government's inability to see the far-reaching economic consequences of its constructive tax directives—its oppressive attempts to curb competition (but undertaken in the name of competition)—leads to a diminishing pie with which to feed the country. This prompts Galt to ask: "What . . . permitted you to hope that you could get away with this muck of contradictions and to plan it as an ideal society?"[37]

THE COLORADO COLONY

The third utopia comprises a small colony of the most productive businessowners and workers who have united in their refusal to continue enabling the unflagging needs of the majority. Two chapters in *Atlas Shrugged* describing the colony are named "Atlantis" and "Utopia of Greed."[38] "Progress can come only out of men's surplus," Rand explains, "that is: from the work of those men whose ability produces more than their personal consumption requires, those who are intellectually and financially able to venture out in pursuit of the new."[39] "It is the value of his own time that the strong of the intellect transfers to the weak, letting them work on the jobs he discovered."[40] Sciabarra contends, "it is the 'pyramid of ability' that explains

---

36. These measures are identified by Heller as a "parody on the verge of surrealism" of President Franklin D. Roosevelt's New Deal business controls. Heller, *Ayn Rand and the World She Made*, 131.

37. Rand, *Atlas Shrugged*, 1050.

38. In an essay explaining the significance of the chapter headings, Ghate says, "The Utopia of Greed," which is Atlantis, "is a realm where the inhabitants proudly and greedily dedicate themselves to the pursuit of their highest values." Onkar Ghate, "The Part and Chapter Headings of Atlas Shrugged," in *Essays on Rand's Atlas Shrugged*, ed. Robert Mayhew (New York: Lexington Books, 2009), 36 (italics in original).

39. Rand, *The Virtue of Selfishness*, 84. This sense of surplus supersedes Marx's meaning; Rand's surplus encompasses the creation of labor for others.

40. According to Rand, "The man at the bottom [of the "intellectual pyramid"] who, left to himself, would starve in his hopeless ineptitude, contributes nothing to those above him, but receives the bonus of all their brains." Rand, *Atlas Shrugged*, 1065. How much credit "the strong of the intellect" deserve for "the bonus of all their brains" is addressed by Hertzka and Bellamy. Hertzka's narrator in *Freeland* declares, "All that we enjoy we owe in an infinitely small degree to our own intelligence and strength; . . . it is to the rich inheritance received from our ancestors that we owe ninety-nine per cent of our enjoyments." Hertzka, *Freeland*, 138. Bellamy advances a similar argument in *Looking*

why the strike works so effectively, by draining the economy of talent."[41] By removing themselves from the larger society, the strikers intend to hasten the demise of the flawed economic model. This theme was foreshadowed in Rand's earlier work, the *Fountainhead*, where Roark asks: "What would happen to the world without those who do, think, work, produce?"[42] Ironically, Saint-Simon had previously envisioned an analogous thought experiment, resulting in France decomposing into a "lifeless corpse."[43]

The prime movers' utopia is transitional, as they foresee the time they (or their successors) will reenter the larger society as its leaders and rebuild the failed economy on a new ideological foundation. Membership in the colony is by invitation only—"based on creative drive and talent, if not genius"[44]—while access and egress to the private valley are subject to close control.[45] Originally, banker Midas Mulligan purchased the valley as a private retreat,[46] but eventually he began selling home sites—but only for gold.[47] The members of the utopian colony deny they have formed a society and claim to have no rules or laws. Their scheme is one of passive-aggressive destruction; their goal, like the anarchists in Dostoevsky's *Devils*, is

---

Backward, 112. Rand does concede, however, that "the knowledge potentially available to man is greater than any one man could begin to acquire in his own lifespan; every man gains an incalculable benefit from the knowledge discovered by others." Rand, *The Virtue of Selfishness*, 32.

41. Chris Matthew Sciabarra, "Manifesto for a New Radicalism," in *Ayn Rand's Atlas Shrugged*, ed. Edward W. Younkins (Burlington, VT: Ashgate Publishing Company, 2007), 29.

42. Ayn Rand, *The Fountainhead* (New York: Signet Books, 1945), 606.

43. Saint-Simon asks, "Suppose that France suddenly lost fifty of her best physicists, chemists, physiologists, mathematicians, poets, painters, sculptors, musicians, writers; . . . These men are the Frenchmen who are the most essential producers, those who make the most important products, those who direct the enterprises most useful to the nation, those who contribute to its achievements in the sciences, fine arts and professions." Saint-Simon, *Henri Comte De Saint-Simon (1760–1825): Selected Writings*, ed. and trans. Markham, 72–73.

44. Alan Clardy, "Galt's Gulch: Ayn Rand's Utopian Delusion," *Utopian Studies* 23, no. 1 (2012): 238–62, 252.

45. The colony or its secret location is referred to either as "Galt's Gulch" or "Mulligan's Valley." Rand, *Atlas Shrugged*, 749.

46. Rand, 746–47.

47. Rand, 727, 747.

to demoralize everyone and make hodge-podge of everything, and then, when society [is] on the point of collapse—sick, depressed, cynical, and skeptical . . . suddenly to gain control.[48]

TAXES IN THE COLORADO COLONY

Since the members of the Colorado colony are the most cognizant and outspoken critics of the federal government's pecuniary and constructive tax systems, it is worth asking whether they imposed any taxes on themselves. At first glance it appears unlikely based on banker Mulligan's assertion: "We are not a state here, not a society of any kind—we're just a voluntary association of men held together by nothing but every man's self-interest."[49] In spite of this denial, however, they evince what Marx calls a "unity of interest"—in contrast to the farmers of whom he says they formed a class only "as a bag with potatoes constitutes a potato-bag."[50] Expounding on the banker's characterization, Galt adds, "we have no laws in this valley, no rules, no formal organization of any kind. . . . But we have certain customs."[51] Rand was a supporter of government and an opponent of anarchy,[52] but her view of

48. Dostoevsky, *Devils*, 748–49. Rand's character Galt says, "When the looter's state collapses . . . when it falls into a level of impotent chaos . . . and dissolves into starving robber gangs fighting to rob one another—when the advocates of the morality of sacrifice perish with their final ideal—then and on that day we will return." Rand, *Atlas Shrugged*, 1067.

49. Rand, *Atlas Shrugged*, 747.

50. This was Marx's description of myriad small French subsistence farmers of whom he said they lack any "unity of interest" since their "individual members live in identical conditions, without, however, entering into manifold relations with one another." Karl Marx, *Eighteenth Brumaire of Louis Bonaparte*, trans. D. D. L. (Project Gutenberg, 2006. Last updated 2013), http://www.gutenberg.org/files/1346/1346-h/1346-h.htm (accessed February 5, 2019).

51. Rand, *Atlas Shrugged*, 714. Bostaph explains that because Rand "assumes no government," she "replaces the word 'law' with the word 'custom' to indicate a less formal agreement." Sam Bostaph, " 'Atlantis' as a Free Market Economy," in *Ayn Rand's Atlas Shrugged*, ed. Edward W. Younkins (Burlington, VT: Ashgate Publishing Company, 2007), 210. Since the beginnings of the colony were only twelve years earlier, however, the use of the term customs appears premature, especially in the declared absence of a society to transmit them.

52. Smith argues that even if the colony lacks a formal government, Rand "is emphatically not an anarchist." Tara Smith, " 'Humanity's Darkest Evil': The Lethal Destructiveness of

"proper government" limits its function to protecting specific moral rights based on an objective code of rules and barring the initiation of force.[53]

Examining the colony in more detail, it becomes clear that although there is not a government (as Rand defines it), the prime movers have formed a society, albeit a secret society.[54] The fundamental rule of the society is its mandatory oath: "I swear by my life and my love of it that I will never live for the sake of another man, nor ask another man to live for mine."[55] A correlative rule is central to the novel's plot and to an understanding of the nature of the strike: "When a man took our oath," Galt explains,

> it meant a single commitment: not to work in his own profession, not to give to the world the benefit of his mind. Each of us carried it out in any manner he chose. Those who had money, retired to live on their savings. Those who had to work, took the lowest jobs they could find.[56]

For this reason, Galt, the brilliant electrical engineer and inventor, works for twelve years as an unskilled track laborer at a Taggart railroad yard.[57] Francisco d'Anconia, heir to the world's largest copper mine, labors as a furnace foreman at a steel mill.[58] And their former philosophy professor Hugh Akston flips pancakes in a diner on Route 86 in the mountains west of Cheyenne.[59]

Non-Objective Law," in *Essays on Ayn Rand's Atlas Shrugged*, ed., Robert Mayhew (New York: Lexington Books, 2009), 342.

53. Rand, *The Virtue of Selfishness*, 109.

54. In her contrast of secret societies with totalitarian movements, Arendt observes, "With secret societies, the totalitarian movements . . . share the dichotomous division of the world between 'sworn blood brothers' and an indistinct inarticulate mass of sworn enemies. . . . It has always been the principle of secret societies that 'whosoever is not expressly included is excluded.'" Arendt, *The Origins of Totalitarianism*, 376–77.

55. Rand, *Atlas Shrugged*, 731.

56. Rand, 747. By taking the "lowest jobs they could find," the strikers sacrificed their personal interests to an ideal opposed to personal sacrifice.

57. Rand, 960.

58. Rand, 998. Francisco was Dagny's childhood friend and college love interest (Rand, 108–9).

59. Rand, 327.

The result of the oath and its corollary is that no surplus is produced and so progress is stopped. The Colorado colony also established rules regarding money and financial transactions as well as trade with the greater society. Gold and silver are the only permissible currency and must be in the form of coins minted by banker Mulligan's Mint.[60] No trade is permitted with the outside world except for those goods Mulligan spirits in from his external source.[61] Another rule states that all transactions between colonists must involve exchanging value for value.[62] This means no gifts or uncompensated arrangements. For this reason, Galt informs Dagny, "there is one word which is forbidden in this valley: the word *'give.'* "[63] "Guests" who stay at Galt's house, for example, must pay for their lodging in gold. Thus, he tells Dagny, "I shall charge you for your room and board—it is against our rules to provide the unearned sustenance of another human being."[64] A similar sounding rule, though with a very different meaning, appears in Bellamy's *Looking Backward.* Dr. Leete declares: "That any person should be dependent for the means of support upon another would be shocking to the moral sense as well as indefensible on any rational social theory. What would become of personal liberty and dignity under such an arrangement?"[65]

Considering this set of clear and objective policies—and the pledge of a former judge to arbitrate disputes[66]—claiming there are no rules and no society is reminiscent of the disingenuous assertion that Wesley Mouch's executive orders are not "laws," merely "directives."[67] Both claims are suggestive of Humpty Dumpty's declaration: "When *I* use a word . . . it means just what I choose it to mean—neither more nor less."[68]

Rand's definition of government, a rephrasing of Weber's, is an agency that "holds a legal monopoly on the use of physical force against legally

---

60. Rand, 727.

61. Rand, 747.

62. Rand, 760; also 410.

63. Rand, 714 (italics in original).

64. Rand, 760.

65. Bellamy, *Looking Backward,* 188.

66. Former judge Narragansett. Rand, *Atlas Shrugged,* 748.

67. Rand, 333. Clardy asserts their society has "shared values, norms, and rituals . . . with people who share a common identity and who interact in any number of ways that are not economic." Clardy, "Galt's Gulch," 257.

68. Lewis Carroll, *Through the Looking Glass,* in *The Annotated Alice,* ed. Martin Gardner (Cleveland, OH: The World Publishing Company, 1960), 269.

disarmed victims."[69] "The source of the government's authority," Rand stipulates, "is 'the consent of the governed.' This means," she says, "that the government is not the *ruler*, but the servant or *agent* of the citizens."[70] "A proper government is only a policeman," Galt declares, "acting as an agent of man's self-defense."[71] Thus, despite its stringent rules—since there is no policeman acting as an agent—it is doubtful that the colonists have fashioned even a quasi (or utopian) government capable of levying taxes.

THE FOURTH UTOPIA

Rand's ideal society is one that permits her ideal men, such as John Galt, to "exist and function," by which she means the society is to be a "free, productive, rational system."[72] "The belief that a good society can be built on the basis of inequality and private property," says Sargent, "is certainly not uncommon, and descriptions of the economic base of such societies deserve notice."[73] The principles of the fourth utopia are defined, although its arrival is expected subsequent to the novel's end. In some respects, at least, the fourth utopia, founded on laissez-faire capitalism, resembles but purifies the first utopia.[74] "Life and production" rather than "death and taxes" are recommended as the "two absolutes" of Rand's moral code.[75] Galt's solution of a strike—the anti-altruistic counterpart of a paternalistic

---

69. Rand, *The Virtue of Selfishness*, 98. Weber states, "Ultimately, one can define the modern state sociologically only in terms of the specific means peculiar to it . . . the monopoly of the legitimate use of physical force within a given territory." Max Weber, "Politics as a Vocation," in *From Max Weber: Essays in Sociology*, trans. H. H. Gerth and C. Wright Mills (New York: Oxford University Press, 1946), 77–78 (italics in original).

70. Rand, *The Virtue of Selfishness*, 110.

71. Rand, *Atlas Shrugged*, 1062.

72. Rand, *The Romantic Manifesto*, 157.

73. Lyman Tower Sargent, "Capitalist Eutopias in America," in *America as Utopia*, ed. Kenneth M. Roemer (New York: Burt Franklin and Company, 1981), 201–2.

74. Rand says, "When I say 'capitalism,' I mean a full, pure, uncontrolled, unregulated laissez-faire capitalism—with a separation of state and economics." Rand, *The Virtue of Selfishness*, 33. In opposition, Hayek explains, "Probably nothing has done so much harm to the liberal cause as the wooden insistence of some liberals on certain rough rules of thumb, above all the principle of laissez faire." Hayek, *The Road to Serfdom*, 17. Hayek specifies that he is using the term liberal "in the original, nineteenth-century sense" (Hayek, ix).

75. Rand, *Atlas Shrugged*, 579.

tough-love cure—forces the United States to suffer the practical consequences of its altruistic moral code: its economic and political demise. Once the collapse of the larger society is complete, the colony of strikers will return and initiate the final utopia, establishing it on a new moral base—self-interest rather than need.

The code Rand and Galt espouse asks what values are necessary for an individual's rational prospering. The fact of our existence, she believes, leads to certain moral conditions under which we must be permitted to live.[76] The right to life, she argues, entails "the freedom to take all the actions required by the nature of a rational being for the support, the furtherance, the fulfillment and the enjoyment of his own life."[77] This is because, she says, "*Rights* are conditions of existence required by man's nature for his proper survival."[78] The challenge of deriving *ought* from *is* in this circumstance does not impress her; in fact, she sees no alternative. Doughney explains, "Rand attempts to deduce 'ought' conclusions completely from 'is' premises, as she believes that this gives all her normative claims objective, factual status."[79] Regarding Rand's position on the *is-ought* problem, Mack explains, "The crux of Rand's central philosophical insight in moral theory is that there is

---

76. For an explication and defense of Rand's argument on this point, see Den Uyl and Rasmussen, *The Philosophic Thought of Ayn Rand*, 63–80. For a critical examination of Den Uyl's and Rasmussen's argument and suggestions on how Rand could have improved her position on this issue, see J. Charles King, "Life and the Theory of Value: The Randian Argument Reconsidered," in the same volume, 102–21.

77. Rand, *The Virtue of Selfishness*, 93–94. At first sight, Rand's view in this regard appears consonant with John Locke's claim that "natural reason . . . tells us, that men, being once born, have a right to their preservation and consequently to meat and drink, and such other things as nature affords for their subsistence." Locke, *Second Treatise on Government*, chap. 5, §25, 18. But whereas Locke attributes this right to God's providence and Natural Law, Rand asserts it as a moral right stemming from our nature as rational beings. For this reason, her view bears an uneasy resemblance to Kant's, of whom she is consistently critical. Kant claims, "Nature gave man reason, and freedom of will based upon reason, and this in itself was a clear indication of nature's intention as regards his endowments. For it showed that man was not meant to be guided by instinct or equipped and instructed by innate knowledge; on the contrary, he was meant to produce everything out of himself." Immanuel Kant, "Idea for a Universal History with a Cosmopolitan Purpose," in *Political Writings*, 2nd ed., trans. H. B. Nisbet, ed. Hans Reiss (Cambridge: Cambridge University Press 1991), 43 (italics in original).

78. Rand, *Atlas Shrugged*, 1061 (italics in original).

79. Lachlan Doughney, "Ayn Rand and Deducting 'Ought' from 'Is,'" *The Journal of Ayn Rand Studies* 12, no. 1 (2012): 151–68, 157.

a far more intimate and profound connection between life and the process of valuation . . . than other moral philosophers have realized."[80] Critical of Rand's logic, Nozick argues, "a right to life is not a right to whatever one needs to live. . . . At most, a right to life would be a right to have or strive for whatever one needs to live, provided that having it does not violate anyone else's rights."[81] One indication of Rand's logical predicament in this effort to derive values from facts is underscored by Henry George relying on the same premise: "a right proclaimed by the fact of [man's] existence," to deny the right to private land ownership—a right required for Rand's argument—and assert the "equal right of all men to use the land."[82]

This final utopia—only outlined through Galt's expressions of its principles—comprises individuals living rationally by recognizing and pursuing their separate long-term self-interests. According to Rand, "the free market is ruled by those who are able to see and plan long-range—and the better the mind, the longer the range."[83] This long-range planning is facilitated by a government whose one task is to defend the (proper) moral rights of individuals. Rand explains that "if one wishes to uphold individual rights, one must realize that capitalism"—in her understanding, a complex of values and rights, not merely an economic model—"is the only system that can uphold and protect them."[84] She acknowledges, however, "A fully free, capitalist system has not yet existed anywhere,"[85] rendering it a utopian quest.

---

80. Eric Mack, "The Fundamental Elements of Rand's Theory of Rights," in *The Philosophic Thought of Ayn Rand*, ed. Douglas J. Den Uyl and Douglas B. Rasmussen (Urbana: University of Illinois Press, 1984), 123–24 (italics in original). Hume is credited with recognizing the problem caused by inferring what we ought to do from purely factual premises. Hume, *A Treatise of Human Nature*, bk. 3, pt. 1, sec. 1, 458, 469.

81. Nozick, *Anarchy, State and Utopia*, 179n. He cites Rand, *The Virtue of Selfishness*, 94.

82. George, *Progress and Poverty*, 338.

83. Rand, *Capitalism: The Unknown Ideal*, 19. "Long-range," extends only to "actual human beings," and not to future generations, which would render it altruistic and utopian. Rand, *The Virtue of Selfishness*, 81.

84. Rand, *The Virtue of Selfishness*, 92. Bostaph notes, "Rand's formal knowledge of economics was relatively limited and . . . her case for the free market is almost entirely ethical and political." Samuel Bostaph, "Ayn Rand's Economic Thought," *The Journal of Ayn Rand Studies* 11, no. 1 (July 2011): 19–44, 19. Rand's informal knowledge of economics includes what she gleaned from her personal acquaintance with economists Henry Hazlitt, Ludwig von Mises, and Alan Greenspan. Heller, *Ayn Rand and the World She Made*, 248–52.

85. Rand, *The Virtue of Selfishness*, 129.

Like Owen, who argues that a change of principle "must be effected . . . by making it appear, first to the few, and then to the many,"[86] Rand sees the promotion of capitalism as a mission initially for the few. "History is made by minorities," she observes, and more particularly by intellectual movements created by minorities.[87] To effect the utopian rebirth she desires, Rand looks to the emergence of "New Intellectuals" as the force behind her moral renaissance. "The battle is primarily intellectual (philosophical)," she stipulates, "not political."[88] By *intellectual* she means the extraordinary combination of "a man who is guided by his *intellect*" and who is also "a thinker who is a man of action."[89] The challenge she sets for this minority is to promote capitalism as a moral ideal and the focus of moral education, rather than as an economic endeavor. Effective moral education, she believes, begins with children and stresses authors such as Hugo and Dostoevsky who portray the type of character "in whose image" the child can "shape his own soul."[90]

In the present age, she reports, the intellectual and the businessman do not communicate; rather they coexist in mutual fear and contempt.[91] The businessman is "the producer of wealth" and the intellectual is "the purveyor of knowledge,"[92] but the code of altruism, she believes, has derailed their potential collaboration. Her solution, an ironic rendering of Plato's paradoxical claim in the *Republic*, is for philosophers to become businessmen and businessmen, philosophers.[93]

---

86. Owen, *A Development of the Principles and Plans on Which to Establish Self-Supporting Home Colonies*, 31.

87. Rand, *Philosophy: Who Needs It*, 273.

88. Rand, 273.

89. Rand, *For the New Intellectual*, 51 (italics in original). She, like Plato, seeks natures who "are few and born only rarely among human beings." Plato, *Republic*, trans. Bloom, bk. 6, 491a–b.

90. Rand, *The Romantic Manifesto*, 99, 139. Lipp says that as much as Rand loved Hugo and Dostoevsky, she disliked Shakespeare and "loathed" Tolstoy. Ronald F. Lipp, "Atlas and Art," in *Ayn Rand's Atlas Shrugged*, ed. Edward W. Younkins (Burlington, VT: Ashgate Publishing Company, 2007), 144.

91. Rand, *For the New Intellectual*, 48.

92. Rand, 21.

93. Rand, 52–53; Plato, *Republic*, bk. 5, 473.

RAND'S "TAX" SYSTEM

This is the most difficult part. Because at this point we depart from the confines of the believable.

—Yevgeny Zamyatin (1884–1937), *We*[94]

Burke observes that "those who are habitually employed in finding and displaying faults are unqualified for the work of reformation."[95] This may explain why those who oppose taxation are an unlikely source of fresh ideas on tax policy or tax reform. Younkins claims that Rand sees income taxes as "antiproductive, destructive, unjust, and immoral."[96] On this point, at least, her view intersects that of Henry George who declares, "Our revenue laws as a body might well be entitled, 'Acts to promote the corruption of public officials, to suppress honesty and encourage fraud, to set a premium upon perjury and the subornation of perjury, and to divorce the idea of law from the idea of justice.' "[97] Indeed, for Rand, the "imposition of taxes" represents the government's "initiation of force,"[98] making it incompatible with individual rights. By the "imposition of taxes," however, she means only "compulsory taxation," which she claims is a "remnant of the time when the government was regarded as the omnipotent ruler of the citizens."[99] Since she also rejects the notions of "the public" (as a rights-possessing entity) and of "the public interest,"[100] the scope of her public policy and of her proposed tax policy are correspondingly truncated. This leaves individual self-interest as the glue bonding her social order together, backed by the reciprocal mandate of rights—the requirement that we recognize the equal rights of others. "The bond of reciprocity unites men," Fuller advises, "not simply *in*

---

94. Zamyatin, *We*, record 27, 136.

95. Burke, *Reflection on the Revolution in France*, 171.

96. Edward W. Younkins, "Economics in Ayn Rand's Atlas Shrugged," *The Journal of Ayn Rand Studies* 13, no. 2 (December 2013): 123–39, 127.

97. George, *Progress and Poverty*, 417.

98. Rand, *The Virtue of Selfishness*, 116.

99. Rand, 118.

100. Rand, 88.

spite of their differences, but *because* of their differences."[101] But honoring the equal rights of others runs the risk that the others will not reciprocate. Thus, Hobbes warns, "he that performeth first, has no assurance the other will perform after."[102] One question this fosters is whether recognizing the equal rights of others is, for Rand, a sacrifice or an equal exchange? It is neither. Honoring the corresponding rights of others—including strangers and moral enemies—is not, for Rand, a call for positive action, it is a call for non-interference.[103] A person's rights, declares Rand, "are his by nature and not subject to your grant or sanction."[104] Thus when Dagny is told, "You have no duty to anyone but yourself,"[105] it means no duty to actively consider and promote the well-being of another, if so doing requires any sacrifice.[106] It does not preclude, but is limited by, recognizing the other's equal rights to life, liberty, and property.[107]

Based on these factors, the taxes she foresees and endorses are not imposed or compulsory—they are voluntary (optional)—and hence not taxes.[108] Swift anticipated her suggestion of a voluntary tax. He proposed taxing men in accordance with the high opinions they hold of themselves in respect to their physical and mental abilities, to which they would self-attest.[109] Rand's scheme rests on citizens' rationality, however, rather than their arrogance. Describing her proposal, she says, "In a fully free society, taxation—or, to be exact, payment for governmental services—would be *voluntary*."[110] Rational citizens, she believes, would voluntarily comply since they

---

101. Fuller, *The Morality of Law*, 23.

102. Hobbes, *Leviathan*, first part, chap. 2, 108.

103. See Rand's discussion in *The Virtue of Selfishness*, 44–45.

104. Rand, *Journals of Ayn Rand*, 436.

105. Rand, *Atlas Shrugged*, 802.

106. Rand asserts, "'Sacrifice' is the surrender of that which you value in favor of that which you don't. . . . If you give money to help a friend, it is not a sacrifice; if you give it to a worthless stranger, it is." Rand, *Atlas Shrugged*, 1028.

107. Rand, *Journals of Ayn Rand*, 354.

108. Rand's utopian stance is countered by Olson, an economist, who explains, "the state cannot survive on voluntary dues or payments, but must rely on taxation." Olson, *The Logic of Collective Action*, 13–14.

109. This was the position of a professor at the Academy of Lagado in Balnibarbi. Swift, *Gulliver's Travels*, 177. Voluntary taxes also appear in Louis-Sebastien Mercer's 1771 utopian *Memoirs of the Year Two Thousand Five Hundred*. Saint-Simon advocated voluntary taxation, as outlined in chapter four.

110. Rand, *The Virtue of Selfishness*, 116 (italics in original).

would "not desire the unearned."[111] Nozick is critical of Rand's overreliance on human rationality. "Miss Rand," he says, "falls into [the] optimistic or Platonic tradition in ethics, believing that there are no objective conflicts of interest among persons."[112] Frye observes that a common objection to utopias lies in their presentation of human nature "as governed more by reason than it is or can be,"[113] a point Rand's argument for voluntary taxation serves to illustrate.[114] Acknowledging the utopian implications of her proposal, she ultimately admits that "any program of voluntary government financing has to be regarded as a goal for a distant future."[115]

VOLUNTARY TAXES

Rand's definition of taxation is at once more limiting and more encompassing than mine. It is more limiting since it refers only to pecuniary taxation; it is more encompassing since it includes both voluntary (uncoerced) and nonvoluntary (coerced) payments to the government. Under her definition, user fees and lottery revenue are taxes, as are other payments requiring neither coercion nor sacrifice. Her definition of taxation does not recognize nonpecuniary government-imposed sacrifices, though such constructive taxes, as noted, play a prominent role in *Atlas Shrugged*.

Voluntary taxation is Rand's suggested replacement for current methods that she believes violate our inalienable property rights. The "naked essence" of taxation, she asserts, is "extortion by force."[116] Instead of coercive methods she submits there are many options for voluntary government financing.[117]

---

111. Rand, 31.

112. Robert Nozick, "On the Randian Argument," in *Reading Nozick: Essays on Anarchy, State, and Utopia*, ed. Jeffrey Paul, 206–31 (Totowa, NJ: Rowman and Littlefield, 1981), 218.

113. Frye, "Varieties of Literary Utopias," 26.

114. Rand, *The Virtue of Selfishness*, 116.

115. Rand, 118.

116. Rand, *Atlas Shrugged*, 757–58.

117. Rand, *The Virtue of Selfishness*, 116. Sechrest wonders how human beings in Rand's world "possess so finely-tuned a sense of justice that they would contribute to the public treasury even if they were not forced to do so, and at the same time possess so little sense of justice that they will kill innocent people in a mad search for their stolen property?" Larry J. Sechrest, "Rand, Anarchy, and Taxes," *The Journal of Ayn Rand Studies* 1, no. 1 (Fall 1999): 87–105, 93.

But since she sees this possibility as "very complex,"[118] and arising in the distant future—and so utopian[119]—she submits but two tentative proposals. The first is a government lottery and the other involves taxing contracts. The protection of contractual agreements among citizens is a vital service and one, she believes, only a government can provide.[120] In recognition of this vital service, only contracts "which had been insured by the payment, to the government, of a premium in the amount of a legally fixed percentage of the sums involved in the contractual transaction"[121]—a voluntary "tax"—would be legally enforceable. Since all credit transactions are based on contractual agreements, the potential revenue, Rand believes, could be substantial.[122] Currently, she explains, this service is "provided gratuitously and amounts, in effect, to a subsidy."[123] Downplaying the immediate need to choose the best method of voluntary taxation—implying that taxes are, after all, only an afterthought—she advises that any system of voluntary government financing "is the last, not the first, step on the road to a free society."[124]

Robert Nozick, whose views we examine in the next section, says her "proposal involves the government charging *extra* to enforce contracts, in order to cover the costs of its other protective functions." He then asks, "Why is this not illegitimate forcible redistribution?"[125] Rand's projected reply is that even if the contract fees are redistributive, the enrichment to those who pay nothing "may be regarded as a bonus to the men of lesser economic ability, made possible by the men of greater economic ability—*without any sacrifice of the latter to the former*."[126] Thus she anticipates Nozick's distinction between a tax system *designed* to be redistributive and one merely having that result.

---

118. Rand, *The Virtue of Selfishness*, 116.

119. Rand, 81. And so not affecting "actual human beings."

120. Rand, 116.

121. Rand, 117.

122. Rand, 117.

123. Rand, 117.

124. Rand, 117.

125. Nozick, "On the Randian Argument," 226.

126. Rand, *The Virtue of Selfishness*, 119 (italics in original).

RAND'S LAND TAX

Because Rand views private property—and by implication private land own-ership—as an inviolable moral right (implicit in the right to life), she sees the government's enforcement of this right as an extension of its function as an agent and not, as George argues, a government-coerced monopoly. For this reason, though she otherwise opposes government intervention in economic concerns, including government-coerced pecuniary taxation, she sees the institution of government-enshrined land monopolies as a moral imperative. The consequence of this institution, however (described in chapter six), is a constructive tax—a device of political control—ensuring that for George, Tolstoy, and others, "the interests of some men are to be sacrificed to the interests and wishes of others."[127]

Part Two:
Robert Nozick (1938–2002): Utopia of Utopias

THE MOST EXTENSIVE STATE THAT CAN BE JUSTIFIED

> They tried to tell her what the doctor had said, but it turned out that though he had spoken very fluently and at great length, it was impossible to reproduce what he had said.
>
> —Leo Tolstoy (1828–1910), *Anna Karenina*[128]

---

127. Rand, 88.

128. Tolstoy, *Anna Karenina*, 108. J. Wolff concedes that "to reconstruct Nozick's arguments and conclusions to make them as coherent as possible . . . is not always a simple matter [because] vital premises of arguments can be scattered over many pages, or missing entirely." Wolff, *Robert Nozick: Property, Justice and the Minimal State*, 2. In his defense, Nozick explains that in contrast to neatly packaged philosophical tracts, he believes there is a place for "a less complete work, containing unfinished presentations, conjectures, open questions and problems, leads, side connections, as well as a main line of argument." Nozick, *Anarchy, State, and Utopia*, xii.

Only formal libertarian analogs link Robert Nozick's utopia in *Anarchy, State, and Utopia* to Rand's in *Atlas Shrugged*. Both reveal a minimal state as the utopian foundation; both see moral rights as inviolable and prior to the state; and both assert that any government function exceeding the protection of our rights to life, liberty, and property necessarily violates those rights. Nozick and Rand also agree that moral philosophy provides the foundation for political philosophy[129] (including tax philosophy). But while Rand selected the medium of a Romantic novel to unleash her utopia,[130] Nozick plied his trade as a philosophy professor. Mack notes that Nozick was an academic and Rand was a nonacademic "from whom Nozick was usually eager to distance himself."[131]

Nozick's utopian quest is for a world where no one's choices forcibly constrain the choices of others. He believes enforcing each person's moral rights—to life, liberty, and property—accomplish this.[132] To achieve his goal, he develops two lines of argument converging on the same conclusion.[133] One argument, aiming at Nozick's anarchist opponent, begins in a state of nature and confronts the practical problem of rights protection its populace faces.[134] This argument follows a progression of stages resulting in a minimal state. "The minimal state," he claims, "is the most extensive state that can be justified."[135] The other line of argument explores a formal utopian world that turns out to be a utopia of utopias within a minimal state framework.

---

129. Rand, *The Virtue of Selfishness*, 33; Nozick, *Anarchy, State, and Utopia*, 6; Nozick, *Philosophical Explanations*, 503.

130. Rand says, "In regard to Romanticism, I have often thought that I am a bridge from the unidentified past to the future." Rand, *The Romantic Manifesto*, vi.

131. Eric Mack, "Non-Absolute Rights and Libertarian Taxation," in *Taxation, Economic Prosperity, and Distributive Justice*, ed. E. Paul, F. Miller, and J. Paul (Cambridge: Cambridge University Press, 2006), 112–13.

132. Some commentators speak of Nozick's theory of natural rights, based (I assume) on his reference to a state of nature. However, since the Natural Law has no relevance to his theory, I describe his inviolable prelegal rights as moral rights. Mack speaks of the "Lockean state-of-nature starting point" employed by Nozick as one where individuals "possess various moral or human rights." Eric Mack, "Nozick's Anarchism," in *Anarchism*, ed. J. Roland Pennock and John W. Chapman, 43–62 (New York: New York University Press, 1978), 43–44 (italics added).

133. Nozick, *Anarchy, State, and Utopia*, 333.

134. Nozick, xi.

135. Nozick, 149.

Both lines of argument illustrate his preference for "process" solutions rather than goal-directed or "end state" solutions.[136]

Commentators are divided on whether Nozick requires (or permits) a system of taxation in his minimal state. There is controversy as to whether his libertarian principles ban all forms of taxation or only taxation on labor, as well as whether the compensation device he employs in his minimal state (mentioned in chapter six and described below) is itself redistributive and if so, whether it is a tax. These matters are discussed in their place as well as the (constructive) land tax he implicitly endorses.

THE DEVELOPING STATE: THE FIRST FOUR STAGES

> Individual liberty in a community is not, as mathematicians would say, always of the same sign. To ignore this is the essential fallacy of the cult called Individualists. But in truth, a general prohibition in a state may increase the sum of liberty, and a general permission may diminish it.
>
> —H. G. Wells (1866–1946), *A Modern Utopia*[137]

Nozick's first line of argument begins with an ahistorical anarchic state of nature. His goal is to show the error in the anarchist claim "that in the course of maintaining its monopoly on the use of force and protecting everyone within a territory, the state must violate individuals' rights and hence is intrinsically immoral."[138] To combat this claim, Nozick attempts to demonstrate how a state (albeit a minimal state) might "arise from anarchy (as represented by Locke's state of nature) even though no one intended this or tried to bring it about, by a process which need not violate anyone's rights."[139]

A central feature of his state of nature is that each person pursues her own remedies for addressing what she perceives as violations of her moral rights, making the whole process unpredictable (and possibly risky) and hindering the goal of upholding everyone's rights. In this setting people

---

136. Nozick, 332.

137. Wells, *A Modern Utopia*, 18.

138. Nozick, *Anarchy, State, and Utopia*, xi.

139. Nozick, xi.

eventually demand a better way to defend their rights than each individually acting as her own policeman, judge, and executioner (what Nozick refers to as "self-help enforcement").

The demand for a division of labor—in particular, a specialized protective agency—creates an entrepreneurial vacuum, setting in motion a progression of events resulting ultimately in a minimal state.[140] Under these conditions, Nozick postulates that a marketplace for private protective agencies will develop. With the advent of this marketplace most people voluntarily purchase protection while the rest (the independents), for various reasons, opt for self-protection. Individuals hire these agencies to perform what Nozick sees as the essential functions of a state: protection against violence, theft, and fraud, and the enforcement of contracts. The transition from a state of nature (first stage), where each person is responsible for defending himself and his rights, to the contractual (voluntary) delegation of this protection to private protective agencies marks the second stage in a five-stage evolution of the minimal state (summarized in Table 2). During this evolution—with the forces of competition and an invisible hand guiding it—a shake-out and consolidation occurs (the third stage), wherein the poorly subscribed protective services relinquish customers to more dominant services. Eventually all but one of the protective agencies is extinguished or subsumed into a larger agency or a network of agencies. While most individuals now receive protection from the dominant agency, some continue to protect themselves in their own ways (the self-insured or uninsured independents).

The result of this consolidation is his fourth stage, what he calls the *ultraminimal state*. At this stage, Nozick explains, the dominant protective agency is not a state, properly speaking. But, he asks, what else is required? A state, he stipulates, must have both a territorial monopoly on the use of force and protect the rights of everyone in that territory.[141] In the fourth stage, he explains, "The dominant protective association may reserve for itself the right to judge any procedure of justice to be applied to its clients [including those procedures applied by the independents]."[142] (This is not a new right, as "no new rights 'emerge' at the group level."[143]) At this junc-

---

140. Nozick, 13 (italics in original).

141. Nozick, 113.

142. Nozick, 101.

143. Nozick, 90.

Table 2. Evolution of the Minimal State

Order	Evolutionary Stage	Characteristics of Change
first	state of nature and of anarchy	Protection of one's self and one's moral rights, including property rights, is an individual's responsibility.
second	emergence from state of nature	Entrepreneurs form protective agencies to fulfill a demand. In the resulting market for rights protection, people contract with one of the competing private protective agencies.
third	shake-out period	Weaker protective agencies succumb to competition. A few dominant agencies emerge; eventually only one survives.
fourth	ultraminimal state	Because one agency is dominant, a noncoercive "monopoly" element occurs in a geographical area, but it only provides protection to paying customers. This disadvantages the independents in their ability to protect their rights.
fifth	minimal state	Everyone in a geographical area receives protection, resulting in a "state-like entity." Protection extends to those who do not pay (former independents), resulting in a de facto redistribution, but violating no one's rights.

ture, Miller claims, "Nozick has to prove that [the one dominant protective agency] can justifiably prohibit the independents from taking action against its clients."[144] The general moral principle Nozick advances for this proof is the clients' right of self-defense "against the dangers of unreliable or unfair enforcement procedures," which, he asserts, "gives anyone the right to oversee others' enforcement of their rights against him." Furthermore, he continues, this means a customer "may empower his protective agency to exercise this right for him."[145]

---

144. David Miller, "The Justification of Political Authority," in *Robert Nozick*, ed. David Schmidtz (Cambridge: Cambridge University Press, 2002), 13.

145. Nozick, *Anarchy, State, and Utopia*, 120.

Nozick's concern in the fourth stage, the ultraminimal state, is that the protective agency's near-monopoly power to enforce rights pertains only to the paying customers, a condition he calls a *de facto* monopoly.[146] For although "no monopoly is claimed," he explains, "the dominant agency does occupy a unique position by virtue of its power."[147] As a result, "Though each person has a right to act correctly to prohibit others from violating rights (including the right not to be punished unless shown to deserve it), only the dominant protective association will be able, without sanction, to enforce correctness as it sees it."[148] Acknowledging this asymmetry of rights enforcement potential, Nozick concludes that a "system of private protection, even when one protective agency is dominant in a geographical territory, appears to fall short of a state."[149] It appears, he explains, that the dominant protective agency "not only lacks the requisite monopoly over the use of force, but also fails to provide protection for all in its territory."[150] The close of the fourth stage is marked by the operation of a dominant protective agency, apparently hobbled by a lack of authority to protect the rights of all in its territory and to impose on everyone a monopoly on the use of force. A minimal state provides these services and no more, making it the focus of his utopian vision. The transition to the fourth stage marks the achievement of a territorial near monopoly on the use of force, but it remains for the fifth stage to create a "legitimate" monopoly by extending this protection to the rights of everyone in that territory.[151]

In the ultraminimal state the surviving protective agency has the ability—though not yet the moral authority—to protect the independents.

---

146. Nozick, 108–9. Hospers explains the distinction between a coercive and a de facto monopoly. "There is coercive monopoly, in which government does not permit competition in a given area of goods or services. There is also noncoercive (or de facto) monopoly, in which more than one firm in a given area is legally permitted, but does not in fact exist. . . . A coercive monopoly . . . can be sustained only by force, that is, by the organization of physical force possessed by the government." John Hospers, *Libertarianism* (Santa Barbara, CA: Reason Press, 1971), 163–64.

147. Nozick, *Anarchy, State, and Utopia*, 108.

148. Nozick, 118.

149. Nozick, 51.

150. Nozick, 25. Nozick continues, without explanation, "But these appearances are deceptive" (Nozick, 25).

151. According to Nozick, "When only one agency actually exercises the right to prohibit others from using their unreliable procedures for enforcing justice, that makes it the de facto state" (Nozick, 140, italics in original).

Nozick sees in this arrangement a continuing threat to the agency's clients in each independent's empowerment as a standalone adjudicator and dispenser of justice.[152]

In summarizing the outcome of the first four stages, Nozick proclaims, "Out of anarchy, pressed by spontaneous groupings, market pressures, economies of scale, and rational self-interest there arises something very much resembling a minimal state."[153] At that point, the missing condition for becoming a state is that it must protect the rights of everyone in its territory.[154] For this reason, he says, the operators of the ultraminimal state "are morally required to transform it into a minimal state."[155]

Though Nozick predicts that the natural workings of the market will ultimately result in the emergence of a single dominant protective agency—a monopoly occurring without government intervention—he recognizes that this is an anomaly and not the predictable outcome for a free market in other services. This leads him to ask, "Why is this market different from all other markets? Why would a virtual monopoly arise in this market without the government intervention that elsewhere creates and maintains it?"[156] The reason he asserts is that "the worth of the product purchased, protection against others, is relative: it depends upon how strong the others are."[157]

THE FIFTH STAGE

A solution which leaves an unaccounted-for residuum is no solution at all.

—Edward Bellamy (1850–1898), *Looking Backward*[158]

---

152. Nozick says that "men who judge in their own case will always give themselves the benefit of the doubt and assume that they are in the right. They will overestimate the amount of harm or damage they have suffered, and passions will lead them to attempt to punish others more than proportionately and to exact excessive compensation" (Nozick, 11).

153. Nozick, 16–17.

154. Nozick, 113.

155. Nozick, 119. He adds, cryptically, "but they might choose not to do so" (Nozick, 119).

156. Nozick, 17.

157. Nozick, 17.

158. Bellamy, *Looking Backward*, 111.

One of Nozick's goals is to show how the minimal state arises from a state of nature, not as the result of a social contract, as Hobbes and Locke had proposed, but as the result of unhindered market forces.[159] His method "differs from social compact views," he explains, "in its invisible-hand structure."[160] The reason his objective is the minimal state is because "any state more extensive violates people's rights."[161] A more extensive state is one that provides goods to some by requiring sacrifices (taxes, redistribution) from others. The minimal state, he stipulates, "treats us as inviolate individuals, who may not be used in certain ways by others as means or tools."[162]

In the fifth and final stage, based on an understanding of what it means to fully possess rights, the dominant protective agency unilaterally asserts its authority to protect everyone's rights. "It becomes a minimal state," Miller affirms, "when it undertakes to provide protective services to those independents whom it has prohibited from using their own enforcement procedures."[163] In so doing, no old rights extinguish nor new rights emerge; the state assumes the authority to enforce the rights of all those it now protects—(potentially) everyone in its geographical territory.[164] Thus, while the residents retain their moral rights, the enforcement of these rights has been delegated to (or appropriated by?) the state.

The "root idea" for Nozick's view of rights and the role of government is "that there are different individuals with separate lives and so no one

---

159. Nozick, *Anarchy, State, and Utopia*, 132.

160. Nozick, 132. Fried observes that the invisible-hand mechanism that results in the minimal state "lacks the two key attributes of the Smithian invisible hand: voluntary, private transactions that produce an optimal outcome (here, the minimal state) without any one trying to produce it." Barbara H. Fried, "Does Nozick Have a Theory of Property Rights?" *Stanford Law School Research Paper* no. 1782031, 1–28, 15 (italics in original; download at SSRN).

161. Nozick, *Anarchy, State, and Utopia*, 149.

162. Nozick, 333.

163. Miller, "The Justification of Political Authority," 13.

164. I say "potentially" everyone based on Nozick's reference to some independents declining to purchase coverage from the dominant protective agency. These may include, for example, "pacifists who refuse to support or participate in any institution that uses force, even for their own self-defense." Nozick, *Anarchy, State, and Utopia*, 131. Murray affirms, however, that Nozick's state, if legitimate, must protect everyone in its territory. Dale F. Murray, *Nozick, Autonomy and Compensation* (London: Continuum International Publishing Group, 2007), 115.

may be sacrificed for others."[165] This, he says, "leads to a libertarian side constraint that prohibits aggression against another."[166] Side constraints are moral limitations on what means are permissible for accomplishing specific ends.[167] "Side constraints upon action," he explains, "reflect the underlying Kantian principle that individuals are ends and not merely means; they may not be sacrificed or used for the achieving of other ends without their consent."[168] Accordingly, neither an individual nor the state may initiate aggression (including force, violence, and fraud) against any individual.[169]

In summary, what Nozick pursues is a state whose legitimacy is beyond question and whose authority is not dependent on a social contract (or tacit consent[170]) but develops under the guidance of an invisible-hand process operating in a marketplace of private protective agencies. As Singer explains, "without any express agreements or over-all intention on anyone's part, people in the state of nature would find themselves with a body that satisfies the two fundamental conditions for being a state: it has a monopoly of force in its territory, and it protects the rights of everyone within the territory."[171]

TAXES, FORCED LABOR, AND THE MINIMAL STATE

This sphere . . . within whose boundaries the sale and purchase of labour-power goes on, is in fact a very Eden of the innate rights of man. There alone rule Freedom, Equality, Property, and Bentham.

—Karl Marx (1818–1883), *Capital*[172]

---

165. Nozick, *Anarchy, State, and Utopia*, 33.

166. Nozick, 33.

167. Nozick, 28–31.

168. Nozick, 30–31.

169. When the state intercedes with force to protect one individual's rights from another's aggression, it is not initiating force.

170. Nozick observes that "tacit consent isn't worth the paper it's not written on" (Nozick, 287).

171. Peter Singer, "The Right to be Rich or Poor," in *Reading Nozick: Essays on Anarchy, State, and Utopia*, ed. Jeffrey Paul, 37–53 (Totowa, NJ: Rowman and Littlefield, 1981), 39–40.

172. Marx, *Capital*, pt. 2, chap. 6, 83.

It may appear (as it has to some commentators) that with the formation of the minimal state the paying customers must sacrifice—"pay extra" to cover the cost of the independents—and therefore pay a redistributive tax.[173] Nozick must reconcile this appearance with his earlier claim that "the state may not use its coercive apparatus for the purpose of getting some citizens to aid others."[174] But once the right to state protection has replaced the independents' rights to self-protection, the question becomes: At whose cost? This leads Robert Wolff to assert that for Nozick, "as for all libertarians, the real problem is how to show that the protective association has a right (or indeed, a duty) to tax its clients in order to 'redistribute' income to those who cannot or will not buy protection contracts and thereby become clients."[175] Nozick, however, does not propose a tax for this or any other purpose.

VOLUNTARY PAYMENTS

Nozick never stipulates that these payments for protection will cease to be made voluntarily,[176] and since he asserts that the formation of the minimal state violated no one's rights, it appears unlikely that he would now condone payments subject to coercion.[177] Rodgers observes, applying Nozick's earlier reasoning, "If individuals cannot force others to pay taxes, neither can the government."[178] Murphy and Nagel concur that for Nozick, as a "rights-based [libertarian] . . . no compulsory taxation is legitimate; if there is to be government, it must be funded by way of voluntary contractual

---

173. The extra cost equals the cost of protection less the cost the independent would have incurred in her self-help enforcement of her rights. Nozick, *Anarchy, State, and Utopia*, 111.

174. Nozick, ix.

175. Robert Paul Wolff, "Robert Nozick's Derivation of the Minimal State," in *Reading Nozick: Essays on Anarchy, State, and Utopia*, ed. Jeffrey Paul, 77–104 (Totowa, NJ: Roman and Littlefield, 1981), 82.

176. For Nozick's definition of voluntary, see *Anarchy, State, and Utopia*, 262.

177. Nozick, 52, 113–14.

178. Lamont Rodgers, "Death, Taxes, and Misinterpretations of Robert Nozick: Why Nozickians Can Oppose the Estate Tax," *Libertarian Papers* 7, no. 1 (2015): 1–17, 16.

arrangements."[179] Sartorius contrasts Hayek's view on taxes, which permits some government coercion, with Nozick's, observing that "For Nozick, there are no exceptions to the principle that the state may employ coercion only to prevent coercion."[180]

Among commentators who believe Nozick *must* use compulsory taxation in his minimal state, Hailwood holds that since the minimal state will protect everyone, including those who do not pay, this "will require compulsory taxation."[181] Feser says Nozick allows "for whatever taxation is required in order to fund the activities of the minimal state."[182] J. Wolff asserts that Nozick's minimal state may levy taxes but only "to fund defence, the police, and the administration of justice."[183] Scanlon claims the minimal state has "the right to force residents to pay for its services whether or not they have consented to do so."[184] Murray adds that since not everyone will contribute voluntarily to support the protective service, there must be "coercive measures such as taxation."[185] Fried concurs: "At some point coercive taxation will be required."[186] Cohen says that Nozick's citizens "are

---

179. Murphy and Nagel, *The Myth of Ownership: Taxes and Justice*, 31. They assert that this is a "conclusion explicitly embraced in Nozick (1974), 110–13, 169–72, 165–8" (Murphy and Nagel, 196n35).

180. Rolf Sartorius, "The Limits of Libertarianism," in *Liberty and the Rule of Law*, ed. Robert L. Cunningham (College Station: Texas A and M University Press, 1979), 87–88. However, since Nozick states that the "principle that prohibits physical aggression . . . does not prohibit the use of force in defense against another party who is a threat, even though he is innocent and deserves no retribution" (*Anarchy, State, and Utopia*, 34), this suggests the unacknowledged possibility of employing preemptive coercion to collect taxes to be used to prevent coercion anticipated as arising from threats.

181. Simon A. Hailwood, *Exploring Nozick: Beyond Anarchy, State and Utopia* (Aldershot: Avebury, 1996), 15.

182. Edward Feser, "Taxation, Forced Labor, and Theft," *Independent Review* 5, no. 2 (Fall 2000), 219.

183. J. Wolff, *Robert Nozick*, 115.

184. Thomas Scanlon, "Nozick on Rights, Liberty, and Property," in *Reading Nozick: Essays on Anarchy, State, and Utopia*, ed. Jeffrey Paul, 107–29 (Totowa, NJ: Rowman and Littlefield, 1981), 107.

185. Murray, *Nozick, Autonomy and Compensation*, 95, 115.

186. Fried, "Does Nozick have a Theory of Property Rights?," 25.

obligated to pay tax to support its police force,"[187] to which Mack replies that Cohen is simply mistaken.[188] In opposition to those who see Nozick's views as implying the need for taxation, Mack says, "Nozick's minimal state does not impose taxation—even to fund its rights protective activities." The impression that it does, he claims, results from Nozick's "ill-chosen language that suggests the contrary."[189]

The fact that the minimal state has a monopoly on force, as well as responsibilities relating to protection, does not establish its right to impose (coerce) taxation. When we consider further Nozick's claim that "the legitimate powers of a protective association are merely the *sum* of the individual rights that its members or clients transfer to the association," and that "no new rights and powers arise,"[190] we should be skeptical that the minimal state will engage in any coercive taxation.[191]

TAXATION AS FORCED LABOR

Some commentators claim that Nozick's rejection of taxation is "not absolute"—an apparent reference to his pointed denunciation of the taxation of labor as "on a par with forced labor"[192]—possibly leaving the door open for

---

187. Cohen, *Self-Ownership, Freedom, and Equality*, 231–32n4. Cohen makes this claim in his summary of Raz's argument regarding Nozick's view of slavery. What is not clear is whether Cohen is saying that Nozick categorically believes this or only that Nozick's view commits him to this view.

188. Eric Mack, "Robert Nozick's Political Philosophy," *The Stanford Encyclopedia of Philosophy* (Summer 2015), ed. Edward N. Zalta, http://plato.stanford.edu/archives/sum2015/entries/nozick-political/ (accessed January 16, 2019). In note 16, Mack says, Cohen "mistakenly takes Nozick's minimal state to engage in taxation. See 89 and 235." G. A. Cohen, *Self-Ownership, Freedom, and Equality* (Cambridge: Cambridge University Press, 1995).

189. Mack, "Robert Nozick's Political Philosophy." The "ill-chosen language" compares Milton Friedman's tax-funded voucher system for schools (allowing for individual choice of schools within an existing tax system) to the funding in Nozick's ultraminimal state (stage four in Table 2). "Under this plan," Nozick stipulates, "all people or some (for example, those in need), are given tax-funded vouchers that can be used only for their purchase of a protection policy from the ultraminimal state." Nozick, *Anarchy, State, and Utopia*, 27.

190. Nozick, *Anarchy, State, and Utopia*, 89.

191. Nozick, 52, 113–14.

192. Nozick, 169.

some other form of taxation. To understand the significance of this issue—whether Nozick condemns all taxes or only those on labor—it is necessary to examine his argument in greater detail. Nozick asks, "if it would be illegitimate for a tax system to seize some of a man's leisure (forced labor) for the purpose of serving the needy, how can it be legitimate for a tax system to seize some of a man's goods for that purpose?"[193] Whether the state taxes all wages or only wages "over a certain amount," he stipulates, "seizing the results of someone's labor is equivalent to seizing hours from him and directing him to carry on various activities."[194] In raising this issue he appears to assume without question that taxation means pecuniary taxation, giving no credence to the fact that forced labor, as explained in chapter one, was the earliest form of taxation. Employing my definition of taxation—as government-required sacrifice for the general welfare—both forced labor and required pecuniary payments are forms of taxation.[195]

Cohen, reflecting on Nozick's claim that taxation is forced labor, says, "It is impossible to argue that an hour's labor that ends up as part of somebody's welfare payment is like slavery, while an hour's labor that ends up as part of a policeman's salary is not, when focus is on the condition of the putative slave himself."[196] Nozick, I believe, would agree. When Cohen questions the difference it makes whether tax dollars from an hour's labor are allocated to welfare payments or a policeman's salary, the issue he raises is the moral question of redistribution. But when Nozick opposes paying welfare *or* the policeman's salary with the proceeds from a tax on labor, it is not because the system's design is redistributive but because the tax was

---

193. Nozick, 170.

194. Nozick, 172. Murphy and Nagel observe, "It is illegitimate to appeal to a baseline of property rights in, say, 'pre-tax income,' for the purpose of evaluating tax policies, when all such systems are the product of a system of which taxes are an inextricable part." Murphy and Nagel, *The Myth of Ownership*, 9.

195. Assuming Nozick's minimal state does require nonvoluntary taxation, as some commentators believe, one possible source, as Bird-Pollan suggests, based on Nozick's view of property, is an estate tax. Since Nozick sees property rights as arising from the moral rights of living individuals, Bird-Pollan asks, should not such rights extinguish at death? The property in question, she observes, "can no longer properly be said to 'belong' to the taxpayer. The taxpayer is dead." Jennifer Bird-Pollan, "Death, Taxes, and Property (Rights): Nozick, Libertarianism, and the Estate Tax," *Maine Law Review* 66 (2013): 1–23, 4. Rodgers offers a libertarian rebuttal. Lamont Rodgers, "Death, Taxes, and Misinterpretations of Robert Nozick," *Libertarian Papers* 7, no. 1 (2015).

196. Cohen, *Self-Ownership, Freedom, and Equality*, 235.

paid under political duress. I will say more on redistribution presently, as it is important to Nozick's tax philosophy.

Cohen's question about the policeman's salary takes on a new dimension if we assume that the policeman's job is itself forced labor: he did not choose to be a policeman but the state has conscripted him. This possibility illustrates an ambiguity implicit in the meanings of required work and of forced labor.[197] As I suggested in chapter four, required work may be required in either (or both) of two ways: in hours and duration, or in kind or type of work. In More's Utopia, for example, the state requires both forms of constructive taxation. However, the required labor of the most degrading trades in Utopia, that of butchering cattle, for example, is forced labor as it is assigned exclusively to slaves.[198]

DIGRESSION: THE AMBIGUITY OF REQUIRED WORK VS. FORCED LABOR

The extent to which forced labor exists in utopias that feature required work (either in amount or type) is a contentious matter, with diverse meanings of *coercion* and *free will* on the line.[199] On Anarres, the anarchic world of Le Guin's *The Dispossessed*, for example, work is a matter of individual choice, though some work assignments stem from "labor drafts"[200] imposed by the "exigencies of labor distribution."[201] Work "is no longer alienated labor," observes Moylan, "but freely chosen, if also necessary and tolerated for the good of the whole."[202] Assigned labor on Anarres is "an immediate,

---

197. Neither Nozick nor his critics appear to make a serious effort to analyze the meaning of forced labor before plunging into a detached, academic, and perhaps flippant debate about whether a tax on labor is or is on par with forced labor. Had they done so, the complexity of the question might have barred their categorical conclusions. One starting point for such analysis is Arendt's discussion of modes of forced labor in Russia. Arendt, *The Origins of Totalitarianism*, 443–44.

198. More, *Utopia*, bk. 2, 55.

199. J. Wolff suggests one criterion for distinguishing required work from forced labor: "Forced labor rarely includes the option of deciding how much labour to do." J. Wolff, *Robert Nozick*, 91. This has implications for the utopias of More, Campanella, Bellamy, and Skinner, each with its requirement of how much labor to do.

200. Le Guin, *The Dispossessed*, 216.

201. Le Guin, 215.

202. Moylan, *Demand the Impossible*, 94.

permanent social necessity,"[203] and each worker "to survive . . . had to be ready to . . . do the work that needed doing."[204] In principle, this work is voluntary; though, in the absence of laws, the evolution of custom and practice provides sanctions against slackers. On Anarres, Tunick explains, "social conscience can be as coercive as laws."[205]

As in *The Dispossessed*, work in Morris's *News from Nowhere* is a matter of individual choice. Though Morris's old Hammond refers to their system as "communism," a lack of political structure suggests a cooperative anarchy.[206] A person's choice, however, as on Anarres, is expected to take cognizance of the relative demand for particular forms of work. Morris's character Dick describes a situation where a hay harvest needs a group of able-bodied workers. While many people voluntarily leave their preferred jobs to partake in the haymaking, one group of workers declines and earns the label "obstinate refusers." Since there are no official sanctions for their refusal, Dick explains, "the neighbours . . . jeer good-humouredly at them."[207]

On Anarres, as in *News from Nowhere*, people work "for the work's sake" and because work is "the lasting pleasure of life."[208] Even so, the inducement of social pressure is in play, as Davis points out, since "all the varied work being done is out in the open and plainly visible,"[209] as it was in More's Utopia (described in chapter two). This is a problem on Anarres for those shirking their work responsibility and who, for that reason, face increasing levels of public scorn, including the loss of "respect of one's fellows" and the negative opinion of one's neighbors, which "becomes a very mighty force."[210]

---

203. Le Guin, *The Dispossessed*, 215.

204. Le Guin, 215. Urgent requests for workers to relocate and perform specific work duties are referred to as work "levies" (Le Guin, 215).

205. Tunick, "The Need for Walls: Privacy, Community, and Freedom in The Dispossessed," 135.

206. Morris, *News from Nowhere*, 134. Robertson describes it as "anarcho-communism." Robertson, *The Last Utopians*, 116.

207. Morris, *News from Nowhere*, 195.

208. Le Guin, *The Dispossessed*, 132. In Morris's *News from Nowhere*, "all work is now pleasurable," 122. Nozick discusses the concept of meaningful work in *Anarchy, State, and Utopia*, 247.

209. Laurence Davis, "Morris, Wilde, and Le Guin on Art, Work, and Utopia," *Utopian Studies* 20, no. 2 (2009): 213–48, 234–35.

210. Le Guin, *The Dispossessed*, 132.

Expressing his view of the declining grip of founder Odo's anarchic teachings on their current social practices, Shevek, Le Guin's protagonist, says, "the social conscience completely dominates the individual conscience, instead of striking a balance with it."[211] "We fear our neighbor's opinion," he continues, "more than we respect our own freedom of choice."[212] He admits, "we're ashamed to say we've refused a [job] posting. . . . We don't cooperate—we obey. We fear being outcast, being called lazy, dysfunctional."[213] These conditions border on Nozick's depiction of forced labor where other people "decide what you are to do and what purposes your work is to serve."[214] "Especially for creative and uncompromising libertarians like . . . Shevek," observes Smith, "the growing stultification of Anarresti society takes on the metaphysical aspect of encircling walls which prevent free thought and action."[215] In the face of these obstacles, people must work or else face banishment from society.[216] Whether the required work on Anarres constitutes a constructive tax, as it does in More's *Utopia* and Bellamy's *Looking Backward*, for example, is a question the reader may decide. The point of my digression was to illustrate the continuum of coercion from required work to forced labor.

VOLUNTARY TAXATION

Nozick's claim that taxing labor is (or is on par with) forced labor would have seemed less contentious to his critics, I believe, if he (or they) had framed the question as suggested here, employing a broader definition of taxation that includes forced labor as one type. By clarifying the meaning of taxation at the outset, his commentators might have avoided another controversy as well: whether taxes include voluntary payments. For some

---

211. Le Guin, 287–88.

212. Le Guin, 288.

213. Le Guin, 287.

214. Nozick, *Anarchy, State, and Utopia*, 172.

215. Phillip E. Smith, "Unbuilding Walls: Human Nature and the Nature of Evolutionary and Political Theory in The Possessed," in *Writers of the 21st Century Series: Ursula K. Le Guin*, ed. Joseph D. Olander and Martin Harry Greenberg, 77–96 (New York: Taplinger Publishing Company, 1979), 95.

216. Someone "who just won't cooperate" is subject to ridicule, or the others "get rough with him, beat him up." Le Guin, *The Dispossessed*, 132. The most extreme cases, including "chronic work-quitters," receive "therapy" on Segvina Island (Le Guin, 148–49).

libertarians, taxation can (and for Rand, to be moral, must) be voluntary. The fact that for Nozick payments to a dominant protective agency were voluntary—prior to that agency's claiming a monopoly on force and emerging as a minimal state—proves neither that they will continue to be voluntary after the transition nor that they will cease to be. Yet their previous voluntary status, together with his theory of property rights (and its qualifying Kantian side constraint[217]), makes it unlikely—as I asserted earlier—that he would permit the minimal state to coerce tax revenues from its citizens.

REDISTRIBUTION: ITS TWO FORMS

More than one commentator sees the protective agency's paying clients as paying "extra" (in the form of compensation) to cover the additional cost of providing protective services to the nonsubscribers (the former independents).[218] When libertarians (of his brand) oppose tax redistributions, he says, it is to "types of *reasons* for an arrangement" that they object, "rather than to an arrangement itself."[219] The purpose of this distinction is to allow him to register his disagreement with redistributive designs (patterns), but not necessarily with redistributive outcomes.

Permitting nonpaying citizens to receive protection from the dominant protective agency *could* be on account of those citizens being otherwise financially unable to afford it. This would constitute a "type of reason for an arrangement"—affordability—aiming to achieve a certain patterned redistributive result. Nozick rejects this form of redistribution because, in aspiring to an overall social good, redistribution by design, he believes, yields rights violations. It is from this perspective that he proclaims that "no moral balancing act can take place among us; there is no moral outweighing of one of our lives by others so as to lead to a greater overall *social good*."[220]

---

217. Nozick, *Anarchy, State, and Utopia*, 28–31.

218. See, for example, Robert L. Holmes, "Nozick on Anarchism," in *Reading Nozick: Essays on Anarchy, State, and Utopia*, ed. Jeffrey Paul, 57–67 (Totowa, NJ: Rowman and Littlefield, 1981), 58; Mack, "Robert Nozick's Political Philosophy."

219. Nozick, *Anarchy, State, and Utopia*, 27 (italics in original). Singer provides an example of a redistributive "type of reason" to which libertarians would object. Namely, we "take from the rich and give to the poor . . . because the poor will benefit more from this redistribution than the rich will suffer." P. Singer, "The Right to be Rich or Poor," 45.

220. Nozick, *Anarchy, State, and Utopia*, 33 (italics in original).

Rather than redistribution by design to achieve some overall social good, what Nozick permits is redistribution resulting from the application of rights-conserving moral principles. His solution is to permit qualifying nonpaying citizens to receive protection paid for by compensation they receive for the loss of their right to "self-help enforcement," a "compelling nonredistributive reason."[221] Accordingly, the minimal state "does not compel some to pay for the protection of others on the basis that otherwise those people would be unprotected. Rather," says J. Wolff, "they must pay compensation for not allowing those others to exercise their natural rights,"[222] a harm inflicted by the state.

Nozick's view of harm and its indemnification is that remedial (what he calls *full*) compensation may make right some wrongs.[223] (Nozick's notion of compensation through the principle of rectification for unjust land ownership was introduced in chapter six.) In this context, the principle of compensation, he says, "requires that people be compensated for having certain risky activities [specifically, "self-help enforcement"] prohibited to them."[224] For this reason, he concludes that the transition to the minimal state violates no one's rights, including those of the (former) independents who receive compensation for the appropriation of their right to self-help enforcement.[225]

Simmel tenders a caveat to Nozick's optimism about the role of compensation. He cautions, "One of the reasons for the numerous injustices

---

221. Mack observes, "This may appear to be enforced redistribution; but it is not. For, the additional charges incurred by the minimal state's paying clients simply are payments that are needed to fund compensation that must be paid if the oversight that is imposed on behalf of the clients' security is to be permissible." Mack, "Robert Nozick's Political Philosophy."

222. J. Wolff, *Robert Nozick*, 47. As Hailwood explains, "this is not a situation brought about for illegitimate redistribute reasons, but for moral reasons of compensation." Hailwood, *Exploring Nozick*, 18.

223. Nozick distinguishes between "full compensation" and "market compensation." Nozick, *Anarchy, State, and Utopia*, 65.

224. Nozick, 83.

225. Nozick, 52, 113–14. Young claims that Nozick is describing restitution rather than compensation. Thus, he says, the formation of the minimal state involves coercion that violates the rights of independents. Fredric C. Young, "Nozick and the Individualist Anarchist," in *Equality and Liberty: Analyzing Rawls and Nozick*, ed. J. Angelo Corlett, 268–75 (Houndsmills, UK: Macmillan, 1991), 270–71.

and tragic situations in life may be that personal values cannot be balanced by or equated with the money that is offered for them."[226]

The compensation Nozick refers to takes the form of a subsidy to the independents for the fees the agency charges for its protective services. One tax-relevant outcome of this process, he says, is that the agency "may have to provide some persons services for a fee that is less than the price of those services"[227] (a potential redistribution of wealth). However, he explains, "No compensation need be provided to someone who would not be disadvantaged by buying protection for himself."[228] In this way, what began as a program to compensate independents suffering the loss of their self-help enforcement of justice (and thus "disadvantaged"), ends up as a subsidy *only* for those who are *also* economically disadvantaged.[229] As J. Wolff observes, "this particular transition has a quite different character from those that went before it,"[230] which were invisible-hand and market driven.[231]

Though Nozick and some of his commentators assume that the paying customers may have to pay extra (via compensation) in the minimal state than in the prior ultraminimal state, the adjusted cost of protection when everyone is protected may net a savings. Since the protective agency is now enforcing its single version of justice, this neutralizes risks the independents previously posed. Furthermore, recalling Nozick's claim that the cost of "protection against others . . . depends upon how strong the others are,"[232] we might anticipate a cost *reduction* upon minimizing (or neutralizing) the

---

226. Simmel, *The Philosophy of Money*, 406.

227. Nozick, *Anarchy, State, and Utopia*, 112–13.

228. Nozick, 112.

229. Commenting on this aspect of Nozick's scheme of compensation, Murray says, "I believe that compensatory rights evolve out of Nozick's work in a way contrary to his intention. That is, the rules of compensation Nozick accepted would likely support broad entitlements to social goods that he would not have wanted to accept." Murray, *Nozick, Autonomy and Compensation*, 131–32.

230. J. Wolff, *Robert Nozick*, 67.

231. While R. Wolff assumes it is "the rich [who will have] to buy protection for the poor" (R. Wolff, "The Derivation of the Minimal State," 82), Nozick suggests that the independents might be "people whose religion prohibits purchasing protection; . . . or misanthropes who refuse to cooperate with or hire any other persons." Nozick, *Anarchy, State, and Utopia*, 131.

232. Nozick, *Anarchy, State, and Utopia*, 17.

strength of the others (the former independents). Thus, if the outcome of these potential cost-saving factors—plus any resulting economies of scale (everyone's rights are now protected in a uniform manner)—means the paying customers do not need to "pay extra," then the question of redistribution (of either kind) is rendered superfluous.

NOZICK'S CONSTRUCTIVE TAX ON LAND PROPRIETORSHIP

To Spencer's proclamation that "either men *have* a right to make the soil private property, or they *have not*,"[233] Nozick affirms they do—at least to that which they are justly entitled. Like Rand, he views private property—and by implication private land ownership—as an inviolable moral right that precipitates the most that can be made of man.[234] And though he denounces government-coerced pecuniary taxation, he levies the constructive tax of government-coerced land monopolies on George, Tolstoy, Wells, and the others who, like Proudhon, view land as like "water, air, and light . . . common things, not because they are inexhaustible, but because they are indispensable . . . to our existence."[235] But while Proudhon claims that land's use "must be regulated not for the profit of a few but in the interest and for the security of all,"[236] Nozick's stance favors the invisible-hand outcome of his entitlement theory of justice (described in chapter six).

UTOPIA: THE MINIMAL STATE FRAMEWORK

The first thing you want in a new country, is a patent office; then work up your school system; and after that, out with your paper.

—Mark Twain (1835–1910), *A Connecticut Yankee in King Arthur's Court*[237]

---

233. Spencer, *Social Statics*, 139 (italics in original).

234. Nozick lists "various familiar social considerations favoring private property," including, for example, the claim that "it increases the social product by putting means of production in the hands of those who can use them most efficiently (profitably)." *Anarchy, State, and Utopia*, 177.

235. Proudhon, *What is Property?*, 73.

236. Proudhon, 73.

237. Mark Twain, *A Connecticut Yankee in King Arthur's Court* (1889) (New York: Bantam Books, 1981), 42.

Though his goal is a minimal state, Nozick asks if such a state can "thrill the heart or inspire people to struggle or sacrifice?"[238] He concedes, "Whatever its virtues, it appears clear that the minimal state is no utopia."[239] In addressing his utopia, Nozick claims that "the ultimate purpose of utopian construction is to get communities that people will want to live in and will choose voluntarily to live in."[240] But, he explains, "there is no reason to think that there is one community which will serve as ideal for all people and much reason to think that there is not."[241] In contrast to other utopias, his ideal is not located in the features of a particular political or economic structure but in the formal requirement that everyone be free to choose her own utopian community. In this respect, his vision differs markedly from Rand's, who insists that utopia is only possible through laissez-faire capitalism.[242] The result for Nozick, says Lomasky, "is that within a libertarian framework there can be no preferred conception that merits the honorific, *utopia*."[243]

Nozick's final product is a utopia of utopias, a "meta-utopia."[244] Utopia, he says, "will consist of utopias, of many different divergent communities in which people lead different kinds of lives under different institutions." His utopia

> is a framework for utopias, a place where people are at liberty to join together voluntarily to pursue and attempt to realize their own vision of the good life in the ideal community but where no one can *impose* his own utopian vision upon others. The utopian society is the society of utopianism.[245]

In making this claim he implicitly assumes that people will prefer a choice among diverse communities over one best form of world organization (for

---

238. Nozick, *Anarchy, State, and Utopia*, 297.

239. Nozick, 297.

240. Nozick, 317.

241. Nozick, 310.

242. Feser reports, "It is usually thought that libertarianism itself requires that everyone live according to a laissez faire capitalist ethos, but that isn't so." Edward Feser, *On Nozick* (Boston, MA: Wadsworth, 2004), 92 (italics in original).

243. Loren E. Lomasky, "Nozick's Libertarian Utopia," in *Robert Nozick*, ed. David Schmidtz (Cambridge: Cambridge University Press, 2002), 59 (italics in original).

244. Nozick, *Anarchy, State, and Utopia*, 312.

245. Nozick, 312.

example, Wells's modern Utopia). The resulting federation ensures individual rights by permitting people—by its "law"—to leave one community for another. "Anyone may start any sort of new community," declares Nozick, and no community may be excluded on "paternalistic grounds."[246] Fowler says Nozick "tends to treat the framework as a market."[247] As a market, it is a "process" rather than an "end state."[248]

But if his minimal state lacks luster, as he objects, his libertarian utopia of utopias provides no additional content but only form. The form comes from the freedom to choose which of a potentially endless series of themed communities of like-minded people to join. Our brief glimpse of Nozick's utopia—about which he knowingly raises as many questions as he answers—indicates a structure and rationale but nothing about the daily lives of the citizens. He does not lobby for libertarian communities but for the ultimate libertarian freedom of choice.[249] "It preserves what we all can keep from the utopian tradition," he tells us, "and opens the rest of that tradition to our individual aspirations."[250] In the end, Nozick asks, "Is not the minimal state, the framework for utopia, an inspiring vision?"[251]

TAXATION IN NOZICK'S UTOPIA OF UTOPIAS

There must in the nature of things be one best form of government, which all intellects, sufficiently roused from the slumber of savage ignorance, will be irresistibly incited to approve.

—William Godwin (1756–1836), *Enquiry*[252]

---

246. Nozick, 324.

247. Mark Fowler, "Stability and Utopia: A Critique of Nozick's Framework Argument," *Ethics* 90, no. 4 (July 1980): 550–63, 558. Reprinted in *Equality and Liberty: Analyzing Rawls and Nozick*, ed. J. Angelo Corlett, 245–60 (Houndsmills, UK: Macmillan, 1991), 253.

248. Nozick, *Anarchy, State, and Utopia*, 332.

249. Cohen notes that "Nozick forbids any act which restricts freedom; he does not call for its maximization." Cohen, *Self-Ownership, Freedom, and Equality*, 32.

250. Nozick, *Anarchy, State, and Utopia*, 333.

251. Nozick, 333.

252. Godwin, *An Enquiry Concerning Political Justice*, 1st ed., bk. 3, chap. 7, 102–3.

The question of taxation in Nozick's utopia has two parts. One involves the tax system the overall framework applies to the individual communities. The other involves the tax system each community adopts as part of its initial design (or perhaps as an afterthought). Unfortunately, a minimal state does not imply a minimal need for finances. As Macey observes, "it is very costly to protect against force, theft, and fraud, not to mention the cost of enforcing contracts."[253] Nozick's utopia, however, shares a common feature with those of Godwin and Owen (and many other utopias) in seeking to remove a critical cause of costly interpersonal friction. Nozick's utopian communities—since they comprise only people who desire to be members (others are free to leave[254])—are unlikely to include malcontents, rival factions, or revolutionaries. People will get along because they live in communities where they fit in, and no one receives admittance who will take more than she gives.[255] This stipulation leads, however, to the possibility that some undetermined percentage of the framework's population will be rejected by their community of choice and will have to settle for a lesser, and hence nonutopian community.[256] It even raises the specter of a segment of the population—like that described by Hernstein and Murray in *The Bell Curve*—who are left behind, an underclass that "must be made permanent wards of the state," and consigned by the rest of the framework's population to a "high-tech and more lavish version of the Indian reservation" to keep them "out from under foot."[257] What Nozick does discuss in connection with this issue is whether the choice made by the individual who may not join her first-choice utopia is thereby a non-voluntarily act. Nozick says no. No one's rights are violated if a person

253. Macey, "Government as Investor," 260. See also Holmes and Sunstein, *The Cost of Rights: Why Liberty Depends on Taxes.*

254. Nozick, *Anarchy, State, and Utopia*, 324. This raises a question: Is a person free to leave a community if she lacks sufficient funds for transportation and to finance a new start in her next community? Simmel observes, "freedom from something implies, at the same time, freedom to do something." Simmel, *The Philosophy of Money*, 400. See also Cohen, *Self-Ownership, Freedom, and Equality*, 58.

255. Nozick, *Anarchy, State, and Utopia*, 301.

256. "Not everyone," says Nozick, "will be joining special experimental communities" (Nozick, 312, italics in original).

257. Richard J. Herrnstein and Charles Murray, *The Bell Curve: Intelligence and Class Structure in American Life* (New York: Simon and Schuster, 1994), 523, 526.

must choose her second, or nth preference.[258] But that is beside the point in the context of utopias.

TAXATION BY THE COMMUNITIES

Just as each community need not be libertarian, each community—with its unique political configuration—is free to rely on voluntary payments or on requiring sacrifices for its general welfare. Unlike the utopian framework, which Nozick says "may not compel redistribution between one community and another," an individual community "may redistribute within itself."[259] Since the overall framework of utopia is indifferent as to what each community taxes or why, some may tax labor or land and others, like in Bellamy's *Looking Backward*, may conscript an industrial army.

TAXATION IN THE UTOPIA OF UTOPIAS

The wider framework of utopia—the "central apparatus or agency"—is responsible for adjudicating "in some reasonable fashion conflicts between communities which cannot be settled by peaceful means."[260] This includes preventing "some communities from invading and seizing others, their persons or assets,"[261] and enforcing the "right to leave a community," as well as other stipulated but unspecified individual rights.[262] Commentators are split on whether Nozick would permit the utopia of utopias to levy taxes. Lacey, for example, "presumes" that the activities of the framework would be "financed by taxing the communities, on a basis they all agree on."[263] My assumption is that the framework operates as a minimal state—since Nozick says they are equivalent[264]—with the citizens replaced by utopian communities. Since he believes that there "is no justified sacrifice of some

---

258. Nozick, *Anarchy, State, and Utopia*, 263.

259. Nozick, 321.

260. Nozick, 329–30.

261. Nozick, 329.

262. Nozick, 330. About the other rights, Nozick says, "Some things about some aspects of life extend to everyone; for example, everyone has various rights that may not be violated" (Nozick, 325).

263. A. R. Lacey, *Robert Nozick* (Princeton, NJ: Princeton University Press, 2001), 68.

264. Nozick, *Anarchy, State, and Utopia*, 333.

of us for others,"[265] the prohibition against taxation arising in the minimal state should pertain as well to the framework of utopian communities.

The picture Nozick outlines of the utopian framework, and of the tax structure necessary to support it, is sketchy. Whether taxes are coercive or voluntary, taxing communities and taxing individuals pose quite different challenges. The communities will tax their own citizens, as noted, each in its own way, or not at all. Communities may also (possibly) tax each other using tariffs on trade, for example, assuming the framework permits it. But how the framework of utopias will tax its constituent communities is a question Nozick leaves unanswered. "What the best form of such a central authority is," he declares, "I would not wish to investigate here. It seems desirable that one not be fixed permanently but that room be left for improvements of detail."[266]

IN CLOSING

> But we must not always exhaust a subject, so as to leave no work at all for the reader. My business is not to make people read, but to make them think.
>
> —Montesquieu (1689–1755), *The Spirit of Laws*[267]

As noted earlier, the libertarian thread in Nozick's utopia permits each community to fashion itself on any political or economic basis. This suggests the possibility that at least one of his imaginary communities will take seriously the recommendation I made in the first chapter of this book and integrate—from the outset—its moral and political principles with a complementary tax system to support and enable the society's goals. Rather than retrofitting its tax system to an existing structure of values and ideals—part of the governmental sausage grinding—its founding mothers and fathers will recognize that openly acknowledging the need for unrequited sacrifice is too important to take up as an afterthought.

---

265. Nozick, 33.

266. Nozick, 330.

267. Montesquieu, *The Spirit of Laws*, bk. 11, chap. 20, 84.

When we build a community from the ground up—a community with a tax system derived from its moral principles—we are bound to gain a broader understanding of taxation and a finer appreciation of our ideal state and its values. The success of this endeavor, however, will rest heavily on the felicity of our judgment in earmarking which aspects of human nature are permanent and which are transient or conditional. When viewing taxes more broadly than revenue, as a government-required sacrifice for the general welfare, we see their force as a partial determinant of any social ends at which we aim and a marker for gauging moral change.

Utopias perform multiple functions, as indicated in chapter one. One of these functions is the timely detection of societal trends promising injury to the general welfare or destruction of the society. "That we escaped the destiny portrayed in George Orwell's *Nineteen Eighty-Four*," writes Brin, "may owe in part to the way his chilling tale affected millions, who then girded themselves to fight 'Big Brother.'"[268] The required sacrifices I label constructive taxes include restrictions on privacy and access to truth, required work or occupation, controls on marriage, restraints on childrearing, enforced eugenic procedures, and legal constraints on the proprietorship of land. None of these can yet be consigned to a static past; nor is this list exhaustive, for the forms of required sacrifice may prove boundless. In a dystopia as well as a utopia, as noted, the tax system should reflect and support the goals of the depicted state. In our own time, however, as tax laws are crafted behind closed doors, with no public hearings—energized by unacknowledged incentives—opaque government is the sacrifice we are asked to endure, and Thoreau's question, "why the schoolmaster should be taxed to support the priest, and not the priest the schoolmaster?"[269] becomes moot.

---

268. Brin, "The Self-Preventing Prophecy," 222–23.

269. Thoreau, *Civil Disobedience*, 277.

BIBLIOGRAPHY

Adler, Mortimer J. *The Idea of Freedom: A Dialectical Examination of the Conceptions of Freedom*, 2 vols. Garden City, New York: Doubleday and Company, 1958.

Albanese, Denise. "The New Atlantis and the Uses of Utopia." *ELH* 57, no. 3 (Autumn 1990): 503–28.

Andelson, Robert V. "Henry George and The Reconstruction of Capitalism." Robert Schalkenbach Foundation. Accessed November 24, 2016. http://schalkenbach.org/on-line-library/works-by-robert-v-andelson/henry-george-and-the-reconstruction-of-capitalism/.

Anderson, F. H. *The Philosophy of Francis Bacon*. Chicago: The University of Chicago Press, 1948.

Arendt, Hannah. *The Origins of Totalitarianism*. Orlando, FL: A Harvest Book – Harcourt, 1968.

Aristotle. *Politics*. Translated by Benjamin Jowett. New York: The Modern Library, 1943.

Aughterson, Kate. " 'Strange Things So Probably Told': Gender, Sexual Difference and Knowledge in Bacon's *New Atlantis*." In *Francis Bacon's New Atlantis*. Edited by Bronwen Price, 156–79. New York: Manchester University Press, 2002.

Bacon, Francis. *New Atlantis*. In *The Works of Francis Bacon*. Edited by James Spedding, Robert Leslie Ellis, and Douglas Denon Heath, vol. 3. Cambridge: Cambridge University Press, (1857) 2011.

———. *The New Organon*. In *The Works of Francis Bacon*. Edited by James Spedding, Robert Leslie Ellis, and Douglas Denon Heath, vol. 4. Cambridge: Cambridge University Press, (1858) 2011.

———. "Of Counsel." In *The Essays or Counsels Civil and Moral*. Edited by Brian Vickers. Oxford: Oxford University Press, 1999.

———. "Of Love." In *The Essays or Counsels Civil and Moral*. Edited by Brian Vickers. Oxford: Oxford University Press, 1999.

———. "Of Marriage and Single Life." In *The Essays or Counsels Civil and Moral*. Edited by Brian Vickers. Oxford: Oxford University Press, 1999.

———. *Of The Advancement of Learning*. In *The Works of Francis Bacon*. Edited by James Spedding, Robert Leslie Ellis, and Douglas Denon Heath, vol. 3. Cambridge: Cambridge University Press, (1857) 2011.

———. *Of The Dignity and Advancement of Learning*. In *The Works of Francis Bacon*. Edited by James Spedding, Robert Leslie Ellis, and Douglas Denon Heath, vol. 4. Cambridge: Cambridge University Press, (1858) 2011.

———. "Plan of the Work," *The Great Instauration*. In *The Works of Francis Bacon*. Edited by James Spedding, Robert Leslie Ellis, and Douglas Denon Heath, vol. 4. Cambridge: Cambridge University Press, (1858) 2011.

Baker-Smith, Dominic. *More's Utopia*. London: HarperCollinsAcademic, 1991.

Barker, Ernest. *The Political Thought of Plato and Aristotle*. Mineola, NY: Dover Publications, 1959.

Becker, Howard. *Outsiders: Studies in the Sociology of Deviance*. New York: The Free Press, 1963.

Bellamy, Edward. "The Economy of Happiness." In Arthur E. Morgan, *The Philosophy of Edward Bellamy*. New York: King's Crown Press, 1945.

———. *Equality*. 3rd ed. New York: D. Appleton and Company, 1897.

———. "How and Why I Wrote Looking Backward." In *America as Utopia*. Edited by Kenneth M. Roemer, 22–27. New York: Burt Franklin and Company, 1981.

———. *Looking Backward: 2000–1887*. New York: Penguin Books, 1982.

Benn, S. I., and R. S. Peters. *The Principles of Political Thought*. New York: The Free Press, 1959.

Bentham, Jeremy. *Anarchical Fallacies*. In *'Nonsense upon Stilts': Bentham, Burke and Marx on the Rights of Man*. Edited by Jeremy Waldron. London: Methuen, 1987.

Bentham, Jeremy, and C. K. Ogden. *Bentham's Theory of Fictions*. Paterson, NJ: Littlefield, Adams, 1959.

Best, Arthur. *Evidence*. Boston: Little, Brown, 1994.

Bird-Pollan, Jennifer. "Death, Taxes, and Property (Rights): Nozick, Libertarianism, and the Estate Tax." *Maine Law Review* 66 (2013): 1–23.

Bloch, Ernst. *The Principle of Hope*. Translated by Neville Plaice, Stephen Plaice, and Paul Knight. Cambridge, MA: The MIT Press, 1986.

Blodgett, Eleanor Dickinson. "The *'New Atlantis'* and Campanella's *'Civitas Solis.'*" *PMLA* 46, no. 3 (September 1931): 763–80.

Bloom, Allan. *The Closing of the American Mind*. New York: Simon and Schuster, 1987.

———. "Interpretive Essay." In *The Republic of Plato*, 2nd ed. Translated by Allan Bloom. Basic Books, 1968.

Bloomfield, Paul. "The Eugenics of the Utopians: The Utopia of the Eugenists." *The Eugenics Review* 40 (April 1948–January 1949): 191–98.

Bok, Sissela. *Lying*. New York: Vintage Books, 1978.

Bostaph, Samuel. "'Atlantis' as a Free Market Economy." In *Ayn Rand's Atlas Shrugged*. Edited by Edward W. Younkins. Burlington, VT: Ashgate Publishing Company, 2007.

———. "Ayn Rand's Economic Thought." *The Journal of Ayn Rand Studies* 11, no. 1 (July 2011): 19–44.

Boyd, William. *The History of Western Education*, 8th ed. New York: Barnes and Noble, 1961.

Branden, Nathaniel. "Counterfeit Individualism." In Ayn Rand, *The Virtue of Selfishness*. New York: Signet Books, 1964.

Brin, David. "The Self-Preventing Prophecy; or How a Dose of Nightmare Can Help Tame Tomorrow's Perils." In *On Nineteen Eighty-Four: Orwell and Our Future*. Edited by Abbott Gleason, Jack Goldsmith, and Martha C. Nussbaum, 222–30. Princeton, NJ: Princeton University Press, 2005.

Broome, John. *Ethics out of Economics*. Cambridge: Cambridge University Press, 1999.

Brown, E. J. *Brave New World, 1984, and We*. Ann Arbor, MI: Ardis, 1976.

Bruce, Susan, ed. *Three Early Modern Utopias*. Oxford: Oxford University Press, 1999.

Burke, Edmund. *Reflections on the Revolution in France*. Oxford: Oxford University Press, 1993.

Butler, Samuel. *Erewhon*. Mineola, NY: Dover Publications, Inc., 2002.

Campanella, Thomas. *A Defense of Galileo*. Translated by Richard J. Blackwell. Notre Dame, IN: University of Notre Dame Press, 1994.

Campanella, Tommaso. *The City of the Sun*. Translated by Daniel J. Donno. Berkeley: University of California Press, 1981.

———. *Selected Philosophical Poems of Tommaso Campanella*. Translated and edited by Sherry Roush. Chicago: The University of Chicago Press, 2011.

Carroll, Lewis. *Through the Looking Glass*. In *The Annotated Alice*. Edited by Martin Gardner. Cleveland, OH: The World Publishing Company, 1960.

Carter, Steven. "The Masks of Passion." In *George Orwell's 1984*. Bloom's Modern Critical Interpretations, updated, edited by Harold Bloom. New York: Chelsea House Publishers, 2007.

Chambers, R. W. *Thomas More*. Ann Arbor, MI: The University of Michigan Press, 1958.

Christensen, Andrew G. "Charlotte Perkins Gilman's *Herland* and the Tradition of the Scientific Utopia." *Utopian Studies* 28, no. 2 (2017): 286–304.

Christian, R. F. *Tolstoy: A Critical Introduction*. Cambridge: Cambridge University Press, 1969.

Cicero. *On Duties* [*De Officiis*]. Translated by Walter Miller. Cambridge, MA: Harvard University Press, Loeb Classical Library (LCL 30), 1913.

———. "On the Manilian Law." In *Orations*. Translated by H. Grose Hodge. Cambridge, MA: Harvard University Press; Loeb Classical Library (LCL 198), 1927.

Claeys, Gregory. *Citizens and Saints: Politics and Anti-Politics in Early British Socialism*. Cambridge: Cambridge University Press, 1989.

———. *Dystopia: A Natural History*. Oxford: Oxford University Press, 2017.

———. "The Effects of Property on Godwin's Theory of Justice." *Journal of the History of Philosophy* 22, no. 1 (January 1984): 81–101.

———. Introduction to *A New View of Society and Other Writings*, by Robert Owen. New York: Penguin Classics, 1991.

———. *Machinery, Money and the Millennium: From Moral Economy to Socialism, 1815–1860*. Princeton, NJ: Princeton University Press, 1987.

———. *Searching for Utopia: The History of an Idea*. London: Thames and Hudson, 2011.

Claeys, Gregory, and Lyman Tower Sargent, eds. *The Utopia Reader*. New York: New York University Press, 1999.

Clardy, Alan. "Galt's Gulch: Ayn Rand's Utopian Delusion." *Utopian Studies* 23, no. 1 (2012): 238–62.

Clark, John P. *The Philosophical Anarchism of William Godwin*. Princeton, NJ: Princeton University Press, 1977.

Coates, Ta-Nehisi. *We Were Eight Years in Power*. New York: One World, an imprint of Random House, 2017. Originally published in *The Atlantic* (June 2014).

Cohen, G. A. *Self-Ownership, Freedom, and Equality*. New York: Cambridge University Press, 1995.

Cooke, Brett. *Human Nature in Utopia: Zamyatin's We*. Evanston, IL: Northwestern University Press, 2002.

Craig, Tobin L. "On the Significance of the Literary Character of Francis Bacon's *New Atlantis* for an Understanding of His Political Thought." *The Review of Politics*, 72 (2010): 213–39.

Criado-Perez, Caroline. *Invisible Women: Data Bias in a World Designed for Men*. New York: Abrams Press, 2019.

Crowther, J. G. *Francis Bacon: The First Statesman of Science*. London: The Cresset Press, 1960.

Cummings, Jasper L., Jr. *The Supreme Court, Federal Taxation, and the Constitution*. Washington, DC: American Bar Association, 2013.

Darwin, Charles. *The Origin of Species*, 6th ed. (1876). In *Works of Charles Darwin*, vol. 16. Edited by Paul H. Barrett and R. B. Freeman. New York University Press, 1988.

Davis, Laurence. "Morris, Wilde, and Le Guin on Art, Work, and Utopia." *Utopian Studies* 20, no. 2 (2009): 213–48.

Dawes, Robyn M. *Rational Choice in an Uncertain World*. New York: Harcourt Brace Jovanovich, 1988.

Den Uyl, Douglas J., and Douglas B. Rasmussen. *The Philosophic Thought of Ayn Rand*. Edited by Douglas J. Den Uyl and Douglas B. Rasmussen. Urbana: University of Illinois Press, 1984.

Dewey, John. "An Appreciation of Henry George." In *John Dewey: The Later Works, 1925–1953*, vol. 3. Edited by Jo Ann Boydston. Carbondale: Southern Illinois Press, 1984. First published in *Significant Paragraphs from Progress and Poverty*. Edited by Harry Gunnison Brown. Garden City, NY: Published for the Robert Schalkenbach Foundation by Doubleday, Doran and Co., 1928.

———. "A Great American Prophet." In *John Dewey: The Later Works, 1925–1953*, vol. 9. Edited by Jo Ann Boydston. Carbondale: Southern Illinois University Press, 1989. First published in *Common Sense* 3 (April 1934): 6–7.

———. Foreword to *The Philosophy of Henry George*, by George Raymond Geiger. New York: The Macmillan Company, 1933.

———. *Human Nature and Conduct*. New York: The Modern Library, 1950.

———. *Reconstruction in Philosophy*. Boston, MA: Beacon, 1957.

———. "Steps to Economic Recovery." In *John Dewey: The Later Works, 1925–1934*, vol. 9. Edited by Jo Ann Boydston. Carbondale: Southern Illinois Press, 1986.

Donno, Daniel J. Introduction to *The City of the Sun*, by Tommaso Campanella. Translated by Daniel J. Donno. Berkeley: University of California Press, 1981.

Dorter, Kenneth. *The Transformation of Plato's Republic*. Lanham, MD: Lexington Books, 2006.

Dostoevsky, Fyodor. *Devils*. Translated by Michael R. Katz. Oxford: Oxford University Press, 1999.

Doughney, Lachlan. "Ayn Rand and Deducting 'Ought' from 'Is.' " *The Journal of Ayn Rand Studies* 12, no. 1 (2012): 151–68.

Engels, Frederick. *Socialism: Utopian and Scientific*. New York: Pathfinder, 1972.

Eurich, Nell. *Science in Utopia: A Mighty Design*. Cambridge, MA: Harvard University Press, 1967.

Faulkner, Robert K. *Francis Bacon and the Project of Progress*. Lanham, MD: Rowman and Littlefield Publishers, Inc., 1993.

Feser, Edward. *On Nozick*. United States: Wadsworth, a division of Thompson Learning, 2004.

———. "Taxation, Forced Labor, and Theft." *Independent Review* 5, no. 2 (Fall 2000): 219–35.

Fisher, Richard. "Henry George: Antiprotectionist Giant of American Economics." *Economic Insights*. Federal Reserve Bank of Dallas 10, no. 2 (2005). Accessed November 23, 2016. http://www.dallasfed.org/assets/documents/research/ei/ei 0502.pdf.

Foucault, Michel. *Discipline and Punish: The Birth of the Prison*. Translated by Alan Sheridan. New York: Penguin Books, 1977.

Fowler, Mark. "Stability and Utopia: A Critique of Nozick's Framework Argument." *Ethics* 90, no. 4 (July 1980): 550–63. Reprinted in *Equality and Liberty: Analyzing Rawls and Nozick*. Edited by J. Angelo Corlett, 245–60. Houndsmills, UK: Macmillan, 1991.

France, Anatole. *The Red Lily*. N.p.: Dodo Press, n.d.

Fried, Barbara H. "Does Nozick Have a Theory of Property Rights?" *Stanford Law School Research Paper* no. 1782031, 1–28; downloaded at SSRN.

Friedman, Milton. *Capitalism and Freedom*. Chicago: The University of Chicago Press, 2002.

———. Interview in *Human Events*, November 19, 1979. Quoted in Richard Fisher, "Henry George: Antiprotectionist Giant of American Economics," *Economic Insights*. Federal Reserve Bank of Dallas 10, no. 2 (2005). Accessed November 23, 2016. http://www.dallasfed.org/assets/documents/research/ei/ei0502.pdf.

Frye, Northrop. "Varieties of Literary Utopias." In *Utopias and Utopian Thought*. Edited by Frank E. Manuel, 25–49. Boston: Houghton Mifflin Company, 1965.

Fuller, Lon L. *The Morality of Law*. New Haven, CT: Yale University, 1964.

Galton, David J. "Greek Theories on Eugenics." *Journal of Medical Ethics* 24, no. 4 (August 1988): 263–67.

Galton, Francis. "Eugenics: Its Definition, Scope, and Aims." *The American Journal of Sociology* 10, no. 1 (July 1904): 1–25.

Gandhi, M. K. *An Autobiography*. Translated by Mahadev Desai. Ahmedabad: Navajivan Publishing House, 1927.

Garnsey, Peter. *Thinking About Property: From Antiquity to the Age of Revolution*. New York: Cambridge University Press, 2007.

Geiger, George Raymond. *The Philosophy of Henry George*. New York: The Macmillan Company, 1933. Reprint. Page references are to reprint.

George, Henry. *A Perplexed Philosopher: Being an Examination of Mr. Herbert Spencer's Various Utterances on the Land Question with Some Incidental Reference to His Synthetic Philosophy*. Repr. N.p.: Elibron Classics, n.d.

———. *Progress and Poverty*. 1879. New York: Robert Schalkenbach Foundation, 1953.

Gerber, Richard. *Utopian Fantasy: A Study of English Utopian Fiction since the End of the Nineteenth Century*. London: Routledge and Kegan Paul, 1955.

Ghate, Onkar. "The Part and Chapter Headings of *Atlas Shrugged*." In *Essays on Rand's Atlas Shrugged*. Edited by Robert Mayhew. New York: Lexington Books, 2009.

Gilman, Charlotte Perkins. *Concerning Children*. Project Gutenberg, 2012. Accessed February 2, 2019. http://www.gutenberg.org/files/40481/40481-h/40481-h. htm. Originally published London: G. P. Putnam's Sons, 1903.

———. "Education for Motherhood." In *Charlotte Perkins Gilman: A Nonfiction Reader*. Edited by Larry Ceplair. New York: Columbia University Press, 1991.

———. *Herland*. Mineola, NY: Dover Publications, 1998.

———. *Human Work*. Lanham, MD: AltaMira Press, a division of Roman and Littlefield Publishers, 2005.

———. "Is America Too Hospitable?" In *Charlotte Perkins Gilman: A Nonfiction Reader*. Edited by Larry Ceplair. New York: Columbia University Press, 1991.

———. *The Living of Charlotte Perkins Gilman: An Autobiography*. Madison: The University of Wisconsin Press, 1935.

———. *Moving the Mountain* (1911). Reprint, n.p, n.d.

———. *Women and Economics*. Mineola, NY: Dover Publications, 1998.

Godwin, William. *An Enquiry Concerning Political Justice* (1793). Oxford: Oxford University Press, 2013.

———. *Enquiry Concerning Political Justice and Its Influence on Modern Morals and Happiness* (1798), 3rd ed. New York: Viking Penguin, 1985.

———. *The Enquirer: Reflections on Education, Manners and Literature* (1798). New York: Augustus M. Kelley Publishers, 1956.

———. *Things as They Are or the Adventures of Caleb Williams*. New York: Penguin Books, 1988.

Goffman, Erving. *Behavior in Public Places*. New York: The Free Press, 1963.

Goldman, Emma. *Anarchism and Other Essays*. New York: Dover Publications, Inc., 1969.

Goodwin, Barbara. "Economic and Social Innovation in Utopia." In *Utopias*, 69–83. Edited by Peter Alexander and Roger Gill. London: Duckworth, 1984.

———. "Taxation in Utopia." *Utopian Studies* 19, no. 2 (2008): 313–31.

Goodwin, Barbara, and Keith Taylor. *The Politics of Utopia*. Oxford: Peter Lang, 2009.

Gottfredson, Michael R., and Travis Hirschi. *A General Theory of Crime*. Stanford, CA: Stanford University Press, 1990.

Gottlieb, Erika. "The Demonic World of Oceania: The Mystical Adulation of the 'Sacred' Leader." In *Bloom's Modern Critical Interpretations: George Orwell's 1984*, updated. Edited by Harold Bloom. New York: Chelsea House Publishers, 2007.

———. *Dystopian Fiction East and West: Universe of Terror and Trial*. Montreal: McGill-Queen's University Press, 2001.

Gough, Val. "Lesbians and Virgins: The New Motherhood in *Herland*." In *Anticipations: Essays on Early Science Fiction and its Precursors*. Edited by David Seed, 195–215. New York: Syracuse University Press, 1995.

Groves, Harold M. *Tax Philosophers: Two Hundred Years of Thought in Great Britain and the United States*. Edited by Donald J. Curran. Madison, WI: The University of Wisconsin Press, 1974.

Gubar, Susan. "*She* in *Herland*: Feminism as Fantasy." In *Charlotte Perkins Gilman: The Woman and Her Work*. Edited by Sheryl L. Meyering. Ann Arbor, MI: UMI Research Press, 1989.

Hailwood, S. *Exploring Nozick: Beyond Anarchy, State, and Utopia*. Aldershot: Avebury, 1996.

Hale, Kimberly Hurd. *Francis Bacon's New Atlantis in the Foundation of Modern Political Thought*. New York: Lexington Books, 2013.

Hall, K. Graehme. "Mothers and Children: 'Rising with the Resistless Tide' in *Herland*." In *Charlotte Perkins Gilman: The Woman and Her Work*. Edited by Sheryl L. Meyering. Ann Arbor, MI: UMI Research Press, 1989.

Hamilton, Alexander. *The Federalist Papers*, No. 36. New York: Penguin Books, 1987.

Hammond, N. G. L. *A History of Greece*. Oxford: The Clarendon Press, 1959.

Hand, Learned. *The Bill of Rights*. New York: Atheneum, 1979.

Hansot, Elisabeth. *Perfection and Progress: Two Modes of Utopian Thought*. Cambridge, MA: The MIT Press, 1974.

Harrington, James. *The Commonwealth of Oceana* (1656). In *The Political Works of James Harrington*. Edited by J. G. A. Pocock. Cambridge: Cambridge University Press, 1977.

Harris, Roy. "The Misunderstanding of Newspeak." In *George Orwell: Modern Critical Views*. Edited by Harold Bloom. New York: Chelsea House Publishers, 1987.

Harrison, John F. C. *Utopianism and Education*. New York: Teachers College Press, Columbia University, 1968.

Hayek, Friedrich A. *Law, Legislation and Liberty*, 3 vols. Chicago: University of Chicago Press, 1979.

———. *The Road to Serfdom*. Chicago: University of Chicago Press, 1944.

Heilbroner, Robert L. *The Worldly Philosophers*, 3rd ed. New York: Simon and Schuster, 1953.

Heller, Anne C. *Ayn Rand and the World She Made*. New York: Doubleday, 2009.

Herman, Edward S. "From *Ingsoc* and *Newspeak* to *Amcap, Amerigood*, and *Marketspeak*." In *On Nineteen Eighty-Four: Orwell and Our Future*. Edited by Abbott Gleason, Jack Goldsmith, and Martha C. Nussbaum, 112–23. Princeton, NJ: Princeton University Press, 2005.

Herrnstein, Richard J., and Charles Murray. *The Bell Curve: Intelligence and Class Structure in American Life*. New York: Simon and Schuster, 1994.

Hertzka, Theodor. *Freeland: A Social Anticipation*. Translated by Arthur Ransom. London: Chatto and Windus, 1891. Reprint, University of California Libraries.

Hertzler, Joyce Oramel. *The History of Utopian Thought*. New York: The Macmillan Company, 1926. Reprint. Page references same as original.

Hexter, J. H. *More's Utopia: The Biography of an Idea*. New York: Harper Torchbooks, 1965.

Hitler, Adolf. *Mein Kampf*. Translated by Ralph Manheim. Boston: Houghton Mifflin Company, 1971.

Hobbes, Thomas. *Leviathan: Or the Matter, Forme and Power of a Commonwealth Ecclesiasticall and Civil*. Edited by Michael Oakeshott. London: Collier-Macmillan, 1962.

Hofstadter, Richard. *Social Darwinism in American Thought*. Boston: Beacon Press, 1944.

Holland, Owen. "Spectatorship and Entanglement in Thoreau, Hawthorne, Morris, and Wells." *Utopian Studies* 27, no. 1 (2016): 28–52.

Holmes, Robert L. "Nozick on Anarchism." In *Reading Nozick: Essays on Anarchy, State, and Utopia*. Edited by Jeffrey Paul, 57–67. Totowa, NJ: Rowman and Littlefield, 1981.

Horan, Thomas. "Revolutions from the Waist Downwards: Desire as Rebellion in Yevgeny Zamyatin's *We*, George Orwell's *1984*, and Aldous Huxley's *Brave New World*." *Extrapolation* 48, no. 2 (2007): 314–39.

Hospers, John. *Libertarianism*. Santa Barbara, CA: Reason Press, 1971.

Houston, Chlöe. "Utopia, Dystopia or Anti-utopia? Gulliver's Travels and the Utopian Mode of Discourse." *Utopian Studies* 18, no. 3 (2007): 425–42.

Howells, William Dean. *A Traveler from Altruria*. New York: Sagamore Press, 1957.

Hudak, Jennifer. "The 'Social Inventor': Charlotte Perkins Gilman and the (Re) Production of Perfection." *Women's Studies* 32 (2003): 455–77.

Hume, David. "Idea of a Perfect Commonwealth." In *Essays, Moral, Political, and Literary*. Edited by Eugene F. Miller. Indianapolis, IN: The Liberty Fund, Inc., 1985.

———. "Of Taxes." In *Essays, Moral, Political, and Literary*. Edited by Eugene F. Miller. Indianapolis, IN: The Liberty Fund, Inc., 1985.

———. *A Treatise of Human Nature*. Edited by L. A. Selby-Bigge. Oxford: Oxford University Press, 1888.

Huxley, Aldous. *Brave New World*. New York: HarperCollins, 2004.

———. *Island*. New York: HarperCollins, 1962.

Ionescu, Ghita. Introduction. *The Political Thought of Saint-Simon*. Edited by Ghita Ionescu. Oxford: Oxford University Press, 1976.

James, William. *The Varieties of Religious Experience*. London: Collier-Macmillan, 1961.

Kahneman, Daniel, and Amos Tversky. "Advances in Prospect Theory: Cumulative Representation of Uncertainty." In *Choices, Values, and Frames*, 44–65. Edited by Daniel Kahneman and Amos Tversky. Russell Sage Foundation, Cambridge: Cambridge University Press, 2000.

———. "Prospect Theory." In *Choices, Values, and Frames*, 17–43. Edited by Daniel Kahneman and Amos Tversky. Russell Sage Foundation, Cambridge: Cambridge University Press, 2000.

Kant, Immanuel. *Critique of Pure Reason*. Translated by Norman Kemp Smith. London: Macmillan and Co., 1964.

———. *First Part of the Philosophical Theory of Religion*, 4th ed. Translated by Thomas Kingsmill Abbott. Reprint, n.p., n.d.

———. "Idea for a Universal History with a Cosmopolitan Purpose." In *Political Writings*, 2nd ed. Translated by H. B. Nisbet. Edited by Hans Reiss. Cambridge: Cambridge University Press, 1991.

———. "Laws." In *Lectures on Ethics*. Translated by Louis Infield. Indianapolis, IN: Hackett Publishing Co., 1963.

———. *Perpetual Peace*. In *Kant: Political Writings*. Translated by H. B. Nisbet. Cambridge: Cambridge University Press, 1970.

Kaplow, Louis. *The Theory of Taxation and Public Economics*. Princeton, NJ: Princeton University Press, 2008.

Kateb, George. *Utopia and Its Enemies*. New York: The Free Press, 1963; Schocken Books, 1972.

Kavka, Gregory S. "An Internal Critique of Nozick's Entitlement Theory." In *Equality and Liberty: Analyzing Rawls and Nozick*. Edited by J. Angelo Corlett, 298–310. Houndsmills, UK: Macmillan, 1991.

Kenyon, T. A. "The Problem of Freedom and Moral Behavior in Thomas More's *Utopia*." *Journal of the History of Philosophy* 21, no. 3 (July 1983): 349–73.

Keynes, John Maynard. "Economic Model Construction and Econometrics." In *The Philosophy of Economics,* 2nd ed. Edited by Daniel M. Hausman, 286–88. Cambridge: Cambridge University Press, 1994.

Kierkegaard, Søren. *Attack Upon "Christendom."* Translated by Walter Lowrie. Princeton, NJ: Princeton University Press, 1944.

Kochin, Michael S. *Gender and Rhetoric in Plato's Political Thought.* Cambridge: Cambridge University Press, 2002.

Kramnick, Isaac. Introduction to *Enquiry Concerning Political Justice and Its Influence on Modern Morals and Happiness,* 3rd ed., by William Godwin. New York: Viking Penguin Inc., 1985.

Krieg, Joann P. "Charlotte Perkins Gilman and the Whitman Connection." In *Charlotte Perkins Gilman: The Woman and Her Work.* Edited by Sheryl L. Meyering. Ann Arbor, MI: UMI Research Press, 1989.

Krutch, Joseph Wood. *The Measure of Man.* New York: Grosset and Dunlap, 1953.

Kumar, Krishnan. *Utopia and Anti-Utopia in Modern Times.* Oxford: Basil Blackwell, 1987.

Lacey, A. R. *Robert Nozick.* Princeton, NJ: Princeton University Press, 2001.

Lakoff, George. *Don't Think of an Elephant!* White River Junction, VT: Chelsea Green Publishing, 2014.

Lasky, Melvin J. *Utopia and Revolution: On the Origins of a Metaphor.* Chicago: University of Chicago Press, 1976; republished, New Brunswick, NJ: Transaction Publishers, 2004.

Lawson, John, and Harold Silver. *A Social History of Education in England.* London: Methuen and Co., 1973.

Le Guin, Ursula K. *The Dispossessed: An Ambiguous Utopia.* New York: Harper and Row Publishers, 1974.

Levi, Margaret. *Consent, Dissent, and Patriotism.* Cambridge: Cambridge University Press, 1997.

Leviner, Sagit. "The Normative Underpinnings of Taxation." *Nevada Law Journal* 13, no. 95 (Fall 2012): 1–27.

Levitas, Ruth. *Utopia as Method: The Imaginary Reconstruction of Society.* New York: Palgrave Macmillan, 2013.

Lewis, Arthur O. "The Utopian Hero." In *America as Utopia.* Edited by Kenneth M. Roemer, 133–47. New York: Burt Franklin and Company, 1981.

Lipow, Arthur. *Authoritarian Socialism in America: Edward Bellamy and the Nationalist Movement.* Berkeley: The University of California Press, 1982.

Lipp, Ronald F. "Atlas and Art." In *Ayn Rand's Atlas Shrugged.* Edited by Edward W. Younkins. Burlington, VT: Ashgate Publishing Company, 2007.

Locke, Don. *A Fantasy of Reason: The Life and Thought of William Godwin.* London: Routledge and Kegan Paul, 1980.

Locke, John. *Second Treatise of Government.* Edited by C. B. Macpherson. Indianapolis, IN: Hackett Publishing Company, 1980.

Lomasky, Loren E. "Nozick's Libertarian Utopia." In *Robert Nozick*. Edited by David Schmidtz, 59–82. Cambridge: Cambridge University Press, 2002.

London, Jack. *The Iron Heel*. New York: The Macmillan Company, 1908. Reprint, n.p.: n.d. Page references are to reprint.

Lorenzo, David J. *Cities at the End of the World*. New York: Bloomsbury, 2014.

Macey, Jonathan R. "Government as Investor: Tax Policy and the State." *Social Philosophy and Policy* 23, no. 2 (2006): 255–86. Reprinted in *Taxation, Economic Prosperity, and Distributive Justice*. Edited by E. Paul, F. Miller, and J. Paul. Cambridge: Cambridge University Press, 2006.

Mack, Eric. "The Fundamental Elements of Rand's Theory of Rights." In *The Philosophic Thought of Ayn Rand*. Edited by Douglas J. Den Uyl and Douglas B. Rasmussen, 122–61. Urbana: University of Illinois Press, 1984.

———. "Non-Absolute Rights and Libertarian Taxation." In *Taxation, Economic Prosperity, and Distributive Justice*. Edited by E. Paul, F. Miller, and J. Paul. Cambridge: Cambridge University Press, 2006.

———. "Nozick's Anarchism." In *Anarchism*. Edited by J. Roland Pennock and John W. Chapman, 43–62. New York: New York University Press, 1978.

———. "Robert Nozick's Political Philosophy." *The Stanford Encyclopedia of Philosophy* (Summer 2015). Edited by Edward N. Zalta. Accessed October 21, 2016. http://plato.stanford.edu/archives/sum2015/entries/nozick-political/.

Macpherson, C. B. *The Political Theory of Possessive Individualism: Hobbes to Locke*. Oxford: Oxford University Press, 2011.

———. *Property*. Toronto: University of Toronto Press, 1978.

Magner, Lois N. "Darwinism and the Woman Question: The Evolving Views of Charlotte Perkins Gilman." In *Critical Essays on Charlotte Perkins Gilman*. Edited by Joanne B. Karpinski, 115–128. New York: G. K. Hall and Co., 1992.

Maine, Henry Sumner. *Ancient Law*. Reprint, n.p.: Nu Vision Publications, 2009.

———. *Lectures on the Early History of Institutions*. New York: Henry Holt and Company, 1888.

Malthus, Thomas. *An Essay on the Principle of Population*. Oxford: Oxford University Press, 1993.

Mannheim, Karl. *Ideology and Utopia: An Introduction to the Sociology of Knowledge*. Translated by Luis Wirth and Edward Shils. San Diego, CA: A Harvest Book, Haircourt, 1936.

Manuel, Frank E. *The New World of Henri Saint-Simon*. Cambridge, MA: Harvard University Press, 1956.

———. "Toward a Psychological History of Utopias." In *Utopias and Utopian Thought*. Edited by Frank E. Manuel, 69–98. Boston: Houghton Mifflin Company, 1965.

Manuel, Frank E., and Fritzie P. Manuel. *Utopian Thought in the Western World*. Cambridge, MA: The Belknap Press of Harvard University Press, 1979.

Markham, F. M. H. Introduction. *Henri Comte De Saint-Simon (1760–1825): Selected Writing.* Edited and translated by F. M. H. Markham. New York: The MacMillan Company, 1952.

Marks, Jonathan M. *What it Means to be 98% Chimpanzee: Apes, People, and Their Genes.* Berkeley and Los Angeles: University of California Press, 2002.

Marx, Karl. *Capital.* Translated from 3rd German ed. by Samuel More and Edward Aveling. Edited by Friedrich Engels. Revised with additional translation from the 4th German ed. by Marie Sachey and Herbert Lamm. In *Great Books of the Western World.* Edited by Robert Maynard Hutchins and Mortimer Adler, vol. 50. Chicago: Encyclopaedia Britannica, 1952.

———. *Eighteenth Brumaire of Louis Bonaparte.* Translated by D. D. L. Project Gutenberg, 2006. Ebook no. 1346. Last updated 2013. Accessed February 23, 2020. http://www.gutenberg.org/files/1346/1346-h/1346-h.htm.

Mayer, Jane. *Dark Money: The Hidden History of the Billionaires Behind the Rise of the Radical Right.* New York: Anchor Books, a division of Penguin Random House, 2016.

McCann, Charles R., Jr. "Apprehending the Social Philosophy of Henry George." *American Journal of Economics and Sociology* 67, no. 1 (January 2008): 67–88.

Mill, John Stuart. *Autobiography.* New York: Penguin Books, 1989.

———. *On Liberty.* Chicago: Henry Regnery Company, 1955.

———. *Principles of Political Economy.* Abridged by J. Laurence Laughlin. New York: Appleton and Company, 1884.

———. "Property and Taxation." In *Essays on Economics and Society,* vol. 5. Collected Works of John Stuart Mill. Toronto: University of Toronto Press, 1967.

———. *A System of Logic Ratiocinative and Inductive.* Honolulu, HI: University Press of the Pacific, 2002.

Miller, David. "The Justification of Political Authority." In *Robert Nozick.* Edited by David Schmidtz, 10–33. Cambridge: Cambridge University Press, 2002.

Montesquieu, Charles de. *The Spirit of Laws.* Translated by Thomas Nugent. Revised by J. V. Prichard. In *Great Books of the Western World.* Edited by Robert Maynard Hutchins and Mortimer J. Adler, vol. 38. Chicago: Encyclopaedia Britannica, 1952.

More, Thomas. *Utopia.* Translated by Robert M. Adams. Cambridge: Cambridge University Press, 1975.

Morris, Donald. "A Case for Company-Specific Public Disclosure of Corporate Tax Returns." *Accounting and the Public Interest* 2015, 15:1, 1–21.

Morris, William. "Bellamy's Looking Backward." *Commonweal* 5, no. 8, June 21, 1889. Accessed September 6, 2017. https://www.marxists.org/archive/morris/works/1889/backward.htm.

———. *News from Nowhere.* In *News from Nowhere and Other Writings.* New York: Penguin Books, 1993.

———. "Useful Work Versus Useless Toil." In *Political Writings of William Morris*. Edited by A. L. Morton. New York: International Publishers, 1973.

Morton, A. L. *The English Utopia*. London: Lawrence and Wishart, 1952. Reprint, Berlin: Seven Seas Books, 1968. Page references are to reprint.

———. *The Life and Ideas of Robert Owen*. London: Lawrence and Wishart, 1962.

Moylan, Tom. *Demand the Impossible: Science Fiction and the Utopian Imagination*. Edited by Raffaella Baccolini. Oxford: Peter Lang, 2014.

Mumford, Lewis. "Utopia, The City and The Machine." In *Utopias and Utopian Thought*. Edited by Frank E. Manuel, 3–24. Boston: Houghton Mifflin Company, 1965.

Murphy, Liam, and Thomas Nagel. *The Myth of Ownership: Taxes and Justice*. Oxford: Oxford University Press, 2002.

Murphy, N. R. *The Interpretation of Plato's Republic*. Oxford: The Clarendon Press, 1951.

Murray, Dale F. *Nozick, Autonomy and Compensation*. London: Continuum International Publishing Group, 2007.

Musgrave, Robert A. *The Theory of Public Finance*. New York: McGraw-Hill Book Company, Inc., 1959.

Nagel, Thomas. *Equality and Partiality*. New York: Oxford University Press, 1991.

Negley, Glen, and J. Max Patrick. *The Quest for Utopia*. New York: Henry Schuman, 1952. Reprint, New York: Anchor Books, 1962. Page references are to reprint.

Nietzsche, Friedrich. *Beyond Good and Evil*. Translated by Walter Kaufmann. New York: Vintage Books, 1966.

———. *Human, All Too Human*. Translated by Marion Faber with Stephen Lehmann. Lincoln, NE: University of Nebraska Press, 1984.

———. *Twilight of the Idols*. In *The Twilight of the Idols and The Anti-Christ*. Translated by R. J. Hollingdale. New York: Penguin Books,1968.

Nisbet, Robert. *History of the Idea of Progress*. New York: Basic Books Publishers, 1980.

Nissenbaum, Helen. *Privacy in Context: Technology, Policy, and the Integrity of Social Life*. Stanford, CA: Stanford University Press, 2010.

Nozick, Robert. *Anarchy, State, and Utopia*. New York: Basic Books, 1974.

———. "On the Randian Argument." In *Reading Nozick: Essays on Anarchy, State, and Utopia*. Edited by Jeffrey Paul, 206–31. Totowa, NJ: Rowman and Littlefield, 1981.

———. *Philosophical Explanations*. Cambridge: The Belknap Press of Harvard University Press, 1981.

O'Donnell, Edward T. *Henry George and the Crisis of Inequality*. New York: Columbia University Press, 2015.

Okin, Susan Moller. *Justice, Gender and the Family*. N.p.: Basic Books, 1989.

Olson, Mancur. *The Logic of Collective Action: Public Goods and the Theory of Groups*. Cambridge, MA: Harvard University Press, 1965.

Orwell, George. *Homage to Catalonia.* London: Secker and Warburg, 1938. Reprint, n.p.: Will Jonson and Dog's Tail Books, n.d. Page references are to reprint.

———. *Nineteen Eighty-Four.* New York: PLUME/Penguin/Harcourt Brace, 1949.

———. "Politics and the English Language." In *Why I Write.* New York: Penguin Books, 2004.

———. Review of "*The Road to Serfdom* by F.A. Hayek." *Observer* 9, April 1944. https://thomasgwyndunbar.wordpress.com/2008/10/09/george-orwell-review/.

———. *The Road to Wigan Pier.* New York: A Harvest Book – Harcourt, 1958.

Owen, Robert. *The Book of the New Moral World.* New York: Augustus M. Kelley Publishers, 1970.

———. *A Development of the Principles and Plans on Which to Establish Self-Supporting Home Colonies.* London: Home Colonization Society, 1841. Reprint, Kessinger. Page references same as original.

———. *Lectures on An Entire New State of Society.* London: J. Brooks, 1830. Reprint, Kessinger. Page references same as original.

———. *The Life of Robert Owen Written by Himself.* New York: Augustus M. Kelley Publishers, 1967.

———. *A New View of Society and Other Writings.* New York: Penguin Classics, 1991.

———. *The Revolution in the Mind and Practice of the Human Race.* London: Effingham Wilson, 1849. Reprint, Nabu Public Domain. Page references same as original.

Owen, Robert Dale. *Threading My Way.* London: Turner and Co., 1874. Reprint, Forgotten Books, 2012. Page references same as original.

Paine, Thomas. *Agrarian Justice.* Accessed September 15, 2017. https://www.ssa.gov/history/paine4.html.

———. *Rights of Man.* In *Common Sense, Rights of Man, and Other Essential Writings of Thomas Paine.* New York: Signet Classic, 1969.

Parrinder, Patrick. "Eugenics and Utopia: Sexual Selection from Galton to Morris." *Utopian Studies* 8, no. 2 (1997): 1–12.

———. "Utopia and Meta-Utopia in H. G. Wells." *Utopian Studies* 1 (1987): 79–97.

Peikoff, Leonard. *Objectivism: The Philosophy of Ayn Rand.* New York: Meridian, a division of Penguin Books USA, 1991.

Pfaelzer, Jean. "Immanence, Indeterminance, and the Utopian Pun in *Looking Backward.*" In *Looking Backward 1988–1888.* Edited by Daphne Patai. Amherst: The University of Massachusetts Press, 1988.

———. *The Utopian Novel in America, 1886–1896: The Politics of Form.* University of Pittsburgh Press, 1984.

Pfohl, Stephen. "The 'Discovery' of Child Abuse." *Social Problems* 24, no. 3 (February 1997): 310–23.

Philp, Mark. *Godwin's Political Justice.* Ithaca, NY: Cornell University Press, 1986.

Piketty, Thomas. *Capital in the Twenty-First Century.* Translated by Arthur Goldhammer. Cambridge, MA: The Belknap Press of Harvard University Press, 2014.

Plato. *Critias.* Translated by A. E. Taylor. In *Plato: The Collected Dialogues.* Edited by Edith Hamilton and Huntington Cairns. New York: Pantheon Books, 1961.

———. *Laws.* Translated by A. E. Taylor. In *Plato: The Collected Dialogues.* Edited by Edith Hamilton and Huntington Cairns. New York: Pantheon Books, 1961.

———. *Republic.* Translated by Allan Bloom, 2nd ed. Basic Books, 1968.

———. *Republic.* Translated by Benjamin Jowett. New York: Vintage Classics, a division of Random House, 1991.

Pocock, J. G. A. Historical Introduction. In *The Political Works of James Harrington.* Cambridge: Cambridge University Press, 1977.

Popper, Karl. *The Open Society and Its Enemies.* Princeton, NJ: Princeton University Press, 2013.

Posner, Richard A. *Law and Literature,* 3rd ed. Cambridge, MA: Harvard University Press, 2009.

Prettyman, Gib. "Gilded Age Utopias of Incorporation." *Utopian Studies* 12, no. 1 (2001): 19–40.

Proudhon, Pierre-Joseph. *General Idea of the Revolution in the Nineteenth Century.* Translated by John Beverley Robinson. Mineola, NY: Dover Publications, 2003.

———. *What is Property?* Edited and translated by Donald R. Kelley and Bonnie G. Smith. Cambridge: Cambridge University Press, 1994.

Rand, Ayn. *Atlas Shrugged.* New York: Random House, 1957.

———. *Capitalism: The Unknown Ideal.* New York: Signet Books, 1967.

———. *For the New Intellectual.* New York: Signet Books, 1963.

———. *The Fountainhead.* New York: Signet Books, 1945.

———. *Introduction to Objectivist Epistemology,* expanded 2nd ed. New York: Meridian, a division of Penguin Books USA, 1990.

———. *Journals of Ayn Rand.* Edited by David Harriman. New York: The Penguin Group, 1997.

———. *Philosophy: Who Needs It.* New York: Signet, 1984.

———. *The Romantic Manifesto.* New York: Signet Books, 1971.

———. *The Virtue of Selfishness.* New York: Signet Books, 1964.

Reeve, Andrew. *Property.* Atlantic Highlands, NJ: Humanities Press International, 1986.

Reeve, C. D. C. *Philosopher-Kings: The Argument of Plato's Republic.* Princeton, NJ: Princeton University Press, 1988. Reprint, Hackett Publishing Company.

Robertson, Michael. *The Last Utopians: Four Late Nineteenth-Century Visionaries and Their Legacy.* Princeton, NJ: Princeton University Press, 2018.

Rodgers, Lamont. "Death, Taxes, and Misinterpretations of Robert Nozick: Why Nozickians Can Oppose the Estate Tax." *Libertarian Papers* 7, no. 1 (2015): 1–17.

Roemer, Kenneth M. *The Obsolete Necessity: America in Utopian Writings, 1888–1900.* The Kent State University Press, 1976.

———. "Utopia and Victorian Culture: 1888–99." In *America as Utopia*. Edited by Kenneth M. Roemer, 305–32. New York: Burt Franklin and Company, 1981.

Rogers, Jennifer. "Fulfillment as a Function of Time, or the Ambiguous Process of Utopia." In *The New Utopian Politics of Ursula K. Le Guin's The Dispossessed*. Edited by Laurence Davis and Peter Stillman, 181–94. Lanham, MD: Lexington Books, 2005.

Rosen, Jeffrey. *The Unwanted Gaze: The Destruction of Privacy in America*. New York: Vintage Books, 2000.

Rossi, Paolo. *Francis Bacon: From Magic to Science*. Translated by Sacha Rabinovitch. Chicago: The University of Chicago Press, 1968.

Rothbard, Murray. *The Ethics of Liberty*. New York: New York University Press, 1998.

Rousseau, Jean-Jacques. *Discourse on the Origin and Foundations of Inequality Among Men*. In *Rousseau's Political Writings*. Translated by Julia Conway Bondanella. New York: Norton, 1988.

Ryan, Alan. *Property and Political Theory*. Oxford: Basil Blackwell, 1984.

Sabia, Dan. "Individual and Community in Le Guin's *The Dispossessed*." In *The New Utopian Politics of Ursula K. Le Guin's The Dispossessed*. Edited by Laurence Davis and Peter Stillman, 111–28. Lanham, MD: Lexington Books, 2005.

Saint-Simon, Henri. *Henri Comte De Saint-Simon (1760–1825): Selected Writings*. Edited and translated by F. M. H. Markham. New York: The MacMillan Company, 1952.

———. *Henri Saint-Simon (1760–1825): Selected Writings on Science, Industry and Social Organization*. Edited and translated by Keith Taylor. New York: Holmes and Meier Publishers, Inc., 1975.

———. *The Political Thought of Saint-Simon*. Edited by Ghita Ionescu. Oxford: Oxford University Press, 1976.

Samuelson, Paul A., and William D. Nordhaus. *Economics,* 14th ed. New York: McGraw-Hill, 1992.

Sargent, Lyman Tower. "Authority and Utopia: Utopianism in Political Thought." *Polity* 14, no. 4 (Summer 1982): 565–84.

———. "Capitalist Eutopias in America." In *America as Utopia*. Edited by Kenneth M. Roemer, 192–205. New York: Burt Franklin and Company, 1981.

———. *Contemporary Political Ideologies: A Comparative Analysis*, 14th ed. Belmont, CA: Wadsworth, 2009.

———. "Edward Bellamy's Boston in 2000 from 1888 to 1897: The Evolution of Bellamy's Future Boston from *Looking Backward* Through *Equality*." *Utopian Studies* 27, no. 2 (2016): 152–81.

———. "A Note on the Other Side of Human Nature in the Utopian Novel." *Political Theory* 3, no. 1 (February 1975): 88–97.

———. "The Three Faces of Utopianism Revisited." *Utopian Studies* 5, no. 1 (1994): 1–37.

————. *Utopianism: A Very Short Introduction*. Oxford: Oxford University Press, 2010.

Sartorius, Rolf. "The Limits of Libertarianism." In *Liberty and the Rule of Law*. Edited by Robert L. Cunningham. College Station, TX: Texas A&M University Press, 1979.

Say, Jean-Baptiste. *A Treatise on Political Economy*, 4th French ed. Translated by C. R. Prinsep. New Brunswick, NJ: Transaction Publishers, Rutgers, 2001.

Scanlon, Thomas. "Nozick on Rights, Liberty, and Property." In *Reading Nozick: Essays on Anarchy, State, and Utopia*. Edited by Jeffrey Paul, 107–29. Totowa, NJ: Rowman and Littlefield, 1981.

Sciabarra, Chris Matthew. "Manifesto for a New Radicalism." In *Ayn Rand's Atlas Shrugged*. Edited by Edward W. Younkins. Burlington, VT: Ashgate Publishing Company, 2007.

Sechrest, Larry J. "Rand, Anarchy, and Taxes." *The Journal of Ayn Rand Studies* 1, no. 1 (Fall 1999): 87–105.

Sen, Amartya. *Development as Freedom*. New York: Anchor Books; a division of Random House, 1999.

Sessions, W. A. *Francis Bacon Revisited*. New York: Twayne Publishers, 1996.

Shakespeare, William. *Hamlet*. In *The Complete Works*, compact ed., 653–90. Oxford: Clarendon Press, 1988.

Shearman, Thomas Gaskell. *Natural Taxation*. New York: Doubleday and McClure Co., 1898. Reprint.

Shklovsky, Victor. "Evgeny Zamyatin's Ceiling." In *Zamyatin's We: A Collection of Critical Essays*. Edited by Gary Kern, 49–50. Ann Arbor, MI: Ardis Publishers, 1988.

Sidgwick, Henry. *Outlines of the History of Ethics*. Indianapolis, IN: Hackett Publishing Company, 1988.

Silver, Harold. *Robert Owen on Education*. Cambridge: Cambridge University Press, 1969.

Simmel, Georg. *The Philosophy of Money*. Translated by Tom Bottomore and David Frisby. Boston: Routledge and Kegan Paul, 1978.

Singer, Joseph William. "How Property Norms Construct the Externalities of Ownership." In *Property and Community*, 57–79. Edited by Gregory S. Alexander and Eduardo M. Peñalver. Oxford: Oxford University Press, 2010.

Singer, Peter. "The Right to be Rich or Poor." In *Reading Nozick: Essays on Anarchy, State, and Utopia*. Edited by Jeffrey Paul, 37–53. Totowa, NJ: Rowman and Littlefield, 1981.

Skinner, B. F. *About Behaviorism*. New York: Alfred A. Knopf, 1974.

————. *Beyond Freedom and Dignity*. New York: Alfred A. Knopf, 1971.

————. *Contingencies of Reinforcement: A Theoretical Analysis*. New York: Appleton-Century-Crofts, 1969.

————. *Cumulative Record*, 3rd. ed. New York: Appleton-Century-Crofts, 1959.

————. "News from Nowhere, 1984." *The Behavior Analyst* 8, no. 1 (Spring 1985): 5–14.

————. *Notebooks.* Edited by Robert Epstein. Englewood Cliffs, NJ: Prentice-Hall, 1980.

————. "The Problem of Consciousness—A Debate." *Philosophical and Phenomenological Research* 27, no. 3 (March 1967): 317–37 (with B. Blanshard).

————. *Science and Human Behavior.* New York: Macmillan Company, 1953.

————. *The Technology of Teaching.* New York: Meredith Corporation, 1968.

————. *Walden Two.* New York: Macmillan Publishing Co., 1976.

Slemrod, Joel, and Christian Gillitzer. *Tax Systems.* Cambridge, MA: MIT Press, 2014.

Smith, Adam. *The Theory of Moral Sentiments.* Indianapolis: Liberty Fund, 1976.

————. *Wealth of Nations.* Amherst, NY: Prometheus Books, 1991.

Smith, H. F. Russell. *Harrington and His Oceana: A Study of a 17th Century Utopia and its Influence in America.* Cambridge: At the University Press, 1914; republished by Leopold Classic Library.

Smith, John Maynard. "Eugenics and Utopia." In *Utopias and Utopian Thought.* Edited by Frank E. Manuel, 150–68. Boston: Houghton Mifflin Company, 1965.

Smith, Phillip E. "Unbuilding Walls: Human Nature and the Nature of Evolutionary and Political Theory in *The Possessed.*" In *Writers of the 21st Century Series: Ursula K. Le Guin.* Edited by Joseph D. Olander and Martin Harry Greenberg, 77–96. New York: Taplinger Publishing Company, 1979.

Smith, Tara. " 'Humanity's Darkest Evil': The Lethal Destructiveness of Non-Objective Law." In *Essays on Ayn Rand's Atlas Shrugged.* Edited by Robert Mayhew. New York: Lexington Books, Inc., 2009.

Solove, Daniel J. *Nothing to Hide: The False Tradeoff Between Privacy and Security.* New Haven, CT: Yale University Press, 2011.

————. *Understanding Privacy.* Cambridge, MA: Harvard University Press, 2008.

Spedding, James. Notes to the Preface to *Novum Organum.* In *The Works of Francis Bacon.* Edited by James Spedding, Robert Leslie Ellis, and Douglas Denon Heath, vol. 1. Cambridge: Cambridge University Press, 2011.

Spence, Thomas. *The Constitution of Spensonia.* In *Pig's Meat: Selected Writings of Thomas Spence, Radical and Pioneer Land Reformer.* Nottingham: Spokesman, 1982.

————. *The Restorer of Society to its Natural State.* In *Pig's Meat: Selected Writings of Thomas Spence, Radical and Pioneer Land Reformer.* Nottingham: Spokesman, 1982.

————. "*The Rights of Man*" (1793). In *Pig's Meat: Selected Writings of Thomas Spence, Radical and Pioneer Land Reformer.* Nottingham: Spokesman, 1982.

Spencer, Herbert. *Social Statics* (1850). Reprint, New York: D. Appleton and Company, 1885. Page references are to reprint.

Stern, Alexandra Minna. "STERILIZED in the Name of Public Health: Race, Immigration, and Reproductive Control in Modern California." *American Journal of Public Health* 95, 7 (2005): 1128–138. Published Online: October 10, 2011. http://doi.org/10.2105/AJPH.2004.041608.

Steuerle, C. Eugene. "And Equal (Tax) Justice for All?" In *Tax Justice*. Edited by Joseph J. Thorndike and Dennis J. Ventry Jr. Washington, DC: The Urban Institute Press, 2002.

Stillman, Peter G. "'Nothing is, but what is not': Utopias as Practical Political Philosophy." In *The Philosophy of Utopia*. Edited by Barbara Goodwin, 9–24. London: Routledge, Taylor and Francis Group, 2001.

Strauss, Leo. *The City and Man*. Chicago: University of Chicago Press, 1964.

Sumner, William Graham. "The Absurd Effort to Make the World Over." In *War and Other Essays*. New York: AMS Press, 1970.

———. "Modern Marriage." In *Essays of William Graham Sumner*. Hamden, CT: Archon Books, 1969.

Suter, Rufus. "Salomon's House: A Study of Francis Bacon." *The Scientific Monthly* 66, no. 1 (January 1948): 62–66.

Suvin, Darko. *Metamorphoses of Science Fiction*. New Haven, CT: Yale University Press, 1979.

Swift, Jonathan. *Gulliver's Travels*. New York: Penguin Putnam, 2001.

Taylor, Keith. *The Political Ideas of the Utopian Socialists*. London: Frank Cass and Company Limited, 1982.

Taylor, Walter Fuller. *The Economic Novel in America*. Chapel Hill: University of North Carolina Press, 1942.

Thomas, John L. *Alternative America: Henry George, Edward Bellamy, Henry Demarest Lloyd and the Adversary Tradition*. Cambridge, MA: The Belknap Press of Harvard University Press, 1983.

Thoreau, Henry David. *Civil Disobedience*. In *Walden and Civil Disobedience*. New York: Barnes and Noble Classics, 2003.

———. *Walden*. In *Walden and Civil Disobedience*. New York: Barnes and Noble Classics, 2003.

Tilman, Rick. "The Utopian Vision of Edward Bellamy and Thorstein Veblen." *Journal of Economic Issues* 19, no. 4 (December 1985): 879–98.

Tocqueville, Alexis de. *Democracy in America*. Translated by Henry Reeve. New York: W. W. Norton and Co., 2007.

Tolstoy, Count Lev. *What Shall We Do Then?* Edited and translated by Leo Wiener. Boston: Dana Estes and Company, 1904. Reprint, n.p., n.d. Page references are to reprint.

Tolstoy, Leo. *Anna Karenina*. Translated by Louise and Aylmer Maude. Mineola, NY: Dover Publications, 2004.

———. *A Confession*. Translated by Aylmer Maude. Mineola, NY: Dover Publications, 2005.

———. *How Much Land Does a Man Need? And Other Stories* (1886). Translated by Louise and Aylmer Maude. Reprint, n.p.: Digireads.com., n.d.

———. *Resurrection*. Translated by Louise Maude. Oxford: Oxford University Press, 1994.

———. *The Slavery of Our Times*. Reprint, n.p. Read Books, 2013.

———. *Tolstoy's Letters*. Translated by R. F. Christian. 2 vols. New York: Charles Scribner's Sons, 1978.

———. *War and Peace*. Translated by Richard Pevear and Larissa Volokhonsky. New York: Vintage Classics, 2008.

Tunick, Mark. "The Need for Walls: Privacy, Community, and Freedom in *The Dispossessed*." In *The New Utopian Politics of Ursula K. Le Guin's The Dispossessed*. Edited by Laurence Davis and Peter Stillman, 129–47. Lanham, MD: Lexington Books, 2005.

Tversky, Amos, and Daniel Kahneman. "Availability: A Heuristic for Judging Frequency and Probability." In *Judgment Under Uncertainty: Heuristics and Biases*. Edited by Daniel Kahneman, Paul Slovic, and Amos Tversky. Cambridge: Cambridge University Press, 1982.

Twain, Mark. *A Connecticut Yankee in King Arthur's Court* (1889). New York: Bantam Books, 1981.

Tyler, Tom R. *Why People Obey the Law*. Princeton, NJ: Princeton University Press, 2006.

Vaingurt, Julia. "Human Machines and the Pains of Penmanship in Yevgeny Zamyatin's *We*." *Cultural Critique* 80 (Winter 2012): 108–29.

Van Doren, Charles. *The Idea of Progress*. New York: Frederick A. Praeger, Publishers, 1967.

Vinton, Arthur Dudley. *Looking Further Backward*. New York: Albany Book Company, 1890. Reprint, n.p., n.d. Page references are to reprint.

Vonnegut, Kurt, Jr. *Jailbird: A Novel*. New York: Dell Publishing Co., 1979.

Waldron, Jeremy. *The Right to Private Property*. Oxford: The Clarendon Press, 1988.

Wasserman, Louis. "The Essential Henry George." In *Critics of Henry George*. Edited by Robert V. Andelson. Malden, MA: Blackwell Publishing, 2003.

Webber, Carolyn, and Aaron Wildavasky. *A History of Taxation and Expenditure in the Western World*. New York: Simon and Schuster, 1986.

Weber, Max. "Politics as a Vocation." In *From Max Weber: Essays in Sociology*. Translated by H. H. Gerth and C. Wright Mills. New York: Oxford University Press, 1946.

Wegner, Phillip E. "On Zamyatin's *We*: A Critical Map of Utopia's 'Possible Worlds.'" *Utopian Studies* 4, no. 2 (1993): 94–116.

Weinberger, J. "Science and Rule in Bacon's Utopia: An Introduction to the Reading of the *New Atlantis*." *The American Political Science Review* 70, no. 3 (September 1976): 865–85.

Weinberger, Jerry. *Science, Faith, and Politics: Francis Bacon and the Utopian Roots of the Modern Age*. Ithaca, NY: Cornell University Press, 1985.

Wells, David Ames. *The Theory and Practice of Taxation*. New York: D. Appleton and Company, 1911.

Wells, H. G. "Discussion." In Francis Galton, "Eugenics: Its Definition, Scope, and Aims." *The American Journal of Sociology* 10, no. 1 (July 1904): 1–25.

————. *A Modern Utopia*. New York: Digireads Publishing, 2011.

————. *When the Sleeper Wakes*. In *Three Prophetic Novels of H. G. Wells*. New York: Dover Publications, Inc., 1960.

Wenzer, Kenneth C. "The Influence of Henry George's Philosophy on Lev Niko-laevich Tolstoy: The Period of Developing Economic Thought (1881–1897)." *Pennsylvania History* 63, no. 2 (April 1996): 232–52.

————. "Tolstoy's Georgist Spiritual Political Economy (1897–1919): Anarchism and Land Reform." *American Journal of Economics and Sociology* 56, no. 4 (October 1997): 639–67.

Westin, Alan F. *Privacy and Freedom*. New York: Antheneum, 1967.

White, Howard B. *Peace Among the Willows: The Political Philosophy of Francis Bacon*. The Hague: Martinus Nijhoff, 1968.

Whitney, Charles. *Francis Bacon and Modernity*. New Haven, CT: Yale University Press, 1986.

Wicksell, Knut. "A New Principle of Just Taxation." Translated by J. M. Buchanan. In *Classics in the Theory of Public Finance*. Edited by Richard A. Musgrave and Alan T. Peacock. New York: St Martin's Press, 1967.

Winfrey, John C. *Social Issues: The Ethics and Economics of Taxes and Public Programs*. Oxford: Oxford University Press, 1998.

Wolff, Jonathan. *Robert Nozick: Property, Justice and the Minimal State*. Stanford, CA: Stanford University Press, 1991.

Wolff, Robert Paul. "Robert Nozick's Derivation of the Minimal State." In *Reading Nozick: Essays on Anarchy, State, and Utopia*. Edited by Jeffrey Paul, 77–104. Totowa, NJ: Roman and Littlefield, 1981.

Wollstonecraft, Mary. *A Vindication of the Rights of Women*. Reprint, n.p., n.d.

Wortham, Simon. "Censorship and the Institution of Knowledge in Bacon's *New Atlantis*." In *Francis Bacon's New Atlantis*. Edited by Bronwen Price, 180–98. New York: Manchester University Press, 2002.

Young, Fredric C. "Nozick and the Individualist Anarchist." In *Equality and Liberty: Analyzing Rawls and Nozick*. Edited by J. Angelo Corlett, 268–75. Hounds-mills, UK: Macmillan, 1991.

Younkins, Edward W. "Economics in Ayn Rand's *Atlas Shrugged*." *The Journal of Ayn Rand Studies* 13, no. 2 (December 2013): 123–39.

————. "Rand's Philosophical and Literary Masterpiece." In *Ayn Rand's Atlas Shrugged*. Edited by Edward W. Younkins. Burlington, VT: Ashgate Publishing Company, 2007.

Zadek, Simon. *An Economics of Utopia*. Brookfield, VT: Ashgate Publishing Company, 1993.

Zamyatin, Yevgeny. *A Soviet Heretic: Essays by Yevgeny Zamyatin*. Edited and trans-lated by Mirra Ginsburg. Chicago: The University of Chicago Press, 1970.

————. *We*. Translated by Natasha Randall. New York: The Modern Library, 2006.

Zimbardo, Phillip G. "Mind Control in Orwell's *Nineteen Eighty-Four*: Fictional Concepts Become Operational Realities in Jim Jones's Jungle Experiment." In *On Nineteen Eighty-Four: Orwell and Our Future*. Edited by Abbott Gleason, Jack Goldsmith, and Martha C. Nussbaum, 127–54. Princeton, NJ: Princeton University Press, 2005.

INDEX

access to truth. *See* truth

Adler, Mortimer J., 130, 160

Albanese, Denise, 144

altruism, 155–56, 238, 239n9, 240, 242n27, 252

A Modern Utopia. See Wells, H. G.

anarchy/anarchist, 81–82, 84–85, 153–56, 209, 222, 246, 258–59

Anarchy, State and Utopia. See Nozick, Robert

Andelson, Robert V., 219

Anderson, F. H., 71n46, 69n36

Arendt, Hannah, 49, 77, 247

Aristotle, 135, 140, 199n11, 206

astrology, 138, 187

Atlantis, 73n61, 244

Atlas Shrugged. See Rand, Ayn

A Traveler from Altruria. See Howells, William Dean

Aughterson, Kate, 145

Bacon, Francis, 68–76, 144–47
  marriage: encouraged by king, 144; eugenic paradox of, 146–47; inheritance tax on, 145; love and, 145–46; prostitutes as tax on, 146; wise laws touching, 145–47
  nature: laws of, 10n22, 69; human, 71

science, 68–69, 74–76

scientists: causes (uncovering hidden), 68–69, 75; eugenics, 146–47; experiments, 147n45; (as) rulers, 74–75; secret society, 68–69, 75

truth, access to: cognitive biases (idols), 69–71, 146; government as obscure and invisible, 73; laws of secrecy, 72, 75; scientists' superior knowledge of, 75–76; tax on, 75

war (avoidance of), 74–75

Baker-Smith, Dominic, 45, 101n63, 143

Barker, Ernest, 10

Becker, Howard, 30, 78

behaviorism, 122–23, 174–83

Bellamy, Edward, 106–14, 189–93
  arts surtax, 110; dependency on others, 248; Dewey, J. (on), 109n116
  economics: competition, 191; equality, 113–14; monopoly (final), 107–108; profit, 94, 108–10, (national), 114; poverty, 191–92; tax assessors and collectors, 5
  education: corrupted by capitalism, 86–87; special avocation, 110–11

Bellamy, Edward *(continued)*
    eugenics, 172, 188n315, 189–93;
        evolution (logical), 107–108,
        109n16, 189n321; freedom,
        248; general welfare, 109, (as
        egalitarian), 114; human nature,
        190–91; justice, 192; leisure, 46;
        marriage, 191–92; Morris, W. on,
        112; past generations (debt to),
        244; punishment, 193; revolution
        (nonviolent), 107–108, 109n116;
        Saint-Simon, H. (contrast
        with), 108; science, 86; society,
        224n148; truth, access to, 86–87;
        war (avoidance), 109–10
    work: boot camp, 110; career
        choice, 94, 110; distasteful jobs,
        113; effort, incentive for, 111–13;
        gender roles, 111; industrial army,
        94, 103, 106–14; inequality of
        ability ("invalid corps"), 113–14,
        137; multiple careers, 110;
        persistent refusal to, 112; required
        labor, 109–11; surplus labor, 105,
        138; women's army, 111–13
Benn, S. I., 23
Bentham, Jeremy, 6, 48, 51, 163, 204,
    231, 265
Bird-Pollan, Jennifer, 269n195
Bloch, Ernst, 101, 135–36
Blodgett, Eleanor Dickinson, 72, 136
Bloom, Allan, 44, 66, 97, 142
Bloomfield, Paul, 150
Bok, Sissela, 67
Bostaph, Samuel, 246, 251
Boyd, William, 157–58
Branden, Nathaniel, 239
Brave New World. See Huxley, Aldous
Brin, David, 44, 282
Broome, John, 200
Brown, E. J., 55

Bruce, Susan, 144
Burke, Edmund, 13–14, 31–32,
    204n33, 253
Butler, Samuel, 173, 179

Campanella, Tommaso (Thomas),
    135–38, 186–88
    Aristotle, 135; astrology, 138, 187;
        childrearing, 166; education, 136–
        37; eugenics, 187–88; "marriage"
        (mating), 187–88; Plato, 187;
        science, 135–36; war (military
        training), 137
    work: assigned occupations, 136–38;
        division of labor, 138; 135–38;
        gender roles, 136; inequality of
        ability (disabled workers), 137;
        surplus labor, 138
capitalism, 219–20, 239n9, 241–42,
    249, 251–52, 277
Carroll, Lewis, 248
Carter, Steven, 182n80
Chambers, R. W., 100, 103
character: force of, 42; Owen, 156–57,
    163, 210–11; Plato (of guardians),
    97
childrearing (state controlled):
    Campanella, 166; Gilman, 80,
    167, 169–70; Hertzka, 170n189;
    Huxley, 196; Owen, 163–66;
    Plato (guardians), 142; Skinner,
    B. F., 181–85; Wells, H. G., 230
Christensen, Andrew G., 118
Christian, R. F., 223, 226n164
Cicero, 17, 101n63, 139
City of the Sun. See Campanella,
    Thomas
Claeys, Gregory: Bellamy, E., 39n160;
    Gilman, C. P., 114n155; Godwin,
    W., 84n126, 157n109, 210n68,
    233n202; Harrington, J., 206;

liberalism, 239n9; Owen, R., 159, 162n137, 166–67, 211n74, 212; Skinner, B. F., 182n276; utopia, 240–41

Clardy, Alan, 245, 248n67

Clark, John. P., 84n122

Coates, Ta-Nehisi, 36n149, 234n211

coercion. *See* tax

Cohen, G. A., 13n35, 204, 231, 267–68, 269, 278n249

The Commonwealth of Oceana. See Harrington, James

competition: absolute advantage, 93–94; Bellamy, E., 191; comparative (relative) advantage, 93–94; George, H., 211, 219; Gilman, C. P., 171; Hayek, F. A., 132; Nozick, R., 260–61, 262n146; Rand, A., 244; Saint-Simon, H., 132–33; Skinner, B. F., 184; Wells, H. G., 151

Conroy, Patrick J., 1

The Constitution of Spensonia. See Spence, Thomas

constructive tax. *See* tax

control. *See* political control

Cooke, Brett, 56, 193–94

Craig, Tobin L., 69

Criado-Perez, Caroline, 117n174, 230n180

crime/criminal, 151, 171, 192–93, 211, 217

Critias. See Plato

Crowther, J. G., 75

Cummings, Jasper L., Jr., 28n102, 29n108

Darwin, Charles, 150n69, 172n212, 189n318

Davis, Laurence, 271

Den Uyl, Douglas J., 238n5, 250n76

Dewey, John: Bacon, F., 69; Bellamy, E., 109n116; ends and means, 10–11, 24; George, H., 205, 213, 216, 218–19

disabled. *See* work

The Dispossessed. See Le Guin, Ursula K.

division of labor. *See* work

divorce (or utopian counterpart): Godwin, W., 152; Goodwin, B., 140n3; Le Guin, U. K., 95; More, T., 143; Morris, W., 154n95; Owen, R., 184n284; Skinner, B. F., 184n284

Donno, Daniel J., 135–36

Dorter, Kenneth, 99

Dostoevsky, Fyodor, 63, 147, 245–46, 252

Doughney, Lachlan, 250

egalitarian: common dining hall as sign: Lycurgus, 99n51; More, T., 46, 100–101, 105; Plato, 44; Zamyatin, Y., 56 general welfare as: Bellamy, E., 114; More, 100–101; Zamyatin, Y., 58 objection to, 109n117

education: Bellamy, E., 110–11; Campanella, T., 136–37; Gilman, C. P., 115, 169; Godwin, W., 86–87, 157n109; Hertzka, T., 169n189; London, J., 87; Mayer, J., 87n141; Morris, W., 115–16, 181n267; Owen, R., 163–66; Plato (guardians), 96–98; Rand, A. (moral), 252; Skinner, B. F., 180–83, 177–79; state's role, 94

egoism, 155–56, 170–71, 240

ends and means, 6–7, 9–11, 13, 17, 23, 39

Engels, Frederick, 129, 210

Enquiry Concerning Political Justice. See Godwin, William

equality: ability, 113; liberty and, 7, 12–13, 155n102, 204; political, 113

Equality. See Bellamy, E.

equal rights. *See* rights

Erewhon. See Butler, Samuel

eugenics (state required):
 authors: Bacon, F., 146–47; Bellamy, E., 172, 188n315, 189–93; Campanella, T., 187–88; Gilman, C. P., 118n315, 149n61, 168, 171–72; Morris, W., 190n327; Wells, H. G., 148–50, 188n315; Zamyatin, Y. (quality control), 188n315, 193–94
 topics: benign neglect, 187; forced sterilization, 35, 150, 172n210; negative, 142, 151, 172; passive-aggressive, 189; population control, 168; positive, 142, 152, 168, 172; procedures, 150–51; selectionist, 188

Eurich, Nell, 69, 99–100, 136

evolution: atavistic, 57, 170; Bellamy, E. (logical), 107–108, 109n116, 189n321; Darwin, C., 172n212, 189n318; Gilman, C. P., 116, 170; Le Guin, U. K., 153, 271; Nozick, R. (of minimal state), 260–61; social Darwinism, 106; utopia as, 153; Wells, H. G., 150n69

experiment(al): Bacon, F., 147n45; Godwin, W., 82n108; Nozick, R., 279n256; Owen, R., 158–59, 163–64; (in) shared sacrifice, 6; Skinner, B. F., 8, 124, 174–75, 183, 185; Wells, H. G., 119

family restrictions: Gilman, C. P. (one-child policy), 168; Huxley, A. ("we decant our babies"),

195–96; Owen, R. ("single family arrangements . . . broken up"), 165; Skinner, B. F. (segregating children from their parents), 184; Wells, H. G. (marriage license restrictions: financial, intellectual, and physical), 147–49; Zamyatin, Y. ("maternal norm" for conception), 194

Faulkner, Robert K., 72–73, 145

Feser, Edward, 267, 277n242

Fisher, Richard, 218

forced labor. *See* work; Nozick, R.

Foucault, Michel, 56n82

Fowler, Mark, 278

France, Anatole, 140

freedom:
 authors: Bellamy, E., 248; Bentham, J., 51, 204; George, H. (restricting), 201; Godwin, W. (of inquiry), 73, 209; Hertzka, T., 228n169; Huxley, A., 173n220; Le Guin, U. K. (responsibility as), 153, 155; More, T. (discipline not), 100; Morris, W., 109; Nozick, R., 232n193, 235, 258, 277; Orwell, G., 79; Owen, R. (character formation and), 158–62, 165; Rand, A., 198, 239n9, 258, 254; Saint-Simon, H. (collective), 125, 130–31; Skinner, B. F., 160, 179–80; Wells, H. G., 51, 119, 150, 201, 228, 259; Zamyatin, Y., 59
 topics: determinism, 157n109; equality and, 7, 12–13, 155n102; free will, 160–61; land and, 201, 204; self-determination, 42, 160–61

Freeland. See Hertzka, Theodore

Fried, Barbara H., 264n160, 267, 268n189

Friedman, Milton, 203, 212, 268n189

Frye, Northrop, 15–16, 255
Fuller, Lon L., 111–12, 253–54,
179n258
future generations: Burke, E., 31–32,
204n33; family, 138; general
welfare, 31, 202; Gilman, C. P.,
118, 169, 173; Harrington, J.
(agrarian law), 207–208; land
ownership and, 202; Rand, Ayn,
31n117, 251n83; Skinner, B. F.,
123; Wells, H. G., 148–50

Galton, David J., 142n16
Galton, Francis, 187, 195–96
Gandhi, M. K., 1–2, 211n74
Garnsey, Peter, 18, 232
Geiger, George Raymond, 213
gender roles: Bellamy, E., 111;
Campanella, T., 136; Gilman,
C. P., 117; Hertzka, T., 114n154;
Owen, R., 165, 184n284; Plato
(guardians), 96–98; Skinner, B. F.,
124, 184; Wells, H. G., 120;
Zamyatin, Y., 193
general welfare:
authors: Bellamy, E., 109, 114;
Gilman, C. P., 117, 119, (organic
nature of), 168–73; Godwin
("general weal"), 81, 84, 210;
Harrington, J., 207–208; Hayek,
F. A. on, 31; Holmes, O. W.,
Jr., 150n69; More, T., 100–101;
Nozick, R., 232n193; Owen, R.
(based on laws of nature), 165;
Saint-Simon, H., 127–28, (organic
nature of), 130–32, 134; Skinner,
B. F., 122–23, 185–86; Wells,
H. G., 119, 121, 148; Zamyatin,
Y., 58
topics: definition, 30–31; egalitarian,
100–101; future generations, 31,
202; "how general is general?," 31;
inequality and, 92; land's affect

on, 198–205; male-biased, 111,
114, 116–17, 140n4, 230n180;
public interest, 1, 61n120, 253;
public welfare, 26, 100, 105,
150n69; social cohesion as, 34;
taxation and, 19, 29–30; tax
protest and, 36
George, Henry, 212–20
capitalism, 217, 219–20;
competition, 211, 219; factors of
production, 215; general welfare,
216–17; inequality, 216, 249;
justice, 216, 219
land: common ownership, 205,
213–14, 216; constructive tax,
213; definition, 214n91; first use
(or acquisition), 233; freedom
(restricting), 201; fundamental
question, 201; lease, 217;
monopoly, 205, 220; private
property in, 213n89, 216; proper
use, 216; rent appropriation
by tax, 215–17; single tax on,
217–18
Malthus, T., 214–15; political power,
213; poverty, 212–17; profit,
219; progress (and poverty), 214;
Spencer, H., 199; Tolstoy, L., 199,
220–22, 226; wealth inequality,
213, 216
Gerber, Richard, 8, 193n349, 196
Ghate, Onkar, 244n38
Gillitzer, Christian, 17, 25–26
Gilman, Charlotte Perkins, 114–19,
167–72
access to truth (cohesion of
conviction), 172–73; civilization,
119; economic progress, 117;
education, 115, 169; eugenics,
118n315, 149n61, 168, 171–72;
evolution, 116, 170
family restrictions: childrearing, 80,
167, 169–70; one-child policy, 168

Gilman, Charlotte Perkins *(continued)*
  future generations, 118, 169, 173;
    general welfare, 117, 119, (organic
    nature of), 168–73; interference
    (friction), 116; marriage, 149n61,
    172n210; moral progress, 170–71,
    173; organic nature of society,
    119, 170, 173; past generations,
    32; population control (based on
    food supply), 168; science, 116,
    118, 169; society (organic nature
    of), 119, 170, 173
  work: her "real job," 114–15; gender
    roles, 117; multiple careers, 115;
    nurturing variety, 115; required
    work or occupation, 117; sexuo-
    economic barriers, 115, 117;
    women's obligatory work, 119
Godwin, William, 81–90, 209–10
  anarchy, 81–82, 84–85; divorce,
    152; education, 86–87, 157n109;
    general welfare ("general weal"),
    81, 84, 210
  government: best form of, 278; evils
    (hidden), 88–89; euthanasia of,
    89–90; self-interested interference,
    81
  individuality, 83; human nature, 8;
    judgment, 81–83, 90; justice, 81,
    83–85, 88–89, 209–10; liberty,
    209; marriage, 83, 152
  moral: autonomy, 81; progress, 82
  nature (commonage of), 88;
    pecuniary tax, 84–85, 88–89;
    poor vs. rich, 88–89; privacy, 41;
    private land holdings, 209–210;
    progress, 82; property rights, 209,
    210n68
  truth: access to, 81–83, 86–87;
    contemplation and, 41;
    experiment and observation,

  82n108; freedom of inquiry, 173;
    government interference with, 82
  work (allocation of, two options),
    91
Goffman, Erving, 60
Goodwin, Barbara: dystopic warnings,
    39; inequality, 92; marriage,
    140n3; mutual control, 42n3;
    Nozick, R., 233n201; pre-
    taxation, 104n89; private property,
    198, 209n66; progressive taxation,
    54n73; promoting order, 46;
    Skinner, B. F., 174–75; taxation
    and society, 7
Gottlieb, Erika, 59, 77n80, 79n90
Gough, Val, 115, 167, 170
government revenue. *See* tax
Groves, Harold M., 217–18
Gubar, Susan, 117n170, 118
Gulliver's Travels. See Swift, Jonathan

Hailwood, S., 267, 274n222
Hale, Kimberly Hurd, 72, 145
Hall, K. Graehme, 118–19
Hamilton, Alexander, 25n86
Hammond, N. G. L., 98
Hand, Learned, 1, 24n83, 30
Hansot, Elisabeth, 191n332
Harrington, James, 206–208
  empire of laws and not of men,
    206; general welfare, 207–208;
    government stability (promoting),
    207; historical materialism,
    208n56; Hume's criticism of,
    208n60
  land: agrarian law (inheritance
    of land), 207–208; future
    generations, 207–208;
    independent variable in
    distributing required sacrifice,
    207–208; primogeniture, 208n59

preventing the concentration of power, 206

Harris, Roy, 78

Harrison, John F. C., 161n136, 164

Hayek, Friedrich A.: coercion, 24, 257; competition, 132; critic of utopia, 41; ends and means, 24; general welfare, 31; interference (with inherent principles), 130n257; laissez faire, 249n74; Orwell, G. on, 132n275; public finance, 2; Saint-Simon, H. on, 132; socialism, 109n116

Heilbroner, Robert L., 159, 166, 219

Heller, Anne, 238n6, 241n19, 244n36, 251n84

Herland. See Gilman, Charlotte Perkins

Herman, Edwards S., 35n143, 64n4

Herrnstein, Richard J., 279

Hertzka, Theodor: childrearing, 170n189; education, 169n189; freedom, 228n169; land ("masterless"), 228n169; past generations (debt to), 224n40; privacy (financial transparency), 61–62; tax (income), 18n154; work (gender roles), 114n154, 124n221

Hertzler, Joyce Oramel, 132, 134, 165, 206n46, 207

Hexter, J. H., 16, 99, 101–102, 104

Hitler, Adolf, 11

Hobbes, Thomas, 68, 86, 89n150, 92–93, 254

Hofstadter, Richard, 150n69, 189, 191n335, 219n124, 239n12

Holland, Owen, 149n66

Holmes, Oliver Wendell Jr., 150n69, 172

Holmes, Robert L., 273n218

Horan, Thomas, 56–57, 80n102

Hospers, John, 262n146

Houston, Chlöe, 74n65

Howells, William Dean, 28, 93, 106, 244n29

Hudak, Jennifer, 171, 173

human nature: Bacon, F., 71; Bellamy, E., 190–91; economics and, 26; eugenics and, 172; flawed, 186; Howells, W. D., 243n29; inequality and, 92; permanent or transitory features, 8–9, 282; Skinner, B. F., 174; utopias, 255; Wells, H. G., 152n78; Zamyatin, Y. (instinct for freedom), 59

Hume, David, 14, 89n150, 208n60, 230, 251n80

Huxley, Aldous: childrearing, 196; conditioning (Pavlovian), 182n276, 196; contraception, 186, 196n372; eugenics, 186n302, 195; family restrictions ("we decant our babies"), 195–96; freedom, 173n220; leisure, 11; marriage, 196; privacy, 49n45, 59; religion, 1, 40n163, 177; science, 80; talent, 96n30; truth, 77n80, 80; work, 195

individualism, 86, 162n137, 239n12

inequality: (of) ability, 91, 113; (and) general welfare, 92; George, H., 213, 216, 249; Hobbes, T. (self-cancelling), 92; Nagel, T., 92n3; natural, 92; Nozick, R. (Kantian side constraint to curb), 265; Plato, 65–66, 93–95; political, 92; Rousseau, J.-J., 92; sacrifice (of), 23, 29; Saint-Simon, H., 131–32; Smith, A., 92; taxes, 25; 55n81; Zamyatin's *We*, 213

injustice. *See* justice

interference: Godwin, W. (with access to truth by government), 81–82; Gilman, C. P. (producing friction), 116; Hayek, F. A. (with inherent principles), 130n257; Saint-Simon (with industry), H., 130; Spencer, H. (with far-seeing benevolence), 189; Rand, A. (with moral rights), 254

invisible hand, 28n103, 92, 112, 189, 260, 246–65, 257–76

Ionescu, Ghita, 127–28

is-ought problem, 214n92, 250

James, William, 38–40

justice: Bellamy, E., 192; distributive, 12, (intergenerational distributive), 31n117; George, H., 216, 219; Godwin, W., 81, 83–85, 88–89, 209–10; injustice (nature of), 140n4; Nozick, R., 232–34, 260, 263, 267, 275–76; Orwell, G., 78–79, 89, Plato, 66, 95, 98; Rand, A., 255n117; Smith, A., 209; taxation, 12, 22, 23n78; Tolstoy, L., 221–22

Jones, Mother, 34n137

Kahneman, Daniel, 71n47

Kant, Immanuel, 31, 33, 160–61, 202, 250n77

Kaplow, Louis, 31n117

Kateb, George, 6, 11, 16, 52

Kavka, Gregory S., 202, 234n205

Kenyon, T. A., 46n27, 103n79

Keynes, John Maynard, 7

Kierkegaard, Søren, 223n143

Kochin, Michael S., 97n39

Kramnick, Isaac, 90

Krieg, Joann P., 169

Krutch, Joseph Wood, 175–76

Kumar, Krishnan, 50, 108, 174, 182n276

Lacey, A. R., 280

laissez faire, 249n74

Lakoff, George, 201

land (division and proprietorship), 197–235

authors: Burke, E., 204n33; George, H., 201–202, 205, 213n89, 214n91, 215–18, 220; Godwin, W., 209–10; Harrington, J., 207–208; Kant, I., 202; Nozick, R., 231–33; Paine, T., 198, 235n216

topics: application for the benefit of the whole, 62; "common ownership" (choice of this term), 202; freedom and, 201, 204; future generations, 198, 202; gender bias, 208, 230n180; general welfare, 198, 200, 202, 205; indivisible, 200; monopoly, 205, 220; moral question, 199–200; political control, 198, 257, 276; primogeniture, 208n59; private property in, 198, 201–204, 205n43; "property," as ambiguous, 203; property rights in, 198, 231–33; proprietorship, 198, 202; question, the, 198, 221; sacrifice, 200, 202; tax, 198, 202; worldviews (rival), 200–201

common ownership: George, H., 205, 213–14, 216; Hertzka, T., 228n169; More, T., 204; Owen, R., 165, 204, 211–12; Proudhon, P.-J., 204n39, 213n89, 214, 232; Spence, T., 214n92; Spence, T., 203n28; Spencer, H., 198–99; Tolstoy, L., 197, 204, 216n110, 223; Wells, H. G., 201, 228–30 first use (or acquisition): George, H., 233; Hume, D., 230; Kant, I., 31; Locke, J., 232; Maine, H. S., 233n204; Owen, R., 211; Nozick, R., 231–33

Lasky, Melvin J., 18

Laws. See Plato

Lawson, John, 163

Le Guin, Ursula K., 152–56, 270–72
    anarchy, 153–56; childrearing, 154; divorce (or utopian counterpart), 95; evolution, 153, 271; freedom (responsibility as), 153, 155; general welfare, 154–55; marriage (partnership "monogamous union" as substitute), 154–55; mutual aid, 154; organic nature of society, 153, 156; privacy, 58n96; social conscience, 272; walls, 200–201; war, 154
    work: distasteful jobs, 113; labor drafts, 155, 270–72

leisure, 11, 46, 110, 120, 180, 269

Levi, Margaret, 33, 34n135

Levitas, Ruth, 9

Lewis, Arthur O., 238, 242n28

liberty. *See* freedom

lie. *See* truth

Lipow, Arthur, 190–91

Lipp, Ronald F., 252n90

Locke, Don, 35n146

Locke, John, 231, 250n77

Lomasky, Loren E., 277

London, Jack: access to truth, 87; education, 87; utopian, 15

Looking Backward: 2000–1887. See Bellamy, Edward

Lorenzo, David J., 191n332, 194

Lycurgus, 99n51

Macey, Jonathan R., 235n213, 279

Mack, Eric, 250–51, 258, 268, 274n221

Macpherson, C. B., 200, 201n21, 203–204, 207

Magner, Lois N., 199n8

Maine, Henry Sumner, 143n17, 233n204

Malthus, Thomas, 14n42, 83n115, 100, 214–15

Mannheim, Karl, 125n225, 126, 133, 200n17, 201, 239n8

Manuel, Frank E., 38, 53, 126, 128, 129n252, 131n268, 133

Manuel, Fritzie P., 38, 133

Markham, F. M. H., 125n226, 127

marriage restrictions, 139–95
    authors: Bacon, F., 144–47; Bellamy, E., 191–92; Campanella, T., 187–88; Gilman, C. P., 149n61, 172n210; Godwin, W., 83, 152; Goldman, E., 152; Goodwin, B., 140n3; Huxley, A., 196; Le Guin, U. K. (partnership "monogamous union" as substitute), 154; More, T., 142–43; Morris, W. (extra-legal), 154n95; Owen, R., 184n284; Plato (sequential/serial), 99, 141–42, 143n20, 147; Skinner, B. F., 183–84; Spencer, H., 188; Wells, H. G., 147–49; Wollstonecraft, M., 152n82
    topics: grouped, 148; laws against interracial or same-sex, 34n138, 140; license, 148–50; monogamy, 140n3, 141n9, 143, 154–55; parental permission, 145; political control, 141–43, 145–50, 154–55; polygamy, 143n17, 146–47; waiting period, 148; wise laws touching, 145, 147

Marx, Karl, 14, 105, 129, 162n141, 246, 265

Mayer, Jane, 87n141

McCann, Charles R., Jr., 217, 220

means and ends. *See* ends and means

Mercer, Louis-Sebastien, 254n109

Mill, John Stuart: character, 156;
community of property, 109n117;
land, 200n12, 217–18; Saint-
Simon, H., 10; taxes, 22–23;
truth, 64

Miller, David, 261, 264

monopoly: Bellamy (final), 107–108;
coercive, 262; de facto, 262;
George (on land ownership),
205, 220; Nozick (on force and
land use), 231, 233, 235, 25–59,
262–63, 264; Rand (on force),
248–49; (on land ownership), 257

Montesquieu, Charles de, 13, 50n47,
54, 66, 145n35, 207n51, 281

moral:
autonomy, 7, 81, 160; entitlement,
231; ideal(s), 56n85, 240, 252;
insight, 100; judgment, 81

progress: Gilman, C. P., 170–71,
173; Owen, R., 164; Rand, A.,
252; Saint-Simon, H., 126, 128;
Skinner, B. F., 9n14, 181; taxes
as gauge of, 36; Wells, H. G.,
51–52, 148

rights: Locke, J., 231; Nozick, R.,
233–35, 258–59, 264; Rand, A.,
250–51

morally neutral definitions: tax, 29;
utopia, 38–39

More, Thomas, 45–47, 99–106,
142–43
afterlife, 103–104; atheists, 32;
childrearing, 103–104; discipline,
100–101; economy, 101–102;
egalitarian, 46, 100–101, 105;
famine, 100; freedom (discipline
not), 100; general welfare, 100–

101; leisure, 11, 46; marriage,
142–43; nature, 10n21; poverty,
100–101; privacy, 44–47; profit,
105–106; punishment, 103n79;
rational, 103n79; required
sacrifice, 100

war: avoidance of, 104–105;
mercenaries, 34n134, 105–106

work: career choice, 103–104, 47,
104, 270; farming, 102–103;
gender roles, 103; multiple
careers, 103–104; slavery, 47, 104;
surplus labor, 104–105; useful
trades, 102; workload, 102–103

Morris, William:
Bellamy, E., 112; commercial
slavery, 109; divorce (or utopian
counterpart), 154n95; education,
115–16, 181n267; eugenics,
190n327; freedom, 109; human
nature, 8; marriage (extra-legal),
154n95; revolution, 109

work: happy and useful, 112;
obstinate refusers, 217; pleasure
in, 112; varying occupations,
115–16

Morton, A. L., 158, 162, 163n148,
208n56, 228n169

Moving the Mountain. See Gilman, C. P.

Moylan, Tom, 153n86, 270

Mumford, Lewis, 66n12, 141

Murphy, Liam, 5, 205n43

Murphy, N. R., 96n27

Murray, Charles, 279

Murray, Dale F., 264n164, 267,
275n229

Musgrave, Robert A., 15

Nagel, Thomas: ethical and political
dimensions of taxes, 5, 12, 18n63,
36; inequality, 92n3; justice or
injustice of taxation, 23n78;

Nozick, R., 266–67; private property, 205n43, 231, 269n194; utopianism, 30

natural rights. *See* rights

nature:
commonage of (Godwin, W.), 88; division of labor by (Plato), 93–95; exploitation of (Saint-Simon, H.), 131; following, 10–11; forces of, 57; intentions (Kant), 250n77; irrational world of (Zamyatin, Y.), 57

laws of: Bacon, F., 10n22, 69; More, T., 10n21; Nietzsche, 11; Owen, R., 10n23, 157, 165

men equal by (Hobbes, T.), 92; perfection of (Swift, J.), 32; rule (Hitler, A.), 11n24; state of (Locke, J.), 231, 264 (Nozick, R.), 258–60, 264–65; secrets of (Bacon), 69, 146; take its course (Spencer, H.), 189

New Atlantis. See Bacon, Francis

News from Nowhere. See Morris, William

Nietzsche, Friedrich, 11, 14, 17, 113n143, 160

Nineteen Eighty-four. See Orwell, George

Nisbet, Robert, 132

Nissenbaum, Helen, 41, 42–43, 61

Nozick, Robert, 230–35, 257–281
anarchy (natural state of), 234, 258–59; children as property, 232n196

coercion: political duress, 270; preemptive, 267n180; taxes and, 267–68

compensation (for loss or violation of rights), 234–35, 273–75; competition, 260–61, 262n146; end-state solutions (consequentialist), 259, 278;

entitlement theory (of ownership), 232–35; freedom, 231, 232n193, 235, 258, 277; general welfare, 232n193; inequality (Kantian side constraint to curb), 265; initiating force, 265n169; invisible hand, 260, 264; justice, 233–34, 260, 267, 275–76

land ownership: George, H. on, 233; justice in acquisition (first use), 231–33; justice in transfer, 232–33; moral right, 231; theory of, 200; what is owned, 234

leisure, 269; market forces, 263–64; mixing labor with land, 232

monopoly: on use of force, 259–60, 262–63, 265, 268, 273; on use of land, 276

patterned outcome, 234, 273; process solutions, 259, 279; property rights, 210n68, 231, 276; protective agency, 260–61; Rand, A., 255–56; rectification for unjust transfers (principle of), 234–35; redistribution, 269, 273–74, 280

rights: conflict of, 233n202; equal, 259–65, 273, 280; moral, 231, 233, 235, 258–59, 264; property, 210n68; to leave utopian community, 279–80

self-help enforcement, 260, 274; self-interest, 263; socialism, 235

state: de facto, 262n151; definition of, 260; evolution of minimal, 260–61; minimal, 258, 262, 264–65, 278; monopoly on enforcement, 262, 265; of nature, 258–60, 264–65; protects the rights of everyone within its territory, 265; ultraminimal, 260, 262

Nozick, Robert *(continued)*
   tax: as coerced extractions or
      voluntary payments, 266–69,
      272–73; as forced labor, 265–66,
      268–70
   utopia: as experimental community,
      279n256; utopian, 15; utopia of
      utopias, 276–81

Oceana. See Harrington, James
O'Donnell, Edward T., 107
Okin, Susan Moller, 232n
Olson, Mancur, 9n14, 254n
operant conditioning. *See* behaviorism
Orwell, George, 47–50, 76–81; access
      to truth, 77–81; capitalism,
      241n25; general welfare, 78, 81;
      Hayek, F. A. (review of *The Road
      to Serfdom*), 132n275; history
      (revision of), 77; justice, 78, 89;
      language and thought, 78–79, 81;
      (no) law, 50; liberty and equality,
      79; poverty, 241n25; privacy,
      80–81; revolution, 16; science,
      79–80; truth, 77–79
Owen, Robert, 146–67, 210–12
   character formation, 156–66,
      210–11
   children: education, 163–66; infant
      school, 163–64; punishment, 158,
      164; reward, 158, 164
   experimental evidence, 158–59,
      163–64
   family restrictions: childrearing,
      163–66; divorce, 184n284;
      marriage, 184n284; "single family
      arrangements . . . broken up,"
      165
   freedom (character formation and
      free will), 158–62, 165; gender
      roles, 165, 184n284; general
      welfare (based on laws of nature),

      165; land, 165, 204, 211–12;
      moral autonomy, 160; moral
      progress, 164; nature, 10n23, 157,
      165; poverty, 162–64, 211; private
      property, 211; profit, 163n148;
      progress, 212; revolution (without
      violence), 210–11, 212n81; rights
      (equal), 165
   tax: evil, 157; (on) labor, 166; (on)
      land, 166; pecuniary, 166
   townships (home colonies, nuclei),
      164–65; war (avoidance of), 157
Owen, Robert Dale, 161n136, 163,
      212n81

Paine, Thomas, 21n71, 32n118, 198,
      235n216
Parrinder, Patrick, 152n78, 187,
      190n327
past generations (debt to): Bellamy,
      E., 244n40; Burke, E., 31–32;
      Gilman, C. P., 32; Hertzka, T,
      244n40; Rand, A., 244n40
Peikoff, Leonard, 238n3
penalty. *See* tax
Pepper, Stephen, 200n17
Peters, R. S., 23
Pfaelzer, Jean, 106, 116, 192n339
Pfohl, Stephen, 78
Philp, Mark, 35, 83
Piketty, Thomas, 12, 19, 25, 235
Plato, 65–68, 94–99, 141–42
   Critias, 73–74; eugenics, 141–42,
      97, 172; general welfare, 66
   guardians: character, 97; childrearing,
      142; common dining, 44;
      education, 96–98; equality, 95–96;
      gender roles, 96–98; "marriage"
      (sequential/serial), 99, 141–42,
      143n20, 147; privacy, 44
   justice, 66, 95, 98; *Laws*, 141, 143;
      progressive tax, 99; tax regime, 18

truth: lies in speech, 66–67; noble lies, 65; true lies, 66–68
war (and avoidance of), 96–98
work: division of labor (adopted by nature), 93–95; myth of metals, 65–66
Plutarch, 99n51
Pocock, J. G. A., 206n46, 208n58
political control: access to truth, 64, 77–81; childrearing and, 142, 164, 169–70, 195–96, 182–85; eugenics, 141, 146–47, 148–50, 171–72, 186–96; family (constraints on), 138, 147–49, 165, 168, 184, 194–96; gender, 111, 114n154, 116–19, 149, 230n180; land ownership as, 198, 201, 213, 257, 276; language use for, 30, 77–81; marriage restrictions, 141–43, 145–50, 154–55; pecuniary tax, 37; privacy deprivation, 43, 46, 49, 51, 54; science, 68, 72–74, 123–24, 126, 175–78, 184–85; state's weighing scale, 55; taxation as, 27; work (required), 92–93, 109–111, 119
Popper, Karl, 9, 14
Posner, Richard A., 49n45, 61, 79
poverty: Bellamy, E., 191–92; George, H., 212–17; More, T., 100–101; Orwell, G., 241n25; Owen, R., 162–64, 211; Saint-Simon, H., 133; Spencer, H., 189; Tolstoy, L., 221–24
Prettyman, Gib, 108
privacy restrictions, 41–62; deprivation, 41–62; expectation of, 59–62; Godwin, W., 41; Hertzka, T. (financial transparency), 61–62; Huxley, 49n45, 59; invasion of, 44, 53, 61n120; Le Guin, 58n96;

More, 44–47; observer effect, 60; Orwell, G., 80–81; Plato, 44; political control, 43, 46, 49, 54; Wells, 51–54; Zamyatin, 56–9
private property. See land
profit: Bellamy, E., 94, 108–10, (national), 114; George, H., 219; More, T., 105–106; Owen, R., 163n148; Proudhon, P.–J., 276; Wells, H. G., 121n205
progress: George, H. (and poverty), 214; Godwin, W., 82; Owen, R., 212; Saint-Simon, H., 126, 129; Skinner, B. F., 9n14
Progress and Poverty. See George, Henry
property (ambiguous), 202–203
property tax on land. See land
Proudhon, Pierre-Joseph: land, 204, 214, 232, 276; property as theft, 213n89; revolution, 16; tax, 25n87
public finance. See tax
public interest. See general welfare
public welfare. See general welfare
punishment: Bellamy, E., 193; More, T., 103n79; Owen, R., 158, 164; Skinner, B. F., 176, 178–79; Wells, H. G., 151

Rand, Ayn, 237–57
anarchy, 246; capitalism, 241, 242n27, 249, 251–52; competition, 244; freedom, 198, 239n9, 258, 254; future generations, 31n117, 251n83
government: definition of, 248–49; interference with moral rights, 254; initiation of force by, 253; monopoly on force, 248–49; role as policeman, 249
individualism, 239n12, 242; justice, 255n117

Rand, Ayn *(continued)*
  morality: altruism, 238, 239n9,
    240, 242n27, 252; education
    (moral), 252; egoism, 240; is–
    ought problem, 250–51; need (as
    moral criteria), 238, 242–43, 250;
    progress, 252
  past generations (debt to), 244n40;
    rationality, 56n85, 254–55
  rights: to life, 250–51; natural,
    254; private property, 198, 203;
    reciprocal nature of, 254
  self-interest, 246, 250–51, 253;
    self-sacrifice, 238n3, 240, 247n56;
    Skinner, B. F., 176n239
  society: no such entity, 239n9,
    245–46; secret Colorado, 247;
    social system, 239, 241
  strike: of essential workers, 244–49;
    nature of, 247; prime movers,
    239–40, 242, 245
  surplus (men's), 105, 244, 248
  tax: constructive, 243–44, 255, 257;
    (on) contracts, 256; definition of,
    255; income, 253; "naked essence"
    of, 235; voluntary, 254, 256
Rasmussen, Douglas B., 238n5,
  250n76
Reeve, Andrew, 198
Reeve, C. D. C., 67, 96n28
Republic. See Plato
required sacrifice: allotment of, 100;
    balance of, 20, 36, 119, 203,
    206; coercion (and) as unifying
    principles, 37; definition, 33–34;
    nonpecuniary and pecuniary,
    6–7, 19, 26–28, 34, 41, 63, 255;
    scalability of, 40; unequal, 23, 29;
    (as) unrequited, 3, 202, 281
Resurrection. See Tolstoy, Leo
revolution: Bellamy, E. ("bloodless"),
    107–108, 109n116, 193; French,

13; Godwin, W., 89; Kateb, G.,
  16; Orwell, G., 16; Owen, R.
  ("without violence"), 210–11,
  212n81; Proudhon, P.-J., 16;
  Saint-Simon, H. (insurrection),
  108, 129; Zamyatin, Y., 54, 57,
  59, 194
rights:
  asymmetry of, 262; (and) duties, 24,
    55, 233n202
  equal: Nozick, 259–65, 273, 280;
    Owen, R., 165; Rand, A., 198,
    203, 253–54, 258; Tolstoy, L.,
    227; Wells, H. G., 51; Zamyatin,
    Y., 55
  inviolable, 257, 258, 276; moral,
    233–35, 243, 247, 250–51,
    258–59, 264, 269n195; natural,
    204, 258n132, 274
  property: Godwin, W., 209, 210n68;
    Nozick, R., 210n68; Rand, A.,
    198, 203
Robertson, Michael, 171, 172n210,
  271n206
Roemer, Kenneth M., 31n116,
  32n120, 191
Rogers, Jennifer, 153
Rosen, Jeffrey, 43, 60
Rossi, Paolo, 71
Rothbard, Murray, 29
Rousseau, Jean-Jacques, 92, 160
Ryan, Alan, 209n66
Ryan, Paul, 238n5

Sabia, Dan, 153, 155
sacrifice. *See* required sacrifice
Saint-Simon, Henri, 125–35
  competition, 132–33; education,
    134; freedom (collective liberty),
    125, 130–31; general welfare,
    127–28, (organic nature of),
    130–31, 134; government, 127,

129, 132, 134; Hayek, F. A. on, 132; industrials, 125, 129–30; insurrection, 108, 129; interference (with industry), 130; moral progress, 126, 128; nature (exploitation of), 131; politics (science of), 126–27; poverty, 133; progress, 126, 129; public opinion, 108; Say, J.-P., 127; scientists, 126–29, 131–32; self-interest, 131; society (organic nature of), 127–28, 131, 133

tax: authority to, 125; power to, 133; voluntary, 34

utopian paradox, 133; war (avoidance of), 129–30

work: ability to (enabling), 134; control of, 131; equality of opportunity, 132; essential workers, 245n43; inequality of ability, 131–32; hierarchy of, 131–32, 134; source of all virtues, 125; useful, 128

Samuelson, Paul A., 93

Sargent, Lyman Tower: Bellamy, E., 111; better social order, 190; bibliography of utopian literature (online), 39n159; eugenic legislation, 186–87; free market, 239n8; Gilman, C. P., 114n155; individual freedom, 13n34; inequality and private property, 249; Le Guin, U. K., 155n102; More, T., 103n9; Rand, A., 238; utopianism as multidimensional phenomenon, 38

Sartorius, Rolf, 267

Say, Jean-Baptiste, 127

Scanlon, Thomas, 267

Sciabarra, Chris Matthew, 244–45

science: Bacon, F., 68–69, 74–76; Bellamy, E., 86; Campanella,

T., 135–36; Gilman, C. P., 116, 118, 169; Huxley, A., 80; Orwell, G., 79–80; political influence on, 64n5, 68n66, 75; resistance to, 173, 175, 179; Saint-Simon, H. (scientists), 126–29, 131–33; Skinner, B. F., 174n223, 175–76, 179, 184, 186; Tolstoy, L. (economic), 221, 224; Wells, H. G., 120; Zamyatin, Y., 59

Sechrest, Larry J., 255n117

self-interest: Godwin, W., 81; Le Guin, U. K., 155; Nozick, R., 263; Rand, A., 246, 250–51, 253; Saint-Simon, H., 131

Sen, Amartya, 100

Sessions, W. A., 146–47

Shakespeare, William, 195, 252n90

Shearman, Thomas Gaskell, 21

Shklovsky, Victor, 55

Silver, Harold, 163

Simmel, Georg, 27, 274–75, 279n254

Singer, Joseph William, 231n188

Singer, Peter, 265, 273n219

Skinner, B. F., 122–24, 173–86
 autonomous man, 160, 179
 behaviorism: behavioral technology, 122–23, 174–83; defined, 174n223; contingencies of reinforcement, 122; control, 123, 175–76; critics of, 175, 176n239; cultural design, 16, 122, 174–75; education, 180–83, 177–79; experimental design, 124, 174–75, 183, 185; operant conditioning, 177–79, 182n276; punishment, 176, 178–79
 Bellamy, E., 124; competition, 184
 family restrictions: childrearing, 181–85; divorce, 184n284; marriage, 183–84; segregating children from their parents, 184

Skinner, B. F. *(continued)*
   free will, 160, 179–80; future
     generations, 123; general welfare,
     122–23, 185–86; leisure, 180;
     human nature, 174; moral
     progress, 9n14, 181; Morris, W.,
     124; progress, 9n14; science,
     174n223, 175–76, 179, 184,
     186; stimulus-response, 182n276;
     surplus labor, 105; taxes, 17, 186;
     utopian community, 8; utopia
     of means, not ends, 174; war
     (avoidance of), 180
   work: distasteful jobs, 124;
     gender roles, 124, 184; work-
     hour equivalency credits, 124;
     workload, 123–24
slavery: More, T., 47, 104; Morris, W.
   (commercial), 109; Nozick, R.
   (forced labor), 265–66, 268–70;
   Proudhon, P.-J. (indirect),
   213n89; Tolstoy, L. (tax as),
   222, 225–26
Slemrod, Joel, 17, 25–26
Smith, Adam: agrarian law (Rome),
   207n51; conscripted labor
   (corvée), 33; canons of taxation,
   23; division of labor, 92; hurt the
   interests of one order to promote
   another, 20; inequality, 92; justice,
   209; justice and equality, 20–21,
   37; pin factory, 93; utopia, 99;
   war, 26–27
Smith, H. F. Russell, 207
Smith, John Maynard, 188n315
Smith, Phillip, E., 252
Smith, Tara, 246n52
socialism, 109n116
society:
   civilized: Holmes, O. W., Jr.,
     150n69; collective action, 19,
     235; common destiny, 235

eugenic pruning, 141, 149;
   founding, 22; general welfare,
   90; goals of, 13, 23; health of,
   39, 127; marginalized citizens,
   151; marriage, control over, 138;
   meaning, 22; no such entity
   (Rand, A.), 239n9, 245
   organic nature of: Gilman, C. P.,
     119, 170, 173; Le Guin, U. K.,
     153, 156; Saint-Simon, H.,
     127–28, 131, 133
   perfection of, 189; sacrifice and
     coercion required, 6, 20, 22,
     37
   secret: Bacon, F., 68–69, 75; Rand,
     A., 247
   segment of: left behind, 279;
     imposing sacrifice on another
     segment as constructive tax, 21,
     27, 202
   state and, 7n8; tax supporting, 2,
     6–7, 16; work supporting, 90–91,
     93–94, 128, 195
Solove, Daniel J., 42–43, 45, 60
Spedding, James, 76
Spence, Thomas, 203n28, 214n92,
   218n120
Spencer, Herbert: eugenics, 188–89;
   interference with far-seeing
   benevolence, 189; land question,
   198–99; law of equal freedom,
   199n8; marriage, 188; nature,
   189; poverty, 189; society,
   perfection of, 189
state (definition), 7n8
Steuerle, C. Eugene, 26
Stillman, Peter G., 38
Strauss, Leo, 66, 97
Sumner, William Graham, 14, 139,
   188–89
surplus labor: Bellamy, E., 105, 138;
   Campanella, T., 138; Marx, K.,

105; More, T., 104–105; Skinner, B. F., 105

Suter, Rufus, 68

Suvin, Darko, 138n315, 194–95

Swift, Jonathan, 32, 45, 74n34, 79, 173, 254

tax: abuse of, 23, 30n112, 253; central need for, 22; coercion and, 37, 205, 255, 262n146, 267–68; conditional, 140n6; conscription as, 33–34; constructive, 2, 34–37 (two types), 140n6; consumption (on), 88–89; corvée as, 33; definition of, 3, 5–6, 12, 28–29; earliest form, 33; economists and, 26; ends and means, 11–13, 23, 27, 208n58; estate, 229, 269n195; ethical question, 25, 29; forced labor as, 29; general welfare, 30–31; government revenue, 2–3, 5, 28, 30, 87; head, 59n107, 140; income, 18n154; inheritance, 206–208, 229n178; (at) initial formation of government, 22–24; in kind, 19n67, 26, 37; land, 88–89; marriage, 140, 147–49; nonpecuniary, 6–7, 19, 26–28, 34, 37; pecuniary, 3, 27, 37; penalty (not), 145, 151, 230; political control (device of), 27, 141, 257; preemptive coercion, 267n180; pre-taxation, 104n89; progressive (graduated), 25, 54n73, 99; promote ends of ideal state, 10; proportional, 25n87; prostitutes as, 146; public finance, 2, 17; quantification for comparison, 37; redistributive, 25, 29; regressive, 25, 89n150; sacrifice (required), 7, 27, 100; slavery as, 29; substitution of (constructive or pecuniary), 34, 78; surplus labor, 104–105; theft, 29; unconditional, 140n6; voluntary, 29, 254–56, 272–73, 280–81; women's obligatory work as, 119; work, 92; zoning as, 54, 229–30

Taylor, Keith: dystopic warnings, 39; mutual control, 42n3; private property, 198; promoting order, 46, Saint-Simon, H., 129, 133; B. F. Skinner, 174–75

Taylor, Walter Fuller, 106, 109n120, 191

Thomas, John L., 199n11

Thoreau, Henry David, 20, 27, 122, 123, 282

Tilman, Rick, 86n137, 191

Tocqueville, Alexis de, 12, 33, 206

Tolstoy, Leo, 220–27; altering forms of social life (choices for), 37; anarchist, 222; Christian, 222n143; George, H., 199, 220–22, 226; justice, 221–22; land, 197, 204, 216n110, 223; moral struggle (personal), 223–24, 226n164; poverty, 221–24; property as root of evil, 220; purity of motives, 226; rights (equal), 227; science, 221, 224; slavery (as tax), 222, 225–26; Spencer, H., 199; (as) wealthy landowner, 227

transparency, 42, 61–62, 64, 282

totalitarian, 49, 76–77, 79n90, 175, 247n54

truth:

access to, 63–90:

Bacon, F.: governments as obscure and invisible, 73; idols (cognitive biases) and, 69–71; scientists' superior knowledge of, 75–76

truth *(continued)*
  education and, 86–87; Gilman,
    C. P. (cohesion of conviction),
    172–73; Godwin, W., 41, 81–83,
    86–87, 173; Huxley, A., 77n80,
    80; language and, 77–81; London,
    J., 87; lying (definition), 67; Mill,
    J. S., 64; opaque government,
    63–64, 73, 282; Orwell, G.,
    77–81
  Plato: lies in speech, 66–67; noble
    lies, 65; true lies, 66–68
  political control and, 64, 77–81;
    self-evident, 203; universal and
    consistent, 77
Tunick, Mark, 155, 271
Tversky, Amos, 71n47
Twain, Mark, 276
Tyler, Tom R., 43–44, 50

utopia: critics of, 14; definition
    (morally neutral), 38–40;
    dystopia (distinction not relevant
    for taxation), 39; ends and
    means, 21, 24, 27, 31, 38, 174;
    language conventions in, 79–80;
    practicality, 15–16; problem, 227;
    vested interests (opposing change),
    85–86, 211n74, 219

Vaingurt, Julia, 57, 193–94
Van Doren, Charles, 128
Vinton, Arthur Dudley, 109–10
Vonnegut, Kurt, 107

Walden. See Thoreau, Henry David
Walden Two. See Skinner, B. F.
Waldron, Jeremy, 27, 204, 232n193,
    233–34
war:
  avoidance of: Bacon, F., 74–75;
    Bellamy, E., 109–10; Le Guin,
    U. K., 154; More, T., 104–106;

  Owen, R., 157; Plato, 98; Saint-
    Simon, H., 129–30; Skinner,
    B. F., 180
  mercenaries (More, T.), 34n134,
    105–106
  military training: Bellamy, E.
    (Vinton, A. D.), 109; Campanella,
    T., 137; Plato, 96–97; support
    from taxation for (Smith, A.),
    26–27
Wasserman, Louis, 215
Webber, Carolyn, 19n67, 22, 33
Wegner, Phillip E., 194n359, 195
Weinberger, Jerry, 73, 74n63
welfare. *See* general welfare
Wells, David Ames, 30n112, 145n35
Wells, H. G., 50–54, 119–21, 227–30,
    147–52:
  Bacon, F. (influence on),
    120; charity, insult of, 121;
    competition, 151; economists, 26;
    education for diversity, 52
  eugenics: evolution, 150n69;
    forced sterilization, 150; future
    generations, 148–50, 188n315
  exclusion and intolerance (overcome
    by education), 52
  family restrictions: children ("sound
    childbearing"), 147–49, 230;
    marriage (financial, intellectual,
    and physical conditions for
    license), 147–49; wise laws
    touching marriage, 145
  freedom, 51, 119, 150, 201, 228,
    259; gender roles, 120; general
    welfare, 119, 121, 148; Hertzka,
    T. (contrast), 228n169; human
    nature, 152n78; idleness, 120;
    indexing humanity, 52–53;
    individuality, 229; initiative, 227,
    229; land ownership, 201, 228–30;
    leisure, 120; to be moneyless as
    sign of unworthiness, 121; moral

progress, 51–52, 148; political control, 201; privacy, 51–54; profit (and general welfare), 121n205; property, 229; punishment, 151; resources (natural, energy from), 227–28; rights (equal), 51

science: experiment (world for), 119; House of Saloman, 120; innovation, 119–20; royalties for inventions, 120n194

tax: breaks, 230; estate tax, 229; zoning (as constructive tax), 54

work: career choice, 120; conditions, 229–30; education for, 52; inequality of ability, 121; minimum wage, 119–21; reserve employer (state as), 121; unskilled labor, 121, 137

zoning (land), 229–30

Wenzer, Kenneth C., 221–22, 224

Westin, Alan F., 43

White, Howard B., 72–73, 75, 147

Whitney, Charles, 70, 74

Wicksell, Knut, 27

Wildavsky, Aaron, 19n67, 22, 33

Winfrey, John C., 20n69

Wolff, Jonathan, 204, 235, 257n128, 267, 274–75

Wolff, Robert Paul, 266, 275n231

Wollstonecraft, Mary, 152n82

worldviews (competing), 196, 200–202, 205

work, 91–138:
  authors:
    Bellamy, E.: career choice, 94, 110; gender roles, 111; incentive for effort, 111–13; "invalid corps," 113–14, 137; multiple careers, 110; required labor, 109–11; surplus labor, 105, 138; workload, 111
    Campanella, T.: assigned occupations, 136–38; disabled

workers, 137; division of labor, 138; gender roles, 136; workload, 138

Gilman, C. P.: her "real job," 114–15; multiple careers, 115; women's obligatory work, 119

Hertzka, T.: gender roles, 114n154, 124n221

Huxley, A.: five grades of workers, 195

Le Guin, U. K.: distasteful jobs, 113; labor drafts, 155, 270–72

More, T.: career choice, 103–104, 270; farming, 102–103; gender roles, 103; multiple careers, 103–104; slavery, 47, 104; surplus labor, 104–105; useful trades, 102; workload, 102–103

Morris, W.: happy and useful, 112; obstinate refusers, 217; pleasure in, 112; varying occupations, 115–16

Nozick, R.: forced labor, 265–66, 268–70

Plato: division of labor, 93–95; myth of metals, 65–66; nature (adopted by), 94–95

Saint-Simon, H.: hierarchy of, 131–32, 134; useful trades, 128

Skinner, B. F.: distasteful jobs, 124; gender roles, 124, 184; work-hour equivalency credits, 124; workload, 123–24

Wells, H. G.: career choice, 120; conditions, 229–30; education for, 52; inequality of ability (disabled and "inferior types"), 121, 137; minimum wage, 119–21; reserve employer (state as), 121; unskilled labor, 121

work *(continued)*
  topics:
    allocation for the general welfare
      (Godwin's two options), 91;
      career choice, 47, 94, 103–
      104, 110, 120, 270; coercion,
      94; distasteful (arduous) jobs,
      113, 124; division of labor,
      92–95, 138, 260; gender roles,
      103, 111, 114n154, 124,
      136, 184; inequality of ability,
      103, 113–14, 137; multiple
      careers, 103–104, 110, 115;
      required amount in hours or
      duration or required in kind
      or type, 93–138; surplus labor,
      104–105, 138; workload,
      102–103, 111, 123–24,
      138
Wortham, Simon, 144

Young, Fredric C., 274n225
Younkins, Edward W., 240, 253

Zadek, Simon, 26n92
Zamyatin, Yevgeny, 54–59, 193–95;
  children (maternal norm for), 194;
  egalitarian (living conditions),
  56; eugenics, 188n315, 193–94;
  freedom (instinct for), 59; gender
  roles, 193; general welfare, 58,
  194–95; Great Operation, 59;
  inequality, 213; nature (irrational
  world of), 57; political control
  (state's weighing scale), 55;
  privacy, 56–59; rationality, 56,
  193; revolution, 54, 57, 59,
  194; rights (equal), 55; science,
  59, 194; transparency (privacy),
  56–58; wall (glass), 57–58
Zimbardo, Phillip G., 42